Defender of the Underdog

Defender
OF THE
Underdog

Pelham Glassford
and the
Bonus Army

HARVEY FERGUSON

University of New Mexico Press
Albuquerque

© 2023 by Harvey Ferguson
All rights reserved. Published 2023
Printed in the United States of America

First paperback printing 2025

ISBN 978-0-8263-6506-4 (cloth)
ISBN 978-0-8263-6807-2 (paper)
ISBN 978-0-8263-6507-1 (epub)

Library of Congress Cataloging-in-Publication data is on file with the Library of Congress

Founded in 1889, the University of New Mexico sits on the traditional homelands of the Pueblo of Sandia. The original peoples of New Mexico—Pueblo, Navajo, and Apache—since time immemorial have deep connections to the land and have made significant contributions to the broader community statewide. We honor the land itself and those who remain stewards of this land throughout the generations and also acknowledge our committed relationship to Indigenous peoples. We gratefully recognize our history.

Cover adapted from image courtesy of Underwood and Underwood, Library of Congress.
Designed by Isaac Morris
Composed in Albertan Pro, Averia Serif

In treasured memory of Jack Pennington Sutton, Gig Harbor, Washington, loving husband and father, dedicated professional, best friend to many, Airborne/Special Forces/Green Beret veteran, and the funniest guy I've ever known.

And for Sally and Greg.

Glassford has immense capabilities for helping make this world a better place.

—ERNIE PYLE, 1939

CONTENTS

PREFACE	xi
MAPS	xv
INTRODUCTION	1
CHAPTER 1. *Beginnings*	3
CHAPTER 2. *Monastery on the Hudson*	13
CHAPTER 3. *A New Officer for a New Army*	23
CHAPTER 4. *On the Border, Prelude to France*	37
CHAPTER 5. *The German Spring Offenses and the Allied Defenses*	54
CHAPTER 6. *St. Mihiel and the Meuse-Argonne Offenses*	66
CHAPTER 7. *Soldiering in Peacetime*	75
CHAPTER 8. *The New Police Chief*	88
CHAPTER 9. *Walter Waters: Glassford's Friendly Enemy*	105
CHAPTER 10. *The Bonus Veterans Arrive*	116
CHAPTER 11. *The Anacostia Flats Camp*	133
CHAPTER 12. *Painting the Bonus Army Red*	144
CHAPTER 13. *Pretext for Expulsion*	155
CHAPTER 14. *No Good Deed Goes Unpunished*	167
CHAPTER 15. *Whitewashing the Expulsion*	186
CHAPTER 16. *Aftermath*	194
CHAPTER 17. *Factories in the Field and Communists on the Horizon*	204
CHAPTER 18. *Sob Sisters and Busybodies*	222
CHAPTER 19. *Ranching, Policing, and Politics*	234
CHAPTER 20. *The Later Years*	241
AFTERWORD	253
NOTES	255
REFERENCES	284
INDEX	292

Illustrations follow page 132.

PREFACE

My introduction to General Pelham Davis Glassford came more than a decade ago when I was researching the life of General Lucian K. Truscott Jr. The two army generals never met, but they came close one day in 1932, when Army Chief of Staff Douglas MacArthur carried out President Herbert Hoover's order to expel 6,000 hungry, destitute World War I veterans from Washington, DC. The expelled veterans were the remnant of the 26,000 members of the Bonus Army, who had trekked to the nation's capital in small groups to peacefully petition for early payment of their promised bonus for having served during World War I. Truscott, then a young, mounted cavalry captain, was part of the army force detailed to drive the veterans out of the city by use of sabers, bayonets, and tear gas. Retired general Pelham Glassford was then the city's police chief, who defied the Hoover administration for several months as he endeavored to feed and shelter the veterans.

    As a retired Seattle Police chief of detectives, I felt compelled to learn more about this intrepid police chief. The more I learned about Glassford, the more I wanted to share his story.

    During World War I, Glassford, at age thirty-five, had become the second-youngest brevet brigadier general in the American Expeditionary Force, then fighting the Germans in France and Belgium. Following his army retirement in 1931, the commissioners of Washington, DC, recruited him to become the city's police chief. Soon after accepting the position, the new chief faced the unanticipated necessity of having to feed and shelter thousands of his fellow World War veterans. Thereafter, essentially alone, he resisted the determined efforts of President Herbert Hoover and his administration, in concert with the District of Columbia commissioners, to drive the destitute veterans out of the city.[1]

Reconstructing Glassford's life was like putting together a puzzle with missing pieces. He never published an autobiography, and no one has previously written his full biography. Unfortunately, his army personnel file, detailing twenty-eight years of service, no longer exists. That file, along with perhaps eighteen million others, burned in a catastrophic fire on July 12, 1973, in the National Personnel Records Center in St. Louis, Missouri. Fortunately, in June 1955, four years before his death, Glassford donated his collected papers to the Charles E. Young Research Library at the University of California, Los Angeles. Among many other things, the papers contain three single-page typed résumés that Glassford had prepared over his career, providing many essential dates, locations, and duties of his army service.

Another document proved to be of significant value. Glassford's first wife, Cora Arthur Carleton, wrote a partial biography of her husband detailing their years together from 1907 to 1932. Titled *One Life Is Not Enough*, the document, unedited and unpublished, is essentially a family memoir, but it provides a wealth of information about Glassford's professional life as well. Cora's chapters recall his years as a student and instructor at West Point, his service in the Philippines and Hawaii, his combat command of a World War I field artillery regiment, his years as an army instructor, and his long-term avocation as an artist.

Also helpful was "The Boys from Las Vegas: The Glassford Brothers in World War I," a partial summary of Glassford's life and that of his brother, William Glassford II. Its author, Thomas L. Hedglen, presented his research at the Arizona–New Mexico Joint History Convention in April 2007, and he was kind enough to provide me with a copy of his presentation. Also, one of Glassford's grandsons, William C. Parke, a professor at George Washington University, shared with me his trove of information about Glassford's ancestors and family, as well as some of Glassford's writings, photographs, and watercolor paintings, the latter primarily painted between 1947 and 1959. Additionally, old newspaper articles proved to be an important source of information in connecting the events of Glassford's life. In years past, small-town newspapers continued to follow their local sons and daughters as they went off to do great things.

Surprisingly little is known about Glassford's youth, his army service, or his life following the Great Depression. In contrast, much is known about the year he served as police chief in Washington, DC, as well as the arrival of the Bonus Army. For guidance with that, I am indebted to authors Paul Dickson and Thomas B.

Allen for their book *The Bonus Army: An American Epic*, as well as Roger Daniels's *Bonus March: An Episode of the Great Depression*. Glassford's year as police chief in the nation's capital was undoubtedly the apex of his life, bringing him from relative obscurity to international acclaim. It remains the singular action for which he is best remembered, relegating his many other accomplishments to the shadows.

Less is known about Glassford's efforts in 1934 to curb deadly agricultural violence between powerful growers and migrant fieldworkers in the Imperial Valley of California. For assistance with that topic, I relied on the in-depth research of Professor Kathryn S. Olmsted, whose book *Right Out of California: The 1930s and the Big Business Roots of Modern Conservatism* provides a thoroughly riveting examination of that subject.

I have chosen *not* to write a narrowly focused biography of Pelham Glassford. Instead, I elected to include the stories of two men whose lives significantly intersected with his and substantially affected his actions. I include in this category his father, army officer William Glassford Sr., and Walter W. Waters, the "friendly enemy" commander of the Bonus Army. I have also given special attention to the monastic West Point that Glassford attended between 1900 and 1904, and similar attention to how astonishingly unprepared the US Army was to fight a world war.

Generous people have assisted me. Especially important are the general's five grandsons: William Parke, James Glassford, Carl Glassford, Robert Parke, and Thomas Parke. I also thank Leslie Stapleton, library director of the Daughters of the Republic of Texas Library, San Antonio, Texas; Diane M. Kasha, manager of the Plaza Hotel, Las Vegas, New Mexico; the library staff and students of the Charles E. Young Research Library at UCLA; and my editor, Gregory McNamee. Most of all, I thank my wife, Margie, whose expertise at genealogical research, skill at resurrecting long-forgotten newspaper articles, and thoughtful recommendations made this book possible.

MAPS

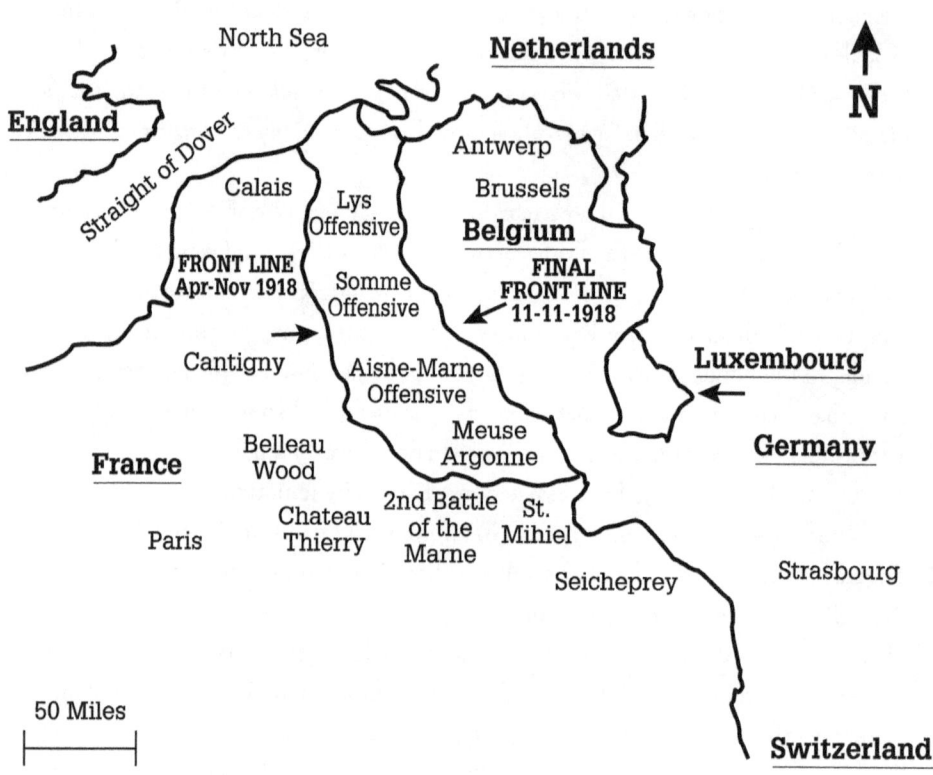

Map 1. General US Battle Area on the Western Front, 1917–1918.

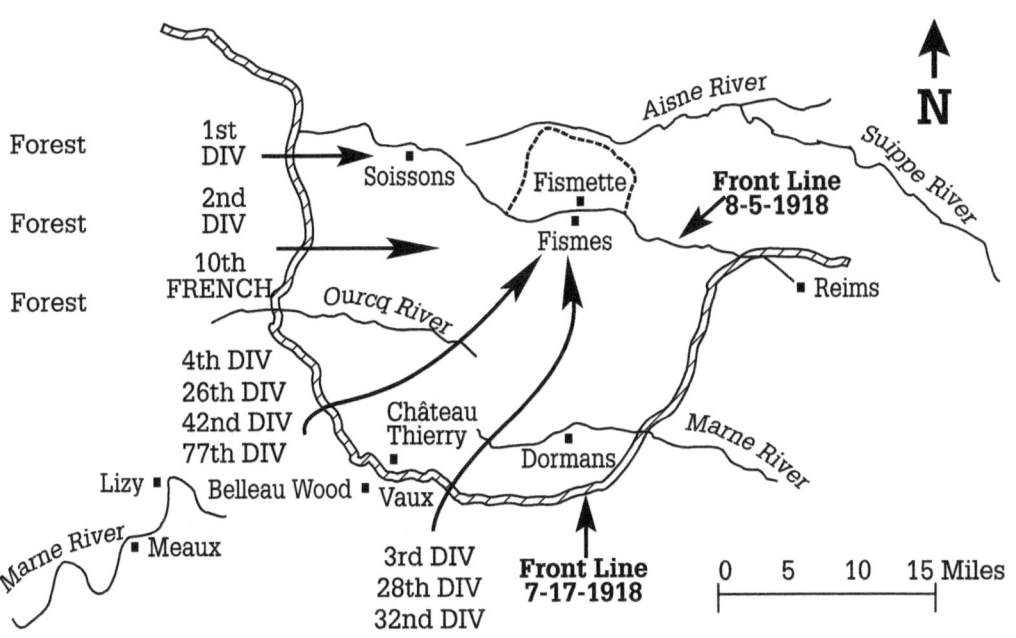

Map 2. German Aisne-Marne Reduction, July–August 1918.

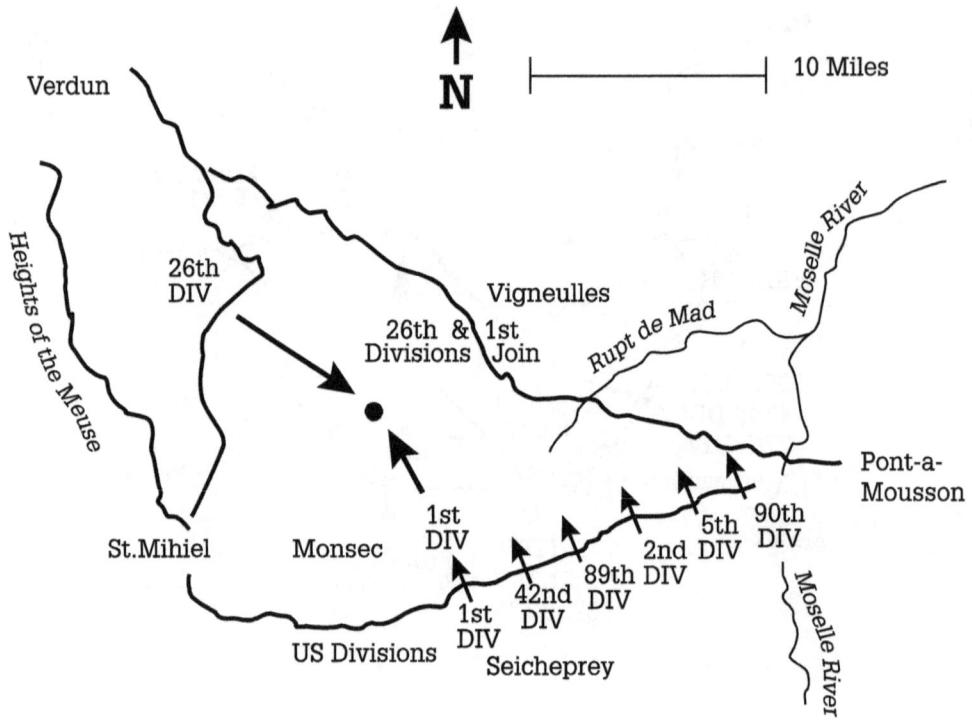

Map 3. Reduction of the St. Mihiel Salient.

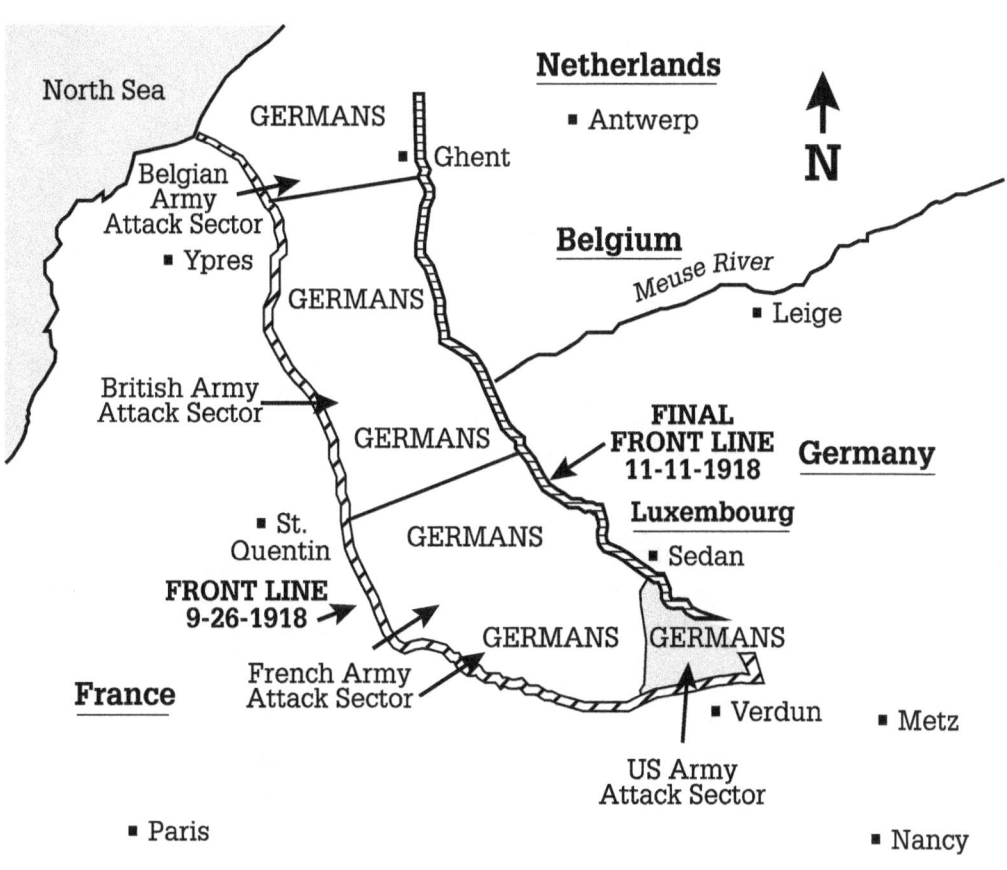

Map 4. Allied Final Assault on Germany, September–November 1918.

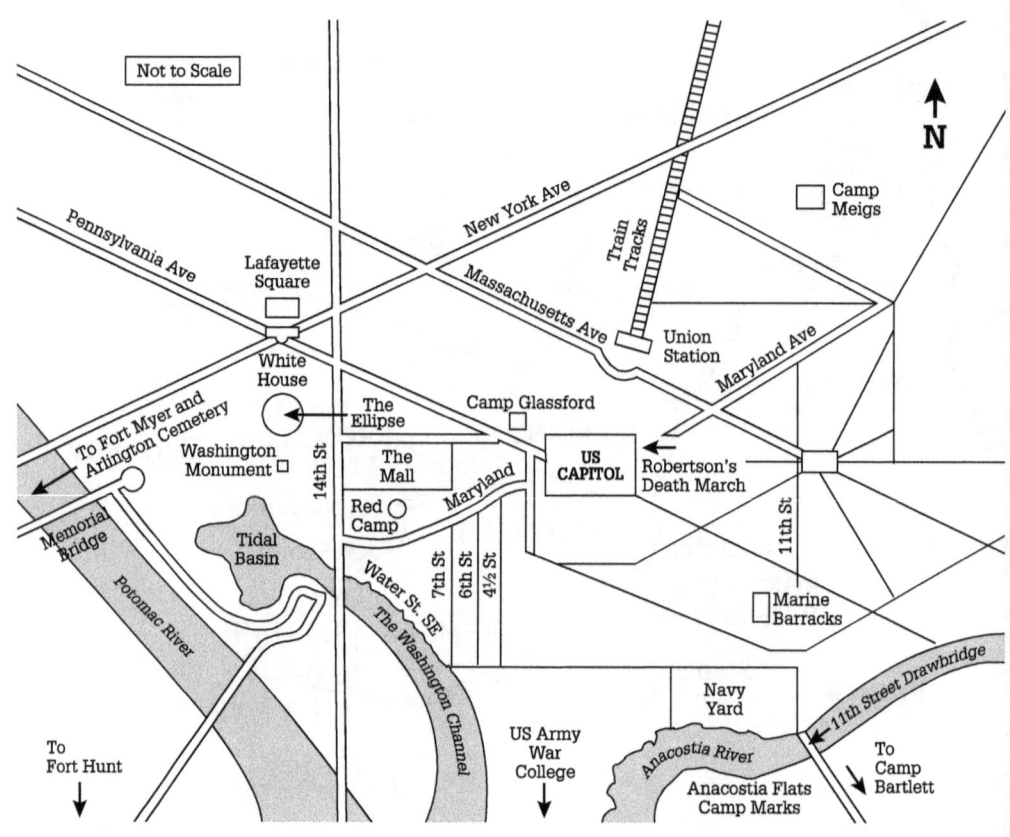

Map 5. Washington, DC, 1931–1932.

Introduction

"WE'RE going to break the back of the B.E.F. Within a short time, we will move down Pennsylvania Avenue, sweep through the billets there, and then clean out the other camps. The operation will be continuous. It will all be done tonight." With that statement, General Douglas MacArthur, the army's youngest chief of staff, told Pelham Glassford, fellow West Point graduate and now police chief of Washington, DC, what was about to happen to thousands of their fellow World War I veterans, now middle-aged and down and out.[1]

The Bonus Expeditionary Force, or BEF, later became known as the Bonus Army. Its members were all World War I survivors. Not all of them had suffered wounds during the war, but the Great Depression had now wounded them all. They had come from across the country to the nation's capital, hopping freights, thumbing rides, and trudging along highways and backroads for thousands of miles. Three years into the Great Depression, most had lost their jobs, their homes, their farms, and often their families. Some who had families brought them to the gigantic "Hooverville" encampment in Washington, DC, now having no other home. In the nation's capital, the veterans found an unlikely ally, Police Chief Pelham Glassford.

Born in 1883, Glassford gained admission to the United States Military Academy at West Point while still just sixteen. The year he began, 1900, verbal, physical, and dangerous hazing of plebes—first-year cadets—was intense. Upon graduation, Glassford, who stood a ramrod-straight six foot three, received his commission in the competitively sought-after field artillery branch. He later served in the Philippines and Hawaii, where he discovered his love for art, adventure, and motorcycles. In 1916 the army rushed him to the Mexican border in response to Pancho Villa's raid on Columbus, New Mexico, and next ushered him to France with the initial deployment of American troops to the war in Europe. The Americans arrived utterly untrained, unequipped, and unprepared to assist the allies.

Following the war, Glassford became one of the army's premier instructors. When assigned to the Army War College in Washington, DC, he found time to join the city's exclusive and vibrant arts community. When the army later reassigned him to Oklahoma, he rode his motorcycle there, taking a 7,000-mile circuitous route, mostly on dirt roads.

His father's serious illness, coupled with glacial-speed army promotions, prompted him to retire early. A later visit to Washington resulted in the District of Columbia commissioners inducing him to become the new police chief. His appointment in late 1931 just preceded the arrival in the capital of 26,000 World War I veterans who came seeking immediate payment of a promised bonus. The DC commissioners and President Herbert Hoover's administration pressured Glassford to forcefully expel the veterans. He stood fast.

In 1934 President Franklin Roosevelt, through his labor secretary, dispatched Glassford to the Imperial Valley of California to mediate between powerful growers and impoverished fieldworkers, then being courted by a Communist labor union. His efforts to ameliorate the situation led to threats on his life, putting him in the greatest danger he had faced since the war.

For much of his life he was a soldier, a fearless and courageous commander. For a year he was a police chief, who, when faced with an enormous and nearly impossible task, accepted the challenge with grace and empathy for his fellow humans. Also, this biography contends that the novice police chief, perhaps without intending to, formulated a model of community-based, problem-solving policing that works as well today as it did in 1932.

He was amazingly generous with his time and money, and he loved risky adventure as much as he loved painting watercolors. His friends called him Happy, "Hap" for short, a West Point nickname that stayed with him for life. His grin was ever present.[2]

CHAPTER 1

Beginnings

PELHAM Davis Glassford descended from sturdy Scottish stock. His maternal grandfather, Samuel Burwell Davis, born in Ohio in 1826, was commissioned as an officer and surgeon during the Civil War and served on General Ulysses S. Grant's staff. During the Vicksburg Campaign, Doctor Davis contracted typhoid fever, which affected him for the rest of his life. Following the war he became the medical director at Fort Marcy, near Santa Fe, in what was then the New Mexico Territory. His wife, Elizabeth, born in Ohio in 1832, accompanied him on the dangerous trip across the plains. The couple initially lived in Santa Fe and then resettled in the small town of Las Vegas, New Mexico, where Davis functioned as the presidentially appointed Internal Revenue assessor. Elizabeth Davis was among the first English-speaking women to reside in what is now the town of Las Vegas, New Mexico. After Samuel's death in 1874, Elizabeth managed a frontier hotel in Las Vegas.[1]

Pelham Glassford's paternal grandfather, John Knox Glassford, was born in Hamilton, Ohio, in 1826. In 1848 he married Augusta M. Lucas, and in 1865 they migrated south to Missouri, settling near Carthage. Four of their children died young, but two survived, one of whom was William Alexander Glassford, who would become Pelham Glassford's father. John later purchased a 290-acre farm of rich Missouri topsoil and, with Augusta, muscled the land into an orchard of 5,500 fruit trees, two miles south of Carthage. The couple marketed fruit locally and as far away as Wichita, Kansas; San Antonio, Texas; and Monterrey, Mexico. In 1882 John and Augusta resettled in the Salt River Valley in the Arizona Territory, where they found the desert landscape surprisingly receptive to growing cotton and fruit. John Glassford retained sufficient ties with Missouri to assist his son and later two grandsons in gaining appointments to the nation's most selective military academies.²

William Alexander Glassford, who would later become Pelham Glassford's father, was born in 1853 near Monticello, Tippecanoe County, Indiana. With his father's assistance, he was admitted to the United States Naval Academy in 1871. While on a Mediterranean cruise for midterm midshipmen, he suffered an acute illness, requiring that he resign from the Academy. By the time he had regained his health, he had lost his appointment but not his desire to become a military officer. He enlisted in the US Army as a private in 1874. Because of his aptitude for electrical engineering, the army assigned him to the Signal Corps. He was promoted to sergeant in 1877, and by 1879 he had won a commission as a second lieutenant. As a signal officer assigned to the Department of Missouri, his primary duty was overseeing the installation and operation of telegraph lines throughout the vast areas of the New Mexico and Arizona Territories. Family lore would later hold that William had captured the Apache chief Geronimo. While not accurate, as will be seen, William did play a significant role in Geronimo's capture.³

The American defeat of Mexico in 1848 resulted in the transfer of an enormous amount of land to the United States, which eventually became the states of Texas, California, New Mexico, Arizona, and parts of Colorado, Utah, Nevada, Kansas, and Wyoming. Seemingly overnight, the American Southwest opened to migration. For those easterners willing to take the risks, the 900-mile-long Santa Fe Trail served as the primary path. The last stop on the trail was the village of Las Vegas, Spanish for "the meadows," situated in the grasslands of the Gallinas River Valley in the New Mexico Territory. The small village sprouted quickly. The Santa Fe Trail began in Independence, Missouri, crossed Kansas, offered a choice of nicking Oklahoma or Colorado—depending on the time of year—and entered the northeastern corner of the New Mexico Territory. Much of the route was wide open, windblown, unprotected prairieland with occasional swollen rivers to ford. The long wagon trains passed through the traditional lands of 30,000 members of various Indigenous American tribes, which on occasion greeted the trespassers with arrows and lances. Other trail dangers included wildfires, hailstorms, blizzards, dust, deep mud, and mosquitoes. For the brave-hearted travelers, the route was not difficult to track; just follow the wagon-wheel ruts.⁴

Upon reaching the New Mexico Territory, the travelers looked forward to arriving at Fort Union, a supply and communications center, situated in a massive grassland flanked by distant mountains. Arriving at the fort meant not only safety but medical care as well. On a typical day, distant dust trails announced the arrivals of as many as 30 to 100 caravans, each of which might consist of up to 200 wagons, representing an enormous migration.[5]

Lieutenant William Glassford visited Fort Union as part of his telegraph duties, sometimes finding it necessary to travel to Las Vegas, New Mexico, thirty miles away, a day's horseback ride. In 1879 the small town, which had begun as a collection of log and adobe houses surrounding a livestock plaza, became the terminus of the Atchison, Topeka, and Santa Fe (AT&SF) Railroad. The arrival of the railroad gave Las Vegas a growth spurt, making it rival Denver, Tucson, El Paso, and Santa Fe.[6]

It soon became clear that Las Vegas needed a first-class hotel. Benigno Romero, a local contractor, obliged by building the Plaza Hotel in 1882. The grand hotel of Victorian style had three floors with fourteen-foot ceilings, tall windows, and a grand facade with a center-top crown. Inside the hotel were thirty-seven guest rooms, a dining room, a saloon, and a large dancehall. Guests climbed and descended the two matching walnut staircases that spiraled from the lobby to the top.[7]

What the hotel and adjacent plaza needed next was a skilled manager, someone smart enough to develop its reputation as the best hotel in the territory but tough enough to handle the rough-and-tumble frontier crowd. The arrival of the railroad regularly brought many visitors to Las Vegas, most of whom were upstanding but some of whom were low down. Jesse James and Billy the Kid purportedly first met in Las Vegas, and dentist Doc Holliday owned one of the two dozen rowdy saloons near the plaza. On one occasion in 1880, local vigilantes, fed up with drifters and outlaws shooting up the town, forcefully extracted three from the jail and hanged them from a windmill derrick on the plaza, and then fired bullets into the swinging bodies. Posters appeared on walls warning twenty-some other suspected desperados to leave town that night or be invited to a necktie party hosted by 100 concerned citizens.[8]

The tough first-ever manager of the Plaza Hotel, which opened in March 1882, would be Elizabeth Davis, now the widow of Dr. Samuel Burwell Davis. Elizabeth had sold their nearby Montezuma Hot Springs resort, popular for curing all varieties of ills and diseases, and accepted the offer to manage the new hotel. Not everyone agreed that she was the best choice. Russell A. Kistler, owner and editor of the *Las Vegas Daily Optic* newspaper, was critical of her appointment: "While we have nothing in particular to heave over into Mrs. Davis's back yard," he wrote, "we have always contended that a hotel the size of the Plaza should be engineered by a man." The Las Cruces, New Mexico, *Rio Grande Republican* newspaper disagreed, asserting, "Mrs. Davis is certainly the queen of hotel-keepers in this Territory, and will make a success of the house, if human efforts can do it."[9]

One who frequently visited Las Vegas was twenty-eight-year-old Lieutenant William Glassford. *The Las Vegas Daily Gazette* reported that the lieutenant commanded the US Army signal service in the New Mexico Territory and now maintained his quarters at the Plaza Hotel. The room rate of $7.00 per week (about $195 in 2021 dollars) was reasonable, but the young lieutenant had other things on his mind; he could hardly keep his eyes off Elizabeth's daughter, Allie. The twenty-three-year-old had lived and worked in the hotel since its opening. No doubt she had noticed the handsome young army lieutenant as well.[10]

Likely having courted for some months, the young couple married, the ceremony taking place on October 24, 1882, within the Plaza Hotel. The Right Reverend George Kelly Dunlop, Episcopalian bishop, officiated. The *Las Vegas Daily Gazette* reported that Lieutenant Glassford was well known in New Mexico and Colorado, having been stationed at Santa Fe in charge of the military telegraph lines, and having built the observatory on Pikes Peak. The *Gazette* described Allie, known by all in her small community, as a " handsome and accomplished young lady."[11]

William and Allie made their way to Fort Leavenworth, Kansas, where, by late March, the couple knew that Allie was expecting. They agreed that Allie would return to the Plaza Hotel and stay with her mother while William remained at Fort Leavenworth but would endeavor to reach Las Vegas for the baby's birth. Presumably, William arrived in time to welcome Pelham Davis Glassford, delivered on August 8, 1883, with the *Las Vegas Daily Optic* noting that the "handsome baby boy" was delivered within the hotel. On August 21 William reluctantly packed and returned to Fort Leavenworth, after which the *Gazette* assured its readers, "The boy is doing nicely and grows an inch a day."[12]

Allie and baby Pelham remained in Las Vegas for two months before joining William in Kansas in October. By 1885 the army had transferred William to the Presidio of San Francisco, where a second son was born on June 6, 1886. William Alexander Glassford II would be called "Bill." Both boys would grow up in a military family. Such a life is not without its challenges. Most military dependents grow up having to change schools and friends every few years because of frequent reassignments and accept occasional absences of the military parent, sometimes sent to a location unsuitable for a family. That was indeed the case when the army dispatched Lieutenant Glassford and his Signal Corps soldiers to the Arizona Territory on a special mission. Allie and the two boys remained in San Francisco for the time being, but they soon returned to Las Vegas to be with her mother.[13]

The lieutenant's mission was to assist in tracking and capturing the evasive Geronimo and his elusive band of Apaches. The army had been attempting that for some time, but the chief and his warriors always seemed to evaporate. Historian Donald E. Worcester describes these Apache guerrilla fighters: "Those who failed to qualify as warriors were treated with contempt. The hardy warrior produced by this exacting process was a relentless and pitiless foe, a master at stealth, surprise, and flight. His endurance was incredible; a warrior on foot could cover seventy miles in a day. Apaches scorned heroics; if they could not gain overwhelming advantage over an enemy by stealth it was foolish to risk battle."[14]

Lieutenant Glassford and his eleven signal soldiers joined the search, bringing with them thirty-seven heliographs, ten telescopes, thirty marine glasses (binoculars), and an aneroid barometer. They immediately began setting up a heliograph system on mountain peaks in the New Mexico and Arizona Territories. The equipment could track and help searchers pinpoint Geronimo's location. Mounted on waist-high portable tripods, the heliographs utilized the combined power of the sun, mirrors, shutters, and Morse code to flash line-of-sight messages from one mountain peak to the next and on to others. The mountain-top soldiers used the telescopes to detect human movement from the dust plumes in the deserts far below, alerting other soldiers by signal the direction and progress of the Apaches. Worcester considered this as military smoke signals, adding that the soldiers could send a twenty-five-word message 400 miles and receive an answer within four hours. Guided by the heliographs, one cavalry troop pursued Geronimo's dust trail, while troops at distant locations positioned for a possible arrival. The pursuit took four months and covered 1,400 miles, but on September 4, 1886, as capture grew inevitable, Geronimo and his warriors, bedraggled and beaten down from the continual pursuit, turned themselves in. The chief "laid his rifle down twenty feet away and came and shook hands."[15]

In March 1887 Lieutenant Glassford reported to his next assignment as superintendent of US Army Signal Service for the Department of Arizona, which included New Mexico, and was headquartered at Fort Whipple, northeast of Prescott, Arizona. In May of that year, Allie and the two boys joined him. By now the lieutenant had found that the climate and beauty of the Southwest pleased him. In a letter to his parents, he suggested that they consider coming west, and recommended that they homestead in the Salt River Valley of the Arizona Territory. That was enough of a pull for John and Augusta Glassford; they journeyed west, staked their claim, found a place to live, and established the first of what would become multiple farms in the Valley, in today's metropolitan Phoenix.[16]

Of course, the two territories were still untamed, as evidenced by an incident witnessed by Allie. On February 26, 1888, the *Arizona Silver Belt* newspaper posted the following story: "Mrs. Glassford brings word of a deed of violence committed at Gallup, New Mexico, while the train was there, on which she was a passenger. If we caught the story correctly, three men were gambling, when the loser became enraged and murdered one or both of his companions. An excited mob arose and at once lynched the murderer, and in lieu of a rope they cut the bell cord out of the coach in which Mrs. Glassford was seated." The article removed any doubt that the territories were still part of the Wild West.[17]

The young Glassford family departed Arizona in June 1889, anticipating William's upcoming assignment to Washington, DC. The transfer to the nation's capital would come with a promotion to first lieutenant. Many in the Southwest knew William well and regretted his departure, since they had essentially adopted him as their telegraph representative.[18]

In Washington Allie enrolled young Pelham in the Weightman public school at Twenty-third Street and M Street NW. For the young family from the desert, Washington must have been quite a contrast. Glassford's new assignment was with the army's national weather service, with duties that included reporting on issues in the far western arid belt. Twenty years previous, Congress and President Ulysses S. Grant had mandated that the army establish and operate such a service, which the army had assigned to the Signal Service. While there, the young lieutenant hoped to dispel the East Coast thinking that Arizona weather was too extreme, later reporting, "It is recorded as extreme yet no one suffers, and sun strokes are unknown. This is usually accounted for from the purity and dryness of the air," adding that the "pure air is a tonic to shattered constitutions, a healing balsam to the consumptive."[19]

Glassford's work was mostly routine, excepting one day in particular; that was when Frances Folsom Cleveland, the wife of President Grover Cleveland, sent an inquiry to the weather service asking what the weather would be for the following day, as she hoped to host a White House Garden party. The lieutenant assured the First Lady that the weather would be pleasant, as it had been for some time. The arrival of a sudden spring snowstorm the next day likely caused the young officer to anticipate a transfer back to the frontier.[20]

The army did not banish Lieutenant Glassford to the desert. On the contrary, it gave him a handsome sword for his eighteen years of dedicated service and dispatched him to Paris, France. His mission was to collect information on "military ballooning, moveable search and signal lights and military telegraphs, and to witness the use of these appliances in connection with military maneuvers during the autumn in France and Germany." In June 1892 the Glassford family boarded the ship that would take them across the Atlantic. The passage must have caused great excitement for the young family and likely some seasickness; fortunately, it was a summer voyage. Pelham, age nine, having begun school in Washington, would continue his education in France. In Paris the family found a flat in upscale Passy, on the right bank of the Seine in the Sixteenth arrondissement, where Benjamin Franklin had once resided.[21]

As Pelham had feared, French would be the only language spoken at the school. He and young Bill found that understanding and speaking French was difficult, although their young, receptive minds stayed afloat throughout their near-total immersion. When the family departed more than a year later, the brothers carried with them a respectable foundation in French language and culture, which would serve each well in his future professional life. William's Paris assignment ended in July 1893 and required that he precede his family to the United States, where he would create the first-ever US Army Observational Balloon Unit, at Fort Logan, Colorado, ten miles south of Denver. Allie, eleven-year-old Pelham, and nine-year-old Bill remained in France for a while, departing from Boulogne-sur-Mer on the *Spaarndam*, a Belfast-built sailing steamship, and arrived in New York on October 2, 1893. By the end of the year, William Glassford had successfully completed his examination for promotion and soon pinned on the silver bars of a captain.[22]

On February 15, 1898, following an explosion, the US battleship *Maine* sank in Havana Harbor, killing 260 officers and sailors. On April 16, 1898, the army ordered Captain Glassford and his Signal Corps unit to report to Fort Wadsworth, New York, and by

June 9 he had been promoted to major. Glassford would serve as chief signal officer for I Corps (the Roman numeral usually being pronounced "eye"). Working under Major General John R. Brooke, Major Glassford and his troops would take part in what would become known as the Spanish-American War. Allie and the boys remained in Colorado for a while but then left to stay with her mother in New Mexico.[23]

American motives in the Spanish-American War were mixed. It seemed reasonable to support Cuba's ongoing revolution for independence from Spain, which appeared to be much like the revolt by the thirteen colonies against England. Newspaper giants William Randolph Hearst and Joseph Pulitzer, aided by public opinion, pressured the president and Congress to demand that Spain relinquish control of Cuba. Others saw the opportunity to acquire Spanish possessions in the Caribbean and Pacific as well. The puzzling explosion and sinking of the *Maine* served as the catalyst. The US Navy had anchored the battleship to protect Americans in Cuba who might find themselves somehow entrapped in the crossfire. A preliminary naval investigation concluded that a mine had caused the explosion, and it suspected Spanish sabotage. More than seventy years later, investigators would ascertain that ammunition stored too close to burning coal in a bunker had caused the explosion from within the ship. But for those with lustful eyes, the explosion had become the needed motive for American expansion. Soon overwhelmed, Spain sued for peace and surrendered dominion of Puerto Rico, Wake Island, Guam, Samoa, Cuba, and other territories. The fighting in the Caribbean ended in less than four months, but the hostilities in the Philippines would continue and require the US Army to station troops there for decades to come.[24]

Likely disappointed that the army had ordered him to liberate Puerto Rico rather than Cuba—where the fighting was sure to occur—newly promoted Brevet Lieutenant Colonel Glassford assumed responsibility for all signal service operations in Puerto Rico. His command of 300 soldiers would take charge of all telegraph lines on the island. During this time, Puerto Rico saw little in the way of hostile gunfire with many Puerto Ricans welcoming the Americans as liberators. Glassford based himself in the telegraph office in Arroyo, from where he could control all telegraph communication on the island.[25]

A few days later, while investigating the contents of a backroom closet in the telegraph office, Glassford serendipitously discovered on the top shelf a cache of old telegraph instruments, hidden beneath decades of dust. A closer inspection revealed that the instruments had once belonged to none other than Professor Samuel B. Morse, inventor of the telegraph and its eponymous code. Glassford learned that Professor Morse and his daughter had often spent their winters in Puerto Rico. The colonel, who for many years had erected telegraph lines in the Southwest, was thrilled at the historic find and ensured that the instruments found their way to the Smithsonian Institution.[26]

On August 9, 1899, Puerto Rico turned dangerous once again when a hurricane made landfall. Colonel Glassford reported to the Adjutant General in Washington, DC, that "a [hurricane] has just passed over the island, prostrating telegraph and telephone lines. Several have been killed. My quarters were wrecked and the signal barracks partially destroyed likewise. Hundreds of native houses were destroyed. The center and south of the Island worse."[27]

Following the war, Glassford remained as chief signal officer on Puerto Rico. By March 1900, having found suitable living arrangements, he sent for Allie and the boys. Now teenagers, Pelham and Bill had most recently attended school in Denver and now resumed their studies on the island, attending the Model School in San Juan. It seems that the family found the island suitable, as the *Santa Fe New Mexican* reported to the folks back home that "Mrs. Glassford and their two sons are with [William], and they all like their station very well.[28]

On September 1, 1900, the *Santa Fe New Mexican* reported that some months before, young Pelham Glassford had gone to Jefferson City, Missouri, to compete for nomination by his representative in Congress for conditional appointment to West Point, and subsequently had scored highest among the twenty-two applicants. One month away from his seventeenth birthday, he received the letter he hoped for: the United States Military Academy had accepted his application to attend. He was due to report immediately for summer camp, which would begin with something called "Beast Barracks," certainly an unsettling name. Suitcase in hand, he began the sea and land journey from Puerto Rico to New York and on to West Point, arriving there on July 24, 1900.[29]

Pelham had received two appointments to West Point. This was due in large part to his grandfather, John Knox Glassford, who, although residing in Arizona, remained well connected in Missouri. Because Missouri was his father's home state, Pelham chose to use that appointment, which had been offered by Senator Francis M. Cockrell; in fact, it had been Pelham's grandparents' residence in Carthage that had allowed Pelham to take the admission test. His second appointment had come from President William McKinley.[30]

Senator Cockrell, a portly man with receding hair and a chin beard almost the length of his face, was not only a successful attorney but a former Confederate general as well. He knew a thing or two about the qualities needed by an officer in battle, having served throughout the Vicksburg Campaign. On May 16, 1863, he had distinguished himself at the critical Battle of Champion Hill. Ironically, Pelham's maternal grandfather, Samuel B. Davis, had also been at Vicksburg, the battle lasting from just-bearable May to intolerably torrid July. It was in the swamps around Vicksburg that the doctor had contracted the typhoid fever that necessitated his medical retirement. Cockrell must have thought highly of the Glassford family. Aside from Pelham's West Point appointment, the senator had given Pelham's father his Annapolis appointment twenty-nine years earlier and would give Pelham's brother Bill his Annapolis appointment two years in the future. The result would be an army colonel, an army general, and a navy admiral.[31]

CHAPTER 2

Monastery on the Hudson

FOLLOWING the American Revolution, the newly formed Congress concluded that it had little need for a standing army in peacetime, finding it "dangerous to the liberties of a free people." Thus, it made no sense to invest in a national military academy. Others, having just witnessed what historian David McCullough termed a "rabble in arms" army, saw the need for a professionally trained officer corps, knowing that the Revolution's successful outcome had "seemed little short of a miracle." Thus, in 1802 a Corps of Engineers school of seven officers and ten cadets constituted the nation's first military academy. Its location was West Point, New York, overlooking a sharp turn in the Hudson River, which originally served as a defensive position to control navigation on the river, should the British or anyone else have in mind to invade. In 1812 Congress reorganized and expanded the school but noted little improvement. Then, in 1817, Sylvanus Thayer, who would become the "Father of the Military Academy," initiated and shaped what became the United States Military Academy (USMA) at West Point. What he had in mind, however, resembled a monastery more than a university.[1]

The USMA Academic Board consisted of the superintendent and a group of permanent professors who exercised near total control over the school. Generally, cadets were not permitted to have money, were encamped during three of the four summers, were required to recite in every class daily, were graded daily, and ranked from high to low weekly. While other colleges and universities of that era had moved beyond rote memorization and standing recitation as ways to educate students, West Point saw no need to alter these practices. Historian D. Clayton James says of West Point, "Once a leader in some disciplines, particularly engineering, West Point had gradually secluded itself from the changing currents of higher education." In the years following the Civil War, the Academy became, in the view of historian Stephen Ambrose, "a small, forgotten, narrowly professional college tucked away in a corner of New York state, paying no attention to the outside world and receiving none in return."[2]

In 1900, the year Pelham Glassford began at West Point, the superintendent was Colonel General Albert L. Mills, USMA, 1879, who oversaw the Academy with his staff, professors, and instructors. At the start of the new century, the Academy had graduated about 4,000 cadets. Of that number, 3.5 percent were sons or grandsons of previous graduates. Ethnically, the new cadets were mostly of Anglo-Saxon Irish, English, Scottish, and German descent. They were exclusively male, overwhelmingly Caucasian, and primarily Protestant. West Point had admitted its first African American cadet, James W. Smith, in 1870, and graduated its first African American cadet, Henry O. Flipper, in 1877. Rather than being harassed, African American cadets were ostracized.[3]

A disturbing change had occurred at West Point in the years after the Civil War. It was then that severe hazing became inculcated into West Point's culture. Unlike other universities, where students chose from numerous extracurricular activities, West Point offered no amusements or organized recreation other than sports, a debating society, and the YMCA. Cadets were permitted to leave the Academy only on horseback but were forbidden to halt or dismount. The result was that hazing emerged as the primary outlet for an abundance of youthful energy. The most enthusiastic hazers at the Academy were the "yearlings," the second-year cadets. Having survived their first year as "plebes," they now relished in hazing the new plebes. Dwight D. Eisenhower, class of 1911, had his own recollections of yearlings: "There's probably no individual in the world more serenely arrogant than the cadet who has just left the ranks of Plebes to become a lordly 'Yearling.'" By the time Eisenhower arrived in 1911, the hazing had become just verbal, but in 1900, during Glassford's tenure, it went well beyond that.[4]

As Pelham Glassford made his way to West Point, he was one of approximately 124 cadets admitted to West Point that year. He was just sixteen, a week shy of his seventeenth birthday, the youngest cadet in his class. Many of the teenagers heading to West Point arrived at the West Shore Rail station at the village of Buttermilk Falls (later Highland Falls), having boarded in New York City, about forty-five miles to the south. Glassford had elected to take one of the steamboats of the Hudson River Day

Line, which had transported passengers since the 1860s, steaming from New York to Albany and back, with stops in between, including West Point. On that July 24, 1900, he was sitting near the ship's railing, prepping for the upcoming West Point entrance examination. With his nose buried in an American history book, he did not see the other West Point-bound teenager approach. Robert N. Danford, from New Boston, Illinois, easily picked Glassford, "a tall, gangling, and very youthful appearing boy," to be a new cadet as well. Danford never suspected that he had just met someone who would be his friend for life. As Danford introduced himself, he concluded that "each [of us] became the first classmate known to the other." The two newbies soon had their first view of what would be their home for the next four years, appearing more like a remote and forbidding penitentiary than a university, backed by rugged granite cliffs and hills of dense trees. Glassford and Danford, along with other new arrivals, suitcases in hand, trudged up the long steep hill in the uncomfortably warm and sticky morning, ensuring that they arrived before noon. They would attend until June 15, 1904, having only a few days off during the winter holidays followed by a two-month summer leave at completion of their second year, which must have seemed an eternity away.[5]

The first stop for the new arrivals was the adjutant's office, where the administrative and testing process was held. Yearling cadets, gray-jacketed with white trousers, waited patiently outside, eager to pounce on the unsuspecting plebes when they emerged. Once the freshmen appeared, the yearlings swarmed them, ensuring that the plebes ran and never walked a step thereafter. The yearlings crowded close to the new arrivals, loudly barking, "Run, run, run!" A barber gave the plebes a quick one-size-fits-all haircut and sent them back to the yearlings, who next ran them to the cadet store to draw uniforms and bedding.[6]

Danford was present when Glassford was given his West Point nickname on his first day, a name that would follow him through life. An upperclassman focused on Glassford and braced him until he managed to assume the preposterous position demanded: exceedingly erect, motionless, chin drawn to the back of the neck, shoulders squeezed back hard, stomach pulled in tight, preferably maintained without appearing to take a breath. Not a single upperclassman provided anything in the way of informative instruction; every word was a growl or a shout intended to intimidate. Glassford attempted to hold in his arms the impossible load just issued to him: a large bundle of uniforms, shoes, laundry bag, blanket, pillow, comforter, toilet articles, bucket, washbasin, broom, chair, table, soap, towel, and mattress. A yearling screamed at him, "Well, Mr. Ducrot, where do you think you are going?" Struggling to avoid dropping any item, the new plebe dared to look the yearling in the eye, who immediately screamed: "You take your slimy eyes off me. . . . Stand up! Get those shoulders back! Drag in that chin! Drag it in. Still more! You are the grossest thing I've ever seen, Mr. Dumbjohn!" Glassford held the brace but dropped the bucket. "Pick up that bucket!" The new cadet quickly scooped it up but somehow dropped the mattress. The upperclassman peppered him with a torrent of demands, seemingly never pausing to breathe. Senior cadets now ringed him, shouting, "Pick up that mattress. Don't be slow!" The mattress would not fold or roll or otherwise cooperate. Glassford found the situation so silly that he "opened his wide mouth and laughed and laughed." Outraged, the upperclassman demanded, "Mister, what's your name? Sound off!" The freshly arrived plebe answered as quickly as his Southwestern drawl allowed, saying, "Mr. Glassford, Sir." "No! Wrong!" barked the upperclassman. "Say, I'm the happy, laughing Mr. Glassford, Sir!"[7]

In saying what he said, the upperclassman unintentionally assigned to Glassford the nickname that he would carry not only through West Point but for life: "Happy," often shortened to "Hap." Plebe Danford likely witnessed the christening. As Glassford's future wife Cora later wrote, "That name which has clung to him through the years, is as much a part of him as is the broad smile in the friendly face. It came to him in 1900, on his first day at West Point." Worse by far was that Glassford found it nearly impossible not to laugh at the ridiculous demands. "That spontaneous, sunny smile, which was as much a part of him then as it is now, and never 'wiped off' for long, no matter how barking the command!"[8]

To intensify the intimidation of each "confrontation," upperclassmen endeavored to get nose-to-nose with the plebes, only an inch or two away. The problem was that the upperclassmen were typically five foot ten or thereabouts; Glassford stood six feet three. Thus, an upperclassman looking directly at Glassford would see his Adam's apple and would have to look up to see him eye-to-eye. Whether Glassford kept his eyes directly forward or dared to look down, there must have been a serious dilution of the attempted intimidation. "Calculated chaos" was how Eisenhower later described his first day at West Point: "Here we were, the cream of the crop, shouted at all day long by self-important upperclassmen, telling us to run here and run there; pick up our clothes; bring in that bedding; put your shoulders back, keep our eyes up, and to keep running, running, running."[9]

It was Glassford's misfortune that 1900, his plebe year, marked the high point of West Point hazing. Historian Barbara Tuchman states, "Hazing had reached an extreme at this time," which would soon result in a Congressional hearing. Two of Glassford's fellow plebes shared his same poor timing: future generals Joseph W. Stilwell, from Yonkers, New York, and Lesley J. McNair, from Verndale, Minnesota. Stilwell, five foot nine and weighing 145 pounds, must have been a more inviting target than Glassford. It was perhaps fortunate for the upperclassmen hazers that they encountered Stilwell long before he earned his acidic nickname of "Vinegar Joe." By March 1901, members of Congress would undertake an investigation of hazing at West Point, but by then the three plebes would be yearlings.[10]

During the summers the Corps of Cadets, plebes through seniors, bivouacked and underwent basic and advanced training, where they learned the basics of soldiering. However, before the plebes could join the annual summer camp with the senior cadets, the new arrivals had to survive "Beast Barracks," a shortened name for Basic Cadet Training. As Eisenhower recalled, "During the three weeks as a Beast, no form of animal life is more obnoxious and pestiferous than the ubiquitous cadet instructor. He—there were many—was all over the place, his only mission, as we saw it, was to torment and persecute Plebes." It would have been relatively easy to obey reasonable orders, but usually the demands were capricious and often idiotic. Even so, any hesitation might result in harsh discipline, possibly leading to dismissal of the plebe or a pressured resignation, and thus succeeded in achieving immediate and unquestioned obedience. Upperclassmen demanded that plebes do such things as squat over upended bayonets; hang by their thumbs; stand on their heads; hold a rifle at arm's length for an extended period; be "sweated" (wrapped in blankets and raincoats during the summer heat); eat excessive amounts of Tabasco sauce, molasses, or perhaps 200 prunes; and run nude through a gauntlet of upperclassmen who dumped cold water on the naked sprinters. Other times the upperclassmen demanded that the plebes sit under the table to eat their meals, engage in staged fistfights with skilled cadet boxers, take scalding steam baths, slide naked on a splintered board, undergo paddling, and do "eagles," which were continuous deep-knee bends with outstretched arms performed over ground spread with broken glass. The intent of Beast Barracks was to weed out those plebes who could not withstand intense pressure and thus might falter in battle.[11]

During the fourth week the intense hazing slacked off and the plebes were integrated into the Corps of Cadets. Upperclassmen and plebes lived in tents and went through the same training, but plebes also did "special duty," which meant that they became the personal servants of the upperclassmen: folding their clothes, cleaning their rifles, sabers, spurs, and shoes, and any other chore demanded. Not every cadet found Beast Barracks to be that difficult. Future General of the Army Omar Bradley saw Beast Barracks as a "great leveler." He later wrote, "There were among us many pampered boys, campus heroes and heartthrobs, prep school snobs and even a few bullies. Hazing knocked the wind out of their sails in a hurry." But future General Douglas MacArthur, class of 1903, later wrote, "Hazing was practiced with a worthy goal, but with methods that were violent and uncontrolled." West Point not only tolerated this hazing, but its faculty, upperclassmen, and West Point alumni supported it; even plebes accepted it as a rite of passage. But what was undeniable was that it was often teenagers doing it to other teenagers, with little supervision.[12]

Following the summer camp, West Point assigned the cadets to their barracks and classes. The organization of the Corps was that of a battalion consisting of six companies, A through F, each having about 100 cadets, assigned by height. The latter was necessary, Omar Bradley remembered, "so that when the corps marched as a group the lines of our hats, rifles and greatcoats would not be jagged. The tallest cadets, including most of the athletes, were assigned to A and F companies, which marched on the flanks and were thus called 'flankers.' The smaller men, called 'runts,' were assigned to B, C, D and E companies, which marched in the middle between the flankers." Glassford, not surprisingly, was a flanker, as were the cadets nearest him, all over six feet, who became good friends. Cadets marched as a group, as they did to most every destination.[13]

During the years that Glassford attended West Point, the professors were all long-term veterans who had essentially owned their positions for decades. Engineers had designed the Academy to educate military engineers, and cadets who excelled at math were the most welcomed. An early West Point professor affirmed, "Like the house that defied the storm, West Point is built on a rock, and that rock is mathematics." Subjects such as history, English, and other topics outside the sciences were considered less important, and the curriculum offered few choices. The teaching method was by rote, with cadets standing and reciting from memory, each expected to do so at least once during each class, with instructors rating their recitation. One of the subjects in which Glassford would lead his class was drawing. While West

Point drawing might include some human figure drawing, it focused more on maps, topography, elements of terrain, survey plotting, linear perspective, color, engineer design, and ordnance. Glassford, already familiar with French and Spanish, also led his class in modern languages. Under intense academic pressure, all cadets looked forward to the annual three-day visit to the Gettysburg battlefield to study the tactics used by both armies. The visit was a rare opportunity to leave the campus.[14]

Discipline was exacting and enforced continually. Cadets received demerits for minor infractions, such as not having properly adjusted one's uniform collar or leaving dust on a windowsill. After nine demerits in a month, cadets had to "walk off" the additional demerits; with rifles on their shoulders, the "area birds" paced smartly back and forth within a defined area, one demerit worked off per hour.[15]

How a cadet did academically over the course of four years determined in which branch of the army he would serve. Those in the top 10 percent could request a specific branch, with most selecting Engineers or Artillery, thought to provide better promotional opportunities. As the top graduate of his 1903 class, Douglas MacArthur, one year ahead of Glassford, chose Engineers. In their 1904 class, Glassford and McNair, surviving stiff competition, chose Artillery, and Stilwell, who hated those "oat blowers" of the horse Cavalry, chose Infantry.[16]

Overarching the West Point academic program was the honor system, which held that cadets will not lie, cheat, or steal, or tolerate those who do. Those convicted were almost always expelled. While it might seem that failure to report an abusive hazing of a plebe by an upperclassman would violate the honor system as an act of omission, quite the opposite was the case. As historian and biographer Carlo D'Este notes, "Hazing produced a code of silence on the part of the hapless plebes, and it became a matter of dishonor to expose upperclassmen who perpetuated such mischief."[17]

In 1898, two years before Glassford's arrival, a serious hazing abuse had occurred that involved plebe Oscar L. Booz. During his first summer camp, upperclassmen designated him as a special duty cadet, detailed to do whatever they demanded. Tired after a long day of drill, Booz refused to do an assigned duty, muttering that the upperclassman could do it himself. The upperclassmen assigned another cadet, known to be a good boxer, to fight Booz in a staged bout. By the second round Booz was on the ground refusing to get up. Weeks of humiliation and ostracism followed, during which upperclassmen forced him to eat Tabasco sauce—the hell sauce—at every meal. Thereafter, his throat became so enflamed that he had to withdraw from West Point, and within two years he died of tuberculosis of the larynx.[18]

Similarly, Douglas MacArthur, the son of a famous army officer, was also given severe hazing. Upperclassmen singled out cadets with military fathers for increased hazing. On one occasion, a group of southern upperclassmen braced MacArthur and made him recite his father's full Civil War record three times, then ordered that he stand immobile for an hour. Three separate groups of upperclassmen then forced him to do spread eagles until he fainted. Once back in his tent, he went into convulsions.[19]

Rumors of MacArthur's severe hazing and convulsions leaked out, and on the heels of the hazing of Booz, resulted in Congress insisting that President McKinley order a special court of inquiry to investigate West Point hazing. In December 1900 the court called MacArthur to testify as a witness under oath. He told the members of the court what had happened but shrugged off his convulsions as simple exhaustion and cramping. Despite persistent questioning, he refused to name the upperclassmen involved, saying that plebes were "not to look at those who are hazing them"; thus, he explained, he never saw who was doing it. After that, the court excused him. He later wrote, "Under questioning I fully explained all the circumstances, but refused to divulge the names of the upperclassmen involved." His denial under oath was unconvincing and most probably perjury, or at least a violation of the West Point honor system. Even so, the Academic Board permitted him to remain at the Academy, and the Corps of Cadets gave him a "bootlick," meant as giving their full approval for his resistance. He later wrote, "I would be no tattle tale."[20]

While Glassford was also the son of an army officer, his father was not famous, and thus Pelham was not singled out for special hazing. On another occasion, however, he felt compelled to report a rather serious violation by one of his classmates. As a result, other upperclassmen made him swallow the hell sauce, endangering his health. Like MacArthur and virtually all the cadets, he refused to name the upperclassmen involved.[21]

Glassford's class finished its plebe year on June 11, 1901. The previous January, Congress had passed a law making it illegal for an upperclassman to do anything "of a harassing, tyrannical, abusive, shameful, insulting, or humiliating nature, or that [might] endanger the physical well-being of such candidate or cadet." As a result, such actions were not only West Point violations, but unlawful. Still, one cadet later wrote in the 1904 *Howitzer* yearbook, "Under pressure we had a meeting in the mess hall, where we passed a resolution to quit the practice of hazing, as far as the four classes assembled were concerned. Our report was incorporated in a report to the Committee. From the results, this did not have a great effect." He added, "We were plebes under the old regime," his statement suggesting something of a badge of courage."[22]

In the summer of 1902, Hap began his long awaited two-month leave, while his younger brother Willian began his plebe year at Annapolis. As had been the case with Hap, John Knox Glassford had assisted grandson Bill in gaining his academy appointment, and like his older brother, Bill was the youngest in his class.[23]

During his first three years at the Academy, Glassford had held the ranks of corporal, sergeant, acting first sergeant, and during his fourth and final year, captain in charge of E Company. He played on the intramural tennis and golf teams. "Happy" Glassford graduated with a respectable standing of 18 of 124. "Whitey" McNair, "nicknamed for his strikingly white hair," edged him out, graduating at 11, and "Joe" Stilwell finished at 32.[24]

As graduation neared, excitement grew. The *Howitzer* featured short poems and descriptions describing each cadet. Of Glassford it said:

> You mavy think he walks on stilts;
> He surely is not stuffed with quilts;
> But Happy he is, a captain to be;
> Though he's young enough still to wear kilts.

The *Howitzer* board offered the following comment as well, likely meant for his fellow cadets, who would be the only ones to understand the significance of the puzzling sentences below:

> In looking at this picture do not think you have seen all, for there is more below, which the camera failed to take in. With a faint, little chuckle, strictly his own, he loves to tell harrowing tales of sentimental scenes in Morro Castle. Although delighting in walks with Cuban maidens on the Plaza, he draws the line on those wearing pink hosiery and yellow garters.[25]

While at West Point, Glassford had done some drawing on his own. One of his early drawings depicts a West Point cadet, shown in profile, wearing a full-dress uniform with a billed hat; the cadet is in the dark, his face and hands lit only by the match he is cupping to light his cigarette. Overall, the drawing appears somewhat amateurish when compared with a drawing Glassford did ten years later, showing much more sophistication. The subject of the latter drawing is a mounted field artillery soldier on a black horse, holding the guidon of Battery B, 1st Field Artillery, 1914, Hawaii. Wrapped around the frame is a banner reading "A Merry Christmas." The improvement is stark, evidencing Pelham's continued improvement over the decade, having benefited from art classes and practice.[26]

His friend Robert Danford, looking back over their four years at West Point, later wrote, "Glassford was a marked and popular man throughout our four years at West Point. Classmates sought his companionship and were always well entertained thereby." As the careers of the two new officers progressed, Danford remembered, "Endowed naturally with a rare gift of leadership, [Glassford] quickly became an idealized leader in the eyes of his enlisted men. . . . He was a champion always of fairness and justice and he pursued these ideas with brutal frankness."[27]

CHAPTER 3

A New Officer for a New Army

IN 1903, while Glassford was in his third year at West Point, Congress passed the Militia Act, also known as the (Charles) Dick Act, which would begin the transition of the various state militias into a single, standardized National Guard, allowing for federalization in an emergency. It fell to the regular army to provide standardized training and equipment for the National Guard units, but it also provided an opportunity to improve relations with the National Guard soldiers. In the next few years, Glassford would have occasion to assist in training two National Guard units, the Missouri National Guard, the state from which he had received his Academy appointment, and the Providence Marine Corps of Artillery, Rhode Island National Guard, with which he would later become closely associated.[1]

Even bigger changes were afoot for the army. It had begun in 1899 with the appointment of a new secretary of the army, Elihu Root. Trim and fit, his face calm, his light-colored hair stylishly parted in the middle, he projected no hint of the intensity with which he approached his work. Within four months of his appointment, he was ready to initiate major changes. Under his firm guidance, the army would no longer be just a chain of coast artillery forts loosely conjoined with a frontier constabulary; instead, it would become a unified national force of active and reserve components capable of rapid expansion to repel a foreign invader. Like the hub of a spoked wheel, the regular army would reach out to the state national guards along the rim. The army's new nonpolitical and merit-based officer corps would lead the way, focusing on simplicity, effectiveness, problem solving, and technological development by utilizing enhanced and coordinated education and training. It was a huge challenge for the new secretary, but Elihu Root had earned a reputation as a smart, tough corporation lawyer who got results. Over the next four-and-a-half years he would essentially reinvent the army, usually against determined resistance. His first effort was the most important: creating a single general staff to replace the ten fiercely independent bureau chiefs who fed, paid, supplied, armed, and administered the army, each focused on his own bureau. Although a commanding general oversaw the bureau generals, he had insufficient power to force change, with the other generals not bashful about calling on their powerful congressional friends for support. Root complained to Congress that no railroad or steel company would dare to operate in such an absurd manner. One who listened to Root's complaint was President Theodore Roosevelt, who in 1903 carried a big enough stick to give Root the general staff he needed. Root's next step was to create an Army War College, which would be charged with creating a postgraduate education system for the officer corps. West Point graduates, including Glassford, would play a vital role in developing what would become known as the army's "school system," a key element that would pay huge dividends in the years to come when the army prepared for World War II.[2]

In the meantime, while the country's population had doubled since the Civil War, the army's size had remained at 28,000 officers and soldiers, sprinkled over seventy-eight distant posts. Congress had temporarily increased its size for the Spanish-American War, but following Spain's capitulation, Congress had trimmed the army back to its prewar size. Confounding that action was the beginning of hostilities in the Philippines. Congress next voted to create what amounted to a temporary army of 65,000 regulars and 35,000 volunteers who would serve until July 1, 1901, after which Congress would reduce the army to 29,000.[3]

The situation in the Philippines was an outgrowth of the Spanish-American War, with the unintended consequence of initiating a transformation of the US Army. No longer would it be a home guard; rather, it would become a colonial army, with a significant percentage of American soldiers serving outside the United States in Cuba, Puerto Rico, Hawaii, and the Philippines. That notwithstanding, in terms of being any kind of global force, the US Army was insignificant. Europe's armies were substantially larger, even before ramping up for the world war: the German army had 620,000 soldiers, the French 560,000, and the British 250,000. By 1907 the American army had fewer than 98,000 soldiers.[4]

Upon graduating from West Point on June 15, 1904, Pelham Glassford, serial number 0–1899, was commissioned as a second lieutenant. He would serve in the Field Artillery and earn $1,700 per year ($47,456). While he and his fellow graduates may have saved some money while at the Academy, many would not have enough cash to even purchase their new uniforms.[5]

On July 11, 1904, the army assigned Pelham Glassford and three other freshly clad "shave tail" West Point second lieutenants to the 20th Battery Field Artillery at Fort Riley, Kansas. They would not have to report, however, until September, allowing them to take a well-deserved summer leave. The army had built Fort Riley in 1852, siting it where the primary emigrant trail from the east divided, one branch going northwest toward what would become the states of Oregon, Washington, and Utah, and the other going southwest toward what would become Colorado, New Mexico, Arizona, and California. After the army had sufficiently subjugated the various indigenous Indian tribes, it closed many of its frontier forts, but it spared Fort Riley, where the Cavalry and Field Artillery, both mounted branches, continued to train and serve.[6]

On his uniform, Glassford wore the crossed cannons of the Artillery Corps, which at that time included the Coast Artillery and the Field Artillery. Despite being a West Point graduate, he knew essentially nothing about field artillery. His training would now be on the job, with senior officers teaching him how to lead the soldiers who would serve under them, accurately fire the cannons, and care for the horses. Glassford would do so well during this training that the *Santa Fe Daily New Mexican* newspaper would later report, perhaps with more ebullient pride than evidence, that he had not only headed his field artillery training class but was also regarded as one of the best horsemen in the army. No doubt some cavalry officers must have scoffed at that.[7]

Following completion of his field artillery training, Glassford remained at Fort Riley, taking charge of a unit of soldiers. By now he had considerable training and experience with the soldiers, weapons, and horses. In 1906 the post commander assigned Glassford an auxiliary duty of organizing a baseball team. The lieutenant did so well that the commander promptly assigned him post athletic director.[8]

On January 25, 1907, the army promoted Glassford to first lieutenant. From May 9 to June 5 he attended temporary duty at a Coast Artillery post to better understand its mission. Coincidently, that same year, what had been the unified Artillery Corps formally separated into the Coast Artillery branch and the Field Artillery branch. Their similarity had been in the science of indirect fire delivery, but their differences in weapon size and mobility were greater. Glassford returned to Fort Riley, serving with the 6th Field Artillery. That same year he attended the Mounted Service School, which later transitioned into the year-long Cavalry School. For Pelham, who graduated at the top of his class, the training combined cavalry tactics with field artillery fire.[9]

As was the case with many mounted officers, Glassford took up polo, a sport both demanding and dangerous. He probably played well enough, but after a few months he decided that he preferred training horses to playing polo. For his personal mount he bought a spirited thoroughbred black colt, many hands high, and named him Taylor Boy, which he trained to the saddle and the cart. Thereafter, still the handsome bachelor, he was frequently seen "with his red-lined Artillery cape draped over the shoulders of the lady of his choice, seated in the cart beside him." In later life he would become well known for his horse-training talent.[10]

On August 28, 1907, the army returned Glassford to West Point to serve as an instructor in the Department of Drawing, where he would teach the topics that he had studied a few years before. His supervisor would be Colonel Charles W. Larned, who had taught him as a cadet, and who undoubtedly had requested his return to the Academy.[11]

Glassford was not the first of his 1904 class to return to West Point to instruct. His classmate Joseph Stilwell had arrived there in February 1906 to teach in the Department of Modern Languages. Stilwell noted in his diary, "First man in [the class of] 1904 back." During the summer, when the cadets attended their summer encampments, West Point instructors undertook other duties. Glassford's assignment was working with the National Guard. In August he instructed field artillery units of the Missouri National Guard at their summer encampment in St. Joseph, Missouri, and in subsequent summers between 1908 and 1911, he provided similar training to the Rhode Island National Guard.[12]

On other fronts, Glassford had met his match while posted in Kansas. There was no denying her beauty: a shock of auburn hair worn long and in trusses, a slender face and nose, dark eyes, and narrow shoulders, often invitingly uncovered. The population of young women at Fort Riley was so small that Glassford and every officer and soldier immediately noticed her, but Pelham's height and good looks gave him the edge over her other would-be suitors. Even though the army had returned him to West Point as an instructor, he had not forgotten her. He took leave from his teaching duties and returned to Fort Riley to marry her. She was Cora Arthur Carleton, born on November 25, 1886, on the campus of Texas A&M in College Station, Texas. She was the first child of a cavalry officer, Major Guy Edward Carleton, a veteran of frontier duty in the West, and Cora Belle Arthur, the major's wife. Like most army brats, Cora had grown up living in such places as Arizona, New Mexico, Minnesota, Kansas, China, and the Philippines. Pelham and Cora, he twenty-four and she twenty-one, exchanged vows in the Fort Riley post chapel on December 25, 1907, the Reverend Frank R. Millspaugh, bishop of the Episcopal Church in Kansas, officiating. Pelham and Cora would go on to rear four children.[13]

During Glassford's first three years as a West Point instructor, he held several positions within the department and had become the senior instructor. As he began the fourth year of a five-year assignment, he learned that Professor Larned had become seriously ill and had left the Academy for extended treatment and was not likely to return. The West Point superintendent appointed Glassford as acting-professor and suggested that he might be interested in a full professorship, a coveted position. The assignment came with full colonel rank and pay and beautiful on-campus quarters, but it would essentially relegate him to an academic professorship for the rest of his career. As Hap and Cora carefully weighed the benefits and limitations of the position, senior officers in the War Department simply gave the professorship to another officer. It seemed that that officer and the superintendent had used Glassford as something of a smokescreen to keep other officers from seeking the position. For Glassford it was an early but valuable lesson in army politics. Cora noted, "So Happy was a guileless and unsuspecting cats-paw, for the first time in his life."[14]

In 1801 an association of sea captains founded the Providence [Rhode Island] Marine Society to protect their ships from attacks by barbary pirates and the British Navy, having concluded that cannons afforded better protection than insurance. The Society later morphed into the Providence Marine Corps of Artillery (PMCA), which, despite its name, had nothing to do with the US Marine Corps. The PMCA eventually evolved into a land-based artillery unit of horse-pulled small cannons, and during the Civil War earned distinction for its skill at Antietam, Gettysburg, Cold Harbor, and other battles. Following the surrender at Appomattox, the PMCA rejoined the Rhode Island Militia, which eventually became the Rhode Island National Guard.[15]

Still at West Point, Glassford's summer assignment was now with the Rhode Island National Guard. In July 1908, despite its impressive history, Glassford found that the unit needed significant improvement. He learned that the soldiers had had a succession of poor commanders and now required better leadership, discipline, and training. He tactfully suggested some drastic measures and reorganization, which the officers and soldiers of the unit, after some protest, accepted. In 1909 and 1910, accompanied by four field artillery sergeants, he again assisted the Rhode Island National Guard. Several officers of the unit had resigned in 1910 and 1911 at their own request, but possibly under pressure. In June 1911 the unit went to Fort Riley for more field artillery instruction, and in July it began its annual encampment at Quonset Point, south of Providence on Rhode Island Sound. That year Glassford was able to report "a splendid showing of the men" in their ability to maneuver, fire, and service their cannons. The officers and men of the unit bonded with Glassford, and he with them. In August Glassford moved on to assist Light Battery A of the Missouri National Guard.[16]

In June 1912, the last year of his five-year West Point assignment, Glassford found himself in something of a standoff with the superintendent, who was about to dismiss three second-year cadets if they refused to confess to hazing another cadet. In this situation, Glassford regarded the hazing incident as mild, but the cadets still declined to confess, resulting in the superintendent calling for a board of inquiry. As a member of the board, Glassford respectfully reminded the superintendent that military and civil law forbade compelling a cadet to testify against himself or the others if doing so would incriminate himself. The situation continued for some weeks, after which the superintendent decided *not* to dismiss the cadets, but instead to confine them to their homes for their sophomore summer. While this lesser punishment might not have been the summer leave the cadets had hoped for, it allowed them to attend their third year of West Point in the fall. In appreciation of Glassford's support, the West Point class of 1914 dedicated its end-of-second-year "furlough book" to Glassford, the first time a class had ever done so for a living officer. The dedication read, "To Lieutenant Pelham D. Glassford: We of the class of 1914, respectfully dedicate this Book as a token of our esteem." Glassford, a defender of the underdog, had simply done what he thought was right. The superintendent learned of the dedication and bluntly accused Glassford of instigating the dedication and threatened to court-martial him. Glassford asserted that he knew nothing of the dedication but was nonetheless proud to have received it. The superintendent dropped the matter.[17]

The Glassford family that had arrived at West Point consisted of Hap and Cora. The Glassford family that departed five years later was substantially larger: Guy Carleton, named after his maternal grandfather, was born in 1908; Cora Elizabeth, who would be called Bettie, was born in 1910; and Pelham Davis Jr., who would be called Pete, was born in 1911. In April 1912 Glassford completed his assignment at the Academy. He took leave until October and by December he and his family were on their way to Fort Stotsenburg in the Philippines, north of Manila. In 1912 his father, Lieutenant Colonel William Glassford, was serving in the Philippines as chief signal officer, and the following year he would become a full colonel. The colonel's wife, Allie, already contemplating their future, was investigating property in Phoenix, Arizona, where she and William hoped to retire and own a farm in four years.[18]

In the aftermath of the Philippine Insurrection (1899–1902), there remained pockets of continuing conflict on a few islands, requiring American soldiers and Marines to hunt down and capture or kill the rebels who refused to surrender. Many army officers, including Pelham Glassford and his father, served tours of duty in the Philippines, the largest of the army's overseas garrisons. When Pelham Glassford arrived in 1913, he was one of more than 9,500 officers and soldiers stationed there. Historian Edward M. Coffman called America's ongoing occupation of the Philippines "the United States' greatest experiment in colonization, and in those early years the Army was the key to success." But what Americans called insurrection, Filipinos regarded as a perpetuation of their independence movement. The Treaty of Paris, which had concluded the Spanish-American War, had neatly passed ownership of the Philippines from Spain to the United States. Filipinos regarded this as little more than a change of masters, and many refused to accept it, choosing instead to continue fighting, with geography as their ally. Some of the 7,000 islanders, most noticeably the Moros, waged an ongoing jungle guerrilla campaign. It was not until 1913 that the Moros accepted defeat, and true independence for Filipinos would not arrive until 1946.[19]

For the Glassford family of five, just getting to the Philippines was a trial. Their ship sailed from San Francisco, passed through the Golden Gate, and entered the immense Pacific Ocean, which was anything but passive. They endured their journey of 7,000 miles over several weeks aboard a crowded military transport ship. Weeks later, the now-veteran ocean sailors disembarked on the dock at Manila Bay, where they saw, heard, and inhaled a world immensely unlike their own. The crowds of people they saw were not only Filipino but also Chinese, Japanese, Spanish, and English, wearing all manner of dress and jointly clogging the streets. A cacophony of traffic noises, shouts, and rapidly delivered and unintelligible speech confused the ears of the new arrivals, while their nostrils registered intense scents, some fragrant, some malodorous. The newcomers brought with them their own military-social network, a two-tiered caste system forbidding officers from socializing with noncommissioned officers (sergeants) and enlisted soldiers. This did not go unnoticed by their respective dependents, with every wife and school-age child knowing whose husband and father was an officer and whose was enlisted. Neither group, however, would ever come to regard the Filipinos as equals; nonetheless, the Americans welcomed the affordable services and products that the Filipinos provided. Commissioned and noncommissioned officers hired Filipinos as servants and purchased what they needed from native merchants and artisans. Soldiers, at the time mostly young first-time enlistees, were pleased enough to find tropical drinks and prostitutes within their meager budgets, thus causing the army to contend with both. Military families learned soon enough that sanitation in the Philippines was far below American standards, necessitating that the Americans first plunge all fruits, vegetables, dishes, and silverware into boiling water.[20]

In 1913 the army posted Glassford to Fort Stotsenburg, which years later would become Clark Air Force Base, about sixty miles north of Manila. During Glassford's duty tour there, the post had the highest malaria rate in the army, necessitating that a sergeant and twelve soldiers work full time eradicating mosquito breeding areas, but never quite succeeding. The islands also provided abundant opportunities to experience, perhaps for the first time, such events as earthquakes, typhoons, horrendous downpours, drenching humidity, and temperatures feeling much hotter than they were. Cora, with three small children in tow, was determined to make the best of it. She found, to her disappointment, that despite an abundance of mosquitoes, their grass-roofed "Nipa" house, resting on stilts, relied on mosquito curtains rather than the more effective screens. Nor did their house on officer row have electricity, and on at least one occasion, another Nipa house collapsed due to the "insidious eating of its vital parts by the ever-present white ants." Hap had other concerns. Still a first lieutenant, he spent most evenings studying for the captain examination—by candlelight.[21]

The post housed a headquarters, infantry regiment, field artillery battalion, four companies of Philippine Scouts (a predecessor of the Philippine Army), a medical unit, and various support units, totaling several thousand troops. At a time when officers throughout the army usually had their afternoons free, officers at Stotsenburg apparently had even more than that. One lieutenant colonel, who arrived two years after Glassford, regarded Fort Stotsenburg as something of a country club: a little work in the morning, then polo, tennis, golf, or riding in the early afternoon, drinks at the officers' club at sunset, and dinner in the evening. He thought of it as "a lazy man's paradise."[22]

One evening, long after taps, when the officers and their families had settled in for the night, there came a disturbing bugle call, summoning all officers to headquarters, on the double. The collected officers, dressed in a variety of night attire, learned that the Japanese fleet was then steaming toward Manila Bay. The reason that the Japanese navy was inbound was not clear, but the ubiquitous rumor mill had it that Japan was furious at California's 1913 passage of the Webb-Haney Alien Land Law. It was applicable to several populations but was targeted primarily at restricting Japanese ownership and long-term leases of property. While Californians were well acquainted with the new law, Americans in the Philippines were not. Senior commanders ordered the officers to muster their troops and report as soon as possible to Corregidor, the small tadpole-shaped island perfectly positioned to block entrance to Manila Bay. Coast Artillery units already assigned there stood ready to defend against an enemy fleet entering Manila Bay and possibly invading Manila. The units from Fort Stotsenburg arrived and initiated their own defensive measures. The atmosphere was tense, with every soldier scanning the horizon for even a distant suggestion of the Japanese fleet. But no fleet appeared. The defenders maintained their readiness, using the additional time to enhance their portion of the overall defense plan. Still, no ships arrived. Some Americans seemed quite sure that Japan would launch an attack but speculated that they would wait until sometime into the future.[23]

The Japanese fleet never arrived, causing the soldiers to become bored. Glassford thought it would be a good training exercise for his soldiers to pull a large cannon to the top of Malinta Hill, a forested and rocky slope, and then emplace the weapon at the very top. The location was ideal for such a weapon, but no troops had ever put one there before. The battalion major discouraged Glassford's request to undertake the effort. Glassford proffered more reasons why it was a good idea, but the major again dismissed it. Glassford accepted the refusal and departed. The next morning, as the battalion major leisurely emerged from his breakfast, he started when he looked up and saw, now straddling Malinta Hill's ridge crest, surrounded by proud soldiers, a large cannon. That morning, after reveille, about 100 soldiers from Battery A had pulled and heaved the heavy weapon to the top. No doubt Glassford had motivated them by saying that the major had asserted: "Nonsense! It can't be done."[24]

The good news for the Glassford family and others of the Stotsenburg field artillery battalion was that Hawaii now needed a second field artillery battalion to join the one already there. The Glassfords were more than ready to leave the Philippines for the more favorable climate of Hawaii, where Pelham would serve at Schofield Barracks, less than thirty miles from Honolulu and 1,000 feet higher in elevation. After the Philippines, the family agreed, Hawaii would be paradise. Hap, Cora, and the little Glassfords, now seasoned sailors, welcomed a few weeks at sea on the cruise of more than 5,000 miles, aboard the US Army Transport *Thomas*, capable of holding more than 1,200 passengers. What the family liked was that on this cruise, they had enough room for an additional Glassford: Little Dorothy "Dot" Seymour Glassford, the newest member of the family, was born in Manila on June 23, 1913, the only Glassford child not born at West Point. What the family had not particularly liked was that at one point the ship's captain had to seek shelter from an approaching typhoon.[25]

As the ship arrived at Honolulu Harbor in August 1913, officers and wives of the sibling battalion were waiting to greet the new arrivals, who were surprised to learn that they would not live in houses but in tents, at least for nine months. As it turned out, tent life was surprisingly acceptable. Large hospital tents were plentiful, and a family could request as many as desired and have them connected to form a multiroom home. The Glassfords settled on a seven-room canvas suite, which provided space for a living room (with four corner posts, a wood floor, and an actual roof), dining room, kitchen, master bedroom, children's bedroom, nurse's bedroom, and a covered porch, the latter with a "superb view of the sea and mountains." Cora found their home to be compact and comfortable, even during the fierce Kona storms, although the tents did sway on occasion. The Kona winds blew in from the west during winter, usually two or three times a year, bringing plenty of wind, rain, and occasional flashfloods. Military families, however, are remarkably adaptable, and the Glassfords made the best of it.[26]

The families of the field artillery battalion already at Schofield looked forward to meeting the newcomers. During subsequent visits to the tent-homes of other officers, the Glassfords noticed that those tents usually had Persian carpets laid over the rough wood floors; moreover, dinner parties were frequent and featured delicious meals served on French china prepared by well-trained Japanese servants. All in all, tent life in Hawaii was remarkably agreeable. Cora found the weather to be refreshing and cool after the hot rains of Manila. The family was happy and soon had its own well-trained servants. The biggest threat to the tents was fire, as portable oil burners warded off the night chill on the high Leilehua plateau and kerosene lamps provided the light. Of course, as had been the case in the Philippines, it was not advisable to walk into the dark kitchen at night and light a lamp: it sent dozens of cockroaches scurrying back to their holes. The family also discovered that they had something of a wakeup call. Every morning Mynah birds arrived. When the sun peeked over the ocean horizon, the Mynahs commenced an extended chorus of songs.[27]

On November 18, 1914, not too soon for Glassford's satisfaction, the army promoted him to captain, assigning him as a battery commander with an auxiliary duty as regimental athletics officer of the First Field Artillery. Thereafter he refereed football games, promoted boxing events, and other similar duties.[28]

In June 1915 more than 100 army officers attended a West Point reunion at the Moana Hotel in Honolulu. By all accounts, the hit of the event occurred when Captain Glassford gave his rendition of a "real, old-time Hula that was quite up to expectations." The five-story Moana, built fourteen years earlier, was the first hotel built in the Waikiki area, boasting seventy-five luxurious rooms, private baths, and even an electric elevator.[29]

While some officers spent their afternoons playing polo or golf, Glassford and a few others preferred racing horses. He competed in a steeplechase held at Schofield Barracks, and later, while riding a thoroughbred mare named Tuolumne, twice raced at the Kapiolani Park racetrack in Honolulu, once finishing second on the one-and-one-half mile course that included eight flights of hurdles. As his regiment's athletic officer, he also organized a baseball league and became something of a regular as a referee at the Schofield Arena boxing matches.[30]

During his time in Hawaii, Glassford discovered two avocations that he would enjoy for most of his life: motorcycles and art. His love of motorcycles began somewhat by happenstance, as a replacement for his White steamer motorcar. The car occasionally shot flames from its steam box, which happened once as the family returned to Schofield Barracks following an outing to Honolulu. As the steamer neared the post gate, it fired off a blast of flames and steam. The guards, unfamiliar with steam motorcars, immediately grabbed water buckets and charged toward the car, deluging the flaming car—and the family inside. Thereafter, the guards took to calling the steamer the "Glassford fire car." When the steamer finally gave out, Hap already knew that he and his family would be leaving Hawaii before long. Rather than buy another car, he purchased a bargain-priced motorcycle, likely one of the few at Schofield Barracks. He became as well known for his loud motorcycle as he had been for his steamer. He fashioned and attached a short board designed to be a side-seat to the motorcycle, which allowed Cora, the daughter of a cavalry officer, to ride sidesaddle as Hap motorcycled the duo to one of the local "hop" dances. When he located and attached a sidecar, he managed to get the four children inside, prompting his friends to call it the "baby carriage."[31]

Glassford had always had an interest in art. One might conclude that a professor of drawing would be an artist as well, but West Point drawing was closer to technical drawing than still-life or figure drawing. Glassford now opened himself to the more creative art.[32]

Glassford managed to find a way to combine motorcycling and art. He enrolled in his first creative art class, which was held on Monday evenings in Honolulu. Hap motorcycled the twenty-eight miles to the class, taught by the well-known artist D. Howard Hitchcock, a studious-looking man with Ben Franklin glasses and a dimpled chin. After each class Pelham motorcycled back to Schofield late at night. He attended Hitchcock's Life Class for a year, never missing a session, despite Kona winds, flooded gulch roads, and liquid red lava flows. By the end of the year, Glassford knew he had artistic talent and had significantly benefitted from the classes.[33]

As Glassford's first creative art instructor, Hitchcock had a seminal impact on the young army officer. Hawaii-born Hitchcock had studied at Oberlin College in Ohio, the National Academy of Design in New York, and the Académie Julian in Paris. In Hawaii Hitchcock and a group of fellow artists initiated the Kilohana Art League. Hitchcock also became an important member of the Volcano School of artists. Hitchcock mostly painted oil and watercolor landscapes of Hawaii, but he also journeyed to Mill Valley and Carmel-by-the-Sea, California, to paint similar scenes. The young army captain took it all in.[34]

Glassford loved adventure. Motorcycles intended for off-road use did not yet exist, but most motorcycles of the day could negotiate dirt, gravel, and similar surfaces, as well as pavement. One day, Glassford, having in mind something a little more exciting, simply told Cora that he was going for a ride. Detaching the sidecar, he set out to ride over Kolekole Pass. At the time, as Cora remembered, no wheeled vehicle had ever done so, and even riding a horse there was ill advised. The path was rugged and mountainous but promised adventure. Embarking on the ride, he climbed for some time, his motorcycle doing well over the demanding terrain. Then, quite suddenly, a portion of the mountain trail under the wheels slid away, taking Glassford and the motorcycle with it. The motorcycle stopped some distance below, resting on top of Glassford, pinning him to a narrow ledge. It was indeed fortunate that some of his own soldiers, on a day hike, heard his shouts from below. Forming a human chain, the soldiers extracted Glassford and got him back up to the trail. Other soldiers had returned to the post to fetch a pushcart into which they loaded the captain. By then Cora had begun to worry. The apologetic husband had suffered no serious injury, but the motorcycle was destined to stay below for a time until his soldiers somehow managed to pull it back up to the trail. Glassford repaired it and returned to riding, but he never again attempted Kolekole Pass.[35]

While at Schofield, Glassford developed a disturbing bronchial cough that had lasted for several weeks. His doctor, likely suspecting tuberculosis, said that Hawaii's mild climate was aggravating the problem and recommended that Glassford return to mainland West Coast for at least six weeks. Probably aware of Mark Twain's apocryphal comment that the coldest winter [he] ever spent was a summer in San Francisco, Glassford thought it best to go there, while Cora and the children remained in Hawaii. Since William Glassford Sr. was then stationed at the Presidio, Hap would be able to visit his parents, along with other friends on the post. Never one to simply sit around, Glassford decided to take a class at the San Francisco Institute of Art while he was there. Without identifying himself as an army officer, he enrolled in a class, wearing his "cits" attire and took in more art technique.[36]

He returned to Hawaii, having found that five weeks in San Francisco had cleared his cough. He was next assigned as commander of Battery B, 1st Battalion. The previous captain had become ill and been evacuated to the mainland for extended treatment. In his absence the battery had suffered neglect and now had lost much of its effectiveness. The soldiers' morale was low, the food worse, and the boredom chronic. Glassford went to work. He recruited a new cook, which took some effort, installed pool tables, and subscribed to magazines for the dayroom. Relying on his experience at Fort Riley, he formed a battery baseball team and got the players uniforms and equipment. Apparently inspired by his enthusiasm, the soldiers themselves formed a boxing club, sought volunteer boxers, and trained them. Glassford got permission to build a lighted boxing ring and enlisted an Irish army chaplain to manage the team. The soldier boxers began entering bouts in Honolulu, where boxing was becoming very popular.[37]

Glassford, the father of two boys and two girls, spent as much time with his children as he could. He built a train system for the boys and dollhouses for the girls, and he taught them basic art techniques. The rustic army post, which had no paved roads or sidewalks yet, provided little entertainment for children, but the beach resort of Haleiwa, on the North Shore, was less than nine miles away.[38]

For most officers and their families, the assignment in Hawaii was special. One army wife, Sarah Truscott, later remembered, "Since [we] left Hawaii we have lived in eleven houses. Each one has had its own place in our hearts, and each one represents a change that has added to our experience . . . but none of them will ever mean more to us than that . . . one." Cora had her own memories: "Slipping around Diamond Head we stood on deck watching the last of our flower leis float back on the waves toward Honolulu, and I mused over the age-old promise that we should come back."[39]

CHAPTER 4

On the Border, Prelude to France

THE army issued Special Orders No. 121: "Under exceptional circumstances, leave of absence for two months and twenty-three days to take effect upon arrival at San Francisco, Cal., on or about August 12, 1916, is granted Captain Pelham D. Glassford, 1st Field Artillery." The Glassford family said their goodbyes to friends and once more readied to cruise the Pacific, departing for San Francisco on the afternoon of August 4, 1916, aboard the US Army Transport Ship *Sherman*, which would eventually dock from where the family had left some years before. They would miss seeing Pelham's parents by a few months, as the army had transferred Colonel Glassford from being the chief signal officer of the Western Department at the Presidio to commander of the signal corps aviation school at North Island near San Diego.[1]

Upon arrival at the Presidio, Glassford was pleased to learn that in September he would attend the School of the Line at Fort Leavenworth. The year-long class of instruction would assist the captain in his career, and if he finished in the top half of his class, he would go on to attend the General Staff School (later renamed the Command and General Staff School), also at Fort Leavenworth. Glassford looked forward to the challenging class. Within days, however, the army notified him that the class was now cancelled. The probable cause was that in March of that year, Pancho Villa, considered a bandit in Mexico, had raided Columbus, New Mexico, resulting in the army rushing thousands of regular and national guard troops to the border to protect against further incursions. Those officers who had anticipated attending the School of the Line would remain in their present assignment, with most expecting to be sent to the border soon. The army notified Glassford that he was to report to the 5th Field Artillery at Fort Bliss, El Paso, Texas, but he would be allowed to finish his leave at the Presidio.[2]

In the meantime, his days were free. Incapable of remaining idle, he sensed an opportunity for adventure. To Cora's surprise he applied for an interim job with the *San Francisco Examiner* newspaper, telling the editor, "I want to learn the newspaper business in three months. It will help me in my army work. Give me the hardest assignment you have." The editor was surprisingly agreeable and hired Glassford as a cub reporter. As part of his duties, the incognito captain rode with ambulance crews to various emergencies, sat in on police court where municipal judges adjudicated misdemeanor arrests, followed fire engines responding to fires and other emergencies, and once visited the morgue. Afterward, if the event merited a story, he wrote a short article in a crisp military-style prose. He enjoyed the work immensely and regretted having to tell his editor that revised army orders now necessitated that he and his family depart San Francisco for El Paso, Texas, where he was to report to the 5th Field Artillery at Fort Bliss. There the captain joined thousands of other army regulars and national guard troops who were undergoing training while at the same time protecting the border from raids by the bandidos of Francisco "Pancho" Villa. On the minds of many, however, was the war in Europe and whether the United States would become involved.[3]

In 1910, Porfirio Díaz, considered by most Mexicans to be a dictator, won reelection as president, a position he had held since 1877. A political rival, Francisco Madero, led a successful rebellion against him, causing Díaz to flee to Spain, leaving Madero to assume the presidency. Three rebel leaders then separately sought to unseat Madero: Venustiano Carranza, Pancho Villa, and Emiliano Zapata, eventually causing Madero to also flee Mexico. Bad blood between Carranza and Villa led to Carranza's forces ultimately defeating Villa's army at the Battle of Agua Prieta, immediately south of Douglas, Arizona, with Carranza then assuming the presidency. Villa, once a general with his own revolutionary army, was now declared to be a bandit, forcing him to go on the run with about 500 of his soldiers, the tattered remains of his army. On March 9, 1916, in need of supplies and angry that the United States had voiced support for Carranza, Villa ordered his bandidos to cross the border and raid Columbus, New Mexico, a collection of adobe houses and buildings three miles north of the border. The small town was home to about 350 residents but encamped there were several hundred troopers of the US 13th Cavalry. At about 4:30 a.m. hundreds of horse-mounted "Villistas" galloped through the dirt streets, firing guns. Over the course of two hours, cavalry troopers engaged the bandidos in a fierce firefight, eventually repelling the attack and forcing Villa's men to flee back to Mexico. When the dust settled, 9 American civilians and 8 cavalry troopers were dead, as were perhaps 100 of Villa's men. The raid on Columbus alarmed Americans, especially those living along the 1,500-mile border from San Diego to Brownsville, in East Texas, who now feared additional raids. President Woodrow Wilson and the US Congress were livid, and the president quickly dispatched US Army General John J. "Black Jack" Pershing to lead a "punitive expedition" into Mexico. The ramrod-straight general was an 1886 West Point graduate who had fought in what the cavalry had called the "Indian Wars." While serving during the Spanish-American War, he had come to the attention of volunteer Rough Rider Lieutenant Colonel Theodore Roosevelt, who, as president in 1905, promoted Captain Pershing to brigadier general, skipping three ranks and passing over more than 800 higher-ranked regular officers. Roosevelt described Pershing in combat as being "cool as a bowl of cracked ice." From March 15 to April 12, Pershing led 6,700 soldiers into Mexico, pushing 300 miles deep into the foreign country, but failed to capture or kill Villa. Now sprinkled along the American side of the border were 48,000 regular troops and 110,000 National Guard soldiers. Even so, after decades of congressional neglect, the US Army found itself barely large enough to pursue Villa and still defend its borders from additional attacks.[4]

On October 23, 1916, Captain Glassford assumed his duties as adjutant to Colonel Charles T. Menoher, 5th Field Artillery Regimental Commander. The balding, cleft-chinned colonel, an 1886 West Point graduate, was highly regarded, but the colonel's superior, a brigadier general, was very unpopular. Another colonel in the headquarters absolutely despised the general, resulting in ongoing turmoil within the regiment. Since both Colonel Menoher and the general had equally strong personalities, Glassford found himself serving as something of a buffer, working hard to keep the peace. In the interim, the mission of the army had now changed from border protection to preparation for the ongoing war in Europe.[5]

Hap and Cora had purchased a house in El Paso, seven miles from the fort. It was the first house they had ever owned, which they bought from the army officer who had built it. The family would see little of Hap, however, since each day he left early in the morning and returned late in the evening, putting in long days overseeing intensive training of field artillery crews. Cora remembered that Fort Bliss was almost bursting with troops. "As far as one could see in any direction, from the high plateau of the post, tents in khaki-colored blocks stretched to the foot of the encircling Mount Franklin range." Without doubt, Hap would have preferred to have been part of the actual pursuit of Villa, but that was primarily a cavalry and infantry operation with limited need for field artillery.[6]

The massive Mexico activation had been valuable in one important way. As General Pershing notes in his after-action report on the punitive expedition, "it provided an opportunity for training officers and men for the development of administrative procedures incident to the operations of considerable forces." It had also opened the eyes of many National Guard officers and soldiers, who, suffering discomfort in the border camps, rethought their commitment to the army. Having experienced hard training and field conditions, scores of older and mostly physically unfit officers resigned their commissions, and unfit enlisted soldiers left the army at the end of their enlistment. This had the unintended consequence of improving an army preparing for war, a needed weeding of deadwood. Still, the US Army was not even close to being ready to go to Europe. The president's next order to Pershing was to build an army of one million soldiers to aid European allies in defeating Imperial Germany. As for Villa, his enemies in Mexico tracked him down and assassinated him in 1923.[7]

The war in Europe, understandably, was the pervasive topic of conversation on the post. Cora crossed her fingers, hoping that Europe would need only American money and munitions but not troops. That was dreaming, of course; France and Britain needed American soldiers, thousands of them, and the sooner the better. Hap and his regiment, Cora was sure, would be going. On a needed break from his duties, Glassford requested and received a short leave. He gathered Cora and their four children and journeyed to northern New Mexico to visit family and friends. On a second trip, leaving the children in the care of others, Hap and Cora spent a few days in Las Cruces, New Mexico, forty miles north of the Texas state line, knowing that it might be their last getaway for some time.[8]

President Wilson's problem, which France and Britain failed to comprehend, was that the United States was pathetically unprepared to go to a world war. The Punitive Expedition had demonstrated just how poorly staffed, trained, and equipped the US Army was. At the declaration of war by the president and Congress, the army had only 5,971 officers and 121,797 soldiers in its regular army, and 174,008 officers and soldiers in the collective National Guards, totaling just over 300,000 American troops, despite the National Guard having an authorized strength of 450,000. Furthermore, the largest combat organizational unit in the American army was the regiment, which usually functioned independently. European armies used the "combat division" as the principle fighting unit; it was about the size of two US regiments and was easily combinable with other divisions to form a corps, which then combined with other corps to form one or more armies. It was now obvious that over the years, the US Army had been parsimoniously neglected. Americans would pay the penalty for that neglect, even though many states still recoiled at the thought of paying for anything larger than a small Coast Artillery corps and a frontier constabulary.[9]

On June 28, 1914, Archduke Franz Ferdinand and his wife, Countess Sophie Chotek, made a goodwill visit to the beautiful city of Sarajevo, Bosnia, which the Austria-Hungary Empire had annexed in 1908. The Archduke was the nephew of Emperor Franz Joseph, and heir to the Empire. Slavs in Bosnia were agitating to sever their country from the Empire and make it part of the Greater Serbian Kingdom. Austrian conservatives in Vienna, including eighty-four-year-old Emperor Franz Joseph, suspected that it would soon be necessary to crush the budding revolt. But the young Archduke hoped to avoid that, reasoning that a friendly visit and an offer of giving the Slavs a greater voice in the Viennese court would be welcomed. As it turned out, his timing could not have been worse: the next day was St. Vitus Day, the anniversary of the 1389 defeat of the Serbs by the Turkish Ottoman Empire. In late June 1914, four young men, collectively armed with six bombs and six semi-automatic pistols, members of the Mlada Bosna (Young Bosnia), intended to assassinate the archduke. As his six-car motorcade passed by, one of the conspirators hurled a bomb. It bounced off the back of the open touring car carrying the Archduke and his wife but struck the next car and exploded, injuring two army officers. The Archduke's driver had seen the bomb in the air and immediately accelerated, hoping he had evaded the assassins. Police quickly seized the bomb thrower, but two other conspirators, not sure what to do, slipped away. The fourth conspirator, Gavrilo Princip, remained ready. The dark-haired teenager focused his deep-set eyes on an approaching touring car. Not yet twenty, he still wore the faint mustache of a teenager. He must have found it incredible when the Archduke's driver, having missed a turn, came to a stop to turn around, by chance doing so almost directly in front of Princip. The teenager jumped on the touring car's running board and fired his pistol twice, striking the Archduke in the jugular and the countess in the stomach, killing both. Princip had intended to kill himself but was arrested before he could do so.[10]

At the time, Europe was a precarious amalgam of committed alliances, each intending to provide protection but also obligating itself to support others. The Austria-Hungary Empire sought to punish Serbia for Princip's assassination of the archduke. Russia, allied with Serbia, readied its war machine. Germany and the Austria-Hungary Empire, fearing attack by Russia, declared war on Russia. Germany also declared war on Russia's ally, France. Germany moved against France, passing through neutral Belgium to avoid French defensives. Britain, allied with Belgium, declared war on Germany. That was just the beginning; in just ten days, bound by obligatory treaties, European countries ignited a world war. The two bullets fired by young Gavrilo Princip led to four years of war and the deaths of nine million soldiers and six million civilians. Because of his youth, Princip was not executed, but died of tuberculosis in prison in 1918.[11]

President Woodrow Wilson found the situation perplexing. Taking office in 1913, he had narrowly won election, in part because of his campaign promise to keep the United States out of a European war; now he was contemplating doing precisely the opposite. His change of mind had begun in 1914, when German soldiers invaded Belgium and France, resulting in American news reports detailing German brutality against noncombatants. Next, German submarines in the North Atlantic began torpedoing neutral American ships, suspecting them of transporting munitions to the Allies. Then, a British passenger vessel, the *Lusitania*, was sunk by a German torpedo on May 7, 1915, off the coast of southern Ireland, killing 1,200 passengers, including 128 Americans. The camel straw came in 1917, when American agents learned through the secret "Zimmerman Telegram" that the German foreign secretary, Arthur Zimmermann, was proposing an alliance between his country and Mexico. Intending to divert American attention away from Europe, Germany promised to assist Mexico in regaining Arizona, New Mexico, and Texas.[12]

Most Americans were concerned about the war in Europe, but being buffered by the Atlantic Ocean, they remained comfortable with neutrality. The Zimmermann telegram changed that. On April 2, 1917, President Wilson declared war on Germany, and a few days later, on Austria-Hungary. Now he needed to motivate Americans to prepare for war. For this he summoned George E. Creel, the olive-skinned, impeccably dressed, and always confident promoter who had helped him with his 1916 political campaign, in which Wilson promised that the country would not go to war. A native of Missouri, Creel was something of an enthusiast in whatever he did. His new mission was the reverse of what he had done in 1916. As chair of the Committee on Public Information, formed on April 13, 1917, Creel set about issuing 6,000 press releases. He also arranged for movie stars such as Mary Pickford, Charlie Chaplin, and Douglas Fairbanks to publicly support the war, and dispatched across the nation an impressive collection of "four-minute men." Their job was to speak at hundreds of rallies and in movie theaters across the country and deliver a short message. In just four minutes—the time it took to a change a movie reel—the four-minute men sold Americans on the need to assist the Allies. While Creel did not change all the minds in America, he changed enough.[13]

Between 1914 and 1917, one horrendous battle in Europe followed another. For Americans, the battles were merely names in the newspaper. For Europeans, they meant hundreds of thousands of deaths. New to the lexicon of Americans were such names as the Marne, Gallipoli, Jutland, Verdun, Somme, and Ypres, all fought and won or lost before the first American soldiers would arrive. Of the 4 million Americans who would serve in the military during World War I, almost 117,000 would lose their lives.[14]

Now in his midfifties but still vigorous, General John Pershing was ready to lead 1 million soldiers of the American Expeditionary Force (AEF) to France. His immediate problem was that the AEF existed only on paper. The embarrassing truth was that the combined army of regulars and National Guard soldiers amounted to less than 310,000. Undeterred, the general developed a plan to build it to 1 million. Once enough soldiers were trained, organized, and equipped, a skilled officer corps would command them in battle. Surprisingly, the French and British generals had something different in mind, very different. They would have preferred that Pershing just send soldiers, perhaps organized into companies and battalions, that French and British commanders could plug into the lines where needed. They thought this could happen rather quickly, and they saw no need for Americans to send officers above the rank of, say, major, and certainly no colonels or generals. French and British commanders could handle the rest. They termed it "amalgamation."[15]

Recognizable by his disciplined handlebar mustache, Joseph Jacques C. Joffre, Marshal of France, quickly disabused his fellow French and British generals of the notion that the Americans would agree to such a plan. Indeed, American Secretary of War Newton D. Baker, attorney and former mayor of Cleveland, had already ordered that "the forces of the United States are a separate and distinct component of the combined forces, the identity of which must be preserved." Joffre thought a more palatable plan would be for Pershing to send just one American combat division to France, which the French army could train for up to six weeks and then assign to a quiet sector of the Western Front; thereafter, when the division was ready, French commanders would move it to a more active sector. Joffre saw some urgency, however, since his *poilus*—common French soldiers—were near their breaking point. Spent physically and mentally, they could endure only if they saw American soldiers in the trenches with them.[16]

General Pershing later reported, "Prior to our entrance into the war, the regiments of our small army were very much scattered, and we had no organized units, even approximating a division, that could be sent overseas prepared to take the field." Fortunately, Pershing had already begun working on that new American combat division. While still on the Mexican border, he had selected the 16th, 18th, 26th, and 28th Infantry Regiments and 5th, 6th, and 7th Field Artillery Regiments for his new combat division, the first organizational unit of its kind in the US Army. His immediate need was to infuse replacements into the selected regiments and accelerate their training. He would do his utmost to staff the new division, now named the 1st Division, with the best officers available. By previous standards, it was huge: the division would have four infantry regiments, three field artillery regiments, and various battalions and companies of machine gun, engineer, signal, cavalry, and auxiliary units, totaling 28,000 soldiers. The new US division would be about twice the size of the European divisions.[17]

As Pershing prepared to leave for France, Secretary Baker outlined the general's mission: "I will give you only two orders, one to go to France and the other to come back. In the meantime, your authority in France will be supreme." The general and his small staff sailed to Liverpool, England, on May 28, 1917, aboard the SS *Baltic*, which was joined by two destroyer escorts, all zigzagging through the Danger Zone. After completing various formalities in England, Pershing and his staff proceeded to Boulogne, France. They had preceded the new American division, which was then still undergoing formation and training. Pershing considered his 1st Division as the vanguard of an army of what he hoped would become seventy divisions. It was fortunate that he already had within this new division perhaps the best junior officer in the army: Captain George Catlett Marshall Jr., then just thirty-six years old, a 1901 graduate of the Virginia Military Institute.[18]

On June 14, 1917, Marshall and his fellow staff officers met for the first time aboard the *Tenadores*, a former United Fruit Company ship. At 7:00 a.m., after waiting for a thick fog to lift, the ship weighed anchor near Governors Island in New York harbor and negotiated its way through the submarine chain at nearby Fort Hamilton. Escorted by the armored cruiser *Seattle* and the former German mail ship *DeKalb*, the *Tenadores* crossed the Atlantic with a small fleet of other ships. On each vessel, navy lookouts at their stations scanned the waters for the ripple of German U-boats periscopes. One well-aimed torpedo could destroy the US Army's premier force.[19]

During their get-acquainted meeting on the ship, the officers had their first look at the organizational structure of their new division, which would have oversized regiments and include subunits and weapons new to them. As Marshall later recalled, "No one of us had a definite conception of the character of the war. . . . Today it is inconceivable that we should have found ourselves committed to a war while yet in such a complete state of unpreparedness."[20]

On June 25 the staff cadre arrived at Saint Nazaire on the French coast, about 275 miles southeast of Paris. Marshall and the others journeyed to Paris on July 14, Bastille Day, to meet with General Pershing at his headquarters on Rue Constantine. By September Pershing had shifted his headquarters to the small walled city of Chaumont, southeast of Paris and closer to the Western Front.[21]

Pelham Glassford was not far behind. Having been promoted to major on June 4 and assigned to the 5th Field Artillery, 1st Division, he was one of thirty-two officers and one war correspondent who departed Hoboken, New Jersey, on the *Tenadores* on July 30. The troopship and its soldiers left in secret, with no fanfare permitted, their families knowing only that their loved ones were now gone. Glassford had previously overseen preparations for the regiment to travel to France. What had surprised him most was that their draft horses and cannons would stay behind, since the French would supply both. On August 5, while still aboard the ship, Glassford pinned on the silver oak leaves of a lieutenant colonel. Expanding an army of 300,000 to 1 million creates a lot of promotions, which can come quickly in wartime.[22]

The ship docked at St. Nazaire on August 13. Glassford was now adjutant of the 5th Field Artillery, a position he would hold until September. It seems likely that only a small percentage of the arriving Americans had ever been to Europe, but for all of them, their stay in Saint Nazaire was too brief. Disappointed at seeing so little of their new surroundings, the soldiers reluctantly climbed into the long line of fifty small French railway "forty-and-eight" boxcars, designed to carry forty soldiers or eight horses. The train could transport up to 2,000 soldiers and their officers, the latter riding in two passenger cars at the end of the train. Once the sergeants had ushered in all the soldiers, the train bumped and clacked its way out of the railyard, jerking from side to side as it built a head of steam to carry the newcomers 450 miles along narrow rails to Gondrecourt-le-Château, 60 miles south of Verdun. One of the first realizations of the American doughboys was that their "Montana peak" campaign hats, which served just fine on the Mexican border, would not work well in France. The small boxcars and the narrow trenches of France and Belgium called for another hat. Before long, the new folding "overseas" cap arrived, which was ideal. Also new to the Americans were their British-made steel helmets, which would suffice until replacements manufactured back home arrived.[23]

For enlisted soldiers and officers interested in promotion, the 1st Division was the place to be. Rather rapidly, privates sewed on corporal and sergeant stripes, sergeants pinned on gold bars as commissioned second lieutenants, and junior officers became senior officers. Members of the new division also sewed on a shoulder patch depicting a large red numeral "1" that would forever identify the division as the "Big Red One." By war's end each new division would have developed its shoulder patch design and nickname. Thus, in September soldiers of the Big Red One welcomed a second American division, the 26th "Yankee" Division, in which Glassford would later serve. The next division to land was the 2nd "Indian Head" Division, which arrived in October and included a brigade (two regiments) of US Marines. Finally, in November, the 42nd "Rainbow" Division arrived. The 1st and 2nd divisions were regular army divisions while the 26th and 42nd were National Guard divisions. The soldiers of the 26th had come from New England, while those of the 42nd had come from throughout the country, whence its "Rainbow" nickname. The 26th and 42nd had served on the Mexican border and were as experienced as the two regular divisions.[24]

Organizationally, each division of 28,000 had two brigades, and each brigade had two regiments. Added to each division was a brigade of field artillery and a battalion (one-quarter of the size of a regiment) of combat engineers. These first four divisions became known informally as the "pioneer divisions," and would be the first American units to see battle. The pioneer divisions would also be the only US combat units to endure the unusually harsh French winter of 1917, one of the coldest in decades.[25]

In mid-October Pershing and the French generals inserted a modest number of 1st Division soldiers into a quiet sector on the Front near Nancy. The Americans were assigned in small groups so that the French could tutor them on trench warfare. For the first ten days, the French officers commanded the US troops; American officers could observe, but nothing more. During this time, the soldiers of each army, French and American, sized up the other. One American officer learned from French officers that French soldiers, generally, seemed to see the Americans as being unaware of danger, reckless, rugged, intelligent, undisciplined, careless, sloppy in dress, aggressive in spirit, and, like the Canadians and Australians, good fighters. Conversely, the Americans usually saw the French as meticulous in method, attentive to detail, slow in completion of a task, thorough, tenacious, good fighters, and good cooks. Most important, the two armies developed mutual respect.[26]

From September 1 through October 17, Glassford served as the secretary (executive officer) of the French artillery school at Saumur, which allowed him to study the methods of French artillery training. For a week thereafter, he held a temporary assignment with G-5 (General Staff Planning) at General Headquarters, AEF, allowing him the opportunity to become acquainted with some of the American staff officers assigned there.[27]

His next assignment, disappointing but not a surprise, was to plan and build from essentially nothing a field artillery school for American Army officers of I Corps, consisting of the Pioneer Divisions. Glassford would direct the school, assisted by Lieutenant Colonel Donald C. Cubbison and Lieutenant Colonel Maxwell Murray. The training site was on the expansive grounds of the now partially destroyed Gondrecourt-le-Château, about 170 miles southeast of Paris. The immediate task of the three officers was to supervise the construction of stables and forty-six huts to serve as classrooms and sleeping quarters for the student officers, expected to arrive by mid-November. Delays caused by autumn rains and a shortage of lumber slowed the process, making the timely opening of the school more difficult. French officers, observing the American artillery school emerge from stacks of muddy lumber, roofing, stoves, and other building materials, marveled at the ingenuity and boundless energy of the Americans, which included having to "acquire" some of the needed lumber from abandoned French barracks.[28]

Most of the arriving students would be "ninety-day wonders," second lieutenants just graduated from the three-month Citizen Training Camps, a forerunner of Officer Candidate School. By graduation the novice lieutenants had received the general training needed to be considered officers, but little in the way of branch-specific training, such as specialized skills for leading infantry, artillery, and engineer units. Since the army had necessarily rushed these lieutenants to France and Belgium, their branch training would have to take place in Europe. Most of the new lieutenants would attend infantry training, which, always having the highest casualty rates, required an abundance of lieutenants; a lesser number would attend field artillery, engineering, cavalry, tank corps, signal corps, and other branch training. Director Glassford, senior instructors Cubbison and Murray, and their staff instructors would turn the new second lieutenants into field artillery officers, at least those with sufficient math skills to master the training.[29]

Glassford's West Point classmate Leslie J. McNair had also arrived in France with the 1st Division. Like Glassford, he was a field artillery officer and had served on the border during the 1916 Punitive Expedition. It was McNair's good fortune that during the expedition he had come to the attention of General Pershing, and that on the Atlantic crossing he had shared a stateroom with George Marshall, future World War II army chief of staff. Upon McNair's arrival in France, Pershing appointed him chief of artillery training and tactical procedures for the AEF; as such, he was Glassford's immediate supervisor. In an October 18, 1917, letter to Cora, Hap wrote that McNair had assured him that the nascent artillery school would have whatever it needed to be operational by November 15. With McNair's support, Glassford accelerated the camp construction, but with weather delays it was not ready to accept students until November 26. As it turned out, the first class of students would not arrive until three weeks later. Given that, AEF General Headquarters approved Glassford's request to visit the frontline for two weeks, the first week to observe French artillery organization and specialization and the second week to similarly visit British artillery training. He wrote Cora, saying, "Have a great job, consisting principally of doing something with nothing. Am working like a Trojan to make good at it, because it's the biggest thing over here at the moment in the field artillery." He quickly got into the rhythm of sleeping on a field cot in his office, arising before dawn, and not returning to his cot until late in the evening. It would be long days and short nights for some time.[30]

Artillery training was not easy. One officer who attended artillery training in France was Missouri National Guard First Lieutenant Harry S. Truman. The future president had already had some artillery training provided by his National Guard unit, but he found the I Corps training to be much more demanding. As his biographer David McCullough writes, "The first week at the artillery school was the most difficult ordeal [that Truman] had ever experienced. After that, the work got harder.... The mathematics was all at the college level.... There was hardly time to get from one class to the next." The students learned every aspect of firing their French artillery cannons both day and night, and how to train and supervise the soldiers who would deliver the rounds as precisely as possible. Truman wrote his wife, Bess, saying, "I've studied more and worked harder in the last three weeks than I ever did before in my life." He recalled that he survived the five-week course having just "slipped through."[31]

Glassford's time at the Front with a French artillery unit came close to causing him serious injury. He wrote Cora that a shell had landed a little more than 200 yards from him, and that a hand grenade had exploded within forty feet. He added that on another occasion the fender of a passing Packard truck had "bowled over" him, sending him "kiting" into a ditch. He explained that he had been on the side of the road attempting to clear the spark plug of an acquired motorcycle when the truck came by unexpectedly close. He also experienced his first gas attack, but he had his gas mask with him and thus was not much affected. Another American soldier described what a gas attack was like: "It is beyond doubt that as a medium for inflicting casualties on the enemy's personnel in trenches and dugouts, gas was a most deadly and effective weapon, and gave maximum return for time and labor expended. A study of the statements of gas casualties inflicted either by or upon the enemy showed that hundreds and even thousands of casualties could be caused by gas within the space of a few minutes."[32]

After Christmas Hap wrote to Cora and included a photograph of himself, saying that he and Murray would soon have another photo taken of themselves wearing their new "tin hats," adding that they were "steel helmets and not so bad." December 28 was the last day of the first artillery class. In another letter home he said that he had "turned into a pretty fierce disciplinarian at the school." He added that the school was "sending a bunch of young men to their regiments that their commanders will be glad to get."33

On December 30, during an interval between classes, Glassford went to Verdun, all the while hoping to be given command of an artillery regiment. He spent the next afternoon with the soldiers of a 75 mm battalion, and at one point he and four others managed to draw fire from a German battery. One of the shells exploded within twenty-five yards, showering them with dirt clods and rocks. For the most part, as with the other soldiers, he could now tell by sound about where incoming shells would strike. He worried, however, about a new German shell that reportedly flew faster than sound, and thus would be undetectable until it landed. The following night he and the others feared that "the 'Boche' might give them a New Year's greeting." It was a clear and intensely cold night under a nearly full moon, but they had a small stove that kept him warm in a "bomb-proof" (bomb shelter). Fortunately, the Germans did not attack. It was a quiet sector of mostly reprisal artillery fire. In an unspoken understanding, each side fired an occasional barrage that was then returned by the other side, shells never coming too close, tit-for-tat. Each side knew, of course, that at some future date each side would likely be ordered to obliterate the other.34

His most exciting news for Cora was that while absent from the school he had found a place to take a "red hot bath in a real bathtub," something he had not had for weeks.35

Upon his return to the artillery school, he was pleased to learn that Murray had been promoted. He wrote Cora that he "felt blue" that his friend would be leaving the school and going to an artillery unit. Glassford, naturally, was anxious for an artillery command himself, but that was not to be. On January 22 he moved on to his next assignment, somewhat sad to leave behind the little school that he, Murray, and Cubbison had worked so hard to build and operate. Glassford served for a week in Pershing's headquarters and then moved on to his new assignment. To his disappointment, it was another artillery school. He would become the director of the artillery school that served the entire AEF. Clearly, it was a very big job, but it was not an artillery command.36

By late January 1918 Glassford's new title was "commandant." Although he was a lieutenant colonel, he had replaced a French two-star general. The site of the new

AEF artillery school was that of the prestigious but now closed French cavalry school at Saumur, dating back to the 1700s, located about two hundred miles southwest of Paris. In years past, American cavalry officers had been eager to attend the famous *École de* Cavalerie. Future general George Patton attended for five weeks, completing classes in riding and swordsmanship, funded by his wealthy wife, Beatrice, who also translated French for him during the trip.[37]

The school was a large institution, providing many conveniences that Glassford had done without at his I Corps school—a bed instead of a cot and even a bathtub. The focus of the artillery school was the same, but now served all US Divisions. Additionally, enlisted soldiers might be selected to attend a class where they could earn both an officer's commission and become artillery-branch qualified. The commandant's work was important, but it was also primarily administrative. His immediate task was to ensure a smooth transition between the departing French instructors and incoming American instructors. For this effort, his boyhood time of studying French language and culture proved to be of significant benefit. Most of the American officers in France who knew French knew only "West Point French," which emphasized elements of grammar but gave little attention to conversation. In fact, as historian Stephen Ambrose reports, one of the French professors at West Point during Glassford's time "concentrated on the grammar and made no effort to teach the cadets to speak the language (he did not speak it himself) or to read the masterpieces of French literature." By now Glassford was essentially fluent in the language and familiar enough with the culture to feel confident in his dealings with the French. In addition, in April, his new assistant commandant was Donald Cowan McDonald, a fellow 1904 USMA graduate whose West Point nickname was "Jennie," likely because of his curly hair. McDonald not only spoke fluent French but also had returned to West Point in 1909 for two years as an assistant professor of the language.[38]

On May 19 Glassford held a ceremony of the first class of former enlisted soldiers who had completed both basic officer training and the artillery school and now were second lieutenants. The school was operating just as Glassford had hoped, but perhaps too well. He worried that he might spend the entire war in a training command. He journeyed to Pershing's headquarters in Chaumont and locked in a promise that he would be given an artillery regiment. In the meantime, the AEF artillery school remained a busy place. Over the course of its existence, it instructed 1,700 commissioned officers, of whom 1,548 successfully completed the course, as well as 3,920 officer candidates, of which 3,393 graduated. In total, 5,620 students attended and 4,941 successfully completed their classes.[39]

In a letter to Cora, Pelham wrote, "I live only for two things—to do my bit, and I hope a BIG bit, toward winning this war, and to see my dear ones again." As with all letters from soldiers, it had been censored and arrived without a stamp, but with "soldier's letter" written across the top. If any envelope bore a return address, it was nothing more than "somewhere in France."[40]

The Field Artillery was a mounted branch, and Glassford loved horses. Draft horses pulled the cannons, but for their personal mounts, Glassford and his fellow officers selected and rode the best horses they could find. Sometimes the horses did not last long; artillery forward-observer Lieutenant George P. Hayes, 3rd Division, for instance, had seven horses shot out from under him as he galloped about scouting positions and directing fire. Glassford, as commandant at Saumur, had access to some of the finest horses in France. He and French Colonel Godeau, commandant of the nearby remount depot, had become early morning riding companions. Godeau delighted in selecting horses for Glassford to try. When Godeau later asked Glassford which horse had pleased him most, Glassford, without hesitation, answered "Kidron." The horse was a thoroughbred chestnut gelding standing sixteen hands, two inches tall, with a white streak from eyes to nose and white stocking rear legs. Hap mentioned in a letter to Cora that he often rode with "Lt-Colonel Godeau, one of France's most favorite Cavalrymen. I wish you could see the beautiful horse I am riding now. Much like my old Tuolumne—only taller and much more beautiful," comparing Kidron with the horse he had raced in Hawaii.[41]

Kidron had been captured from the Germans in 1917 and was subsequently trained at the French cavalry school. Sometime later, Colonel Godeau's orderly, holding Kidron by a lead rope, arrived at Glassford's quarters. The orderly told Glassford that Colonel Godeau had departed for the Front but that he was presenting Kidron to the American commandant "for his own use," adding that it was "an official gift made . . . by French authorities." Almost nothing could have pleased Glassford more than this generous gift. He looked forward to taking Kidron home after the war. Unfortunately, while Glassford was away, General Pershing paid a visit to the artillery school, with Glassford's officers supplying Kidron to the general for his use during his visit. Pershing was a cavalry officer as was his aide, Colonel John G.

Quekemeyer, who was also a friend of Glassford. Quekemeyer told Pershing what the general already knew, that Kidron was "too fine a horse to be exposed to the front." The following day an unexpected message arrived at the artillery school from General Pershing's headquarters directing that Kidron be shipped to General Pershing's headquarters. Thereafter, Kidron became General Pershing's favorite mount.[42]

Sometime later, when Glassford was able to do so, he went to Pershing's headquarters to retrieve Kidron. Saddle in hand, Glassford looked about for his horse. When Glassford saw Quekemeyer he asked about his horse. Quekemeyer smiled and simply walked Glassford into General Pershing's headquarters, saying to the general that Glassford had come for his horse. Pershing found it most humorous that Glassford thought he would be taking Kidron. As Glassford remembered, "The usually austere general almost went into hysterics," and then explained that the horse had turned an ankle and could not walk the forty kilometers to Glassford's headquarters and would have to stay at Pershing's headquarters. Thereafter, General Pershing sent a photograph of himself astride Kidron with a notation saying, "To P. D. Glassford, with cordial regards. John J. Pershing." At war's end, Pershing would ride his beauty of a horse in victory parades in Paris and London. Glassford later remembered, "The last time I saw Kidron was soon after the war, at the quartermaster stables in Washington, D.C. He was still Pershing's favorite horse."[43]

CHAPTER 5

The German Spring Offenses and the Allied Defenses

PERSHING hoped to have 650,000 soldiers in France by June 15. American doughboys, most with a modicum of training, continued to arrive on French shores. Because the army had had too few rifles stateside, some soldiers had drilled with wooden rifles and now had to be taught how to care for and shoot their real rifles. The army would eventually organize sixty-four combat divisions for the world war, but not all would be sent to Europe. Of those US divisions that served in France, five were trained by the British rather than the French. The British assumed that these five divisions would remain with them, but Pershing eventually demanded that they be sent to France. A compromise resulted in three of the divisions going to France, and two, the 27th and the 30th, remaining to fight with the British. Private William F. Clarke was assigned to the 27th "New York" Division. His experiences as a young doughboy, as recollected from his memoir, are likely representative of how most privates experienced the Western Front, whether they served with the British or the French. Unlike Glassford and his fellow officers, Clarke's view of the war would be from the bottom up. By the time he disembarked from his troopship in May 1918, soldiers of the pioneer divisions had learned much they could pass on to the newly arrived divisions.[1]

One of Clarke's early memories was being supplied in France with his uniforms and equipment:

> From now on we would carry all we owned on our
> backs in our packs, which, other than toilet articles,
> were a pair of woolen socks, a suit of "long-johns,"
> two blankets, a shelter half which was one half of a

pup tent, a tent pole, tent pins, a pair of shoes, an overcoat, and a slicker or rain coat. Also included was a short trench shovel, a Bowie knife, a revolver and ammunition, first-aid kit, mess kit, and canteen for water. I may have forgotten an item or two, but when we got this mess of stuff rolled into a pack and on our backs, it weighed 70 pounds.[2]

His first ride on a French train was memorable. He and his fellow soldiers rode in boxcars. Painted on the sides of each boxcar was "40 hommes-8 chevaux." Clarke recalled, "Forty men could get into one of these cars if they all stood up, and eight horses might be able to make it, also standing up. I don't know if the French Poilu traveled so crowded, but we never did. . . . There were a few times later on when we had to shovel the manure and smelly straw from the cars before we could or would ride in them."[3]

The AEF would grow to 1.2 million, with troops arriving at the rate of 250,000 a month. During the World War, more than 380,000 African Americans served, with 200,000 sent to France, 40,000 of whom served in combat regiments. The others, designated as "service troops," performed such duties as unloading ships, driving trucks, caring for horses and mules, and similar jobs. Earlier the army had formed two "colored" combat divisions, the 92nd "Buffalo" and 93rd "Blue Helmet" Divisions, but then shipped only detachments of each to France. Those in the 92nd Division were segregated and served for the most part under white American officers; those in the four regiments of the 93rd Division, including the famous 369th "Harlem Hellfighters" Regiment, were not segregated and served under French officers.[4]

Still under pressure to amalgamate his army, Pershing instead offered four regiments of African American soldiers to the French. Why Pershing selected these regiments is suspect, but the French were delighted to have them. Each regiment served with a French division, the only American soldiers to be "amalgamated." The 93rd Division soldiers wore the rounder French blue helmet rather than the flatter olive-drab British American helmet, the only American soldiers to do so. Having previously commanded colonial divisions, French commanders were quite pleased with the African American soldiers. It would take more than thirty years for the US Army to desegregate, being forced to do so by President Harry S. Truman, former World War I artillery captain.[5]

General Erich Ludendorff, Germany's supreme commander, whose drooping mustache mirrored his perpetual frown resting above a double chin, intended to launch five major offensives before American troops, hundreds of thousands of them, landed and became battle ready. He was relatively certain that if he failed, he would have no possibility of winning the war, or even negotiating a favorable armistice. He decided to initiate his offenses in the spring and summer along a 200-mile section of the Western Front, part of the 440-mile trench system that linked the North Sea coast of Belgium to the mountains of Switzerland. It was Ludendorff's good fortune that by October 1917, Vladimir Lenin's embryonic Bolshevik government had disengaged Russia from the war, allowing for the return of forty-eight German divisions from the Eastern Front. Ludendorff now had 3.5 million soldiers ready to attack on his command, going up against 3.9 million Allied soldiers. Ludendorff was sure that a trained and equipped American army would not become operational before 1918. He suspected that the arrival of American troops would not change the course of the war.[6]

On March 21, while Glassford trained artillery students at Saumur, Ludendorff launched his first offensive, Operation Michael, between St. Quentin and Montdidier in Northern France, on the Somme River. The attack lasted until April 5. Four days later he sent forth his second offensive, Operation Georgette, this time to the north of his first offensive. The second attack lasted until April 29. Each attack intended to split apart the French and British armies and, with luck, fully destroy the weaker British Army. Thus far, however, the Germans had pushed only significant salients—bulges—in the frontline, driving deeper into France.[7]

Ludendorff had employed some new tactics, developed by his cousin, General Oskar von Hutier. The tactics were frightening harbingers of the German blitzkriegs of the next world war. Instead of relying on long-distance artillery barrages over several days, Ludendorff used shorter, rolling barrages, immediately followed by numerous assault teams, each made up of fourteen *Sturmtruppen* (stormtroopers). Instead of bolt action rifles, these soldiers fired automatic rifles, light machine guns, small mortars, and flame throwers. The teams bypassed Allied strongpoints, leaving those to be attacked by aircraft and heavier units that followed.[8]

During his second offensive, Ludendorff took the occasion to give the rookie Americans a harsh lesson in what to expect from the German army. On April 20, south of Verdun near Seicheprey, France, a contingent of the 26th Yankee Division suffered a stunning attack. Hundreds of German cannons sent forth a rolling barrage, followed by the advance of 600 stormtroopers, in turn followed by 2,600 regular German soldiers. The Germans quickly overwhelmed the 600 Yankees. When the Germans retired in the evening, they had caused significant casualties and dragged with them 136 American prisoners for interrogation. As historian S. L. A. Marshall notes, "It was an isolated event, staged by the Germans to humiliate the Americans and defer the shaping of an all-U.S. Army."9

Pershing and the French generals agreed that the Americans had thus far experienced only defensive warfare. It was time for them to attack. The 1st Big Red One Division was the most qualified and would endeavor to reduce Ludendorff's salient near Montdidier. But before the 1st Division could initiate its attack, Ludendorff had launched his third offensive, Operation Blücher, which lasted from May 27 to June 5, and dealt the Americans a punishing blow. This offensive, coming between Reims and Soissons, was an elaborate feint designed to make the French believe that the German target was Paris. Ludendorff's real intention, however, remained to separate the French and English armies. He was betting that the French would pull substantial reserves from elsewhere if it appeared that Paris was in jeopardy. As it turned out, the feint was so successful that Ludendorff concluded that he might, indeed, be able to capture Paris, and Paris in German hands would alter the course of the war.10

The Germans had two possible routes to Paris, and both were largely unprotected. The first was from Soissons and the other was from Fismes, southeast of Soissons, both roads converging on Château Thierry on the Marne River, just fifty-six miles east of Paris. By June 3 German troops had established a bridgehead on the Marne. French generals urgently requested that Pershing send American divisions to help. Two were available and reasonably close, the 2nd and the 3rd, both Regular Army divisions; their mission would be to hold the Germans at the Marne. The 2nd Division, consisting of one brigade of soldiers and one brigade of Marines, not only stopped the Germans but managed to launch a counterattack through Belleau Wood. When warned by a French officer that the Marines should retreat, Captain Lloyd Williams scoffed and said, "Retreat, hell! We just got here." The Germans would come to call the Marines "Devil Dogs." Frustrated, Ludendorff shifted his focus, still aiming for Paris but now approaching from Reims, southeast of Fismes. The task of the 3rd Division was to shut down the entrance to the Surmelin Valley, leading to Paris from the south side of the Marne. The order by the

3rd Division commander to his soldiers was simple: "Don't let anything show itself on the other side [of the Marne] and live." General Pershing would later say of the 3rd Division, "On this occasion a single regiment of the Third Division wrote one of the most brilliant pages in our military annals." As the French units withdrew, the stubborn soldiers of the 3rd Division simply refused to budge, earning the division its nickname "Rock of the Marne," which endures to this day.[11]

About six weeks earlier, on May 30, the army had offered Glassford the position of second in command of Fort Sill, Oklahoma, which in 1911 had become the headquarters and home of the Artillery School. Hap knew Cora would want him to accept the offer, but he also knew that she would understand why he could not. Then, quite suddenly, the army simply ordered Glassford to return to the United States. Furious, he hurried to AEF General Headquarters at Chaumont to remind the general staff of their commitment to give him an artillery command. His refusal to return to the United States somehow resulted in Pershing promoting him to full colonel and giving him command of an artillery regiment. AEF headquarters had come through. Glassford took command of the 103rd Field Artillery Regiment, formerly part of the Rhode Island National Guard and now part of the 26th Yankee Division. Apparently, officers of the regiment had held to their behind-the-scenes efforts to have Glassford assigned to their division. Glassford could not have been more pleased; finally, he had a wartime artillery command. He wrote to Cora saying, "On the fourteenth anniversary of my graduation from West Point, I take command of the 103rd F.A."[12]

On June 9 Ludendorff launched his fourth offensive, Operation Gneisenau. Hap wrote to Cora, "Expect to go to the Front. . . . Am delighted to get away, and into the REAL game!" A minor problem was that Glassford was unsure of the whereabouts of his regiment, but by the evening of June 15 he had located it. He reported to the 51st Field Brigade Commander, General Dwight E. Aultman, who offered Glassford his congratulations and assured him that the spread-winged eagle insignias of a full colonel were on the way. That evening, Glassford observed the loading of an artillery regiment for rail transport and was surprised when told that moving it to a new location required 7 trains of 50 cars each, with each train requiring 17 flatcars for guns and vehicles, 30 boxcars for soldiers and horses, 2 cars for officers, and a baggage car for the train crew, 350 cars in all.[13]

Having earlier relieved the soldiers and Marines of the 2nd Division, the soldiers of the 26th Division were now positioned near Chateau Thierry, waiting for further orders. The doughboys were pleased that this sector was quiet, the weather was good, and their rations and mail had found them. Not so pleasing was that German snipers and artillery shells occasionally found them as well. Glassford had assumed command of his regiment on June 15, 1918. The very next day, June 16, the Germans attacked the 26th Division's position at Xivray-Marvoisin, east of St. Mihiel. The Germans shattered the peace at 3:00 a.m. on Sunday morning. The attack was a near-copy of the heavy raid at Seicheprey two months previous, which had devastated elements of the 26th Division. This attack began with a twenty-minute artillery gas and high explosives preparation, followed by three columns of German infantry, each of which divided into three smaller columns, primarily aimed at Marvoisin with a flanking movement at Xivray. Five hundred *landwehr* (garrison troops, usually older men) and German infantry soldiers emerged in the morning mist, aided by eighty stormtroopers and forty pioneers (combat engineers) using twenty trench mortars. The likely mission of the Germans was to capture American soldiers for interrogation, but the defenses of the Yankees held, and the doughboys repulsed the attack. One battery of Glassford's 155 mm howitzer cannons fired ten shells in seventy seconds, a record for the AEF. About sixty Germans were killed, dozens of wounded were carried away, and numerous German weapons littered the ground. The 26th Division had taken casualties as well, 28 killed, 107 wounded, and 47 seriously gassed. Glassford had no doubt that he was now in the "real game."[14]

In an earlier letter he had admitted to Cora, "I'm green as grass after so much school work, and must knuckle down and work." Following the attack on June 16, he wrote in another letter, "It has been most interesting and I am tired to a frazzle. . . . They all blame me," he quipped, "making my arrival the sole cause [of] the Boche trying to welcome me to their vicinity!" He spent the day walking throughout the regimental area, greeting old friends and introducing himself to those he did not know. By June 30 Hap wrote to Cora, "This Regiment is a first-class outfit. We are beginning to get team-work, and I'll soon have the best Regiment over here." He also praised the French 155 mm howitzers, which he called a "fine cannon," adding that since his arrival his men had fired 3,000 shells. He failed to mention that his soldiers were fond of referring to the cannons as "snub-nosed, bell-mouthed hussies" who were not to be denied.[15]

The 26th Division was as pleased with Glassford as he was with them. Major Emerson G. Taylor, acting chief of staff of the 26th Division, would later say that Glassford was "soon to prove himself one of the most conspicuous and able officers the Division ever possessed."[16]

Glassford's regiment was one of the division's three artillery regiments: the 101st, the 102nd, and 103rd, the last of which he commanded. The first two regiments fired the French 75 mm cannon, while Glassford's regiment fired the larger French 155 mm howitzer. His regiment consisted of three battalions, each of which had two artillery batteries, with each battery having four guns, for a total of twenty-four howitzers. Each battery had 210 officers and soldiers. When medical, supply, and staff personnel were added, Glassford's regiment totaled 1,728.[17]

The French 75 mm cannon was primarily an antipersonnel weapon, useful for stopping enemy attacks, cutting paths through wire defenses, and protecting the advance of infantry movements. Glassford's regiment fired the larger Schneider 155 mm howitzer, model 1917, and, like the 75 mm cannon, was designed and manufactured in France. Considered a heavy cannon, the 155 mm was primarily an antibunker weapon. It could fire four ninety-five-pound shells per minute at steep angles up to 42 degrees for more than 12,000 yards (6.8 miles). The weapon proved itself when attacking organized enemy works, such as artillery batteries, concrete fortifications, shelters, trenches, and dugouts. The latter, usually protected on the sides and lightly covered on top, were still vulnerable from overhead. The howitzer was also capable of landing shells behind protective defilade, such as steep hills and deep forests, and could fire even when situated within deep valleys.[18]

At first glance the weapon resembled a grossly oversized Civil War cannon. It had a large tube mounted on a carriage that was attached to two very large wagon wheels and an axle, with double iron trails to the rear, like massive bent arms resting on the ground. Ten stocky workhorses towed the cannon by its trails, the tube pointed to the rear. During setup the cannon rested on its two wheels and two trails, the latter capable of being spread apart for increased stability. The howitzer could fire seven different shells, but most often fired high explosive and gas-filled shells. A well-trained crew could fire up to five rounds per minute. After twenty shots the crew greased the bore and cooled the tube. While Glassford was pleased with his regiment, he intended to make it even better. He was stern with his officers, expecting them to drill their crews so well that each task became automatic during battle. Officers soon learned that he abhorred inefficiency and was intolerant of excuses.[19]

When the World War had begun, French Marshal Ferdinand Foch was a corps commander, but thereafter he quickly rose to chief of staff. Now in his midsixties, his twisted handlebar mustache had turned gray but he remained vigorous. Once it became clear that the Allies could not succeed without one overall supreme commander, the decision makers concurred that Foch was the best choice. With the Americans now landing soldiers in large numbers, Foch was ready to go on the offensive. Reducing the Aisne-Marne salient—the big dent the Germans had made in the frontline—would be where he would begin. His intent was to restore the frontline to where it had been before Ludendorff had attacked. Foch set his launch date for July 18. Three days earlier Ludendorff had launched his fifth and final offensive, Operation Marneschutz-Reims, but it had fizzled.[20]

Foch's assignment for the Americans was to reduce the Aisne-Marne salient. In essence, the German third offensive had made a huge dent—a bulge or salient—in the frontline, pushing it south. Now the Americans were going to hammer it out so that the line was straight again. The original line had run from Soissons in the west to Reims in the east, but now part of the line was thirty miles to the south, near Château Thierry. The primary hammering would be done by the American 1st and 2nd Divisions and the French 1st Moroccan Division. These divisions would hammer on one side of the dent; that is, from the west. The secondary hammering along various parts of the bottom would be done by the American 26th, 42nd, 4th, 77th, 3rd, 28th, and 32nd Divisions. These divisions would drive generally north, aiming for midway between Soissons and Reims. Eventually, all the involved divisions would meet and merge into one force. Since the Germans were determined to hold the territory, it would take the rest of July and half of August for the Allies to complete the mission, but a victory would constitute a turning point of the war.[21]

By July 9 the 26th Division had relieved the 2nd Division along an imaginary line linking the villages of Torcy, Belleau, Bouresches, and Vaux, all just northwest of Château Thierry. The Division had occupied the area essentially for the purpose of denying it to Germans, but it stood ready to immediately go on the offensive when required. Every soldier in the division suspected that an attack was coming, but no one knew where or when. As one officer later wrote, "But secrecy was imperative. The great counter-stroke was to be delivered as a complete surprise to the confident but much-extended [German] infantry." On July 17 a subtle clue was sent to the American infantry colonels, saying simply, "No working parties will be sent out tonight." At 10:15 p.m. the corps commander sent an order to the division commander stating that forward movement of the 26th Division would commence at 4:35 a.m. the next morning. Division staff and line commanders now had just six hours to organize, transport, and notify all unit levels from division down to platoon as to the specific part each would play in the operation. It did not help that a raging storm of lightning, thunder, and torrential rain turned the ground into a slippery and muddy mess.[22]

It had taken the artillery commanders ten nights to secretly bring up the big guns. Their next job was to prepare a secondary artillery barrage zone to protect the primary defensive line. The infantry soldiers, having no fortified trenches, shelters, or barbed wire in front of them, relied on their trusty entrenching tools to shovel out foxholes a foot or two in depth, hoping that they would not have to occupy the holes for long. At the forward outposts, doughboys discovered that they now inhabited a ground of horror. Everywhere there were reminders of the 2nd Division soldiers and Marines who had earlier died in these woods: "Shapeless fragments of what once were men hung in the jagged branches of trees, blown there by shells; stiffened shapes were found by the new troops, lying still unburied where they had fallen before German machine-gun nests in the rocky hollows. A grisly odor of death hung heavy in the summer air around the stone hunting lodge near the eastern skirts of the woods, and the men there came to move and talk as when they know that ghosts are watching them." Then, quite suddenly, orders arrived. The Division moved from defense to offense. The Champagne-Marne defensive battle now migrated into the Aisne-Marne offensive battle, becoming the second battle of the Marne. Throughout the campaign Glassford's regiment would be called upon to support not only their own 26th Division, but the 42nd, 28th, and 4th Divisions as well.[23]

As the regimental historians later wrote, "From the time of the first advance, on July 21st, until relief, the guns of the Regiment, under the command of Colonel Glassford, were continually kept well to the front, always on the heels of the infantry. It is probably safe to say that never before did six-inch howitzers prove themselves so mobile, so thoroughly worthy of the name 'field artillery.' It was here that they gained the nickname, 'Glassford's trench mortars' that was to stick to them until the end of the war." Glassford kept his regiment at a gallop. While a heavy gun regiment would usually be at the rear, Glassford's troops often passed the normally lighter and faster regiments and went into action sooner.[24]

Armies in defense prefer elevated positions; armies on the offense dread having to attack elevated positions but doing so is often critical. On July 18 Glassford's regiment delivered destructive fire around the Etrepilly Plateau, Belleau, and Hill 204, leading to the capture of Torcy. Two days later, supporting the French on several targets, the 103rd helped take Hill 193. For a quarter of an hour, Glassford directed all his batteries to concentrate fire on the woods and ravines where soon doughboy infantry would advance four kilometers. As division historians later wrote, "This fire was not the typical barrage, advancing in regular progression at a fixed rate, but rather a series of terrific concentrations on places which were probable machine-gun nests or other centers of resistance." Glassford's forward observers tracked the German infantry continually and adjusted fire as needed, providing near-perfect artillery support. One artillery captain said of Glassford's written orders, "They emphasize above all other things the need of rapidity of movement without breaking the liaison with the infantry."25

At the end of the first day, the Division had reached its objective and the Germans were retreating. Glassford relied on his liaison officers but knew that situations can change quickly; accordingly, he never hesitated to go forward himself. On one such occasion he mounted his motorcycle and followed an infantry armored car into Trugny. Knowing the division infantry officers would be focused on other matters, he was able to see the situation with the eyes of an artillery commander and revised his cannons accordingly. He agreed with Marshal Foch, who asserted, "To make a reconnaissance correctly one must do more than reconnoiter."26

He recalled in a later letter to Cora, "We were ordered to concentrate EVERYTHING at a certain hill, just over the lines, at a certain hour, just before dark. We had not registered in that direction, so [another officer, two soldiers and] I sneaked out with a [communications] wire to a farm house not far therefrom, and adjusted one battery after another, myself—peeping through some shell-holes through the upper story. At the designated time the pounding began, and the hill looked as if it were on fire, there was such smoke and dust."27

Glassford's assigned vehicle was a standard army olive-drab Dodge touring car, but his preferred "command vehicle" was a sputtering two-cylinder motorcycle on which he zipped about, maintaining close contact with his twenty-four separate gun crews and headquarters. He frequently went forward to meet with infantry officers to ensure the best liaison possible. On July 19 he wrote to Cora, "It is GREAT—this movement and thrilling activity—I am thrilled to the bone with it all! . . . Traveling light, with only a small roll and the sleeping bag, a light pillow, my field glasses, and a forty-five. It is great!"[28]

The accuracy of the 103rd Field Artillery Regiment came to the attention of General Pershing. When AEF headquarters asked the colonel how he did it, he explained that in the evenings he would sometimes go into the valleys on his motorcycle to scout out and mark enemy position coordinates on his map. Early the following morning, he would give the information to his artillery crews so they could fire on the unsuspecting targets. When reminded that what he was doing was dangerous, he quipped that he had not been caught yet. Before long, his soldiers were boasting that they had "the highest-ranking artillery scout in the American Expeditionary Force." As Cora recalled, his soldiers were calling him the colonel "in front of the front."[29]

In a memorable event, Glassford needed to know if the town of Sergy remained in enemy hands. Frustrated at not getting the information he needed quickly enough, he rode his motorcycle into the town, which was very quiet. As Cora later reported, "Upon reaching the main street, Germans began pouring out of the houses, and there being nothing else to do, Happy simply went on at full speed, turned a corner, rode around the block, and returned to his own lines—miraculously unscathed—Probably the Germans were too astonished at his appearance to fire on him!" But the Colonel came back with the information he needed. He later reported to Cora, "Our supremacy in artillery is doing the work, their artillery fire is desultory."[30]

Finally, in early August, the Regiment rotated off the frontline for a much-needed rest. Other units of the 26th Division had been relieved already, but the artillery regiments had been detached to support other divisions. When they were finally released, Glassford admitted, "We hated to be pulled out of the fight—this regiment had made a greater advance against the Huns than any other American regiment, so far—We need a rest and need it badly." The men were tired, the horses dragging, the officers expressionless, and the guns in need of overhaul.[31]

Glassford's circuitous battle route thus far had taken his regiment through the villages of Torcy, Belleau, Bouresches, Vaux, and Château-Thierry, all roughly 100 miles northeast of Paris. The cost of success was high: the Regiment had suffered thirteen killed and fifty wounded. Overall, during the Aisne-Marne Offensive, the Germans had skillfully retreated, forcing the Allies to pay for every mile retaken.[32]

The doughboys, especially the infantry, had their own complaints about the war. The soldiers grew to hate their small neighbors—rats and scabies that shared their sleeping accommodations. Private Clarke of the 27th Division remembered:

> There was no way to get rid of these rats and there was no other place for us to sleep.... We just went to sleep, pulling our lone blanket over our heads.... During the night the rats played games, chasing each other over the mounds of blanketed soldiers. During our service ... we all acquired a large colony of cooties. As a result, we suffered from scabies, that skin disease caused by our parasitic friends. We had few opportunities to bathe. We had no opportunity to launder our underwear.... We never undressed except for our shoes and puttees. There is nothing so personal as a cootie, but hundreds of them infesting your clothes and bodies were sometimes almost unendurable.... It laid its eggs in the seams of our underwear and uniforms. Our body heat produced generation after generation of them.... Little sores and scabs would form all over the body.

The rats and cooties drove the soldiers crazy, but the German artillery and bombers were out to kill them. The night bombers instilled the most fear. Clarke remembered:

> We heard in our dreams the [German] bombers coming over, the whumps in the distance from the exploding bombs. The dreams turned into reality and before we could move, we were hugging the ground as the explosions ripped up the flying field not more than a few hundred yards from us. There is something terrifying about night bombing. There seems to be no defense against it for the individual soldiers. In the darkness of night, the bomber is just a noise in the sky. He cannot be seen. His exploding bombs creep closer and closer. One spot of ground is about as safe as another. In your fear you hug the ground and claw and claw with your fingers to make a hole in the ground, praying and praying that the next salvo will miss you.[33]

CHAPTER 6

St. Mihiel and the Meuse-Argonne Offenses

AS part of the Regiment's refitting, the soldiers were deloused and issued new clothing. Glassford was unhappy that during the campaign his soldiers had not been reissued socks, underwear, shoes, or blankets, all of which had deteriorated from continued use. Even his officers were stripped to essentials. The army's supply system, likely focused on outfitting new arrivals to France, shortchanged the frontline soldiers. Still, he reported to Cora that his regiment was "a great bunch of men. They are always singing and joking when you consider that all our marching and over half our firing is done at night. You can understand that an artilleryman's existence is no pipe-dream."[1]

On August 8 a highly unusual event occurred at La Ferté-Sous-Jouarre. Glassford celebrated his thirty-fifth birthday by giving a party for his soldiers. As the regimental historian notes, "Everyone by order resumed the civilian status, and for one bright hour there were no buck privates, no captains, no majors, no colonels." Since the regiment now had some downtime, they also worked in a little baseball and other entertainment.[2]

In a letter home Hap wrote, "We are out of the line for a couple of weeks, in a beautiful part of France, far from the noise of battle. We are reequipping, drilling, and getting ready for more work. The people of this beautiful little town where I am situated have given 'the Americans from [the battle] of Château-Thierry' a great welcome. Feel that I have made an improvement in the Regiment, in spite of difficulties." Glassford mentioned that he had heard that his old classmate and good friend, Robert M. "John" Danford, had been promoted to brigadier general. Hap added, "Am not a bit jealous though. In fact, I doubt if I would accept a star if offered, so much in love am I with my present job. . . . It is simply great to command a Regiment of real red-blooded Americans, and to feel that they are back of you to a man."³

A story about Glassford and his executive officer, Lieutenant Colonel Everitte Chaffee, circulated around the regiment. It seemed that in late July, during a heavy rainstorm, the two were under a tarpaulin studying a map and discussing tactics. Soldiers who passed by could hear "Chaffee's deep rumble matching Glassford's drawl" as they discussed the matter. Then everyone heard the unmistakable whine of a German 105 mm shell, followed by an air-splitting explosion not one hundred feet away, and in the ensuing silence Glassford was overheard saying, "Would you mind pulling down that canvas on your side, Chaffee; this map's getting wet."⁴

The next task that French Marshal Foch handed the AEF was the reduction of another bulge in the frontline, the St. Mihiel Salient, an operation that would last from September 12 to 16. For the first time General Pershing would have his own American sector. If the Americans reduced the salient, they could move on to capture the city of Metz, an important rail junction. Doing so would also allow the Americans to achieve full-partner status with the other Allied forces. The difficult part was that the Germans were in a stronger position than were the Allies.⁵

To do the planning for the operation, Pershing sent for Lieutenant Colonel George Marshall of the 1st Division. Marshall had been considered for command of a regiment and a promotion to full colonel, but the call from Pershing changed that. Soon permanently affixed to General Headquarters, Marshall immersed himself in planning at a much higher level. Previously, he had focused on feeding, clothing, training, and transporting 1st Division troops. Now he contended with such things as the flow of replacements, ammunition supply, horse availability, ocean tonnage, ports of debarkation, supply lines, large scale training, and gathering tanks and artillery from other allies for the entire AEF. It seems he was penalized for being too good a planner.⁶

A tense disagreement surfaced early. Marshal Foch, top allied general, wanted control of some of Pershing's divisions. Pershing refused. Foch insisted, demanding that he supply the needed soldiers. The argument continued until the American general pulled from his pocket a letter of instructions from President Wilson, which read, "While our army will fight wherever you may decide, it will not fight except as an independent American army." Foch stood up and walked out of the meeting. Pershing's refusal to cooperate would come at a high price, however. The following day the AEF general agreed not only to reduce the St. Mihiel Salient, but thereafter to immediately move his army to the Meuse-Argonne. Having successfully kept his First Army intact so he could attack the St. Mihiel bulge, Pershing now had to uphold his other commitment. Marshall must have cringed when he heard what Pershing had promised. Marshall and his staff had just twenty-four days to plan two major battles, which would include transporting more than a half-million soldiers and their cannons, vehicles, and horses over sixty miles on terrible roads at night, fight one battle, and then move to the next battle almost without pause.[7]

The geography of the St. Mihiel Salient was that of a right triangle having been formed when the Germans pushed south, putting another bulge into the original frontline. The mission of the Americans was to eliminate that bulge, pushing the frontline back to where it had been before. At the top of the triangle was Verdun, on the old frontline; directly south of Verdun at the base of the triangle was St. Mihiel, on the new frontline. About fifteen miles east of St. Mihiel was Seicheprey, where earlier 3,200 German stormtroopers had delivered a punishing assault against the 26th Division. Now the town would serve as the starting line for an American drive north. Lined up east of Seicheprey, from left to right, were six American divisions at the base of the triangle: the 1st, 42nd, 89th, 2nd, 5th, and 90th. All the divisions would push north, aiming toward Verdun, twenty-five miles distant. The 1st Division would constitute the primary effort. About halfway up between St. Mihiel and Verdun Glassford's 26th Yankee Division would come in from the west in a flanking movement, and then join with the 1st Division at Vigneulles, near the center of the triangle. The battle plan of the 26th required that it secretly move into position by September 9. Troop movements, often forced marches through villages, could be done only at night; movement ceased during the day and the soldiers and their equipment remained concealed. Once the 26th Division artillery arrived, instead of being emplaced in gun pits as was the usual case, the weapons were simply kept hidden in the brush. Additionally, there would be no advanced registering of targets for fear of alerting the Germans. The horses, too, were kept back for a few hundred yards. The American attack force was large enough that the salient—bulge—was expected to collapse within a few days. Artillery would play a key role, with 3,000 artillery cannons concentrated for the initial preparation needed to clear the path. The attack also had to take into consideration the *massif* of Montsec, a towering fortress of German observation and associated artillery, blocking all routes north.[8]

At 1:00 a.m. on September 12, the American artillery sent forth a massive barrage all along the frontline, the rounds rumbling, whining, shrieking, and screaming.

At 5:00 a.m. the artillery went silent and the infantry doughboys of the 1st, 42nd, 89th, 2nd, 5th, and 90th moved northwest, while the infantry of the 26th moved southeast. Thereafter, by established procedure, the soldiers moved 100 yards every four minutes, following rolling artillery barrages. When the 1st and 26th Divisions conjoined and closed the gap, the German strongpoint of Montsec folded and the entire salient collapsed. German soldiers were either retreating or surrendering, along with their large stores of ammunition, machine guns, and field pieces. In all, 16,000 German soldiers surrendered and 443 cannons were captured. The battle lasted only two days but provided combat experience for thousands of recently arrived American soldiers.[9]

On September 23 Glassford had another bit of good fortune when he narrowly escaped being seriously hurt or killed by an enemy shell. The incident occurred when Glassford and his adjutant, Major Norman D. MacLeod, and Marine Colonel Hiram I. Bearss, commanding the 102nd Infantry Regiment, were on a hilltop gauging the effectiveness of an artillery box barrage below. The three officers heard a large round approaching and immediately fell prone, but a piece of shrapnel struck Glassford in the chin. He later quipped that being taller, it had taken him longer to reach the ground. He ignored the wound until he was back in the camp, where someone told him that he had blood streaming down his neck. In a letter to Cora he minimized, "Had a lucky escape this morning about one A.M. when an Austrian 88 mm lit in the road only a few feet from me. Got only a scratch on the chin, and a piece of shell went through the collar of my trench coat.... Your four-leaf clover is doing its work! This is the narrowest escape I have had."[10]

The Yanks now moved rapidly to the Meuse-Argonne, which would become the pivotal battle for the AEF. All along the Western Front, the collective Allied armies took their positions for a major drive, each in its own sector. The French would initiate two drives across the extended frontline, while the Belgians, British, and Americans would each initiate one. The frontline curved somewhat, so that the Belgians and British faced east, the French northeast, and the Americans north. The Belgians would push to Ghent, the British to Mons, the French in two drives to Hirson and Mézières, and the Americans to Sedan.[11]

Pershing's mission was to assist the advance of the French army on his left flank, essentially protecting its right flank. He concluded that his best option was to align his nine divisions side by side and at the same moment catapult them forward as rapidly as possible. But first he had to get there.[12]

Moving the American army to the Meuse-Argonne was a Herculean effort.

What had looked extremely difficult on paper now looked utterly impossible on the ground. There were more than 500,000 soldiers in nine divisions, with the divisions having to share 900 trucks for transporting soldiers and a million tons of ammunition and supplies. There were about 3,000 cannons with caissons and their horses, which alone required 300 miles of road-space, and all of it had to be moved at different rates of speed along three muddy and terribly deteriorated roads in absolute darkness. The trucks could drive the distance to and from in one night and return for more loads, but the horse-drawn cannons required three to six nights to arrive. Amazingly, Pershing and his staff, especially Marshall, managed to do it.[13]

The next part was even more difficult. Once in position, the commanders looked north and beheld a threatening terrain that ran perhaps fifty miles from Verdun in the south to Sedan in the north. Colonel Hugh A. Drum, a cigar-chomping graduate of Boston College, then serving as the 1st Army Deputy Chief of Staff, called it "the most ideal defensive terrain I have ever seen or read about." It was a twenty-mile-wide valley with hazards on both sides. The eastern flank presented the unfordable Meuse River backed by the elevated Heights of the Meuse, while the western flank included the dense and elevated Argonne Forest, with the Aire River on one side of the forest and the Aisne River on the other. Compounding the situation, the Germans had occupied the valley since 1914 and still inhabited engineer-built fortifications replete with numerous observation positions and artillery emplacements. Although the Germans had just five divisions positioned in the valley, they could summon fifteen additional divisions within five days.[14]

Pershing later wrote, "Following three hours of violent artillery fire of preparation, the infantry advanced at 5:30 a.m. on September 26, accompanied by tanks." The attack got off to a good start, but by nightfall the American divisions began to falter. The dense morning fog had restricted vision, which had caused confusion. The terrain proved to be exceedingly difficult to negotiate, causing some artillery weapons to bog down in mud. Messages sometimes arrived at the wrong units, and some needed supplies never arrived. Perhaps worse was that some soldiers, having become separated from their units, waited to be found instead of searching for their units. Pershing had hoped to advance eight miles but achieved only three. Confusion turned to stagnation, which invited paralysis. The elevated guns of the Germans continued to drop high explosive and gas shells on the doughboys below.[15]

On October 1, after a brief pause to reorganize, Pershing's attack rebounded. He demanded better coordination among his units, better cooperation between his officers, and better liaison between the infantry and the artillery. Pershing's biggest problem, however, was that the German artillery emplaced on the Heights of the Meuse continued to drop shells onto the valley floor. The main attack continued. Pershing's generals encountered one impossible problem after another. The AEF commanding general rushed in four more divisions but never took the pressure off his generals. Colonel George Marshall later wrote, "General Pershing gave hourly evidence of those rare qualities that make successful leaders of great armies. He continually demanded fresh efforts . . . and was intolerant of the pessimistic reports . . . He inspired the weak-hearted . . . and made all of the higher commanders realize excuses were taboo and that the attack must be driven home."[16]

This would be a sustained battle and would last until November 10—the day before what would come to be known as Armistice Day. Glassford's 26th Division, having been at St. Mihiel, was not called upon to be one of the nine divisions in the main Meuse-Argonne drive. Pershing now assigned it, along with the 79th, 81st, and two French divisions, to dislodge the German artillery from the Heights of the Meuse. Midway through this battle, Glassford received some unexpected news. On October 6 he wrote Cora, "The paper today [October 1st] announced my appointment as Brigadier-General. I wonder if you know it tonight and feel as happy as I do? It was a very great surprise, and I can hardly believe it yet! Am waiting in breathless anticipation what the change will involve. But I am, too, unhappy at leaving this Regiment, and I hope even now, to stay long enough with it to go through one more scrap." He was pleased that Lieutenant Colonel Alden Twachtman, in whom he had great confidence, would assume command of the regiment. Glassford's new assignment was as commanding general of the 152nd Field Artillery Brigade, the brigade to which he was now assigned. Not only did he remain with his division, he remained with his brigade, but now in command of his old regiment and the other two regiments.[17]

Fortunately for the Yanks, the German army, having battled for four years, showed unmistakable signs of fatigue. As the American First Army struggled to its feet, many German soldiers laid down their arms, knowing they were beaten, wanting to quit the war while still alive.[18]

In an October 21 letter to Cora, Hap said, "Yes, I guess it is all right to tell you I was in the St. Mihiel Salient scrap. It was not as dashing, from an artilleryman's point of view as the Château-Thierry drive. . . . The latter is the greatest experience I have ever had."[19]

But an additional and invisible enemy stalked the doughboys: a devastating influenza. The cold, ongoing rain, lack of hot food, wet uniforms, wet blankets, and living in flooded dugouts weakened the resistance of the soldiers to the invisible enemy. Because the sickness was first reported by the free press in Spain, it became known incorrectly as the Spanish Flu. While two or more strains of flu were present in Europe, at least one was carried by American replacements from Fort Riley, packed tightly in troopships and rushed to France.[20]

The sickness would continue over the next two years to infect 500 million worldwide and kill 50 million, including 650,000 in the United States. It affected many AEF divisions and went on to ravage Europe. The 26th Division evacuated significant numbers of ailing soldiers and officers in key positions at every level were forced to surrender their commands. But even those soldiers who did not contract the flu were exhausted and in need of hot food that never arrived because of impassable roads. The doughboys looked gaunt, stooped, feverish, sunken-eyed, mentally absent, and wretched.[21]

Nonetheless, the war had to continue. Belgians, British, French, and Americans steadily pushed against the front, driving against the Germans. In a letter to Cora, Hap wrote, "Am writing this at odd moments during a coup-de-main by our troops—office fighting I call it. Sitting at a desk, directing an office staff force who are getting messages, sending them out, and in general controlling the artillery support of the infantry attack. . . . If things break right, we will have some quick action to perform in order to ensure our infantry [retains its] gains. . . . We are very anxious to gain and hold a certain RIDGE." One gets the sense that the office-bound general would have much preferred to have been on his motorcycle and back in the fight.[22]

His next letter, dated October 27, two weeks before the Armistice, was disconcerting. He had developed a bronchial disorder with a severe cough and fever, requiring medical treatment. An army doctor feared that he had contracted influenza or tuberculosis and ordered him evacuated to a hospital in Bordeaux for treatment. Hap later recounted:

> Am writing in bed at an evacuation hospital. Was sent in last night, and the nurse says I am due for a train ride today, back to one of the base hospitals near Bordeaux. My beloved doctor (Blanchard) has been watching me, and says I need a rest. Have been hitting a pretty heavy pace lately, with a slight breakdown, showing fever.

Have had a cough, too, for a long time. Yesterday he called-in Dr. (Lieutenant Colonel) Morris, one of the best lung-specialists in the U.S. He had to come a great distance. He went over me and found that I have no tuberculosis, but that I might quickly develop it if not given a little rest and sunshine, outside a dugout. I am to have a couple weeks of sick-leave in the south of France. They have promised to keep my place open in the Division if I get back within a month. I hated like the deuce to leave just while there was heavy fighting going on, and good work to be done.[23]

Glassford's cough went away, allowing him to depart Hospital 114 in Bordeaux, which housed thousands of soldiers. He felt fine but had disliked the forced inactivity. On November 9, two days before armistice, he wrote to Cora, "Here am I in Bandol, on the Mediterranean at last, enjoying the sun and warm weather and the good food. Lunched in Marseilles, and it was wonderful." He said he had not liked Bordeaux, but Bandol, between Marseilles and Toulon, was great. He knew he was not yet completely well, and wrote to Cora saying, "Must take things easy, for I find that I tire quickly, and must go back to work full of energy and spirit."[24]

He was very displeased when he discovered that his sketchbook from the front was missing, likely pilfered when he was hospitalized. Soon it was time for him to track down his division, which he had left north of Verdun, but now was reportedly marching to Luxembourg. He finally located it at Neufchatel in time for Thanksgiving dinner. Former brigade commander Brigadier General John H. Sherburne had "returned to his well-loved artillerymen, relieving General Glassford who had done so finely with them."[25]

Finally, the war reached an armistice on the eleventh hour of the eleventh day of the eleventh month. American costs were high: 53,500 battle deaths, 63,000 from disease and other causes, and 204,000 with debilitating wounds. For all intents and purposes, the war had ended when Ludendorff knew that Germany could no longer win. When Germany's allies defected, Ludendorff extended peace feelers, hoping for a truce without reparations. When the British and French balked at that, Ludendorff agreed to a new civilian government and then fled to Denmark, while Kaiser Wilhelm II abdicated and absconded to the Netherlands.[26]

The role of the American artillery, including Glassford's regiment and brigade, had been immense. Of the Meuse-Argonne battle alone, Pershing later wrote, "The artillery acquitted itself magnificently, the barrages being so well coordinated and so dense that the enemy was overwhelmed and quickly submerged by the rapid onslaught of the infantry." He noted that "artillery once engaged was seldom withdrawn and many batteries fought until practically all the [draft] animals were casualties and the guns were towed out of line by motor trucks." Colonel Marshall remarked: "But war is a ruthless taskmaster, demanding success regardless of confusion, shortness of time, and paucity of tools. . . . to succeed, [commanders] must demand results, close their ears to excuses, and drive subordinates beyond what would ordinarily be considered the limit of human capacity. Wars are won by the side that accomplishes the impossible. Battles are decided in favor of the troops whose bravery, fortitude, and, especially, whose endurance, surpasses that of the enemy's; the army with the higher breaking point wins the decision."[27]

The keys to Allied victory were several: stopping the German spring offenses, the continued arrival of American troops, putting the Allied armies under one supreme commander, and the nonstop pursuit of the German army. Perhaps an underappreciated factor was the British blockade of Germany: during the war 40,000 German civilians died of starvation or undernourishment, and German conscripts in the later years were generally twenty pounds lighter and two inches shorter than conscripts in the early years.[28]

On February 8, 1919, Glassford assumed command of a different brigade, the 152nd Artillery Brigade of the 77th "Liberty" Division, the National Guard of New York. Most of its soldiers came from New York City. He and the division would remain in Malicorne, France, northeast of Saint Nazaire, until April 29, 1919, when they were scheduled to return to the United States. General Glassford's reassignment to the 77th Division troubled him. He had wanted to return home with his 26th Division soldiers with whom he had fought the war. He admitted to Cora, "I really feel more upset over this change in brigades than I dare admit, even to myself. But will soon settle down to a normal frame of mind."[29]

CHAPTER 7

Soldiering in Peacetime

FOR his service during the war, the army awarded General Glassford a Distinguished Service Medal, a Silver Star Citation for gallantry, and the Order of the Purple Heart for his battle wound. The Silver Star Citation, awarded for gallantry in action, was to be affixed to the World War Victory Medal, but in 1932 the secretary of war would convert all Silver Star citations to Silver Star medals.[1]

The war was over, but US occupation forces remained in France for a while. Glassford's brigade was billeted in the Haute-Marne area of the Champagne-Ardenne region of France, scattered among twenty-some villages. It was pleasant, but it was not home. Occupation duties included such things as collecting weapons from German soldiers, operating prison camps, guarding railroads, patrolling borders, enforcing various civil ordinances and regulations, and ensuring that German soldiers wore only civilian clothing four days after having arrived home. One American soldier had a special duty—serving as a translator. Private John Warns had been drafted in April 1918 from Wentworth, South Dakota, an area with a large population of German American immigrants. He had served with the 89th "Rolling W" Division. Like most soldiers, he had departed the United States with less than thirty days of training, but then received six weeks of additional training in France. Fluent in German, his occupation duty was to arrange billeting for American soldiers in German homes. He wrote in a letter home, "We pick the finest homes for our quarters and the people treat us to anything the town has. In finding 'quarters' for the boys, I always make the rich take the largest number of boys as they are the real cause of the war. The poor I let off as easy as possible." Warns also became quite fond of the local Riesling wine. In another letter he said,

"Dear folks, if wines like that could be had at home instead of rotten whiskies there never would be any prohibition talk."[2]

Private Bill Clarke of the 27th Division spoke of his occupation duties: "Every American soldier in France and elsewhere wanted to go home, not tomorrow, not next week, not next month, but today." Finally, after a rough winter passage across the Atlantic, Bill remembered, "When we entered New York harbor we were welcomed by a flotilla of small steamers, ferry boats, and launches of every size and description. The whistle of every ship in the harbor, and all the factories bordering its shores, were blasting a deafening welcome."[3]

On April 20, 1919, General Pelham Glassford departed Brest, France, aboard the USS *Agamemnon*, formerly known as the SS *Kaiser Wilhelm II*, a German passenger ship now used as a US Navy transport. The ship docked at Hoboken, New Jersey, on April 29, loaded mostly with 6,000 happy soon-to-be-civilians, elated to be within view of New York City, the Big Apple. There was another passenger on board, however. Before Glassford left France, Colonel Copley Enos, 77th Division, had given Pelham a gift: a beautiful four-month-old purebred police dog, born on November 11. Glassford decided to call him Scrapper and take him home. The puppy was oak brown with black coloring here and there, monstrous paws, and, according to Pelham, "awkward as a cow." Having had General Pershing "appropriate" Kidron, the odds are that Glassford never mentioned Scrapper to the commanding general. Young Pelham Jr. and Guy would get a dog.[4]

Cora and the children had been living in Danville, Kentucky, where her father, Guy Carleton, commanded nearby Camp Zachary Taylor. It had been twenty-two months since Cora and the children had seen Hap. The family made its way to the Hoboken dock and anxiously awaited. When Cora saw him in the distance, she later remembered, "But for me all restraint was thrown to the winds, and for the first time in my army experience, I ignored and disobeyed the properly constituted authority of a military guard, and ducking under the chain, pushed him aside and ran into my husband's arms." It was hugs and kisses all around. It would have been even better if Hap could have gone home with his family that day, but he had to remain on Long Island, New York, for a time to demobilize his brigade.[5]

On May 13 Glassford reported to the Office of the Chief of Field Artillery at Fort Sill, Oklahoma, home of the Field Artillery School. His tour of duty there would last until July 31. Since June 30 he had been wearing the gold leaf insignia of his permanent rank, major, having been reduced three grades in rank. It was no surprise to him or the others who reverted to their permanent ranks since the army's rapid expansion at the beginning of the war now necessitated an equally rapid reduction at the end. The prewar army had had about 5,800 officers, but at the height of World War I, it had 200,000 officers. Those officers who chose to remain in the army accepted the reduction, some having to revert to previous enlisted ranks. Many recently commissioned officers from the Officer Training Camps—now 48 percent of the officer corps—returned to civilian occupations. And not surprisingly, with the war now over, many citizens and members of Congress renewed their reluctance to fund a peacetime standing army of any significant size. Prospects for promotion were bleak.[6]

Younger brother Bill Glassford had also participated in the war, and like Hap, had been decorated. In October 1918 he had been the captain of the USS *Shaw* (DD-68), one of four steam-powered destroyers based at Queenstown, Ireland, to protect Allied ships from German U-boat wolfpacks. On October 9 the four destroyers were escorting the British troop transport *Aquitania*, which carried 8,000 American soldiers. As required, the troopship and its four destroyer escorts zigzagged their way into the English Channel toward their destination of Southampton, England, sixty miles ahead. In misty weather and rough seas, the officer of the day on the *Shaw* ordered the helmsman to set the rudder full port to execute the next turn. The helmsman attempted to do so but shouted that the rudder had jammed and was inoperable. Captain Glassford knew that the *Aquitania*, executing its own turn, would bear down on them within minutes with the *Shaw* in its path. He ordered his destroyer full astern, hoping the *Aquitania* might miraculously avoid a collision. Instead, the bow of the troopship severed ninety feet of the bow of the *Shaw*, causing the latter to immediately take on water. The troopship passed by as the severed bow drifted away and sank. Glassford ordered all crew except seven officers and twelve sailors to the stern for immediate transfer to another destroyer; the remaining officers and crew rushed below to close off all forward hatches and investigate the steering gear, soon ascertaining that a screw had somehow loosened and jammed the rudder. In the engine room, now flooded with three feet of water, crew members managed to contain all fires and restart one of the steam engines. Divers went over the side and cleared away rigging from the *Shaw*'s masts that was fouling the screws. Ninety-six minutes after the rudder jammed, Captain Glassford determined that he once again had steering control, steam in two engines, both screws operating, and bilge pumps working. When another destroyer offered to tow the *Shaw*, Glassford requested instead that the other destroyer simply lead the *Shaw* to the nearest port, which was forty miles away. By the time Glassford docked the damaged destroyer, he knew that two officers and ten sailors had been killed in the collision. A subsequent court of inquiry determined that once the steering had jammed the collision was unavoidable. For his immediate and decisive orders, the Navy awarded Bill Glassford the Distinguished Service Medal. The *Shaw* underwent repairs and later found service with the US Coast Guard doing Prohibition patrol.[7]

In 1912 William Glassford Sr. had been one of three candidates considered for the position of Chief of the Signal Corps of the entire US Army. That post went to another officer, but in March 1913 William achieved the rank of full colonel, serving as Chief Signal Officer for the Western Division. Looking forward to their retirement years, he and Allie acquired considerable property in Arizona, and in 1915 established a personal headquarters at the recently built deluxe Hotel San Marcos in the Salt River Valley, about twenty-five miles from downtown Phoenix. From this location they could oversee their farm property in the vicinity. That changed somewhat in April 1916 when the army assigned Colonel Glassford to be the commandant of its nascent Signal Aviation School at Rockwell Field, North Island, Coronado, near San Diego. Unsure where its new air service best fit, the army assigned it to the Signal Corps, much as it had done with the National Weather Service and later the balloon unit. Thus, Colonel Glassford became the first Chief of Army Air Service, which in the future would become the Army Air Corps and eventually the US Air Force.[8]

Having now reached army mandatory retirement age, William retired in October 1917, despite vigorous protests from his admirers, asking the army to keep him on active duty. The Colonel and Allie made their way to Phoenix, where they bought a brick cottage, which they subsequently enlarged and remodeled. Having spent a few years in the Pacific Northwest, William and Allie also bought a summer home in Port Townsend, Washington, an area the Colonel had discovered while overseeing the laying of the underwater telegraph cable from Seattle to Alaska. The home overlooked Port Townsend Bay and Admiralty Inlet and was to become a delightful retreat for use by all the Glassfords—themselves, their children, and their grandchildren.[9]

The senior Glassford had been in government service for forty-two years, but he had no intention of spending his retired days in a rocking chair. Along with tending crops and managing livestock on his farmland, he continued his interest in Arizona water issues. On April 29, 1922, as chair of the Organization Committee of the National Reclamation Association, he addressed the full group, advocating for dams on the Colorado and Gila Rivers to provide drinking water, electric power, and irrigation for 2.5 million acres in Arizona.[10]

On August 1, 1919, Major Pelham Glassford began his duties as an instructor at general service schools at Fort Leavenworth, Kansas. It was odd to instruct at an army school that he had not attended, the result of his urgent transfer to the Mexican border followed by his deployment to France. Most officers who served at Fort Leavenworth during this time found it to be a pleasant assignment, and there seems little doubt that Hap, Cora, and the children liked it. Guy was now eleven, Elizabeth nine, Pelham eight, and Dorothy six. Scrapper, the newest member, became "a big hit with the family and everyone else." The small post had two unusual neighbors, but they seldom bothered anyone: The United States Disciplinary Barracks, for military prisoners, and the United States Federal Penitentiary, for civilians convicted of federal crimes.[11]

Midway through his third year of instructing, Glassford received orders to report to Fort Sill as a field artillery instructor. General Hanson E. Ely, Commandant of the Fort Leavenworth service school, summoned Glassford and asked if that was his preference. Glassford replied that it was not, and that he would much rather remain at Fort Leavenworth and attend the full course as a student, part of which he was already teaching. General Ely arranged to keep him there as a student but required that Glassford continue teaching his class. The major agreed and graduated from the School of the Line in 1922, and then from the General Staff School in 1923, both with high marks. On his off time, Glassford created the Fort Leavenworth Dramatic Club, arranged for Kansas City orchestras to perform on the post, and started a new Field Club, which would lead to the building of a golf course. Cora noted, "Happy cannot bear for a moment to be without occupation."[12]

His next assignment was to attend the Army War College in Washington, DC. Before reporting there in 1923, he used some of his plentiful leave time. It was summer and an ideal time for a father-son bonding trip. He and Guy embarked on a two-week camping trip in Missouri, driving there in a "newly acquired but ancient Ford touring car," filled with a tent and blankets. Along the way, Glassford happened upon an old friend who had also been a field artillery officer in France. J. C.

Farley now owned a circus, Farley Shows, which he moved from town to town, and it always needed workers. Seeing it as something of another adventure, father and son, one might say, ran off and joined the circus. They worked as carneys, operating the wheel of fortune, barking to hustle visitors to the various shows, and painting signs with outrageously promising claims. It must have been a memorable summer for Guy, who was not yet twelve. Their summer circus days over, the two returned to Washington, but not before Farley unsuccessfully offered Pelham the manager's position for next year's season. Glassford still had some leave time, so he and Cora gathered the children and Scrapper and piled into a new Ford, taking a family road trip through Missouri, Illinois, Indiana, Ohio, Pennsylvania, and West Virginia. There was not enough room inside the car for Scrapper, so he stretched out along the full length of a baggage rack attached to the running board, attracting disbelieving looks from people on the street who saw the traveling Glassfords go by.[13]

In the spring of 1919, at the direction of Communist International (Comintern) Moscow, radicals in America formed the American Communist Party. That same year authorities suspected radicals of setting off bombs at or near the homes of various US government officials, including J. Mitchell Palmer, US attorney general. Palmer subsequently formed an antiradical unit and put in charge a little-known attorney named J. Edgar Hoover. Hoover's agents arrested 6,000 aliens and subsequently deported 556. By the time the 1920s roared in, bringing speakeasys, flappers, and jazz, the Red Scare of 1919–1920 had faded. Now home from the war, Pelham Glassford probably read the news accounts of the bombings and deportations with mild interest. That was not the case with J. Edgar Hoover, who busily built a radical file of thousands and monitored many.[14]

More important to Pelham Glassford and his contemporaries was the "hump." By 1932 the army had more than 4,200 officers—nearly a third of the officer corps—aged thirty-seven to forty-three, of whom 1,885 were captains and 234 were lieutenants in their forties. Seniority promotions and a mandatory retirement age of sixty-four combined to create a huge promotional logjam. Thus, as General MacArthur later noted, "an officer in the 1930s would have to wait thirty-six years for the possibility of becoming a full colonel." Glassford accepted that he would remain a major for some time to come. Added to the paucity of promotions was the pay issue. Between 1908 and 1928, army pay had increased 11 percent while the cost of living had jumped 87 percent. Then, between 1928 and 1935, army pay decreased by 15 percent while the cost of living during the Great Depression decreased by 20 percent.[15]

On April 2, 1923, Glassford reported to the yearlong course at the Army War College, the army's most prestigious service school. The course was held at the Washington Barracks, south of the Capitol between the Washington Channel and the Anacostia River. By graduation he had done so well that he was one of five student-officers invited to remain at the War College as a full-time instructor, an invitation he readily accepted. When he had been a student there, the Glassford family lived in the city on Ontario Place, which Cora remembered as the "crowded year in the small house in town." Now he was an instructor and rated quarters at Washington Barracks, where he, Cora, and the children lived in one of the "big houses on the line." The house had ample bedrooms for the family, and extra rooms for Pelham to have an office and an art studio. It did not take long for the artist in him to surface.[16]

His office was on the first floor and his art studio was on the second. As Cora remembered, "How he loved that room, and how cold he kept it!" He purposely kept the French doors wide open, keeping the air in his studio fresh. One of his first art projects was a standing screen, which he constructed and then artfully painted for placement in a particular room, keeping it in harmony with the decor. The beauty and novelty of his screens became popular, and soon he was painting them on order.[17]

Encouraged, he entered some of his works in various art exhibits. On March 1, 1925, the *Washington Sunday Star* reported that Glassford was exhibiting six screens during a two-week showing at the studio of Mrs. Guy Sandifer on Connecticut Avenue. At the showing, the patrons seemed to most favor Glassford's screen adaptation of a window panel done by James McNeil Whistler, the panel being housed in the Peacock Room of the Freer Gallery at the Smithsonian. The *Star* article noted that Glassford had studied at the San Francisco Institute of Art, trained under Hitchcock in Honolulu, taken classes at the Kansas City Fine Art Institute while stationed at Fort Leavenworth, and might consider retirement in 1930 to devote his time to art. He next entered his screens in an exhibition held by the Washington Arts Club. Three weeks later a *Washington Evening Star* art critic attended the exhibition and praised Glassford's decorative watercolor screens as being beautiful, noting that both were oriental in style, one a floral design and the other a peacock design.[18]

More encouraged, he made time to attend the art school of Felix Mahony, a well-known painter, illustrator, lecturer, and teacher in Washington, known for teaching the concept of "dynamic symmetry," which involved the methodical use of an overlay grid of rectangles and triangles to aid an artist in positioning and balancing the elements of the painting. Cora recalled, "This instruction and discipline in color handling so enhanced [Hap's] own valuation of color; I am sure that [Mahony's] course contributed much to his later composition and execution of his [art]." Hap soon got an opportunity to use Mahony's instruction when the owner of a new restaurant and nightclub commissioned Hap to decorate the large space in complete pirate motif, with each room resembling something of a pirate den. Cora remembered, "That staircase wall was the masterpiece of the work, with its tropical foliage, snakes swinging from tree branches, mischievous monkey faces and purple parrots," along with "heroic size pirates, treasure chests yawned with golden pieces of eight pouring from broken sides." He painted watercolors as well and sometimes sought to capture views of the city. Cora wrote that she and Hap would occasionally rush out in the early evening to the National Mall so that Hap could capture and paint the "ethereal blue light of the twilight, just when the daylight was fading, and the lights twinkled out in fairy gold along the Mall. How many evenings did we get in the car and run over to the parkstand, and for but a few moments Happy would paint, paint fast, before those delicate blue tones left the light and the [Washington] Monument itself."[19]

Hap had one special tree at the National Mall that he loved to paint, a hemlock with branches almost touching the ground. One Sunday afternoon, after Christmas, snow on the ground, Hap and Cora hurried to the National Mall so that Hap could paint the tree again. The children had gone to play ice hockey on the Washington Channel, which ran alongside the Army War College. Skating at that location, quite suddenly, Guy and a young friend, Cameron Sweeney, fell through the ice into the slow tidal stream, their heavy skates and clothing tugging them down. Guy surfaced and used his hockey stick to keep himself above the ice. Seeing Cameron struggling a short distance away, Guy broke the ice so he could reach Cameron and keep him afloat. Along the shore, Scrapper had followed the boys and now began furiously barking and running back and forth in a frenzy. Guy kept yelling for Scrapper to bark. An army sergeant in the vicinity heard Scrapper's barks and then saw the boys. He saw a wooden plank and dragged it down to the shore perpendicular to where the boys were out in the broken ice. The sergeant went prone and inched his way out onto the ice, pushing the plank in front of him. Reaching the boys, he instructed Guy to grab the plank. Guy followed the order and was then able to pull himself and Cameron out of the water. The sergeant put one boy on each arm and pushed himself and the boys back to shore. Major General Hanson E. Ely, Commandant of the War College, whom the Glassfords knew from Fort Leavenworth, had watched the rescue. General Ely, along with his aide, Captain Boone, took the boys to Boone's nearby quarters and got them warmed up. About this time Hap and Cora returned home. Glassford's "striker" (a soldier who served as a combination personal servant and driver) was waiting for them. Upon greeting them, he immediately assured them that the boys were okay and then related the story. Thankful for a "daring sergeant, the General's quick care, and Scrapper's dog-alarm," Hap and Cora found the two boys asleep in a bed at Captain Boone's quarters.[20]

For reasons unknown, Scrapper took to leaving the confines of the War College on occasion, sometimes for a day or more. On one occasion he returned home, but with a rope around his neck, which he had chewed through to free himself. Later, he simply disappeared. The family suspected that he had been stolen or picked up and taken to the dog pound, although Hap checked several times and never found him there. A car may have hit him, or perhaps he was enticed to go elsewhere. As Cora wrote, "We finally accepted the belief after his last appearance that our beloved Scrapper could not return to his home."[21]

The Glassfords were members of various Washington social circles, but naturally they were most involved in Army War College social life. On one memorable occasion the Glassfords hosted a good friend of Hap from the war, Colonel Alden Twachtman, who had taken Glassford's place as artillery regimental commander when Glassford was promoted to general. Alden was the son of the well-known American Impressionist artist John Henry Twachtman. Alden was also a member of the Army Reserve. Like Pelham, Twachtman was a muralist, but unlike the major he sported a bushy mustache and beard that tapered to a point. A 1906 graduate of the Yale School of Fine Arts, Twachtman had also attended the École des Arts in Paris. Alden's primary career was that of an architect at a large New York firm, but in his spare time he painted and drew. During the war, as time had permitted, he had sketched many scenes of what he saw, and fortunately, his sketchbook, unlike Hap's, did not disappear.[22]

The reunion of Pelham and Alden resulted in their collaboration on painting a mural in the YD (Yankee Division) Club in Boston. They had collaborated many times in battle, and now they did the same in art. As Cora remembered, "The subject which had been chosen was a map of the terrain over which the Yankee Division had fought in France, and featured that part of the country on which it had won its greatest honors. The little towns with their names, the hills which were taken by the infantry, and the 'objectives' where the guns had conquered, all were there cleverly delineated on the map, and made so that anyone might read the story of the gallantry of the Division."[23]

The 1926 annual dinner of the YD Club took place at the Wardman Park Hotel in Washington. As the former members of the Division enjoyed their annual dinner, Glassford served as emcee. Many of the members had come down from Boston, including the former division commanding general, Clarence R. Edwards, who spoke about ongoing plans to erect a memorial in France to honor those Yankee soldiers who gave their lives. The only honorary member of the division was there as well, foreign correspondent George Rothwell Brown, who had been embedded with the Division during the war. Along with several one-minute sketches and a good deal of singing, there were also some three-minute speeches, enforced by one of those new-fangled traffic signals—displaying a green light to go and a red light to stop. The last order of business was to set the date for the next reunion.[24]

That same year, the Washington Handicraft Guild changed its name to the Washington Society of Arts and Crafts, hoping to expand and broaden its activities, and installed Pelham Glassford as its president. The Society opened a headquarters on Seventeenth Street, which included sales and exhibition rooms. A few months later Glassford had a showing of his decorative screens, ranging from conventional to modern, and using media from block-print style watercolors to oil on canvas with thick impasto rising from the surface, all later described by critics as quaint and interesting.[25]

Thereafter, a serious incident happened within the family. In April 1926, Guy, now eighteen, simply disappeared. When he did not return after a few days, Pelham posted missing flyers throughout the area, with two photographs of Guy and a comprehensive description: "About 6' tall. Weight about 160. Slender but powerful. Heavy dark brown hair. Brown eyes. Age 18 (Nov. 12, 1926). Self-reliant, resourceful, and gentlemanly. Three years in high school. Eagle Scout (Boy Scouts of America). Anxious parents desire to hear of him or from him and to know that he is safe and well." Glassford, not surprisingly, could not simply dash off a missing person flyer; it had to be compelling and capture the eye to be effective. Perhaps without intending to, the proud parent talked up his missing son: "Favorite sports golf and swimming (excellent at both). Also good at football, baseball (catcher), canoeing, basketball, and track." Eventually, perhaps having seen one of the posters, Guy reappeared, although there seems to be little information about the circumstances of his absence. It is possible that Guy simply rebelled, as do many teenage boys. Pelham's glowing description of Guy may have been Pelham's message to Guy that his parents valued him.[26]

When Glassford completed his assignment at the Army War College, he had instructed there for three years. Before that he had taught at the Command and General Staff school for four years, and before that had been an assistant professor at West Point. A fair conclusion is that the army regarded him as one of its premier instructors. It is also fair to say that at each of those schools he had some impact on his students, some of whom would go on to become World War II generals. He also had a positive effect on the Washington art community; as the president of the Washington Society of Arts and Crafts, he was successful in getting a space in a downtown building where the artists could meet, have studios, and display their art.[27]

Glassford's personal life, however, stumbled. On January 1, 1927, for reasons little publicized, he and Cora separated. She returned to San Antonio with the younger children, living in Alamo Heights with her parents while maintaining attachment with Washington. Hap and Cora would not formally divorce until 1932. If Hap was seeing another woman, no rumors seemed to have appeared in the papers, although most male reporters—the majority then—winked at wandering husbands. And, of course, in the Washington arts community, Glassford was surrounded by admiring women and socialites. Rather than agitate about the possibilities, Cora may have simply retreated to Texas, and Guy's mysterious disappearance some months earlier may have been an indicator of a stressed family.[28]

In July Glassford placed a newspaper advertisement offering for sale a Stearns-Knight five passenger touring car. The ad described it as "never abused, in splendid condition, capable of long service with low upkeep . . . [and] excellent in appearance, and available at the sacrifice price of $375 ($5,829) due to owner's intended departure." Likely with considerable reluctance, Pelham left the sophisticated city of Washington for the still-frontier state of Oklahoma. His new assignment was as commander of the 1st Field Artillery Regiment at Fort Sill. He had taken the long route getting there, riding his motorcycle and logging 7,000 miles—many on dirt roads—before arriving at the post. His route from Washington had been across the country to the Northwest, then down the Pacific Coast, and back through the Southwest to his new assignment.[29]

In 1928 the army promoted Glassford to the permanent rank of lieutenant colonel and once again assigned him to Washington, where he served a year in the Inspector General's Department, then two years as Chief of Mobilization Branch, Operation and Training Division, War Department General Staff.[30]

He was still an artist, however, and being back in Washington was a delight. In December 1929 he had another showing, sponsored by the Washington Society of Arts and Crafts in conjunction with Industrial Arts. A *Washington Post* art critic described his tall screen in Chinese design done in oil on Bristol board as being most attractive and noteworthy. By now Glassford was well known in the Washington arts community. His murals and screens quickly found accommodating walls in homes and buildings. He purchased a large townhouse in Georgetown, with ample bedrooms and bathrooms for his family. He set it up the way he wanted, relishing his art studio on the top floor. One journalist described his house as being both ridiculous and delightful, and his friends took to calling it the "Borneo Embassy" for its unlikely combination of military discipline and Bohemia.[31]

Glassford was now in his midforties, and his children would soon to be adults. In 1930, Guy, an Eagle Scout, had been accepted at West Point, no doubt to the joy of his parents. But a year and a half later he resigned for little known reasons. His brother, Pete, graduated from McKinley Technical High School in Washington and was also accepted at West Point, beginning his studies on May 10, 1931, and graduating four years later. Elizabeth was now nineteen and looking forward to a fashion career of modeling and design, and sixteen-year-old Dorothy was focused on finishing high school.[32]

At the other end of the family, Hap's father, William, having retired some years ago, had become ill and could no longer handle the responsibilities of his Arizona farms. In early June he departed Phoenix for treatment at the Letterman Hospital at the Presidio of San Francisco. In July 1931 Pelham Glassford retired from the army "at his own request," moving from active-duty lieutenant colonel to retired brigadier general. He later wrote, "I could see no future by remaining in the peace time army. . . . There seemed little prospect of regaining my war-time rank much before reaching the retirement age." It seems likely, however, that his father's serious illness was a primary driver in Pelham's retirement.[33]

William Sr. died in the hospital on August 6, 1931. Pneumonia had set in, and he passed three weeks later. Many friends from the old days attended his funeral. He was buried with full military honors at the National Cemetery at the

Presidio. Local newspapers lauded him with more pride than accuracy as the frontier Indian fighter who had captured the treacherous Apache Geronimo.[34]

Hap's mother, Allie, was now in her seventies and contending with William's death. Whether she would be able to manage the extensive farmlands was at question, and there was also the summer home in Port Townsend. Brother Bill was still on active military duty with the navy and preferred to remain that way. Allie, Pelham, and Bill had to decide how best to care for and manage the 325 acres, or perhaps consider selling everything. Exactly how they arrived at the decision is unclear, but Hap retired with the intention of taking the lead role in settling his father's estate and overseeing the properties.[35]

CHAPTER 8

The New Police Chief

AFTER declining several employment offers, including superintendent of the Rhode Island State Police, Pelham Glassford relocated to what was now his mother's home in the Salt River Valley near Phoenix, Arizona, planning to oversee the farms and paint watercolors. Then, in September 1931, another offer arrived: the Veterans of Foreign Wars (VFW) unexpectedly invited Glassford to come to Washington, DC, for a month or so to plan and direct a major event—an Armistice Day jubilee and costume ball. The VFW wanted Glassford to undertake the re-creation of what Paris must have looked like on the night of the original Armistice Day, thirteen years previous. Its promotion promised "A Bit of Paris," and would be held in the Washington Auditorium on, of course, November 11. The VFW had already acquired an office for the retired general's use, located in the House of Representatives Office Building. For Glassford, something of a natural emcee, the money-raising event for the VFW to assist veterans was too inviting to pass up, and it promised to be a lot of fun. The Arizona farms could get by without him for a month or so.[1]

Glassford put aside a painting in progress, cleaned his brushes, and handed off farm management for a few weeks to the reliable foreman. The retired general packed a few bags, caught a train to Washington, and located his small office in the House Office Building, finding it suitable. Hearing that he was back in town, old friends dropped by and were joined by new friends, many of whom offered to help with jubilee preparation. Soon his friends labeled his office below the rafters "the Owl's Nest." Those who met him for the first time were impressed by his grace, charm, and good nature. Newspapers reported that retired general Pelham Glassford, former Army War College instructor, General Staff member, and well-known local artist, was back in town to make "A Bit of Paris" a reality.[2]

One city official took a special interest in Glassford's arrival, having known him in the army. Retired major general (two stars) Herbert B. Crosby was now one of Washington's three DC commissioners, charged with managing the city. A native of Kansas, he had graduated from West Point in 1893 as a cavalry officer. More recently, he and Glassford had served together at the Army War College, where Crosby was the assistant commandant from 1924 to 1927, and Glassford was a student and instructor. Following his retirement, Crosby had been appointed DC commissioner in 1930, joining Major John C. Gotwals, retired army engineering officer, and Lieutenant Colonel Luther H. Reichelderfer, retired MD and army reserve officer. Crosby, always smartly dressed, his short hair parted in the middle, maintained the look of a soldier. He focused on police and fire matters, while Gotwals oversaw sanitation and public works, and Reichelderfer served as the Board of Commissioners president. Appointed by the president and approved by the Senate, the DC commissioners functioned as something of a combined mayor and city council, overseeing the various city departments. All three had served with the army in France during the war.[3]

The DC Metropolitan Police Department had a history of corruption, and in 1931 it was the subject of a federal investigation focused primarily on complaints of officers using "third degree" tactics—unnecessary or excessive force—to gain compliance from suspects. Not yet formally under federal investigation was the probability that some police officers were ignoring Prohibition and profiting from overlooking sales of illegal liquor. In January 1920 the Eighteenth Amendment had taken effect, prohibiting the manufacture, distribution, and sale of liquor throughout the country. That was not a new problem for the DC commissioners, as Washington, DC, had already outlawed liquor in November 1917, making the nation's capital a dry city even before Prohibition. No doubt many world war veterans, upon returning to their hometown of Washington, were disappointed to learn that Prohibition now forbade them from drinking the French wine they had come to appreciate. The DC commissioners were well aware of the earlier "man with the green hat" exposé, in which George L. Cassidy, a veteran of the Western Front, had become the high-end booze supplier for scores of members of Congress. Cassidy even had accommodations in the House Office Building. He was fond of quipping that he had a better congressional attendance record than many of its members. By happenstance, he had been wearing his green fedora in 1925 when law enforcement officers arrested him for bootlegging, thus earning him his moniker. No longer welcome in the House of Representatives, Cassidy became the go-to supplier for thirsty senators. Arrested and jailed again in 1930, he took the occasion to mention to the *Washington Post* and the *New York World* reporters that he had more keys to congressional offices and desks than anyone in history. The upcoming federal investigation, not surprising, would focus exclusively on police officers and not the representatives and senators who illegally bought the booze.[4]

With a police corruption scandal ongoing, it seemed an appropriate time for the DC commissioners to undertake a major police housecleaning, and to announce that they had begun a search for a new chief of police. They wanted a new chief who would renew citizen confidence in the department. Normally, a senior commander from within the police department or one with executive police experience with another agency would be the preferred candidate, but because the three commissioners were all retired army officers, it made sense to consider another of their kind for the chief's position. Likely having read that Glassford was back in town, the DC commissioners began thinking about him as a contender. In late September, when Glassford happened to visit the DC Building—Washington's city hall—to obtain a permit to transform the Washington Auditorium into 1918 Paris, Commissioner Crosby took the occasion to renew their acquaintanceship. As the two chatted, William W. Bride, the corporation counsel—the District of Columbia's chief legal officer—"just happened to be walking by" and joined in their conversation. Neither Bride nor Crosby mentioned the police chief position to Glassford, but the next day Crosby telephoned him and said he was bringing over a box of Havana cigars to have a smoke with his old friend. He walked over intending to sell the police chief job to the former Army War College instructor, no matter how many cigars it took. Through the Cuban haze, the two traded war stories and shared memories of France. Then, quite suddenly, Crosby announced, "I have a surprise for you. You are going to be our next chief of police." Glassford was indeed surprised and managed nothing more than a blank stare. Crosby quickly added that five minutes after he and Bride had chatted with Glassford, they were ready to offer him the job. Later, talking with news reporters, Glassford said, "I was practically 'drafted' as Superintendent of the Washington police." Crosby again visited with Glassford, who by now had warmed to the idea of becoming police chief, but under two conditions: he would have to finish his work on the jubilee, and he would need the option of withdrawing if he chose to do so. Crosby assented to both. Because of his mother's situation, Pelham needed to go to Arizona and discuss the job offer with her.[5]

Apparently with his mother's approval, Glassford returned to Washington and met with Crosby, saying that he would accept the chief's position, but he needed assurance that he would have adequate authority to reform the police department. Crosby assured him that he would have a free hand to do so. To what extent they discussed the ongoing police corruption probe is unclear, but Glassford had resided in Washington on and off for a decade before his retirement and undoubtedly had a fair idea. Of course, in those years he had read the news accounts with the eyes of an army officer, not a police chief. He also suspected that his relationship with Crosby could be problematic. Crosby had outranked him in the army and now would be his superior in municipal government. Glassford remembered, "There would always have to exist a status between us, I felt, that could prove difficult were I to accept the offer."[6]

News reporters heard about Glassford's job offer and wanted to know what law enforcement experience he had. He chuckled that in years past he had been ticketed for running a red light and again for speeding on his motorcycle. Journalists tended to like the forty-eight-year-old police chief immediately. One reporter recalled Glassford saying that he knew his new job would not be an easy one and that he was sure to make mistakes, but that he promised to learn all he could about policing. He assured the reporter that he would learn his job on the street and not in a swivel chair. The reporter later described the new chief as being debonair, unconventional, open-minded, confiding, and courteous. Reporters also appreciated that he had once been a cub reporter for the *San Francisco Examiner*.[7]

The jubilee would be as authentically French as possible—even the money. The only acceptable currency would be French francs, at the exchange rate of ten francs per dollar. Glassford and South Dakota Representative Royal C. Johnson, on behalf of the VFW, extended an early invitation to President Herbert Hoover. Without committing to attend, the president sent his greetings and best wishes for a successful jubilee, knowing that it would benefit disabled soldiers, a cause that all Americans supported.[8]

The night of the event, "Director-General" Glassford did his best to greet many of the 15,000 attendees as they walked into "Paris on Armistice Night, 1918," a jubilee and costume ball. The crowd was replete with politicians, generals, admirals, ambassadors, and other notables. General John Pershing was the guest of honor. Other dignitaries and spouses included President Herbert Hoover; Chief Justice Charles Evan Hughes (whose son Charles Jr. had been at one time Glassford's military aide in France); British ambassador Sir Ronald Charles Lindsay; Secretary of War and Mrs. Patrick J. Hurley; Secretary of State Henry L. Stimson; and Army Chief of Staff Douglas MacArthur. Most of the dignitaries hosted balcony parties, while the lesser known and younger crowd populated the main floor. Some of the latter had agreed to act as French gigolos available for a franc a dance, *gigolettes* selling cigars, and Salvation Army lassies dispensing donuts and soup from a dugout. Fortune tellers and alluring snake charmers slithered about while huddles of veterans gathered and sang the old war songs, their ignored spouses chatting in their own huddles. Decorated balconies resembled the houses overhanging the narrow streets of Montmartre, and once again open for business were the American Bar, Moulin Rouge, Les Folies Bergères, Café de la Paix, and a *salle de jeux*, a game room. Everyone seemed to agree that the event had been a tremendous fête, just like those held that night in Paris.[9]

The novice police chief would soon become intimately familiar with the fluctuating status of the Bonus Bill. The whole thing had begun shortly after Armistice Day when a wealthy farmer from Virginia, W. Bruce Shafer Jr., traveled to Washington to lobby for doubling the money that soldiers had earned during the world war, seeing it as something of a "bonus" for their risks and sacrifices. It was no secret that civilians working in the war industries, safe at home, had made far more money than had the soldiers. Shafer's idea was to give some measure of compensation, a gratuity, to the veterans to reduce the disparity. Many members of Congress favored the idea, seeing it as a readjustment to amend the discrepancy between civilian and military pay. By May 1920 there were seventy-five various bonus bills under Congressional consideration, and in March 1922 the House and Senate passed the World War Adjusted Compensation Act. In September Republican President Warren G. Harding promptly vetoed it, saying that while the veterans would receive no money, Americans would always be thankful. The president maintained that the most important priority of Congress was implementing a tax reduction, not a soldier's bonus. On August 2, 1923, Harding died of a stroke while in office. His successor, former vice president Calvin Coolidge, made it clear that as president he, too, had no interest in giving the veterans a bonus.[10]

Undeterred, in March 1924, with the assistance of the American Legion and the Veterans of Foreign Wars, the House and Senate passed another bill, which granted a bonus but with its payment delayed until 1945. President Coolidge vetoed that bill as well, saying, "Service to our country in time of war means sacrifice." The Senate overrode Coolidge's veto. The new law gave each veteran about $1,000 ($16,092), but not until 1945. Essentially, it was an insurance policy, collectible two decades in the future by the veteran or a named beneficiary. Some veterans saw it as something of a retirement gift; others were sure that they would never see their "tombstone bonus." There was no doubt, however, that the Bonus Bill now constituted a legitimate debt; it was money that belonged to the veterans. Conveniently, the 1924 Congress had handed off the payment obligation to the 1945 Congress. Texas Representative Wright Patman saw that as nothing less than an obscenity. As an enlisted soldier who had earned an officer's commission during the war, he ran for Congress in 1928, telling every group he spoke to that the veterans deserved a "square deal." He contended that it was an outrage that soldiers had earned $1 ($16) per day while shipyard workers and other war industry civilians had received $20 ($322) per day. He reminded his fellow Texans that Congress had also given big bonuses to corporations for their war efforts.[11]

In March 1929, just months before the stock market crashed, newly elected President Herbert Hoover assured Americans that their future was "bright with hope." One year later the country faced its biggest economic crisis in its history. Three years later, 28,000 businesses had failed, annual income from farms had fallen by $3 billion, and 8 million people were jobless. Democratic Representative Wright Patman submitted a bill calling for immediate payment of the veterans' bonus. The bill never made it out of committee.[12]

The stock market crash of October 1929 caused tremendous economic pain. Now, with more resolve, veterans renewed their demand for immediate payment of their bonus. The VFW still supported the bonus payment, but the American Legion now preferred funding assistance only for disabled veterans and dependents of veterans killed in action. By December 1930 President Hoover made clear that he would not support a bonus and became highly critical of Patman and those members of Congress who supported his bill. In early 1931 Patman reintroduced his bill, this time aided by a show of publicity: on January 21 nearly 1,000 veterans paraded along Pennsylvania Avenue to the Capitol. Patman and about 100 other members of Congress joined them. Nevertheless, the Senate continued to oppose the Patman bill, and Hoover vowed to veto it.[13]

The House Ways and Means Committee began hearings on the bill on January 29. One of those testifying was Joe T. Angelo, who had been the batman (personal orderly) of Major George S. Patton during the world war, and who had clearly saved Patton's life. Now an unemployed riveter, Angelo told committee members that he feared that his inability to pay his taxes would result in the loss of his house, which he had built himself. He and a friend had walked almost 150 miles from their home in Camden, New Jersey, to the nation's capital to testify. He described his wartime actions that had earned him a Distinguished Service Cross, adding, "I came to show you that we need our bonus." He later added, "I did my duty. All I ask is a chance to work or a chance to get my money on my certificate."[14]

President Hoover ignored the hearings and on February 26, 1931, he vetoed the immediate payment bill. The following day Republican Representative Royal C. Johnson of South Dakota, a world war veteran, succeeded in gaining approval for veterans to borrow against their bonus. Hoover opposed that bill as well. As historian T. H. Watkins notes, Hoover firmly believed that local communities and their charities should take care of their people, not the federal government, which would advise but nothing more.[15]

On October 21 and 22, 1931, the *Washington Post* reported that the Department of Justice had indicted 18 Washington, DC, Metropolitan Police Department officers for using excessive force on prisoners. To lessen additional negative publicity, the DC commissioners quickly discharged 85 officers using the guise of physical disabilities; thus far, the DC commissioners had ordered 107 officers to undergo physical examinations. On November 1 the commissioners medically retired the chief of police, Henry G. Pratt, with what the *Washington Post* described as unusual speed. Pratt's backdoor medical retirement had been rushed through, apparently to avert a further congressional inquiry into the police department. The DC Board of Surgeons had conducted a quick medical examination, which concluded that Pratt was completely disabled, having high blood pressure, heart issues, poor vision, and dental problems. Journalists reported that the DC commissioners and federal officials were very reluctant to discuss the situation. In response to media inquiries, Commissioner Crosby stressed that incoming Police Chief Glassford would have a lot of "free rein in reorganizing the department after he assumes command." A news account reported that Crosby and Glassford had parallel thinking on how to reorganize the police department and would harmoniously follow each other's suggestions.[16]

Glassford later wrote, "The day I took over command of the Washington police, I found myself in the jungle of politics." Crosby may have forgotten to brief Glassford on how the local District of Columbia government worked. It was unlike any other city government in the country. Glassford would soon find that he had five bosses. The first was the president of the United States, who also served as the mayor of Washington, but seldom involved himself in city issues. The second was the board of DC commissioners, which oversaw municipal responsibilities, not unlike a city council. The third and fourth were the House and Senate committees that determined the municipal budget, including that of the police department. And the fifth was the collective members of the House and Senate, all of whom were very used to getting their way. Glassford would see that the divisions and flexibilities of the government made for easy evasion of responsibility.[17]

As Glassford later remembered, "Congress was in session when I took command, and one influential gentleman after another would call and ask, 'What can you do for my friend so-and-so?'" The new chief told them he did not work that way; he had not worked that way in the army, and he would not work that way in the police department. The callers were not pleased to hear that he would not bend the rules. Aside from Congress, political pressure also came from interests within the city and within the police department. Not long after he had pinned on his badge, he had a minor conflict with Crosby about which lieutenant to promote to captain. Crosby favored one individual whom Glassford thought was capable but weak, preferring another lieutenant. Crosby increased the pressure, and Glassford gave way. "It was one of those things about which one cannot make an issue," he remembered, "but it was an incident that showed clearly how things would go."[18]

An editorial in the *Washington Post* noted that Pratt's real error had been in failing to hold his police inspectors—the rank above captain—accountable, saying that some had shielded others accused of wrongdoings. The *Post* advocated that the DC commissioners give the new chief enhanced power to improve hiring, forbid unnecessary and excessive force, and handle minor discipline without invoking lengthy Trial Boards.[19]

Historian Irving Bernstein describes the new police chief as having a zest for living, adding that he was a patriot without a commitment to class, ideology, or a political party, and seemed to be without personal ambition. Historian Roger Daniels notes Glassford's "distinctly flamboyant, bohemian streak, as well as a deep-seated humanitarian impulse."[20]

On November 24, in his first public address, he affirmed to the Traffic Advisory Council that he favored full enforcement of all traffic regulations, which were then undergoing a wholesale revision. Sometime later he announced promotions of a new lieutenant, precinct commander, and inspector. He also began building a good reputation as he zipped about on his police motorcycle, smoking his pipe, keeping the peace with a wave or a friendly comment. Those who had expected an office-bound police chief quickly realized that he was more likely to be on the street than on the phone. Fleta Campbell Springer of *Harper's Magazine* later wrote that he seemed to be competent, honest, and without political ambition, even though he held a position of power—a rarity in the nation's capital.[21]

At its thirteenth Plenum meeting in 1931, the American Communist Party resolved to focus its efforts on organizing the unemployed. Senior-level Communists now demanded that their street-level comrades take full advantage of the Depression and recruit new members. When no progress resulted, the Party bosses concluded that their underlings must be slacking. To motivate them, the leaders ordered that they immediately recruit enough new workers to stage a huge National Hunger March in Washington. Just three weeks after taking office, Chief Glassford now faced his first major challenge. At least one, maybe more, Communist-led hunger marches would be coming to Washington, and his department would have to handle them. Concomitant with these marches, but only distantly related, was the sudden emergence of homeless military veterans flocking to the nation's capital seeking help. Neither the Communist leadership nor the War Department had expected this latter phenomenon, but the Communists quickly saw it as an enormous opportunity. The War Department Military Intelligence Division (MID) and the Secret Service took the threats very seriously, dusting off Plan White, the blueprint for handling insurrection in the nation's capital.[22]

Glassford remembered, "I had been in command scarcely a month when the series of marches on Washington began." On December 2 Vice President Charles Curtis called a meeting of various members of Congress, the Secret Service, the Park Police, the Capitol Police, and the Metropolitan Police. Curtis demanded that law enforcement officers undertake rigorous preparations to protect the White House. No doubt the new Metropolitan police chief raised eyebrows when he calmly suggested that the marchers were just "tourists" who had already received an abundance of what they were seeking: publicity. He thought it best to feed and shelter them until such time as they broke the law. They were, he reminded the others, American citizens whose rights to petition and assembly needed to be respected. He said he was ready to accept full responsibility for their conduct.[23]

While the new police chief likely did not realize it, he was about to solve his first large-scale police problem. The vice president focused exclusively on protecting the White House—by force; Glassford focused on protecting the entire city, but without denying citizens their right to petition their government as allowed by the US Constitution. He knew the hunger marchers were coming and that violence was possible, perhaps even likely. His job, as he likely saw it, was to get the marchers in and out safely, satisfied that they had adequately delivered their message. Since they were hunger marchers, feeding and sheltering them would be a kindness that would likely increase their satisfaction and, he hoped, send them on their way sooner. Of course, he also had to invisibly prepare for the possibility of a riot. Within two days Glassford knew that three columns of hunger marchers, riding in 1,144 trucks, would arrive in Washington on December 7, from various locations around the country, with the intention of holding a huge conference on unemployment, after which they would march to the White House. The march was Communist-sponsored, and many of the participants were functionaries from throughout the country. The caravan arrived on December 6 but consisted of just 71 trucks loaded with 1,570 marchers. Herbert Benjamin was their advance field representative and earlier had assured news reporters that the marchers were coming to ask for unemployment insurance, which they hoped President Hoover would consider. At this point, as far as Glassford was concerned, the marchers were likely Communists but not criminals. For help with sheltering them, the chief had the assistance of Lieutenant Colonel Ulysses S. Grant III, grandson of the Civil War general and president, and an active-duty army officer, assigned as director of the Department of Public Buildings and Public Parks. Grant knew of several dilapidated buildings—now government property—that were empty and slated for demolition that could shelter the new arrivals. With those buildings as a backup, Glassford investigated the local missions and nearby army camps first. He would also find ways to feed them.[24]

The chief arranged sleeping space for them at the Central Union Mission in the Old Presbyterian Church, as well as at a nearby Salvation Army property.

For overflow, a nearby National Guard camp south of Bolling Airfield was available and could accommodate 400 marchers in its barracks. Fort Myer, across the Potomac River in Arlington, could house 325 in tents and had 600 blankets to help ward off the December cold. If still more space was needed, a tourist camp agreed to accommodate some marchers. Glassford's officers had previously designated a location where Washingtonians could drop off food, blankets, and cots, and Glassford already had offers of 1,000 pounds of coffee and bread. Various charities said they could turn the donated food into hot meals. Glassford regarded protecting the hunger marchers as part of his duty, as well as the smart way to handle them, reasonably confident that the marchers would move on once they had delivered their message. If some got out of hand, he had his entire police department to call on, as well as the National Guard.[25]

To manage the December 6 march, Glassford assigned 4 police inspectors and 1,400 Metropolitan Police officers. Should more officers be necessary, he could call on several hundred detectives who could don uniforms. He agreed to allow the marchers to carry banners, normally not permitted, but required, at the insistence of Vice President Curtis, that they put them aside before reaching the Capitol grounds. Glassford also assigned personal security officers to Senator Tasker Oddie, Republican from Nevada, and Representative Hamilton Fish, Republican from New York, both vociferous critics of the Communists. Glassford further assigned some of his officers to assist the Capitol Police and the Park Police. He had already designated the marchers' route, which included Pennsylvania Avenue, and thus satisfied the marchers' desire for public recognition of their message.[26]

The hunger marchers likely expected—perhaps hoped—that the police would mistreat them and were surprised when Glassford and his officers treated them as upstanding citizens instead. As the trucks rolled into the city, the riders loudly sang "Internationale," a French socialist song now adopted by the American Communists. US Army Captain Charles H. Titus of the MID had surreptitiously infiltrated the group during previous meetings and rallies and reported that most of the marchers were indeed hungry. As was usual at the time, the captain reported their ethnic makeup, noting that the group was about a third Jewish, a third Negro, a third white of varied backgrounds, and a quarter female.[27]

The marchers held their primary meeting that night in the same Washington Auditorium where Glassford had directed the jubilee. Various speakers took the stage and denounced Hoover, Curtis, the Socialist Party, the American Legion, Wall Street, and the American Federation of Labor (AFL) union. Some even complained about the food provided them. One who was in the auditorium reporting on the gathering was writer John Dos Passos, who regarded himself as a socialist but not a communist. He later wrote, "When I left the hall to catch a train, the Brigadier General [Glassford] was sitting in the audience in mufti [civilian clothes], placidly smoking his pipe, while [William Wolf "Will"] Weinstone thundered a *Daily Worker* editorial into the mike." Glassford later told reporters that the group's "threatening communistic tenor of speeches" merited some watching.[28]

The next day thousands of spectators turned out to witness the march, supervised and escorted by officers on motorcycles and in scout (patrol) cars. Following the march, uniformed police officers monitored the situation until midnight. As it turned out, the number of police and spectators dwarfed the Communists. Glassford, with pipe clamped firmly between his teeth, rode his blue police motorcycle up and down the route. What surprised most of the spectators was the sight of "colored" and white marchers walking side-by-side, shouting and singing, certainly an unusual sight in the segregated nation's capital. Vice President Curtis, having met with Glassford, had agreed to allow the marchers to carry their banners, but only if their messages did not attack the government. Most messages were variations of "National Hunger Strike March to Washington, Dec. 7, 1931, Column 1, Unemployment Insurance." No problems occurred during the march. When some of the hunger marchers arrived at the mission that night, they found twenty-two world war veterans already there, Glassford having earlier arranged their stay. When the Communists appeared, the veterans decided to sleep at another location, later explaining to news reporters that they and the marchers were different. At this point Glassford had little reason to suspect that other veterans around the country were meeting in small groups and wondering how they could get an early payment of their bonus.[29]

What the hunger marchers had desired most from President Hoover was that he at least accept their draft of proposed legislation for unemployment insurance. He refused. Nor were the marchers admitted to the floors of the House or Senate, but at least one person there received their petition. The marchers left on December 8, still shivering in the December cold, vowing to return in February, but with a much larger group. Upon departing, the marchers had to squeeze into just forty-five trucks, as some of the drivers, still unpaid, had driven their trucks away early. The *Washington Post* gave Glassford "high marks" for his handling of the situation, saying that it had been "magnificent," adding that the marchers had hoped to be abused but instead were treated with courtesy. Irving Bernstein later wrote, "The National Hunger March had been a flop. Instead of an army, the communists had mobilized a corporal's guard. Glassford had outsmarted them." Glassford's actions were an early form of a formula used by police today to address problems: scan, analyze, respond, assess.[30]

Contrasting Glassford's handling of the Washington hunger marchers was the handling of the March 7, 1932, Communist Ford Hunger March at the Ford River Rouge plant at Dearborn, Michigan. A force of 3,000 Communists marched from Detroit toward Dearborn to demand that Henry Ford disband his spy network, reduce the accelerated speed of production, and grant the right to organize. As the Communists arrived some distance from the plant entrance, a line of more than thirty police officers warned them to stop. The marchers then began throwing rocks, striking some officers, forcing them to retreat. A second line of police, security guards, and firefighters next stopped the marchers at the Ford employment gate, greeting them with tear gas and icy water sprayed from an overpass. When police gunfire killed one marcher, the other Communists retreated to a nearby field. Later, a car exited the factory gate, carrying several security men and Harry Herbert Bennett, Ford's notorious chief of security, well known for his elaborate spy network and use of strong-arm goons. When Bennett emerged from the car, someone threw a piece of cement, which struck him and caused him to fall to the ground, bleeding and unconscious. Police then opened fire with pistols and a submachine gun. Bullets killed four marchers and wounded fifty or sixty others. The response proved to be a publicity bonanza for the Communists, complete with martyrs. On March 12 the four bodies lay below a huge red banner displaying Lenin's portrait and the words "Ford Gave Bullets for Bread." The funeral procession consisted of 10,000 marchers, with an estimated 30,000 spectators. After much singing of "Internationale" and a host of radical speeches, comrades lowered the bodies, draped in red, into a common grave, within sight of the Ford factory. Thereafter, Harry Bennett installed machine gun positions at the Ford estate. For the Communists, it was difficult to imagine a more powerful message. The Hoover administration had Glassford to thank for not having a similar spectacle in Washington. The Communist Party continued its search for ways to radicalize unemployed workers, the hungry poor, and downtrodden veterans, but it managed to set hooks in only a few. The Party failed to comprehend that the down-and-out people were essentially capitalists who just needed a slice of the pie, even a sliver. They knew little about communism and had no interest in learning. The Hoover administration would misread the situation as badly as had the Communists.[31]

Glassford's new position entailed much more than handling protest marches, of course. Learning as he went, the new chief did the kinds of things police chiefs do, most mundane, some serious. During December he addressed various parking issues; ordered traffic tickets prepared in triplicate to prevent "fixing"; attended a Boys Club boxing match with Commissioner Crosby; considered a request from one of his inspectors to demote four detectives who had mishandled a homicide investigation; decentralized some detective units from headquarters to precincts; created three efficiency ratings for detectives; and changed the boundaries for the eleven precincts and three DC headquarter areas.[32]

To enhance officer education, the chief ordered talky short films for in-service training and ordered that the "rookie school" (police academy) include quizzes and examinations, as well as lectures by attorneys, criminologists, and skilled investigators. He next purchased the department's first teletype so that his department could send and receive messages with the nearby Baltimore Police Department and other departments similarly equipped. And on December 30, just before the New Year's celebration, he refused his first proffered gratuity, forwarding to Prohibition agents the three bottles of champagne, a flask of Benedictine, and two bottles of rye whiskey that a bootlegger had mailed to him. Glassford had decided on his first day as chief that for the duration of Prohibition he would not drink alcoholic beverages.[33]

As 1932 began, often regarded as the cruelest year of the Great Depression, President Hoover assured news reporters that there were no starving people. In fact, San Francisco and New York reported that 110 had died of malnutrition, mostly children. Home foreclosures had become a routine occurrence, and almost 3,000 banks closed their doors with more to follow.[34]

Another hunger-march group was on its way to Washington, but the Hoover administration would regard this group differently. It was an even longer caravan of old trucks and jalopies, scheduled to arrive on January 7, 1932, led by a veteran army officer and chaplain who had his own radio program. Father James R. Cox, a Roman Catholic priest, was associated with the Old Saint Patrick's Church in Pittsburgh.

He had sent an evening telegram from Gettysburg to the DC Metropolitan Police reminding them that his six-mile caravan of 3,000 vehicles carrying a "Jobless Army" of 11,000 to 15,000 orderly Pennsylvanians would arrive the next day. Their intention was to present to the House of Representatives, Senate, and President Hoover a petition. On his radio program, to which millions of listeners tuned in, Father Cox said that the Hoover administration needed to do more to aid those in distress. The *Washington Post* asserted that these visitors were good men and not "aliens" like the previous group of hunger marchers. The government gave Father Cox royal treatment, and President Hoover allowed a small delegation to meet with him, likely not suspecting that Father Cox would take the liberty of informing the president that his administration was acting like an ostrich. The president assured the priest that the White House was playing close attention to the problem. For Glassford's Metropolitan Police officers, the march had been a headache like the last one, but with fewer problems. As before, he and his officers did a commendable job of handling the marchers.[35]

On January 22, 1932, following congressional approval, President Hoover implemented his Reconstruction Finance Corporation (RFC), which would lend $2 billion to banks, railroads, and insurance companies in hopes that its trickle-down effect would aid the economy. A second radio priest, Father Charles E. Coughlin, wondered aloud why the government gave money to bankers and railroads but not to veterans when it had no obligation to the former and ignored its obligation to the latter. Will Rogers quipped that it appeared that the bankers were the first to go on the dole. As historian Donald Lisio notes, "At the very time Hoover's rapport with the newsmen was rapidly deteriorating, Glassford's was just as rapidly improving."[36]

In late January, Chief Glassford, a member of St. Paul's (Episcopal) Parish, spoke at the annual evening event in honor of its namesake. Two years earlier he had used one wall of the Parish House to paint "Christ and the Children." In other parts of the city, the new chief had become aware of a growing number of homeless and penniless families arriving in the city. He proposed a trial program through April that permitted his officers to provide $2.00 ($40) for food or gas to needy families encountered during the evening hours, with a social agency later reimbursing the officers. It was a small but novel way to assist what appeared to be increasing numbers of homeless people.[37]

In February, in line with modern business practice, Glassford designed for each police geographical beat a loose-leaf compact portfolio, indexed and kept up to date. Each portfolio would serve to monitor the characteristics of the area, including events and concerns of the day, complaints received, speakeasies, gambling dens, houses of ill repute, warrants served, and so forth. Using the portfolio, the beat officer going off duty would update the beat officer coming on duty. Commanding officers would oversee the program. In March, noting an increase in panhandling, Glassford visited the Volunteers of America Mission to meet some of the panhandlers and share a meal with them.[38]

Prohibition remained a problem. Glassford advised the DC commissioners that he needed more officers to enforce the law, specifying that while Metropolitan officers had arrested 6,375 inebriates in 1922, they had arrested 16,408 in 1931. He added that he would like authority to confiscate cars used to transport illegal liquor, most of which seemed to be coming from outside the city. Newspaper letters to the editor suggested that the police chief should pay more attention to "real" crime, a variation of the speeder who tells the traffic officer that he should be out arresting bank robbers instead of harassing drivers, to which the officer might respond, "I thought you were the getaway driver."[39]

Glassford did not forget his army friends. On March 20 he attended a West Point reunion held in Washington, DC, during which he participated in a humorous skit. Douglas MacArthur was in the audience and enjoyed the antics. Glassford, like most West Point cadets and officers, idolized MacArthur: top graduate of his West Point class; awarded two Distinguished Service Crosses and six Silver Stars during the World War; the most decorated American soldier of the war; appointed as the youngest superintendent of West Point; and now serving as the youngest chief of staff, a soldier's soldier, but still congenial. Most officers revered him.[40]

Of a more serious nature for Chief Glassford was the March 27 protest in front of the Japanese Embassy by thirty self-described Communists. They were outraged that the Japanese army had invaded Shanghai, China, and now vented their anger at the local embassy. Glassford was on the scene overseeing the forty officers who were monitoring the unauthorized gathering. When the situation suddenly turned violent, the officers moved in and arrested the participants, resorting to batons and blackjacks. Arrested and taken to the precinct, the Communists refused to give their names. When their attorney arrived and demanded their immediate release whether they identified themselves or not, Glassford promptly had his officers escort the attorney out of the precinct. News reports over the next few days alleged excessive force by the police, but the DC commissioners dismissed those as false claims. Chief Glassford wrote a letter to the American Civil Liberties Union asserting that the media reports had "immensely exaggerated" the police use of force.[41]

Having completed five months as police chief, Glassford departed Washington to visit Philadelphia, Newark, New York City, Providence, and Boston to investigate innovations employed by those departments. Supplied with a few fresh ideas, he started his drive back to Washington, where, among other things, he intended to improve traffic enforcement and update methods of analyzing and tracking homicide statistics.[42]

Throughout April the chief engaged in other routine police matters: he worked nights to address a rash of thirty robberies having occurred during the previous week; he met with members of Congress to solicit funding for replacement police vehicles; he worked with the corporation counsel to develop a system of gradually increasing traffic fines; he adopted the new Scotland Yard fingerprint system; and he personally conducted three raids in which undercover officers surprised gamblers by arriving in taxicabs, netting 285 arrests.[43]

On May 11 Glassford initiated a new Crime Prevention Division, utilizing vice and precinct detectives, aided by identification and fingerprint personnel, to surveil known and suspected criminals actively involved in illegal activity. Detectives eventually arrested more than one hundred individuals and developed enough evidence on sixty to request criminal charges. Glassford expected a 25 percent decrease in crime.[44]

CHAPTER 9

Walter Waters: Glassford's Friendly Enemy

THE president remained confident that his Reconstruction Finance Corporation was already pulling the knocked-down economy to its feet; thus, he had no hesitation when he vetoed Patman's Bonus Bill. The president also knew that veterans could now borrow against their bonus—with interest, of course. Things were looking up: the economy was improving, and the Bonus Bill was dead. Or so Hoover thought. Black Tuesday, October 24, 1929, had been the beginning of the stock market plunge. The resulting Depression took not only jobs but hopes as well. Now, three years later, few shared the president's optimism. To some World War veterans, the veto of Patman's bill must have sounded like the familiar bugle call of assembly.[1]

In the Great Northwest on the soggy side of Oregon, veteran Walter Warfield Waters was quite sure that the US government owed him his bonus. He knew payment was not due until 1945 but considering that the Depression had been in place for three years, he thought it reasonable that the government pay him now. Thousands of other World War veterans felt the same: if the country could not help them find jobs, then it should advance their bonus. Born in Burns, Oregon, on January 9, 1898, Waters was reared in Weiser, Idaho, at the confluence of the Weiser and Snake Rivers, back when the Snake ran wild, untamed by dams. The town's 2,600 residents farmed, tended orchards, and raised livestock in the mild, semiarid climate. But the small town offered little for a teenager who was anxious to see more of the world. Standing six feet tall and 180 pounds, with wavy blond hair and intense blue eyes, Waters made his way to Boise. There he joined the Idaho National Guard in 1916 and was sent to Mexico for service with the Punitive Expedition.[2]

When that enlistment expired, he joined the Oregon National Guard, and was subsequently deployed to France with a medical detachment of the 146th Field Artillery Regiment of the 41st "Sunset" Division. His division, the fifth to arrive in France, endured some of the fierce winter of 1917–1918. As a combat medic, he treated wounded from the battles of Saint-Mihiel, Château-Thierry, and the Meuse-Argonne. Following the Armistice, the army assigned his division occupation duty. In June 1919 he returned to Idaho having earned sergeant stripes and an "excellent character" notation on his discharge papers.[3]

In civilian life his own medical problems required a stay of several months in a hospital. Once well, he found intermittent jobs as an auto mechanic, car salesman, farmhand, and bakery assistant. In 1925 he said goodbye to his family and left Idaho, hitchhiking to Washington state to work fruit harvests. He met Wilma Anderson, petite and attractive, and married her. In December 1930 they moved to the outskirts of Portland, Oregon, where he found work in a cannery, rising to become assistant superintendent. When the depressed economy swept away that job, they moved to Portland. They had managed to save $1,000 ($16,284) by then, but that quickly dwindled, necessitating that they pawn many possessions. By March 1932, with little of value remaining, they were broke. Now the days of hunger arrived more frequently. He had not worked in eighteen months, and by now he and Wilma had two little girls. The couple found a two-room apartment in a poor part of Portland and struggled to pay the rent. Like many unemployed men, listening to the radio filled the day. He met other veterans in his neighborhood who were just as strapped as he was, and who passed on stories about other veterans they knew who were hopping freight trains to Washington, DC, to demand their bonus, saying that the Constitution permitted it. Waters read the Constitution and saw that, indeed, it promised that "Congress shall make no law respecting an establishment of religion, or prohibiting the free exercise thereof; or abridging the freedom of speech, or of the press; or the right of the people peaceably to assemble, and to petition the government for a redress of grievances." He thought the best place to petition the government would be where it was headquartered.[4]

He disliked the term "bonus" because it sounded like a gift; he preferred "compensation," which recognized that the soldiers, at great risk and hardship to their lives, had earned only a fraction of what civilians in the war industry had earned. Veterans grumbled to one another that the government must have the money because the newspapers reported that it had lent money to big corporations and railroads and extended credit to foreign countries.[5]

Waters attended a meeting on March 15, 1932, at which several hundred of the 1,800 veterans or so who lived in Portland had gathered. He listened to various speakers complain about Hoover, Congress, the Bonus Bill, and the sorry state of the country. Like most veterans in the room, he was slender, any body fat having disappeared during the first few years of the Depression. His light-colored hair contrasted with his olive skin, and his tight lips suggested that he had forgotten how to smile. He asked if he could speak and received permission to do so. He stood and began talking, words coming surprisingly easy. He proposed that at least 300 of them hop a freight train that very night and head to the nation's capital. He speculated that they might attract a few hundred more veterans along the way and might arrive with a force of 1,000. What was most important, he stressed, was that the group would need to demonstrate military discipline all along the route. His speech, he admitted, had fallen flat.[6]

He attended a second meeting in April, this one led by George Alman, a lumberjack with hard muscles but a soft voice, who said he was tired of standing in breadlines. Alman had heard Waters speak at the previous meeting and invited him to do so again. On April 23 Waters delivered the same message as before, adding that there was no difference between hunger in Portland and hunger in Washington, DC. His reception was somewhat better than before, with some veterans warming to the idea of going to the nation's capital. That same day a Portland newspaper had run a one-paragraph article announcing yet another upcoming veterans' meeting. One historian later noted that the veterans were "tired of watching their children grow pale on a diet of stale donuts and black coffee, tired of community neglect, tired of official gabble, tired, above all, of waiting."[7]

On May 1, 1932, certain that President Hoover would veto any bonus, the House Ways and Means Committee killed the Bonus Bill. The Portland veterans saw the Committee's action as an insult and began holding meetings more frequently, attracting more veterans. Finally, on May 10, about 200 committed to go to Washington, a journey that would turn out to be an eighteen-day rough ride to the nation's capital. The group had yet to elect a leader, but rules emerged anyway, based on commonly shared military experience. The agreed-to basics were that every man had to show discharge papers proving that he was a veteran, to take an oath to uphold the Constitution, and swear allegiance to the American flag. In addition, every man had to agree to obey the law and follow the orders of the soon-to-be-elected representatives. The men then elected their commander and other supervisors and divided themselves into companies of forty members each. All concurred that the commander should go ahead by car and arrange for food and transportation for the others, who would follow by hopping freight trains. Waters was elected one of the lesser commanders but with the grandiose title of assistant field marshal. To announce their departure, 250 veterans paraded through downtown Portland under a fluttering banner announcing: "Portland Bonus March-On to Washington." More veterans joined the group at the parade. Likely with some misgivings, the long-term, out-of-work veterans embarked on an odyssey: roughly 300 veterans, 3,000 miles, and $30 ($603) total in their pockets. They knew the law forbade hopping freights, but hobos did it every day. They headed for the Union Pacific railroad freight yard. Their bonus had become their "symbol of hope and security."[8]

In mid-May they stood alongside the tracks, jovial, nervous, excited, and smiling as they saw the blinding headlight of the freight engine in the distance and soon heard the earsplitting whistle of the night train. Each man picked up his knapsack or bundle, anxious to get on with the long and predictably uncomfortable journey, tensely standing ready to hop aboard. The locomotive and its line of boxcars, its deafening whistle blowing continuously, screamed by at fifty miles per hour. The veterans stood stunned. Trainyard switchmen told the fuming veterans that the next train would not arrive until the following night. The commander had already departed with their $30 to set up arrangements at the next stop. Now penniless, the men wandered by any restaurant or bakery they found still open and wondered aloud if there might be any extra food around. A few establishments had some, and a local veteran's chapter brought bread and coffee. Some of the veterans reconsidered their commitment to the journey and drifted away, but some new veterans took their places.[9]

The next day hostile negotiations began between Union Pacific Railroad officials and the veterans. The officials forbade the veterans from riding, warning that they would run the train through them, to which the veterans dared them to do it. The officials next contended that there were no empty cars available, and, anyway, a tunnel ahead would scrape off anyone riding on top. In that case, the veterans warned, train officials should find some empty cars, because the former soldiers intended to ride on top, scraped off or not. The next evening the night train approached but slowed and then stopped. The engineer got out and spoke with the train officials. The engineer returned to the engine, blew his whistle, and opened the throttle. At the sound of the whistle, as planned, 280 veterans rushed forward to the boxcar ladders and scaled to the tops. For some of the veterans, it must have been reminiscent of hearing the whistle blow in 1918 and climbing out of the trenches. The engineer slowed and stopped and climbed down again from his engine to talk with the officials. A train official then approached the veterans, pointed to some empty cattle cars, and said that if they wanted to ride in those, the engineer would hook up the cars. The veterans climbed in, kicked aside the dung left by the previous riders, and settled in.[10]

    The next stop was Pocatello, Idaho, three days later. Once they arrived the veterans located their commander, who told them that he had been unable to collect any donations but would soon go forward and try the next town. Locals confided to several veterans that they were pretty sure that he had already collected some donations. By then he had managed to slip away. Some days later he vanished for good. Waters grew disgusted with the indiscipline of some of the veterans, who panhandled money but kept it for themselves, leading to suspicion, jealousy, and grumbling. Waters, still a lesser commander, conferred with a few associates and asked one of the veterans, a former army bugler, to blow assembly. As the veterans gathered, Waters climbed to the top of a freight car. With the commitment of an evangelist, he made it clear that unless they could all be gentlemen he would abandon the ride. In short order the veterans elected the forty-four-year-old former medic as their commander, with authority to organize and discipline the group.[11]

    Waters assembled his new headquarters team. Mickey Dolan, a former prizefighter, would oversee six appointed military police (MPs), personally selected by Waters. A former supply sergeant, Jim Foley, known for his honesty, would supervise those veterans allowed to solicit donations for the group. Another trusted veteran would manage their money, food, tobacco, and other supplies. Veterans who were former railway workers became the transportation committee and a medic squad formed to treat sickness and injury. Finally, a bugler would regulate the day by sounding up to fifteen standard army bugle calls. Reorganized companies of forty veterans each selected their captain, lieutenant, and sergeant. Absolutely forbidden was drinking, unauthorized panhandling, and antigovernment—communist—talk. Rather than go ahead of his men, as the now-missing commander had done, Waters would remain with the group. To fund their new treasury, the veterans asked for and received permission from city officials to stage a short parade in Pocatello, flanked by four veterans walking along the sides, hat in hand, accepting donations. Waters and his team would sustain this organization and discipline throughout the trip, even though their treasury seldom exceeded $35 ($704). The men were soon calling themselves the "Bonus Expeditionary Force," or the BEF. Waters and only a few of them thought they would get their bonus.[12]

In Cheyenne, Wyoming, a former army officer, now working for the railroad, arranged for the men to have a hot meal. It took a week to reach the next stop, Council Bluffs, Iowa. There, the mayor and the American Legion provided additional supplies to the group and allowed them to bathe for the first time since they had left Portland. When the BEF learned that a little girl in the local hospital needed blood, every veteran volunteered to donate. As local citizens took note of the disciplined conduct of the veterans, donations followed. Along the way, more veterans enlisted in the BEF.[13]

The next challenge was the Wabash Railroad, which absolutely refused to allow the veterans to ride on any train. As Waters negotiated with Wabash officials, his transportation committee members quietly positioned themselves along the long line of rail cars. Then, as the engineer started his engine forward, he heard the loud hissing of air brakes, after which some of the freight cars became uncoupled. The engineer backed up and recoupled the train; as he throttled again, he heard more hissing and the train pulled apart at another coupling. Waters then followed the officials to the office, where one of them telephoned the senior manager. Waters heard only one side of the conversation, but it seemed clear that the local police and the sheriff had no interest in inserting themselves into the dispute. Waters then mentioned that he could stop all the interference if the engineer could manage to find a few empty cars. The officials, now comprehending the situation, arranged for the empty cars to be coupled, and the train departed with its now more than 300 passengers, bound for St. Louis. Thus far, only those towns along the route knew anything about the BEF.[14]

The St. Louis Police Department got word that what sounded like a renegade band of veterans was inbound from Oregon. As the train arrived at the St. Louis yard, scores of officers in pairs stood every fifty feet, ready to respond to any threat of burning, looting, or pillaging. Waters, amused, concluded that this might be the entire police force, and told the bugler to sound assembly. The veterans unloaded from the boxcars, fell into formation, and upon command, marched into the yard. Veterans and police officers watched each other, not sure what might happen next. A short time later the police chief, Joseph Gerk, a pioneer in the use of police radios, arrived on the scene. Quickly scanning the situation, he reduced the number of officers to six, complimented the veterans on their discipline, and made a five-dollar donation to their food fund. Another police problem solved. The group proceeded to East St. Louis, Illinois, twelve miles east on the eastern side of the Mississippi River.[15]

Waters sent his transportation committee to collect information on eastbound trains; they determined that the Baltimore and Ohio (B&O) would be the best train. That afternoon, May 22, B&O officials arrived in the trainyard and presented Waters with a court-ordered injunction forbidding the BEF from riding on any B&O train. Waters tried reasoning with them, but the officials were intransigent, dismissing any attempt at compromise. The BEF became equally stubborn, refusing to leave the yard. For three days neither side budged. Chief Special Agent P. J. Young, head of the B&O Railroad Police, arrived on the scene, along with two dozen of his deputies, whom the hobos usually called "railroad bulls." Young attempted to persuade Waters to find another way east, but Waters refused, saying the BEF had traveled more than 2,000 miles, had a little more than 800 miles to go, and they were not about to stop now. Young said that he would have the engine removed from any train the veterans boarded, and then increased his railroad police force to eighty. He next secretly ordered train crews to continually shunt individual railcars here and there. Waters's transportation members told him that the B&O was doing it to bewilder the BEF. Waters developed his plan. At 10:00 p.m., an eastbound train arrived and stopped. Waters blew his whistle and two columns of veterans quickly climbed to the tops of cars. Young immediately confronted Waters, telling him that no train would leave the yard if veterans were on it; Waters replied, in that case, no train would leave the yard. Veterans slept on the tops of cars that night. By morning, Young had assembled a force of 150 railroad police, likely provided by other railroads. Local police arrived, but only to monitor the gathering crowd of spectators. The American Legion and VFW brought food for the veterans. By noon the next day, no train had departed the yard. Local news reporters wrote about the standoff, and national news reporters picked up the story, publishing it nationwide with headlines announcing that the Bonus Marchers had held up the train. Waters could not have purchased better publicity for what was now being termed the "Bonus Army." Still, no trains moved.[16]

Waters next used the only weapon he had, the threat of resignation. He pointed out to Agent Young that he had 300-plus disciplined veterans who would stay that way, but only if Waters remained in charge. He argued that it would be better to let the BEF depart on a freight train than for the town to have to contend with 300 homeless men roaming the streets of East St. Louis at night. At 3:00 p.m., Waters warned, he would relinquish his authority and urge his lieutenants to do the same. Headlines reported that Waters had threatened the railroads, and Special Agent P. J. Young informed the railroad's vice president of Waters's threat. The B&O vice president held firm and dictated that no nonpaying person would ride the train. When the BEF leader pointed out that hobos were riding B&O trains daily, Young shrugged and left. He returned later and confronted Waters, announcing that he had orders to arrest him. Waters asked why he was being arrested. Young said it was because he was the leader, to which Waters replied that he was no longer the leader, just a veteran like all the others. Headlines from New York to San Francisco reported that the BEF seemed to be outmaneuvering the railroad. If Chief Special Agent Young had any tool in his toolbox other than a hammer, he failed to use it.[17]

By May 25, the third day of the standoff, several thousand spectators were on hand to witness the drama. The B&O contacted the governor, who dispatched five companies of National Guard soldiers to stand by in the yard, just in case. The American Legion arrived but could only offer suggestions. During this time the transportation committee noticed unusual activity in the yard: freight engines moved a variety of railcars here and there, but always toward Caseyville, seven miles away. When the veterans saw a caboose and engine disappear that way, they knew what was happening and began running on foot toward Caseyville. Spectators caught on as well and jumped into their cars, driving alongside the veterans, beckoning them to hop in. The veterans were some distance away when the train prepared to pull away. As the engineer sounded his whistle and turned up the steam, the train's steel wheels moved forward slightly but then began slipping, screeching, squealing, and sparking along the tracks, clearly unable to find traction. As it had turned out, a few veterans had earlier secreted themselves on the soon-to-depart engine. By the time the engineer had coupled the engine to the train, the veterans had scampered to the tops of some of the cars and hand-tightened the brake wheels, closing the iron shoes against the iron wheels. The veterans spent another night on the tops of railway cars. As Waters later wrote, "It was the 'Battle of St. Louis' that brought to the Bonus Army its first large following." The five companies of National Guard soldiers still stood by. At this point unnamed sympathizers drove Waters to Washington, Indiana, to arrange for additional assistance with transportation.[18]

Sheriff Jerome Munie arrived on the scene. He was the opposite of Chief Special Agent P. J. Young. Local folks recognized Jerome by his full head of silver wavy hair, wire-rimmed glasses, and friendly face. Sheriff Munie brought to the problem what it needed: fresh eyes, no invested ego, and a willingness to go around entrenched opponents to end the standoff. He called on friends in labor unions as well as private citizens to assemble a fleet of fifty roadsters, sedans, and trucks to caravan the veterans forward. That solved the sheriff's problem, but it became the problem of others. By now millions of Americans knew that the Bonus Army was on its way to Washington. Along the route, mayors and governors saw the advantage of shuttling the human hot potato eastward. Other veterans from throughout the country read about what was happening and headed for Washington by boxcar, truck, automobile, and foot, responding to the publicity that the Portlanders had engendered.[19]

In Zanesville, Ohio, the veterans learned that they had become national news. By then a telegram from Representative Patman, Bonus Bill author, was waiting for Waters, asking to meet with him to discuss matters as soon as he arrived in Washington, DC, preferably sometime ahead of his men. Also waiting in Zanesville to meet with Waters was a US Secret Service agent from the Cincinnati office, who wanted to discuss sensitive matters with him. The agent took Waters to a hotel, where the Bonus leader learned that the Secret Service had had the group under surveillance for some time and would continue to keep an eye on them. The agent stressed that it was very important that Waters remain in charge of his men for the sake of the president's safety. This was the first time that anyone outside the BEF had mentioned President Hoover since their trip began. Perhaps more important, the veterans heard that Washington, DC, Metropolitan Police Chief Pelham Glassford had announced that the veterans would be allowed to remain in the city for only forty-eight hours.[20]

Waters knew he would soon meet Patman and probably concluded that he would meet Glassford as well. However well or badly the meetings went, he knew he had fulfilled his commitment to bring the BEF to the nation's capital.[21]

Ohio authorities continued the truck transport of the BEF eastward until the Pennsylvania officials took over, who in turn handed off the problem to Maryland authorities. In Cumberland, Maryland, Waters learned that other veterans, having become aware of the Portland veterans' trek, were now also on their way to Washington. Next, he heard that Police Chief Glassford was waiting to meet with him. An American Legionnaire paid Waters's train fare, allowing him to ride the 2:00 a.m. train from Cumberland to Washington, 135 miles southeast, in a passenger seat rather than on a boxcar floor. The Bonus Army leader now had appointments to meet Patman at 8:00 a.m. and Glassford at 9:00 a.m., both at Police Headquarters. Waters reminded himself that he had left Portland intending to bring the veterans across the country and nothing more.[22]

Waters knew of President Hoover, of course, and now he was about to meet a US representative and a police chief. In the coming months, the former army sergeant would never meet any of Glassford's superiors—the three commissioners of the District of Columbus who managed the city. The DC commissioner who would take the lead in contending with the veterans would be Glassford's primary superior, Herbert Crosby, who in turn reported to President Hoover. In the next few months, the uneducated, unemployed, and undaunted former army sergeant would go up against some of the most powerful men in Washington, including the president. In this process, he and the BEF would have a most unlikely ally: Police Chief Pelham Glassford, the veterans' best friend in Washington.

President Herbert Clark Hoover did not cause the Great Depression, of course, but many Americans held him responsible for it, primarily because he seemed to be doing so little to aid them. He was born 1874 in West Branch, Iowa, the son of a blacksmith and a seamstress, both Quakers. Orphaned at age nine, young Hoover lived with an uncle in Oregon. At fourteen, Hoover quit school to clerk at his uncle's real estate business. He later attended Stanford University, graduating in 1895. For twenty years he worked as a mining engineer and financier, becoming exceptionally wealthy in the process. At the onset of the World War, he was called on to arrange passage home for 120,000 Americans then stranded in Europe, and he later procured food for starving Belgians caught in the war zone. In 1917 Democratic President Wilson asked him to become the US food administrator, overseeing the rationing of domestic food so that Allied armies could be fed. Following the war, Hoover headed an agency addressing famine in parts of Europe, including Soviet Russia. Republican President Harding next appointed him secretary of commerce, during which he assisted the victims of a devastating Mississippi River flood. When

Republican President Coolidge declined to seek a second term, the voters elected Hoover as president, his first elected office. Somewhat overweight, the new president seldom smiled, and when he did, it often came across as a smirk. Secret Service Agent Edmund W. Staling, head of the Presidential Protection Detail, described the president as a "poor speaker" and said, "He was handicapped by the fact that he thought of humanity as an abstract quality instead of a collection of highly differentiated personalities."[23]

The ongoing Depression led to President Hoover's creation of such agencies as the Federal Farm Board, the Federal Drought Relief Committee, and the Reconstruction Finance Corporation, all in hopes of reviving the economy. He initiated various public works programs and lent money to assist the states as well. Nonetheless, he adamantly refused to provide any relief to the unemployed, which between 1931 and 1933 increased from 7 million to 11 million. The starving Belgians and flood victims had been relatively passive; that would not be the case with the Bonus Army. Hoover would later refer to Bonus Army members as "supposed veterans," leading commentator Walter Lippmann to wonder how Hoover could "justify the fact that he never took the trouble to confer with the bonus marchers." Throughout the boxcar ride across the country, the BEF never forgot the insult of May 1 that spurred them on their way—the killing of Patman's Bonus Bill by the House Ways and Means Committee. Other veterans, having heard about the Oregon BEF, formed their own groups, and trekked to Washington, DC.[24]

CHAPTER 10

The Bonus Veterans Arrive

IN mid-April Chief Glassford was driving back from New York to Washington, DC, and while passing through New Jersey came upon something of a spectacle. There he saw 75 to 100 bedraggled men walking along the side of the road, happily singing, and waving at passing cars and trucks. The man in front carried an American flag and several others displayed banners reading "Bonus or a Job" and "The trenches in 1918, the benches in 1932." One man trundled a pushcart holding the coats and other possessions of the men, and most surprising, as Glassford saw, "On top of the whole heap rode a baby girl." He was curious and pulled to the side of the road. Upon seeing his Washington license plates the men cheered and flocked around him. They said they were veterans bound for Washington and asked him what to expect when they arrived. They chatted for a while and offered him a flyer titled, "Don't Let the Bankers Fool You," which they hoped he would pass on to Mr. Hoover. Glassford declined the flyer, wished them well, and drove away. He was impressed, however, with the "quiet determination in the demeanor of the men." He remembered, "They faced the prospect of a 200-mile weary march, 200 miles which I was to cover in six hours, but which [would take] them 30 days of dogged plodding."[1]

Glassford wondered how many other veterans were doing something similar, now suspecting this might be just the vanguard. If thousands arrived, as seemed possible, it would no longer be a District of Columbia problem but a national problem, requiring action by the federal government. Within two weeks he received word that other groups were coming from Tennessee and Texas, and press reports said that railway guards in New Orleans had fired shots to scatter some veterans there. The worst was in Cleveland, where some veterans had temporarily commandeered a train. Glassford knew he had been fortunate with the two hunger marches his officers had handled, but now he was uncertain about how best to manage the arrival of thousands of veterans. To him it was obvious that the veterans would have to be fed and sheltered until they got an answer regarding their bonus. There was, he realized, the potential for rioting and bloodshed, which might disgrace not only his police department but the district and national governments as well. He now focused on dissuading the veterans from coming, telegraphing governors and urging them to do what they could to stem the flow, appealing to railroads to block the advance of the free-riders, and asking the American Legion and Veterans of Foreign Wars to use their influence to keep the men at home. But the chief knew what he needed most was for Congress to vote on the bill, up or down, which would likely curb the crusade.[2]

He met with the DC commissioners, asking for instructions. Their advice was to treat the veterans as tramps and shuttle them off to any charity that would feed them and then ensure that they moved along, the sooner the better. Glassford recalled that that advice had floored him. The success of the hunger marches had set something of a precedent. The DC commissioners and the Hoover administration had allowed those groups to parade and petition Congress, but now it seemed that the DC commissioners wanted to treat World War veterans as hobos. If that would be their position, then he wanted a written policy to guide him and his department. The DC commissioners refused, saying that he should handle it on his own authority. He later wrote, "These [veterans] were not coming to Washington as tourists; they were coming to appeal to the National Government, and I felt that it was unfair to place the burden wholly upon the residents of the District of Columbia."[3]

Historian Roger Daniels says of the arrival of the Bonus marchers, "Inconceivable as it may seem today, the only public official in all of Washington who had the wit to initiate any action was the relatively new chief.... No one else was willing to take any responsibility; no one seemed to understand . . . that exceptional times called for exceptional measures."[4]

By May 24 Glassford was certain that more veterans were on their way, the large group from Portland, Oregon, for certain. Having been on the rails and roads for more than two weeks, they were due to arrive in the city the following week. Glassford met with Secretary of War Patrick J. Hurley, asking for some assistance but assuring Hurley that his police officers needed no "military personnel." Hurley said he could provide some tents and accommodations, if necessary. The chief then checked with the Washington area army, navy, and marine installations, but they all declined to lend any equipment; nor could the American Legion, VFW, and Red Cross provide much help. Newspapers were suggesting that anywhere from 70,000 to 1 million veterans might come, complaining that local missions were already at capacity. Glassford hoped that only a few thousand veterans would arrive. He did not know Hurley well, but he sensed a reluctance by the secretary to become involved.[5]

Patrick J. Hurley was born in the Choctaw Nation in Oklahoma in 1883, the son of a coal miner of Irish heritage. Hurley attended Bacone Indian College in Muskogee, where he played sports and edited the school newspaper. In 1905 he graduated from the National University Law School in Washington, DC, after which he returned to Oklahoma and practiced law, becoming wealthy in Tulsa real estate. Always well-dressed and manicured, he became active in Republican politics, becoming President William Taft's choice to be the Choctaw Nation's national attorney. A National Guard captain, he served in the Judge Advocate General's Office in Washington and was later sent to France during the World War, where he experienced combat as an artillery officer. He rose to lieutenant colonel, receiving a citation for gallantry. He returned to Oklahoma and represented clients involved in banking and oil. As chair of the 1926 Republican Party Convention, he coordinated Hoover's Oklahoma presidential campaign, which in 1929 resulted in Hurley's appointment as secretary of war. As such, he urged President Hoover to appoint Douglas MacArthur as army chief of staff.[6]

Glassford must have felt suddenly alone. Officials in Washington seemed content to ignore the recent arrivals and the reports of more veterans on the way. Then Secretary of War Hurley declared that the federal government would give no recognitions to the veterans. He did assent, however, to Glassford's request for some bed sacks (sleeping bags), tents, and rolling kitchens. After being reminded, Hurley supplied the items through an army officer, who informed the chief that they were available for pickup at Fort Myer, adding that the DC commissioners would have to pay for them. Glassford knew that the veterans had a constitutional right to come to Washington to petition the government, but he also knew that "hungry men were riotous men." Still, Commissioner Crosby would not change his position. Glassford saw that he had two choices in dealing with the veterans: "feed them or fight them."[7]

Crosby, the other DC commissioners, and members of Congress, never hesitated to offer suggestions, but nothing in writing. "I have listened to a thousand different suggestions on this subject," Glassford fumed, "so far, the responsibility has rested entirely on my shoulders. I am not taking suggestions from anyone. You are my superior officers. I am ready to obey your written orders." None arrived. Glassford later wrote, "I followed the policy I had adopted in the first place."[8]

This should not have been Glassford's problem to solve; it was bigger than a police department; bigger than a city government. It was a national problem. Feeding "floaters" and shuttling them along would work for only so long; there were too many veterans on their way, and they came on a mission. Glassford now had a police problem to address, albeit much, much larger than most. Since the DC government was of no assistance, the chief and his officers would have to solve, or at least mitigate, the growing problem. Also aware of the problem, Chief of Staff General MacArthur and his staff reviewed Plan White on May 25, which detailed the response in the case of insurrection in the city. That same day, in a bold but risky move, Chief Glassford simply went to the Capitol and the White House. He had decided to go over the heads of his superiors in search for others in the nation's capital who might help. Extending his long elbows, the tall police chief bumped his way into the middle of the buck-passing bureaucrats, determined to do what he thought was right. No one had ever accused him of timidity; that had not been the case when he had scouted behind enemy lines on the Western Front, and that would not be the case now, when he anticipated the arrival of thousands of veterans to the nation's capital. He already knew the answer to the problem: Congress needed to bring the bonus issue to a vote, yes or no, to halt the influx of veterans. He believed that the sooner the bill came out of committee and was acted upon by the House and Senate, the sooner the veterans would stop coming. At the Capitol he hoped to meet with Indiana Republican Senator James Eli Watson and Illinois Democratic Representative Henry Thomas Rainey to state his proposal. He met with Watson and had a friendly conversation but received no commitment, and he never managed to meet with Rainey. Instead, he met with Representative Wright Patman, whose Bonus Bill was now dead. He next visited Walter B. Newton, a prim and studious-looking man fond of wearing Ben Franklin glasses, who formerly had served as a Minnesota representative, and now was Hoover's executive secretary. Glassford asked Newton to present his proposal to President Hoover, suggesting that if Hoover favored a vote, Congress would consider it, and the BEF situation would fade away. Newton agreed to think it over but offered nothing more. Glassford, new to Washington politics, was about to learn that politicians focus on reelection, not solving problems.[9]

Had his plan worked, observers would have applauded it; instead, it revealed that the new police chief was an outsider who did not know his place, a political novice who had failed to investigate the president's entrenched position relative to the Bonus Bill before visiting the White House. He knew he was violating the chain of command, but then Crosby had said that it was a police matter, so the chief did it anyway. Complaints from the White House were immediate, finding the DC commissioners unaware.[10]

Hoover's confidential secretary telephoned Glassford, chiding him for embarrassing the Hoover administration, adding that news reporters had already heard about his visit. Glassford likely encountered reporters who asked why he was at the White House. The president's secretary then asserted that Glassford should have told the reporters that he was at the White House on personal business. Puzzled, Glassford replied matter-of-factly, "When I tell them anything, I tell them the truth." Each must have been astonished at the other. Next, a White House staff member called Commissioner Crosby and complained, as did others. Visiting Crosby's office, Glassford found two members of Congress, one a Republican and the other a Democrat, already there. As Glassford later wrote, "They were raising the devil about my attitude toward the BEF." Speaking to Commissioner Reichelderfer, they accused Glassford of encouraging the veterans to come to the city by feeding them, adding that other members of Congress felt the same. The chief could see that the DC commissioners were under pressure to expel the veterans. Other officials of the White House and Congress complained directly to Glassford. "One prominent official," Glassford recalled, "told me bluntly: 'If you don't change your attitude the president will peremptorily dismiss you.'" To Glassford it must have seemed ironic: he was simply trying to get Congress to do its job—vote on the bill—but members of Congress were complaining to his superiors, essentially accusing him of not starving the veterans sufficiently to encourage them to leave and suggesting that he force them out if they refused. The chief found himself in no man's land, once again. Commissioner Crosby, clearly irritated, admonished him, "Do you understand that if you continue these activities the president may order you summarily removed?" Glassford thought for a moment and replied, "Under the circumstances, such an action would be of great value to me." Crosby backed off, no doubt fearing that firing

Glassford would mean that the DC commissioners would have to take responsibility for the problem. It seems likely that Glassford thought of resigning and returning to Arizona, letting the commissioners deal with the problem, but that was not in the chief's character. His natural inclination was to defend the underdog, and it appeared that there were a lot of them in town and more coming.[11]

Why was Congress so reluctant to vote on the Bonus Bill? The answer was in the politics. The president was a Republican and had already said that he would veto the bill if it reached him. The Senate had a Republican majority of 50 percent to the Democrats' 48 percent and would almost certainly support the president, so overriding his veto would be next to impossible. The House had begun the term with a Democratic minority but would finish with a majority of 51 percent to 48 percent. Thus, the House Democrats could pass the bill, but it would have almost no chance of becoming law. If the bill ever came up for a vote, which way each House member voted carried with it the potential for offending either the veteran voter block or the nonveteran voter block, and in the Great Depression both were suffering equally. Thus, letting the bill die quietly had some attraction.

On May 27 Glassford encountered the first sizable contingent of veterans, about 100, who had temporarily settled down in Judiciary Square, at 6th Street NW and D Street NW, northwest of the Capitol. These were not the Oregon veterans but another group. Glassford noticed that their clothing was worn and shabby but displayed various medals and patches for bravery and battle wounds. He approached them and was pleased when they cheered his arrival. The long-legged police chief, wearing his standard uniform of billed cap, blue dress blouse with badge, white shirt and tie, motorcycle britches, and tall boots, sat down on the grass with them and listened. He was impressed with the group's leader, a southerner, who led the discussion and voting relative to their proposed rules, which were to institute military discipline, forbid liquor, discourage panhandling, reject subversive propaganda, and obey the law and the Constitution. Glassford then had a realization: "What was ahead was suddenly disclosed to my mind. This was not a local police problem; this was the beginning of a national movement. These men had come to demand their bonus." But on a more mundane level, they were also concerned about the safety of their small amount of cash, and asked Chief Glassford if he would oversee it, essentially becoming their treasurer. He agreed, knowing that "in doing so he had a double motive." His participation would serve as "a way of monitoring the group, which he believed had to be done as an alternative to tragedy." What he did not agree with—though he remained silent—was their purpose in coming to Washington, seeing it as a mistaken objective. Nonetheless, no veteran would ever hear him say that. At the same time, he was impressed with the men. "Of material things they had nothing, but all were holding on to the principles of patriotism and country." He knew that they had come because they were idle and miserable and needed work and were seeking "the one thing in the world they had of value, asking for the one thing that stood between them and hunger." He had hoped the federal government would assign them to designated army camps; now he saw that it had no interest in doing so.[12]

He began visiting the impromptu and self-selected veteran camps day and night, getting to know the veterans. Since the groups had usually elected their leaders, he worked through them. Having served in the same army, often on the same battle fronts, he and the beaten-down veterans became friendly. His worst fear was that veterans who had survived the greatest war in history would be killed in the nation's capital. "To avert such a tragedy became one of my chief purposes, and to attain it every resource at my command had to be used."[13]

A young cavalry captain, Lucian K. Truscott Jr., was then serving as a troop commander at nearby Fort Myer, across the Potomac River from Washington. His primary duty was setting up and escorting funerals—most of them for World War veterans—at Arlington National Cemetery, adjacent to the fort. "Early in May," Truscott remembered, "veterans began arriving in Washington . . . in ever increasing numbers." Some of the Fort Myer soldiers hired the veterans to do kitchen police work and stable cleaning to help them earn a little money. Truscott knew of General MacArthur, of course, and he knew Commissioner Crosby from when the latter had been the chief of cavalry, but Truscott had never met or heard of Pelham Glassford until the veterans started arriving. Thereafter, he read about the former army general—now police chief—almost daily.[14]

Anticipating the arrival of Waters and his Oregonians, along with other inbound veteran groups, Glassford and Patman still hoped that Congress would bring the Bonus Bill to a vote. Glassford told reporters that if Congress voted to deny the bonus, it would put an end to the veterans coming to Washington. Wright Patman backed him, saying that the longer it took to vote on the bonus, the more veterans there would be in the city. Glassford told gathered reporters that his officers were now registering veterans to mark the start of their forty-eight-hour visit, but if that failed, he would need federal assistance, warning that empty stomachs would invite problems. This, the last opportunity to derail the Bonus March near its onset, was lost when members of Congress chose to do nothing.[15]

Pennsylvania veteran Harold B. Foulkrod and his small coterie of veterans were making it difficult for members of Congress to do that, and at the same time they were doing a service to the other veterans in town. Foulkrod had served in both the British and American armies during the World War and had suffered four wounds as a result. While he had no connection with Waters, they were soon working in tandem. Foulkrod and his veterans sat on the Capitol steps daily and ensnared unsuspecting members of Congress, requesting that they sign a petition to resuscitate the Bonus Bill. They had already collected more than 90 congressional signatures of the 145 they needed.[16]

On May 27, having resolved that it was in the best interest of the District of Columbia to feed and shelter the veterans, Glassford took Foulkrod and four other veterans to visit Camp Meigs, near Bolling Field, northeast of Union Station. He suggested that they might want to set up their camp there and let them know that he had already solicited some food and lumber donations from merchants, private citizens, and veteran organizations. If Foulkrod and the others would escort arriving veterans to the camp, then Glassford would provide rolling kitchens, pup tents, and bed sacks for them. He hoped the veterans would eventually build temporary structures for housing. If he could keep the veterans somewhat out of sight, he reasoned, there would be fewer complaints. The problem was that the veterans wanted to be in the public eye, putting pressure on Congress to pass the Bonus Bill. Meanwhile, Glassford was working on setting up boxing and wrestling matches as a way of raising money to feed the veterans.[17]

The chief next learned that perhaps 2,000 more veterans had arrived from other parts of the country. Still to arrive was Waters's Oregon group of 300-plus, whose "Battle of East St. Louis" had plastered the issue onto national headlines, unintentionally encouraging other veterans to come. Of major concern to Glassford was a report that a group of avowed Communist veterans had also arrived, calling themselves the Workers' Ex-Servicemen's League (WESL). He was certain that there would be conflict between them and the other veterans, necessitating that he shelter the Communists separately.[18]

Having gone ahead of his men, Waters arrived in Washington, prepared to meet with both a representative and a police chief. Patman, he suspected, would be something of an ally; Glassford was a question. He might be reasonable and easy to work with, or he might be another cop in the mold of Chief Special Agent P. J. Young, railroad bull. Adding evidence to the latter was Glassford's announced rule that veterans could remain in Washington for only forty-eight hours.[19]

On May 29 at 8:00 a.m. Waters sat down with Representative Patman. The meeting went well, considering that for some time Patman had had serious reservations about the Oregon veterans coming to Washington. He began by complimenting Waters on the conduct of his group, adding that he had heard many reports saying as much. He admitted that he was very concerned, however, that others might think that he—Patman—had instigated the cross-country trip and asked Waters to avoid saying anything that might encourage that belief. Waters readily agreed.[20]

For the Oregonian, the 9:00 a.m. meeting with Chief Glassford, fifteen years his senior, went much better than he expected. Waters remembered, "I was agreeably surprised by his appearance. Here was certainly no hard-boiled disciple of the old police school." Waters found the police chief to be very human, friendly, courteous, and considerate. The veteran leader found it difficult to comprehend that he was having a conversation with a former brigadier general. Glassford informed Waters that he made arrangements with the Maryland governor, whose National Guard was already trucking in Waters's group, to bring the men directly into Washington and unload them at 8th and I Streets SE. Their billets would be in a vacant wooden building that had once served as a department store, and a meal would be waiting for them. When Glassford asked Waters for his estimate on how many veterans from around the country might arrive in the next two weeks, Waters estimated 20,000 based on various telegrams he had received. Glassford expressed dismay, having in mind a much smaller number. Waters later conceded that his estimate had not been accurate. As it turned out, it was more than 22,000, but it would take longer than two weeks for them to arrive. In the future, BEF registration records would reflect that at one time or another, more than 28,000 veterans had come to Washington. For various reasons, some veterans had arrived but then chose not to stay. At its peak there would be 26,000 veterans in the city, a majority from Indiana, Missouri, and Oregon, bedding down in at least twenty camps. Waters said of his Portland veterans: "It was the rock that started the landslide."[21]

The line of sixteen trucks, escorted by police motorcycle officers, arrived in the heart of the city to friendly waves of curious spectators. Knowing the men would be hungry, Glassford had gone to the Fort Myer commissary, spending $120 ($2,414) of his own money to buy food. That evening, the new arrivals, tired and worn from their nearly 3,000-mile, 18-day journey by rail and road, enjoyed a dinner of hot stew, milk, bread, and coffee. Better yet, they could look forward to a breakfast of coffee, oatmeal, and milk. Glassford put a police captain in charge of the veterans' food supply with a budget of 7 cents per day per veteran.[22]

Glassford had an advantage in working with the veterans; it was the same advantage he had in working with DC and federal officials. Like many army officers, he prided himself on being apolitical, doing his duty irrespective of politics. As historian Irving Bernstein notes, "In the committed world of 1932, [Glassford] was an unusually free spirit."[23]

The Secret Service, like the army, had already infiltrated agents into the various veteran groups. The undercover agents remained hyperalert for the slightest hint of Communist veterans who might attempt to radicalize the others. Secret Service Agent Edmund William Starling, chief of the White House protection detail, later remembered, "Our agents were among them, keeping us informed of the number of radicals in every group, and checking on the influence they had with the men. Generally speaking, there were few Communists, and they had little effect on the men's thinking. The veterans were Americans, down on their luck but by no means ready to overthrow the government." In that regard, the veterans were no different from most Americans struggling during the Great Depression. For his book *Hard Times*, author Studs Terkel interviewed well over 100 Americans, one of whom was Ed Paulsen. Paulsen remembered, "We weren't greatly agitated in terms of society. Ours was a bewilderment, not an anger. Not a sense of being particularly put upon. We weren't talking revolution. We were talking jobs."[24]

As the Oregon veterans sipped coffee and munched their meal, Officer John E. Bennett welcomed them with a friendly admonition: "Fellows, you're welcome here, but the minute you start mixing with Reds and Socialists, out you go." Bennett pointed out that the marine barracks and several army posts were all close by. Waters answered for the group, saying that if they discovered any Reds in the group, they would drag them to the district line, adding that he and his men had come here under the same flag they fought for in France. Like Ed Paulsen and most Americans, Waters and his men wanted work, not rhetoric. Glassford made a point of selecting police officers who had served in the military to work with the arriving veterans.[25]

The next day Waters found himself not in deep water, but at least over his head. Having brought 300-plus veterans to Washington, he was now the elected "commander" of more than 1,300 veterans in the city. As their leader he emphasized that his plan was to stay in Washington until Congress passed the Bonus Bill. Period. But there was some good news for Waters and the others. Glassford had announced that he would not enforce his forty-eight-hour limit unless it became necessary to do so. The bad news for Waters, individually, was that it seemed that the DC and federal administrations now intended to hold him personally accountable for the actions of all the veterans. He had brought only a few hundred; now there were well over a thousand, and he had warned Glassford that there might be 20,000. By what authority DC and federal officials intended to hold Waters responsible, they never specified; on the other hand, Waters had already determined that a threatened resignation could get results.[26]

While Waters had some natural leadership ability, he had no real training or experience in overseeing large numbers of men. For a year or so, during the World War, he had been a sergeant supervising a squad of perhaps a dozen medics. The army had never commissioned him as an officer, nor had it given him supervisory or managerial training. He had, for a short while, been an assistant superintendent of a cannery, but nothing more. Now, and in the months ahead, federal and DC officials, including Glassford, would endeavor to hold him accountable for the actions of all the veterans, under the assumption—based on no evidence—that he possessed the education, training, skills, and leadership experience comparable with that of an army colonel commanding a regiment. An Idaho boy, Waters must have felt like he had been tossed into the Hells Canyon waters of the raging Snake River, managed to get on his back with his feet pointed downstream, and now hoped to dodge all the rapids, rocks, logjams, and plunging waterfalls ahead.

The BEF commander made clear to news reporters that his Oregon veterans would not associate with the veterans from other states unless those veterans accepted Oregon group rules, which included refraining from drinking and panhandling, always being in possession of discharge papers, and behaving like gentlemen. When the veterans subsequently agreed to those rules, Waters organized them into six companies, with each company electing its captain, lieutenant, sergeant, and mess detail. He next set up a National Headquarters of the BEF, which for the time being would conduct its business in a small house on 11th Street SE that previously had served as an undertaker's parlor—perhaps not the best omen. The house was the property of Carlos Alfonso Don Zelaya, a concert pianist who was also a 1910 West Point graduate and friend of Glassford. Zelaya allowed the BEF to use the house free of charge. It is likely that the Bonus Army followed the same rule as the US Army rule: RHIP (rank has its privileges). Thus, it seems likely that Waters and his top lieutenants bunked here most of the time and not in the various camps.[27]

On May 31 the Bonus Expeditionary Force became official. Waters, at the suggestion of Glassford and some other veterans, agreed to remain as commander, and Glassford agreed to continue as secretary-treasurer. The police chief, perhaps on his own, persuaded the local Marine Reserve unit to provide first aid and basic medical services for the veterans, and Jimmy Lake, a local sports promoter, volunteered to set up a boxing event to raise money for the veterans. By now, Glassford and his officers realized that they had a new community, apart from city residents, with which to contend. There were many problems and addressing them would require the police and veterans to work together.[28]

On June 5 Waters collapsed, likely stressed from too many problems and too little sleep. In his absence the veterans themselves formed an executive committee of sorts and on June 8 asked Waters if he would continue as the commander. He agreed and was pleased when he learned that recently donated money had allowed Glassford to add $5,000 ($100,576) to the BEF treasury; additionally, some food had also been donated. Waters was disappointed, however, when rumors circulated that Glassford was turning the nation's capital into a "hotel for bums" and might be fired as a result.[29]

Now as a sanctioned commander, Waters needed a command staff. He chose lumberjack George Alman, whom he knew from the Portland meeting, as his primary aide and billeting officer. For his bodyguard, he selected former boxer Mickey Dolan. He also appointed a secretary, supply officer, and several squads of veterans to constitute his intelligence service. Their job would be to detect and remove radical veterans who had inveigled their way into the BEF. A second task of these veterans would be to casually befriend police officers, keeping their ears alert for information that might be useful to Waters and his staff. Harold Foulkrod would head the legislative committee and continue to accost and pester members of Congress to sign the petition to bring the Bonus Bill out of committee. Waters set up the various camps along both military and state lines. While smaller camps might house veterans from just one state, larger camps would include veterans from up to five states. Eventually, Waters would oversee more than twenty camps, and in each of them every veteran had to present his discharge papers whenever he passed through the chow line.[30]

Glassford and Waters did their best to manage the increasing number of veterans, while the DC commissioners did their best to ignore the whole situation as did the federal government. President Hoover was always too busy to meet with Waters or any of the Bonus marchers, but still managed to greet and chat with a heavyweight wrestling champion, members of a sorority, a group of adolescent essay winners, and various dignitaries. Ignored by the Hoover administration, the veterans continued to trickle in. Small groups from all over the country arrived, having a common objective and now using army culture as the binding to keep them together. Despite his limitations, Waters seemed to have the skill to keep them together and focused. The BEF commander and the police chief got along surprisingly well. Waters would later say of General Glassford: "He chose, fortunately, to see that the veterans did not starve. He strove to prevent the use of force against us." Waters and the other veterans never forgot, of course, that Glassford was a police chief first and an ally second. Some veterans faulted Waters for appearing to be too cozy with the chief.[31]

Even before the first veterans had arrived, there were already thousands of unemployed people residing in DC. Having received little help in the past three years, they accepted their fate and hoped for better times. The veterans were not so docile; each had come to Washington for a job or his bonus, not a handout. Glassford's aim was simply to keep the veterans from starving until Congress got around to voting on the Bonus Bill. Officer John Bennett reported to the chief that 600 veterans were now in the main camp and another 700 were sleeping in various parks and vacant buildings. Those at 12th and D Streets soon joined with others at 8th and I, and Waters held to his commitment to prohibit Communist veterans from entering the camps. When his intelligence veterans caught two men distributing radical fliers among the veterans, the two became the first discipline examples. A kangaroo court ordered that each man receive ten welts from a belt, followed by expulsion from the camp. Glassford continued to solicit food from merchants, many of whom were kind enough to help. One of the more unusual donations came from the Carrol Fish Company, which delivered four 150-pound turtles.[32]

As a warm June arrived, Glassford continued to review reports and news stories, attempting to gauge how many more veterans were en route. As each group appeared, Waters met with them personally and delivered the firm message of no drinking, no panhandling, no radical talk. If they could not abide by that, they were not welcome in the camps. After Waters briefed the new arrivals, other veterans directed them to the registration tent where one of Glassford's officers took their names and military serial numbers, giving close attention to their discharge papers. When the new arrivals asked where they could shower, a resident veteran usually pointed toward the sluggish, oil-sheened Anacostia River.[33]

The police chief had earlier acquired lumber and tar paper for shelters and now had three army field kitchens. He was pleased when General MacArthur, maybe out of West Point kinship, offered to provide an army field hospital to assist Major Don S. Knowlton, MD, of the 6th Marine Reserve Brigade. President Hoover approved these loans and donations but kept it secret, most probably because his conservative friends and associates might disapprove. The most common medical problems were colds, congestion, stomach problems, toothaches, sprains, sore feet, and body vermin. The Marines held sick call twice daily but struggled to keep up with the demand. Some medical and dental associations in the city teamed up and eventually set up a fifty-bed hospital at John Marshall Place Park. Additionally, several local drugstores donated medical supplies.[34]

The BEF accelerated its efforts to lobby members of Congress. Foulkrod's group worked daily to acquire the needed signatures to qualify the bill for further action. Glassford continued to petition governors throughout the country to do everything possible to keep their veterans from coming to Washington, knowing that many of the governors would not do so, fearing that offending veterans might cost them a reelection. Glassford also knew that some members of Congress were encouraging the veterans. What was frustrating was that he knew that if Hoover, Hurley, the DC commissioners, and some local newspapers collectively pressured Congress, the matter would come to an early vote. Earlier, Representative Henry Thomas Rainey had confided to Glassford that to prevent any embarrassment, it was best to let the bill stayed buried in committee until Congress adjourned. In other words, do nothing and hope the problem does not blow up before the August recess. Yet another problem was that more Communist veterans now appeared in the city. Although Glassford was confident that most of the veterans would ignore the newcomers, he feared that some veterans might do much more than that.[35]

The police chief searched for more ways to feed the veterans. An upcoming boxing match, arranged by Major Harvey L. "Heine" Miller, Marine Reserve, would take place in the Washington Auditorium. Miller, a former boxer, agreed to referee the matches. There would be no admission charge, but everyone involved hoped that the fans would donate generously. Meanwhile, Dixie BBQ arrived at the camp with enough pork to feed 1,500 hungry veterans. By now the veterans had taken their measure of Glassford: they knew that he acted rather than talked, was firm but friendly, and could be depended on.[36]

News reporters took their own measure of the chief. He seemed to want nothing for himself, was not beholden to anyone for his job, and was not a game player. When reporters asked for information, he did not put them off. On occasion, while seated on his police motorcycle, he borrowed an envelope and wrote out a statement, which without exception was neat, short, and on point. He was just as fair and open with his officers, and he was pleased that they were up for the challenge ahead. "The police under my command," he remembered, "worked loyally and worked hard. It was a terrific strain upon every man in the force, most of them doing a good job, using tact and patience, maintaining order, enforcing the law, and with an absolute minimum of trouble and arrests."[37]

On June 1 the *Washington Post* published an editorial critical of the BEF. The paper acknowledged that while the veterans had a right to come to Washington, once they had petitioned Congress it would be best for them to leave. If more veterans arrived, the *Post* warned, they would soon overrun the city, giving Chief Glassford justification in ordering them to leave. In the present economy, the newspaper admonished, Congress would be foolish to pass any Bonus Bill and lashed out at the "demagogues" in Congress who led the veterans to believe that the bill would pass if they just "howled" long enough. The *Post*'s conclusion was that the veterans had been "duped."[38]

One who disagreed with that editorial was an exceedingly wealthy woman, well known in Washington and throughout the country. Ironically, her husband, Ned McLean, owned the *Washington Post*. Her name was Evalyn Walsh McLean, and in her jewelry collection she held both the Hope Diamond and the Star of the East Diamond. Her father, Tom Walsh, had emigrated from Ireland in 1869 at age nineteen; an apprentice carpenter, he worked his way to Golden, Colorado, where he labored as a bridge builder for the Colorado Central Railroad. Like many others in Colorado at that time, he contracted gold fever and began mining, suffering boom and bust over the years. When Evalyn was ten years old, her father announced: "Daughter, I've struck it rich." He moved the family to Washington, DC, where Evalyn transitioned from Colorado tomboy to Washington socialite.[39]

On one late evening in early June, Evalyn saw a dusty truck roll by the front of her mansion. Men were standing in the bed of the truck, which had a bed sheet hanging down the side on which was written "BONUS ARMY." She had read news accounts of the Bonus veterans who had arrived, stating that they were going hungry. After midnight she woke her young son, Jock, thinking that it would be good for his education to see these men. She drove through their camp, seeing "plain evidence of hunger in their faces." Some men were lying on the sidewalk using an arm for a pillow, others shuffled around, and a few were trying to bum cigarettes. Then she saw Chief Glassford, whom she knew socially. She approached him and announced that she was going to buy coffee for the men; he offered to go with her and suggested Childs' Restaurant, one of the early restaurant chains, which was still open at 2:00 a.m. When a waiter arrived, McLean asked, "Do you serve sandwiches? I want a thousand. . . . And a thousand packages of cigarettes." She said she needed them right away, adding, "I haven't got a nickel with me, but you can trust me. I am Mrs. McLean." Hearing this, the manager soon joined the conversation. After some discussion Glassford bought the coffee and Mrs. McLean bought the sandwiches and cigarettes.[40]

The following day she went to the Red Cross and spoke with Judge John Barton Payne, the director. He agreed to provide some flour but nothing more, since the situation was not a true emergency. When she learned that the Salvation Army was already helping, she asked the director there what the veterans might need that she could provide. He agreed to investigate, and the next day he visited her at her mansion, saying that the BEF needed a large tent to use as a headquarters. She ordered one sent from Baltimore and then invited Waters to come to her house, where they soon became acquainted. She later provided books, radios, and some sleeping cots for the camps. She learned that some wives and children had now come with their veteran husbands, so she visited the house that Glassford had arranged for them to use. When she saw that the women and children were sleeping on the floors, she filled the house with sleeping cots, and donated to them some clothing belonging to her son and daughter. She remembered one Bonus Army wife saying, "I guess my child can starve in a fifty-dollar [$1,006] dress as well as in her rags."[41]

That night she called Vice President Charles Curtis, whom she knew well. She later wrote, "Charlie Curtis told me that he was calling a secret meeting of senators, and would send a delegation of them to the House to urge immediate action on the Howell Bill, which would provide money to send the bonus army members back to their homes." Mrs. McLean was not the first person to incorrectly assume that the veterans, perhaps having realized that they had erred, would welcome transportation home. On the contrary, they had come on a mission and intended to stick with it. Waters came to her house a few days later, seeking help in feeding the men. With him was his wife, Wilma, who had arrived in Washington likely after a long bus trip. Mrs. McLean allowed Wilma to bathe and then sleep in one of her guest rooms—the one her father had designed for the royal visit of King Leopold II. Mrs. McLean later reflected on how President Harding would have handled the situation. "Harding would have gone among the men and talked with them in such a manner as to make them cheer him and cheer their flag. If Hoover had done that, I think, not even troublemakers in the swarm could have caused any harm."[42]

Figure 1. Colonel William Alexander Glassford, 1853–1931. Ourfamilytree.org. Courtesy of Professor William Parke, Georgetown University.

Figure 2. Allie Seymour Davis. 1858–1937. Courtesy of William Parke.

Figure 3. Wedding of Cora and Pelham Glassford, December 25, 1907. Courtesy of William Parke.

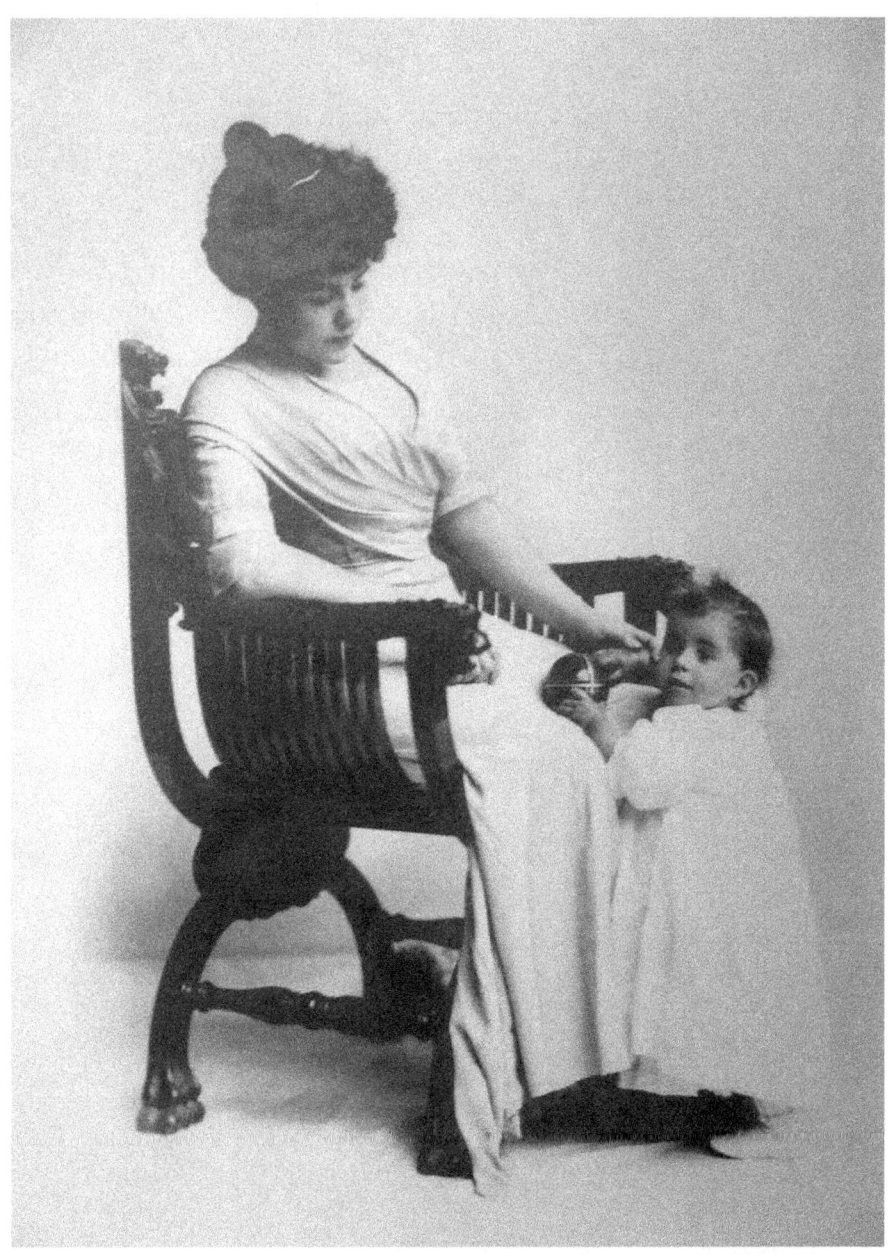

Figure 4. Allie Glassford and baby Pelham. Courtesy of William Parke.

Figure 5. Glassford extended family. From left: Pelham Glassford, Grandmother Elizabeth Davis, Cora Glassford, Col. William Glassford, Allie Glassford, William Glassford II (Pelham's brother). Circa 1910. Courtesy of William Parke.

Figure 6. General John J. Pershing, Pancho Villa, Alvaro Obregon, and others. International Bridge, El Paso, Texas–Juarez, Mexico, 1914, two years before Villa's raid on Columbus, New Mexico. Courtesy of the Aultman Collection, El Paso Public Library, El Paso, Texas. (Image inadvertently reversed).

Figure 7. Pelham with his children. Clockwise from top: Guy Carleton, with tie; Cora Elizabeth "Bettie"; Dorothy Seymour "Dot"; Pelham Davis, Jr, "Pete." Circa 1917. Courtesy of William Parke.

Figure 8. General Pelham Glassford, 1918. Courtesy of William Parke.

Figure 9. French 155 mm Howitzer used by American troops, including Glassford's regiment. US Army Signal Corps photograph, National Photo Company Collection (Library of Congress).

Figure 10. Police Chief Pelham Glassford, Washington, DC, 1931–1932. Harris and Ewing Collection, Library of Congress.

Figure 11. Chief Pelham Glassford with motorcycle, 1931–1932. Harris and Ewing Collection, Library of Congress.

Figure 12. Veterans on freight trains. Underwood and Underwood, Library of Congress.

Figure 13. Bonus Army stages huge demonstration at the Capitol. Underwood and Underwood, Library of Congress.

Figure 14. Bonus Army veterans bathing in the Tidal Basin of the Potomac River, Washington, DC. Underwood and Underwood, Library of Congress.

Figure 15. Police Chief Pelham Glassford inspects Bonus Army Anacostia Camp, Washington, DC, June 1932. Underwood and Underwood, Library of Congress.

Figure 16. Bonus Army veterans in building shelter. Underwood and Underwood, Library of Congress.

Figure 17. Bonus Army veterans pushing truck through mud. Underwood and Underwood, Library of Congress.

Figure 18. Chief Glassford chats with Bonus Army leader Walter Waters and another veteran, 1932. Unknown photographer. Courtesy of William Parke.

Figure 19. General Douglas MacArthur directing the expulsion of the Bonus Army from Washington, DC, 1932. Underwood and Underwood, Library of Congress.

Figure 20. Migratory fieldworker's shack on the edge of a frozen pea field. Imperial Valley, California. Photographer Dorothea Lange. Farm Security Administration, Office of War Information Photograph Collection, Library of Congress.

Figure 21. Migratory fieldworker picking melons in the Imperial Valley, California. Photographer Dorothea Lange. Farm Security Administration, Office of War Information Photograph Collection, Library of Congress.

Figure 22. Watercolor of Lucille Kathryn Painter by Pelham Davis Glassford, 1936. Courtesy of William Parke.

CHAPTER 11

The Anacostia Flats Camp

THE increasing number of arriving veterans quickly taxed all the locations that Glassford had previously identified. If thousands more came, as he now feared, he would need more space. On June 2 he announced his plan to use the Anacostia Flats, a swampy, mosquito-infested, muddy riverbank, as a tent city for 4,000 veterans. The chief had received permission to do so, once again, from Lieutenant Colonel U. S. Grant III. The camp was close to the Capitol but on the other side of the sluggish Anacostia River. The planned tent city would become the main camp of the BEF, except it would never have enough tents. The veterans would have to improvise. Two weeks later, according to Waters, the riverbank resembled a combination picnic ground, tourist camp, trash pile, and Congo village, all splattered onto a mud flat. Subsequently, every junk pile within walking distance became a source of miscellaneous objects and material that could be carried or dragged back to the camp, with car bodies and old bed frames considered good finds. Boards, picket fences, pieces of canvas, and doors were among the items that found new life on the flats. One man located a casket and used it as his bed. Two fire hoses supplied drinking water, the river served as communal bathtub, and the mid-June rains ensured additional misery. The veterans may have been duped, but the daytime flies and the nighttime mosquitoes were delighted. Most veterans found the Anacostia mud to be stickier and stinkier than the mud they had known so intimately in France. The more fortunate veterans were those who had use of tents that the police chief had personally borrowed from the National Guard, which proved more helpful than the regular army.[1]

For the police chief, the mud flat's location provided another benefit: they were on the other side of Anacostia River, linked to the city center by the 11th Street wooden drawbridge. On the Capitol and White House side of the bridge, Glassford would maintain in readiness a small force of officers supplied with tear gas and other weapons, who could immediately raise the drawbridge in an emergency, thus localizing any disorder. Unsure of how many more veterans were coming and of what caliber they might be, Glassford knew he would be remiss if he failed to have an emergency response team ready to confront mass disorder or violence. He hoped for the best but had to plan for the worst. Once his defense plan was in place, he sent a confidential memorandum to the DC commissioners outlining his potential response, the first sentence of which emphasized that no disorder had occurred or was expected, but that his department stood ready to respond to any serious situation. He further recommended that the DC commissioners be prepared to declare an emergency, summon the National Guard, and employ the White Plan to protect the nation's capital from civil disorder. Of interest was that he did not suggest the regular army.[2]

When a news reporter asked the police chief if the veterans were dangerous, he answered, "No, except the danger of gradual rust which attacks those with no occupation and no incentive. They're just middle-aged men out of a job." That same day a Senate subcommittee of two senators reviewed a proposal to provide $75,000 ($1,508,642) to assist transient groups coming into DC to promote legislation, obviously aimed at aiding the veterans. Glassford was pleased with the offer, but his bosses, the DC commissioners, opposed it.[3]

On June 4, not long after sending the confidential memorandum to the DC commissioners, Glassford received a report saying that avowed Communist leaders John T. Pace of Detroit and C. B. Cowan of Cleveland were coming to Washington with some underlings. Pittsburgh police subsequently arrested Cowan just before he tried to slip away, but Pace, a slender, former Marine, bankrupt contractor, and recent convert to the Communist Party, evaded arrest and made his way to the nation's capital. Glassford made a mental note to meet with Pace.[4]

The Communist International (Comintern) in Moscow pressured Earl Browder, secretary general of the American Communist Party, to do more to foment a Communist revolution in the United States, adding that impoverished veterans looked like prime targets. Thus, Pace, the street-level leader of the Workers' Ex-Servicemen's League, was charged with infiltrating the Bonus Army. In the following weeks, despite his best efforts, his minions would have no luck in doing so, and they showed the lumps and bruises to prove it. In the future, when up to 26,000 veterans encamped in Washington, there would never be more than 210 Communist veterans, less than 1 percent of the total. Waters recalled, "Most of the men in the BEF, typically Americans, had never met a 'Red' until their arrival in Washington." To Waters's dismay, considering their small numbers, Pace and his group managed to attract considerable attention from some in the press who seemed anxious to brand the entire BEF as Reds. Even so, Waters's task, as dictated by the police chief, was to keep his non-Communist veterans from assaulting Communist veterans who unwisely came into a Bonus Army camp. Surprisingly, the problem was even smaller than thought. Pace, their leader, knew that the bulk of his Communists were not dedicated Communists or revolutionaries at all, just hungry men in search of food. He also knew that it was probable that a few of his men were undercover federal agents. He calculated that he could trust only about twenty-five.[5]

The Senate subcommittee reviewing the requested appropriation of $75,000 not only disapproved it but also urged the DC commissioners to restrain Chief Glassford, falsely accusing him of announcing the availability of free food and shelter.[6]

In early June, Emanuel Levin, editor of the Communist *Daily Worker* newspaper, along with some associates, opened a storefront at 905 I Street NW. Levin had in mind for Pace and his comrades to stage a "monster demonstration" in downtown Washington on June 8. Glassford learned of it and alerted the BEF that the veterans might be interested in staging a parade the evening before. Waters was ill again but his lieutenants planned the parade for the evening of June 7 along the route specified by Glassford: "Seventeenth and Constitution Avenue to Pennsylvania Avenue and down the great ceremonial boulevard to the Peace Monument at the foot of Capitol Hill." George Alman and Harold Foulkrod led the parade of veterans, who wore shabby clothes but displayed shining medals as they marched along. One veteran wore his Medal of Honor and others wore their Distinguished Service Crosses, Silver Star citations, and the French Croix de Guerre. William A. Butler, an African American, displayed his Distinguished Service Cross and Croix de Guerre as he walked side-by-side with white veterans, an act practically shouting that while the US Army segregated its soldiers, the Bonus Army did not. The veterans paraded according to their states of origin, carrying upright American flags. They included city men from New York, farm workers from Tennessee, coal miners from Pennsylvania, and various others representing at least forty states. About 8,000 veterans marched to the applause of perhaps 100,000 spectators. The veterans held their heads high for another reason: Foulkrod had announced that they were very close to the 145 votes needed to bring the Bonus Bill to a vote.⁷

While the veterans' parade was a huge success, the Communist monster demonstration the next day was a bust. Pace quickly called it off, opting instead for a parade. When only 160 spectators appeared, he cancelled the parade as well. By mid-June it was clear that the Communist effort to use the BEF to stage a revolution had failed. Indeed, Glassford and Waters found themselves spending an increasing amount to time trying to protect the Communists from the other veterans.⁸

June brought with it sweltering temperatures and high humidity that made life in the camps even more miserable, especially in the Anacostia camp, now named "Camp Marks" after police Captain Sidney J. Marks, who had helped the veterans in many ways. Only two meals were served, with breakfast being coffee and bread, and dinner usually mulligan stew ladled into a veteran's repurposed tin can. On rare occasion a third meal was served. Folded newspapers often served as plates, and fingers sometimes substituted for knives, forks, and spoons. Food was never plentiful but burying garbage and digging latrines were daily chores. To complicate billeting issues, by the end of June, 220 women and children had arrived with their male veterans, many families having been evicted from their previous housing. Some women refrained from coming to Washington with their men because they found it easier to receive state charity without them. The number of women and children would grow to 1,100. At his father's suggestion, young Guy Glassford sometimes assisted with the veterans, setting up and running a soup kitchen, getting lumber distributed for shelters, and doing similar tasks. Journalist Mark Sullivan, a friend of the president, would later say that walking among the men one would "recognize instantly their complete harmlessness," adding that a misplaced purse or lost child would be safer among them than in most cities.⁹

Marine Major Knowlton continued to provide medical care, now assisted by four medical officers and six navy corpsmen. More extensive care could be found eleven miles away at Fort Hunt, where a field hospital was in operation. As time went on, a few showers were erected, requiring that a veteran spend the better part of the day in line in hopes of getting a quick and cold shower. The odds were slim, however, with 700 veterans for each shower. Many veterans found that their old friends from the World War—lice—came for a reunion.¹⁰

By now the veterans looked gaunt; even so, they dressed as though they hoped someone might offer them a job any day. Suit pants and coats, long sleeve white shirts with ties, and fedoras with the front brim snapped down were the usual well-worn attire. Those who had been farmers continued to proudly wear their caps and overalls. Every veteran had scuffed shoes or boots with little heel remaining, and some had cardboard stuffed between the soles of their feet and the soles of their shoes. On hot days, they took off their jackets and rolled up their sleeves. Waters affected a new look, something more suitable for a commander: white shirt with bow tie, jodhpurs, tall riding boots, walking stick, and lanyard with whistle. Some accused him of strutting, remarking that the job had gone to his head. He had, indeed, become more demanding, requiring that arriving veterans immediately report to the BEF military police, who would verify that they were documented veterans. What Glassford and Waters had once envisioned—an army-like camp with streets and barracks—was now just another giant "Hooverville," as such encampments around the country were being called. The Washington, DC, Hooverville was one of the largest at 15,000 inhabitants and still growing.[11]

Waters, never especially healthy, collapsed once again and had to step down as BEF commander. In his absence, Glassford met with George Alman, who had assumed the acting-commander position. Surprisingly, Alman admitted to being a Communist, but he had no association with Pace or any other Communist, nor did he ever proselytize. Glassford passed on to Alman an ultimatum from the DC commissioners: The district government intended to provide trucks on June 9, which would take veterans fifty miles in the direction of their home; thereafter, the city would not provide food or shelter. With that, the commissioners thought they had solved the problem—the one they were sure Glassford had created. When Alman advised the chief that even more veterans were due to arrive soon, Glassford replied that he might still be forced to shut down the camps and stop the food supply. Upon hearing that, Waters quickly regained his health and resumed his command position, calling a press conference. He told the assembled news reporters that Kaiser Wilhelm had not been able to run these men out of France in eighteen months, and the DC commissioners would not be able to do it in a week. The veterans, he asserted, were staying until the Bonus Bill passed.[12]

On June 9 Police Captain Marks arrived with the DC trucks to take the veterans fifty miles away from Washington. The captain was not surprised when not even one veteran accepted the fifty-mile offer. Apparently, the DC commissioners,

The Anacostia Flats Camp

who had never visited a camp or talked to a veteran, had somehow concluded that the veterans, who had struggled for weeks to get to Washington, would leave the city only to have trucks dump them fifty miles out of town. The commissioners might cut off their food and shelter, but the veterans were pretty sure that there was nothing to eat fifty miles away either. The men decided that the odds were better by staying in Washington. Disabused of the notion that they had solved Glassford's problem, the DC commissioners contemplated more drastic actions.[13]

The police chief, wary of more Communist veterans coming to town and provoking problems, formed a special unit to maintain surveillance on the headquarters at 905 I Street, which almost everyone now called the Red Camp. He had necessarily transitioned his Special Investigations and Missing Persons Unit into an ad hoc Red Squad, which worked with both the MID and Secret Service. Since the MID seemed to regard every rumor or overheard remark as accurate intelligence, Glassford likely kept close watch on his detectives.[14]

Waters's military police veterans continued to eject suspected Communists from Camp Marks and the other camps, sometimes roughly. For Glassford, there had been few problems with the Communists, but he thought that might change with the arrival of John Pace, who had a reputation as an "energetic field commander." Pace and the Communists occupied a separate vacant building. Glassford, knowing that Pace had participated in the Dearborn riots, decided to meet with him, having heard that he was a "dangerous and fearless leader." Glassford later wrote, "I felt that the better I knew Pace the better I could anticipate his moves. Much to my surprise I found him to be an affable good-natured individual, with a very engaging smile." Glassford inspected their billets and talked with Pace's men but did not sense any great potential for danger. The chief noted, "Most of Pace's men . . . had joined the Workers' Ex-Service Men's League without knowing what it portended, and were much more interested in food than revolution." Thereafter, Glassford visited them frequently. Checking Pace's Detroit police record, the chief saw that Pace had once attempted to chloroform an alderman. When Glassford asked the Communist leader about that, Pace smiled and replied, "You're damn right, that alderman deserved to be chloroformed." Glassford later wrote, "I got to know Pace so well that I was willing to trust him." Sometime later, Glassford went to see Pace and found him and his staff planning to picket the White House. Glassford, miffed, said, "See here Pace. . . . I haven't had a day off since the bonus marchers arrived in this city—I'd like to go away for the weekend; how about an armistice on this picketing business until my return." Pace said, "All right, General, how would noon Monday suit you?" Glassford returned at noon on Monday and found that Pace and his men had paused during the weekend but now had returned to planning the picketing as promised. Glassford, as he had promised, saw to it that the Communist veterans received their share of donated food.[15]

Glassford knew that even though Pace was the field commander, the Communist activities were being orchestrated by the committee in New York, through the office in Washington. Glassford again met with Waters and told him to curb his military police and the other veterans as well. Waters complied but found it no easy task to keep his veterans from thrashing the Communists.[16]

The unexpected appearance of the local health director at the camps fooled no one, nor did his announcement that conditions at the Anacostia Flats camp could easily result in the spread of various contagious diseases, which might necessitate a quarantine. Waters found the health director's report to be exaggerated and clearly aimed at hastening evacuation of the veterans from DC. Nonetheless, the Bonus leader instituted safety measures and appointed veteran Doak E. Carter as the BEF sanitation officer. Many veterans were indeed sick from various ailments, and about 350 lined up each morning for sick call. Waters decided to prohibit visitors from coming to the camps and required all newly arriving veterans to report to Camp Marks first for medical inspection before being registered. Meanwhile, the DC commissioners sent telegrams to the nation's governors urging them to do everything possible to keep their veterans at home, which Glassford had done months earlier with little success. The state governors, now having heard from both Glassford and the DC commissioners, pledged to do what they could, which was probably little. New York governor Franklin Roosevelt, however, offered to send trucks to pick up any New York veterans willing to return.[17]

Glassford redoubled his efforts to relieve congestion in the camps, with Waters agreeing to send all new arrivals to Camp Meigs or Camp Simms instead of Camp Marks. Glassford had also requested use of Fort Hunt and Fort Foote, both in Maryland, but received no answer. Veterans continued to arrive.[18]

On June 8 General Douglas MacArthur gave the commencement address at the University of Pittsburgh, after which he was scheduled to receive an honorary doctorate degree. The liberal faction of the student body staged a protest against his invitation, but MacArthur spoke anyway, saying, in part: "Pacifism and its bedfellow,

Communism, are all about us. In the theaters, newspapers and magazines, pulpits and lecture halls, schools, and colleges, it hangs like a mist before the face of America, organizing the forces of unrest and undermining the morals of the working man. Day by day this canker eats deeper into the body politic." As far as the general and his staff were concerned, it was Communism that threatened the nation, and the BEF had to be involved. Waters could see that the Hoover administration intended to alter public opinion about the new arrivals, and the quickest way to do that was to brand them as Reds. MacArthur's address in Pittsburgh said nothing about the threat of fascism, even though Mussolini had been building his police state since 1927 and Hitler had published *Mein Kampf* in 1925, in which he linked Communism to the "Jewish Conspiracy."[19]

Waters's concern was that the Hoover administration made no attempt to distinguish the thousands of patriotic veterans from the 200 Communist veterans. He feared that some newspapers anxious for a headline might paint the entire BEF red.[20]

Two days later, likely ignited by his own flamboyant oratory, MacArthur ordered his nine geographically based corps commanders to investigate and report to him the names and numbers of Communist organizations passing through their corps areas posing as Bonus Marchers. The corps commander in Baltimore thought it probable that Bonus Marchers were indeed passing through and might cause trouble, but not because of any Communist influence. Another corps commander reported that the Bonus Marchers were not Communists but vehement anti-Communists. Not satisfied with those reports, MacArthur ordered his intelligence division to investigate the BEF leaders in Washington. His officers reported that of the twenty-six men who seemed to be BEF leaders, only three were Communists. General Perry L. Miles, commander of the Washington Military District and the 16th Infantry Brigade at Fort Myer, reported that "the greater part of the bonus marchers have thus far resisted all attempts of the communists to gain control of them, but there are a number of well-known communist leaders here and are claiming credit for the instigation of the march."[21]

From mid-June through mid-July, the camps continued to function as they had, showing no indication of closing. Fortunately, the Washington Hooverville now had "the Hut," courtesy of the Salvation Army, which had been helping the veterans from the beginning. The Hut was an enormous green tent where the veterans could write letters, borrow books, and play cards and checkers. On occasion, the staff passed out magazines, clothing articles, and sacks of tobacco for roll-your-own cigarettes. By now Camp Marks had about 15,000 veterans, wives, and children sharing tents, shacks, and lean-tos. For many of them the camp had become their only home. The recent arrivals sheltered as best they could by using materials dragged from local junkyards, hoping for a modicum of protection and privacy. Soon the camp had its own barbershop, and occasionally some of the more talented veterans staged a vaudeville show. Glassford, as he had done from the beginning, continued to motorcycle through the more than twenty camps, stopping to chat and making himself approachable to anyone with a concern or a suggestion.[22]

Amid the junky flivvers and rusting car bodies, a visitor might see many American flags on poles, rickety tables nailed together as meal tables, all variety of barrels and tubs for hauling water, dugouts with makeshift roofs, an occasional stray dog, seemingly unattended small children running and laughing, still reasonably useable broken chairs, rusty bed frames, car seats, fence sections, and signs with such messages as: "Hard Times Are Still 'Hoovering' Over Us." One veteran brought his burro to the camp. When he asked the animal if it liked Hoover, it shook its head; when he asked it if it favored the Bonus Army, it nodded. Summer rains soon turned the camp into a huge mud bog that attracted even more bugs. Colds, dysentery, and skin eruptions increased.[23]

News reporters—not considered as "visitors"—continued to come to the camps daily. On June 10, John Dos Passos, who earlier had attended the Communist rally in the Washington Auditorium, now toured the main camp while on assignment for the *New York Republic*. He described the veteran camp as a "flimsy encampment of tents and tar-paper and packing-crate shelters beside the muddy Anacostia River in the southeastern part of the city." The racial integration within the BEF was the second-biggest story after the BEF itself, but only a handful of reporters captured it. Roy Wilkins, then a young journalist for the NAACP's *Crisis* magazine, rode the train from New York to Union Station in DC and made his way to the Anacostia camp. He later wrote that the Bonus Marchers had set up a "raggedy camp in the shadow of the Washington Monument." Wilkins took in the incredible scene, later concluding, "For years the US Army had argued that General Jim Crow was its proper commander, but the Bonus Marchers gave lie to the notion that black and white soldiers—ex-soldiers in their case—couldn't live together." Here Wilkins saw "Black men and white men, veterans of the segregated army that had fought in World War I, lined up together for company messes, served together in camp councils, pulled K.P. duty and M.P. duty equally, perspired in sick bays side by side." He stopped to listen when he heard music and then saw an old piano top precariously perched on a wooden crate. There, "a white kid and a black kid took turns playing it. As the black player tickled the keys, the 'St. Louis Blues' trickled its way across the camp." Wilkins returned to New York "feeling a renewed sense of faith in the goodness of poor folks." Thomas Henry, a reporter for the *Washington Evening Star*, noted that in the camp he detected no rebellion, dissension, or crime. On one occasion, when Glassford saw a group of white and black veterans punching and shoving, he pushed into the middle and pulled them apart, saying, "We're all veterans together and there'll be no fighting among veterans."[24]

On June 12 there was some good news: the BEF had a new friend. His name was John Henry Bartlett, former governor of New Hampshire, former president of the US Civil Service Commission, former first assistant postmaster general, a member of both the International Joint (Boundaries) Commission and the National Press Club, and the author of three books. With his receding hairline, wired glasses, dimpled chin, and tailored suits, he was an impressive figure. More important for Glassford and Waters, he was also a generous landowner. He owned thirty-eight acres in southeast Washington, on the other side of the Anacostia River. He thought the acreage large enough to provide camping space for up to 9,000 veterans. He already had 100 tents in place and 100 more promised. Camp Simms would serve as the reception center for the new Camp Bartlett, soon to be established at 23rd Street SE and Alabama Avenue SE, south of the Bartlett property. Glassford, unsuccessful in his efforts to use other camps, was pleased to hear about Camp Bartlett.[25]

On June 13 the *Washington Post* reported an alarming story that workers had found "a bomb" or "dynamite" in an abandoned building associated with the veterans. As it later turned out, it was not a bomb at all, but an inert German grenade, its powder and cap removed, someone's souvenir from the World War. Still, Glassford sensed that the newspapers were turning against the veterans, and with Congress anxious to adjourn, the situation could change and not for the better. He had known for some time that the army was conducting ongoing riot training at Fort Myer. "I saw that this was the beginning of the end, and realized that on the eve of a presidential election politics would reign as soon as Congress adjourned." Cavalry Captain Lucian Truscott, stationed at Fort Myer, recalled, "There was a feeling of unease in official circles, and a restless, troubled feeling throughout the city. No one knew what to expect. . . . Meanwhile, troops were being thoroughly trained in the tactics of riot duty."[26]

Foulkrod's small team of veterans, having worked tirelessly to garner the 145 signatures, had now achieved their goal. The bonus issue would go to a vote; the veterans could do little now but wait outside the Capitol for what they hoped would be good news. Overall, the camps were functioning well enough; the food was adequate, and the medical system was somehow treating the 18,000 veterans, most of whom were at the Anacostia camp.[27]

In mid-June Glassford publicly suggested a proposal to encourage veterans to return home. In exchange for their bonus, each veteran would be granted up to ten acres of federal land, which the veterans could transform into self-supporting farms. The chief saw it as "the means of working out a settlement of this problem, which at present baffles everyone who realizes that the Bonus cannot be paid in cash." By now, Glassford was actively searching for ways to avoid having Hoover call out the army. Other observers suggested another novel way to fund the bonus: since Prohibition was scheduled to end in 1933, why not a penny tax on each bottle of beer sold? Neither attracted interest.[28]

On June 19, according to Waters, several outsiders approached him about creating and leading a national "Khaki Shirts" organization, perhaps a third political party consisting of former soldiers. To Waters it resembled the Fascists of Italy. He wrote that he disapproved of the idea, especially that of a third party, and told the men who had approached him that the BEF needed both Democratic and Republican support. He later denied that he had ever become a member but acknowledged that he had entertained the idea for a time. Three of his men, on their own, joined the Khaki Shirts and operated it independently of the BEF until it died several months later, apparently of no concern to the Hoover administration one way or another. One of Waters's objections to the portentous Khaki Shirts was that it would fracture the Bonus Army into a collection of rival organizations, and he had no interest in broadening the BEF's base to include nonveterans.[29]

Representative Patman, pleased with his list of 145 signatures, once again put forth on the House floor the Bonus Bill. He was even more pleased on June 15 when the House passed the bill by a vote of 211–176. The matter next moved to the Senate. Glassford seemed certain that the Senate would be less amenable to the bill and that problems might erupt in the camps. The next day, a penetrating morning rain beat down on the shacks and tents on the muddy Anacostia Hooverville.[30]

CHAPTER 12

Painting the Bonus Army Red

ON July 16, in anticipation of the Senate's vote on the bill, Waters ordered 6,000 veterans to go to the Capitol Plaza, where they congregated outside the Capitol in small groups. Later, to flex more muscle, he summoned the veterans still at the Anacostia camp, about 13,000, to come to the Capitol as well. The Anacostia veterans gathered and walked toward the 11th Street Bridge on their way to the city center. Police Assistant Superintendent L. I. H. Edwards, in charge of the security force at the bridge, was startled upon seeing the mass of veterans approaching. Misinterpreting the movement as an aggressive action, he ordered his officers to raise the drawbridge. The veterans, stunned at seeing the bridge suddenly rise, had no choice but to stop, not sure what to make of the police action. Traffic in and around the bridge quickly came to a honking standstill. Edwards quickly realized his error and ordered the bridge lowered. The veterans crossed the bridge and walked to the Capitol, not happy with the police officers, who seemed as bewildered as the veterans. In a short while, Glassford, too, was surprised to see thousands of veterans coming his way and ordered his reserve officers forward, just in case. It was a serious miscommunication. Fortunately, Glassford and Waters corrected the situation in time. Neither knew about the bridge raising until one of Waters's men reported it.[1]

Inside the Capitol the speeches continued. As darkness arrived, Waters called for a mobile kitchen to come to the Capitol and serve coffee and stew to the veterans. The US Army Band, which usually played concerts there on Friday summer evenings, reported for duty and began its usual performance, no doubt to the delight of the veterans and everyone else in the area. At 9:30 p.m., Oklahoma Senator Elmer Thomas, a supporter of the veterans, emerged from the Capitol and sought out Waters, whispering the bad news: The Senate had tabled the bill until the following year. Waters, thoroughly disappointed, returned to the plaza and called his men forward and addressed them, telling them the disappointing news that the Bonus Bill had failed, sixty-two to eighteen. He saw it only as a temporary setback and was about to assure his men that they would stay until 1945, when everyone present heard a spontaneous and unified roar from nearly twenty thousand angry, disappointed men, followed by heated words and hesitant movements. It appeared that the men might charge the Capitol at any moment. A tense Waters watched the veterans, unsure what might happen. Standing with him was Elsie Robinson, a syndicated Hearst columnist, but more important, a highly regarded friend of the veterans. She leaned close to Waters and urged him to tell the veterans to sing "America." Waters agreed, shouting, "Comrades, let us show them that we can take it on the chin. Let us show them that we are patriotic Americans. I call on you to sing 'America.'" The attentive army band leader signaled his players to join in with the melody. The veterans obeyed, singing that song and others. By the time the singing had ended, the mood of the veterans had calmed. They grumbled and cursed but slowly made their way back to their camps. A trusted friend, a quick-thinking band leader, and the perfect song staved off what might have been an ugly scene.[2]

The drawbridge incident, followed by the Senate's action, irked the veterans, many of whom concluded that Glassford must have double-crossed them. When Waters demanded an apology for the drawbridge raising, Glassford provided it without hesitation, later writing, "It was a mistake to have done so and the entire police department recognizes it as such." Glassford wisely accepted responsibility for the bridge raising, even though Waters was more responsible for the miscommunication. Had the Bonus commander shared his summons for more veterans with Glassford or any other police commander, the misunderstanding would have been averted. The following day, the *Washington Evening Star* and the *New York Times* praised the BEF for its calm response in the face of very disappointing news.[3]

The Senate had not defeated the bill, however. Had that been the case, the disappointed veterans might have begun drifting away, since most of them knew that there was only the slightest chance that the bill would pass. Instead, the Senate had tabled it. When the bill next saw daylight, it would be the headache of the 1933 seventy-third Congress, whose members would likely curse the senators who had left the mess for the new Congress to clean up. It was no secret that the Senate disfavored the bill and that President Hoover would veto it, but tabling it satisfied no one save the current senators, intent on slithering out of Washington as soon as they adjourned. The president, the DC commissioners, and Glassford would surely have preferred a decision that concluded the matter one way or the other. Waters must have had feelings of leaving Washington, but he had publicly obligated himself several times to stay in Washington until the veterans got their bonus. About a thousand veterans and family members packed their paltry possessions and left, hoping to find something—anything—better somewhere else. The mood of those who stayed worsened. On June 18, to signal that the veterans would not depart, Waters ordered veteran identification cards issued, with the first card going to Patman and the second to Glassford. Each yellow "Official Membership Card" had a space for the bearer's service number and read, "This is to certify that _____ is a member at large of the Bonus Expeditionary Force and is in good standing."[4]

A June 20 *Washington Post* editorial gave all the reasons why Glassford's proposal to grant vacant farmland to the veterans would not work: the land was not suitable for planting, the government was taking it out of cultivation to maintain prices, the cost of the plan would surpass the bonus, and the veterans would continue to agitate for the bonus anyway. After scorning the Chief's proposal, the only idea that the editorial proffered was for the veterans to go home, get relief from their states, and wait to be "reabsorbed" by the industrial system with all the other workers. The editorial neglected a salient point: the plan would send the veterans home, and the land would belong to them indefinitely. A better editorial would have told Glassford what he could do rather than what he could not do.[5]

Waters invited retired Marine Major General (two star) Smedley Darlington Butler to address the veterans. While Glassford thought highly of Butler, having him rally the veterans to stay in Washington was the last thing that the chief needed. Butler was perhaps the most atypical Marine general in the history of the Corps. His biographer, Hans Schmidt, labeled him perfectly as the "Maverick Marine." Butler prided himself on being the enlisted Marine's general, and always considered any situation with their view in mind. He had fought in Cuba, Honduras, Nicaragua, Panama, and Haiti, as well as in Mexico, the Philippines, and China. To his disappointment he had arrived in France too late to have much of a combat command with the Marine brigade. At five feet nine inches and 140 pounds, he was not a big man, but he epitomized the consummate warrior. The Corps was his life, and on occasion one might see part of his eagle-globe-and-anchor tattoo that ran from his throat down to his waist. Smedley, a mediocre student, never attended college, and he had little use for Marine officers who had, especially those from Annapolis. Commissioned as a second lieutenant, he was most at home when he was bushwhacking in the jungles during the so-called banana wars, where he twice earned Medals of Honor and was breveted as a captain while still a teenager. He preferred roughneck and uneducated Marine officers, and disliked office-bound staff officers who garnered attention from high-level Washington politicians. He resented the Navy's control over the Corps when it was exercised by "admirals-without-ships." After thirty-three years in the Corps he concluded, "I spent most of my time being a high-class muscle man for Big Business, for Wall Street and the bankers. In short, I was a racketeer for capitalists." When he addressed the Bonus Army, he assured them that they had as much right to petition Congress as did the US Steel Company, and he urged them to "stick it out," adding that the real "treasury raiders" were the industrialists. He and his son, Smedley Jr., ate with the veterans and spent the night at their camp. In 1935 he published a book titled *War Is a Racket* and went on a speaking tour for the League Against War and Fascism.[6]

While Glassford and Waters disagreed on the wisdom of Butler addressing the veterans, they were in concert on the necessity of negotiating with John Henry Bartlett regarding the establishment of a semi-permanent colony of veterans on his property. It looked promising.[7]

About this time, eight former German soldiers, now naturalized US citizens living in Hudson County, New Jersey, arrived in Washington to visit the Bonus Army veterans, bringing with them 2.5 tons of food. All eight had been on the Western Front for at least three years, had suffered wounds at least twice, and had been decorated. They were intimately familiar with the suffering and sacrifices that the American combat veterans had endured during the war and simply wanted to offer their support.[8]

On June 22 Glassford and various congressional representatives petitioned the railroads to allow BEF members to return home for free, this time riding in passenger cars. Glassford estimated that about half of the BEF had returned home already, mostly in small groups. Waters admitted that the BEF had lost members, but he assured Glassford that more enlistees were on their way. He speculated that the BEF still numbered 19,000. Somewhat confirming this was the report by a police captain that he was still feeding about 15,000. At the very least, perhaps 7,000 had departed the camps. Glassford suggested to Waters that the BEF should self-evacuate, leaving a nucleus to further the bonus cause, perhaps living in semi-permanent quarters on the Bartlett property. Waters insisted that more veterans were on the way.[9]

Glassford had other problems with which to contend. Now that the Senate had tabled the Bonus Bill and Congress was anxious to adjourn, the DC commissioners adopted an aggressive attitude. Those members of Congress who had strongly supported the veterans were due to leave Washington soon, making it easier for the DC commissioners to consider how best to rid the city of what they saw as vile veterans. Crosby publicly criticized Glassford, contending that he had been too soft on the BEF, adding that he should force them out on his own authority. It was clear to Glassford that the DC commissioners, unsure what might happen, adamantly refused to accept responsibility for whatever did happen. Thereafter, Crosby attacked on another front; on June 27 he publicly criticized Glassford of being derelict in his duties because he had failed to enforce an ordinance requiring all occupied buildings to be connected to sewers, likely a noncriminal code violation. Glassford was certain that Crosby wanted him to evict the veterans from the camps while shielding the DC commissioners from its consequences. The chief balked at the sewage complaint, knowing that there were many alleys in the city more unsanitary than the Bonus camps, and a forced eviction could lead to a riot. He invited the commissioners to visit the camps, which brought a refusal. The commissioners, with consent of the president, could have fired Glassford, but they declined, likely preferring to pressure his resignation instead.[10]

The Pennsylvania and B&O Railroads agreed to return veterans to their hometowns for one cent per mile, about a third of the standard rate; other railroads considered doing the same. Glassford hoped that national veteran organizations would donate the funds to pay the veterans' fare. The BEF treasury had $4,000 ($80,461) on the books, and the veteran population seemed stable. Some veterans had left but a similar number of latecomers had arrived. Washingtonians still drove by the Anacostia camp daily, where there was always something worthwhile to see.[11]

Glassford and Waters viewed the BEF situation differently. The police chief urged Waters to encourage the veterans to think about leaving, saying that while the BEF treasury still had a few thousand dollars, it decreased daily. Furthermore, he was hearing complaints about more veterans drinking and panhandling, and the

DC commissioners were increasingly vocal about the sanitation issue in the camps. The chief pointed out that the veterans could better advocate for the bonus issue in their home states, adding that he had sent a list of veterans' names organized by state to Congress, asking those representatives to advocate funding their veterans' train fares. Waters maintained that the BEF still had enough money in their fund and that more veterans were arriving than were leaving. He stressed that the veterans were intent on staying, and when their food finally ran out, he doubted that the federal government would stand by and watch them starve.[12]

As evidence of their commitment to remain in Washington, the veterans published the first issue of *The B.E.F. News*. The June 25 initial run of 25,000 copies sold out in just eight hours. The sales of the paper provided pocket change for those who hawked the papers.[13]

The situation, already stressed, began to unravel. Some of the remaining veterans did choose to drink and panhandle more often and felt less obliged to cooperate with Waters and his staff. On June 25, likely feeling he was losing control over the veterans, Waters resigned—once again—as the BEF commander. He explained his resignation did not mean that he was quitting the BEF, but because thousands of veterans had arrived since he had first become commander, the newer veterans should have the right to elect a commander of their own choosing. Whether it was a power play or an attempt to jump from a sinking ship, it worked. Asked to run for reelection, Waters agreed to do so, but with a formidable caveat that he would have to have the powers of a dictator. Apparently, the veterans, having little to lose, were willing to do that, and on June 29 reelected him. He proceeded to ban all committees and rivals and threatened to build a force of 500 shock troops, seeming to relish in his flirtation with fascism. Ironically, MacArthur and his staff, intent on protecting Washington from a Communist uprising, were inexplicably oblivious to the election of a budding fascist leader in the mold of Mussolini right in their own city. Waters promised to have his military police forcefully remove any veteran who failed to follow his orders.[14]

It did not take long for the chief to hear about the threat, and he wasted no time in reminding Waters that he had very limited power and that he most certainly would not have any shock troops. Waters later wrote that he apologized to Glassford for his outburst, but he contended that thereafter the BEF veterans followed his orders.[15]

Glassford was disappointed when the national veteran organizations declined to fund the $90,000 ($1,810,570) for the veterans to travel home by train.

His next move was to have his motorcycle officers deliver letters to congressional representatives asking them to fund at least 30 percent of the train fare for veterans to their home states. To feed the veterans he opened his wallet once again and bought $775 ($15,589) in food on June 30 and $600 ($12,069) on July 1. The following day, when 500 new veterans arrived from Michigan, he spent another $600 to feed them. Most disturbing for Glassford was that the veteran count was once again increasing. On July 1 his police commanders estimated that 21,000 veterans were still in the city, with more on the way.[16]

In early July an undisclosed New York donor funded Waters's flight to New York to solicit donations by speaking in movie theaters and on the radio. Meanwhile, in Washington, BEF members Harold Foulkrod and Doak Carter handled affairs, including a BEF parade. Glassford assigned fifty police officers to the parade and permitted the BEF military police to assist. Not wanting any of his officers to panic and fire a shot, he instructed them to leave their revolvers in the precincts, which they did. For a police chief, this was highly unusual; while an army general might issue such an order to ensure absolute secrecy for an upcoming surprise attack, a police chief almost never would.[17]

President Hoover urged Congress to provided $100,000 ($2,011,522) on July 7 for train and travel fares to send the veterans and their families home. As an inducement, those who applied received free coffee and doughnuts. The train fare, however, was not a gift but a loan with interest against their 1945 bonus and came with a time limit: if not used by July 15, it was void. Cynics suspected that Hoover and the Republicans wanted the eye-sore tattered veterans out of sight before the presidential campaign season began. About 1,100 veterans returned home. Those who remained in the camps seemed to regard the loan and time limit as a slap in the face. Some veterans accepted the tickets and promptly sold them to locals for cash. A less resentful president and more forgiving Congress might have seized the opportunity to provide the train fare as a gift without the time limit simply to have the veterans depart Washington.[18]

Pace applied for and received a permit for about 200 WESL comrades on July 8 to parade along Pennsylvania Avenue. They reconsidered, however, when they saw about 2,000 BEF members lining the street, some palming brickbats (broken brick pieces) and cobblestones, anxious to break up any Communist demonstration. Pace canceled the march.[19]

A new group of veterans from California arrived in Washington in mid-June. They had begun their journey with 2,600 members, but along the way the group had dwindled to less than 1,000 intrepid travelers. Their leader was a slender former navy sailor and now occasional Hollywood actor named Royal W. Robertson. He was hard to miss; as the result of a broken back, he wore a "steel brace attached to his head with a leather strap under his chin" to hold his head motionless. He made it clear immediately that he had no interest in mixing his Californians with the BEF. He told his men to bed down on the Capitol grounds, where he intended for them to camp until Congress adjourned. Some BEF members joined with Robertson's group, at least for the evening. Waters was not pleased, but he invited Robertson and his men to come to the camps. Robertson replied, "Well, I'm going to wait a few days until I see what it's all about. We came to Washington to petition Congress, not to picnic." Vice President Curtis was outraged when he learned that the men were sleeping on Capitol grounds. Certain that such conduct was illegal, he demanded that the Capitol Police, which had jurisdiction, handle the matter. The following night, the small force of Capitol Police officers turned on the lawn sprinklers, explaining unconvincingly that the sleeping veterans might damage the lawn.[20]

The novelty of a campout on the Capitol grounds attracted some 10,000 vehicles loaded with sightseers who came to watch. Glassford's officers ignored the campers that night, but the chief knew he would have to do something. He told Robertson he would have to keep his men moving if he wanted to be on the Capitol grounds. Robertson formed his veterans in single file, some carrying flags, and had them trudge nonstop around the Capitol grounds. News reporters found the spectacle to be great copy and immediately dubbed it "the death march." It did not take Glassford long to see that Robertson's men were practically sleepwalking. He suggested to the Californian that he split his group and have half picket the Capitol while the other half slept in a nearby vacant lot. Robertson and his men agreed. Waters was clearly irritated that Robertson's headline-grabbing antics put him in the spotlight and the BEF commander in the shadows. Thomas R. Henry, *Washington Evening Star* news reporter, added insult by writing that Robertson seemed to be a real leader, an obvious barb at Waters. Glassford knew that the BEF was loyal to Waters, but he could see that they also supported the actions of Robertson's men. The last thing Glassford needed was to have thousands of BEF members leave the camps and come to the Capitol and join in the death march.[21]

By July 14 Vice President Curtis could no longer contend with the offensive and undignified actions of the veterans continually parading below his window. Earlier that day Glassford had attended the usually routine meeting of the Capitol Police Board, which oversaw the small Capitol Police Department. The board consisted of the vice president, the Senate sergeant-at-arms, the House sergeant-at-arms, the Capitol architect, and Glassford, as chief of the Metropolitan Police. Glassford always found these meetings to be aimless and futile. At this meeting, however, one member of the board demanded that troops be summoned to handle the marching matter. Glassford mollified the request, and the conversation moved on, allowing him to return to police headquarters. The vice president was still in attendance when Glassford left.[22]

A while later the police chief was in his office when Commissioner Crosby telephoned. As Glassford remembered, Crosby was "much flurried and asked why I had called out the Marines to take over command of the Capitol situation." It took a moment for Glassford to realize that after he had left, someone had ordered a detachment of Marines from the Washington Navy Yard to come to the Capitol. Indeed, sixty Marines in full field gear, armed with rifles and bayonets, rode streetcars to the Capitol. There, Robertson's parading veterans, thinking the Marines had arrived for ceremonial reasons, lowered their flags in salute. Crosby asked Glassford to join him in MacArthur's office immediately. The two arrived and were soon joined by Admiral Henry V. Butler Jr., commandant of the Navy Yard. Also attending were Deputy Chief of Staff Van Horn Moseley and General Perry L. Miles, ranking army troop commander in Washington. Butler told them that the vice president had called out the Marines and ordered them to report to Glassford at the Capitol. The police chief and Admiral Butler then went to the Capitol, finding that the Marines had been there for about ten minutes before returning to their barracks. Glassford mumbled that he was "fed up with hysterical meddlers." An ad hoc meeting of the Capitol Police Board determined that the Senate Sergeant-at-Arms David S. Barry had summoned the Marines. "Mr. Barry adopted a very arrogant attitude," Glassford remembered, "asserting he would call all the Marines in the country if he saw fit, and that Vice President Curtis had wanted the Plaza and grounds cleared." Glassford had never seen the usually mild vice president so upset, still insisting that the grounds must be cleared. Glassford knew that doing so was unwise, as members of Congress made speeches there daily, and many BEF members dropped by in support of the Californians. Glassford later wrote, "I believed that if I used force to drive them from the grounds, it would be answered by the entire 20,000 men encamped in and around the city coming to their aid. If that happened the tragedy I was seeking to avert would be precipitated." Facing the vice president, Glassford asked directly, "Is that an order?" Curtis replied that it was not an order, but added, "I give no consent for these violations." Glassford took that as just another suggestion, seeing that even the vice president did not want to accept responsibility. Had it been an order, the police chief would have obeyed, but it was not. The meeting ended with Curtis and Barry still angry. Glassford went to see Connecticut Senator Hiram Bingham III, well known as an academic and explorer before becoming a senator. Glassford explained the situation to Bingham, saying that Curtis still favored using force. Bingham called President Hoover and had a long telephone conversation with him. Glassford heard Bingham say, "The fuss is absurd. There is no occasion for soldiers, and the men wouldn't understand the use of force against them." The conversation continued, but when the Senator finished the call, he said to Glassford, "Herbert Hoover does *not* want force used on the Capitol grounds."[23]

By July 15, the deadline date for the president's travel loan, only 1,736 veterans had applied for funds and of that number, only 1,545 had departed. Counting new arrivals, including Robertson's men, the number of veterans had increased. The president, anxious to be rid of the BEF, extended the deadline to July 25.[24]

The next day, July 16, was the last day of the 1932 congressional session. Robertson suspended the death march. Waters, over the course of the day, dispatched his veterans to the Capitol for a mass demonstration, totaling 5,000 in the morning, 10,000 by noon, and 17,000 by the afternoon. When Glassford arrived on his blue police motorcycle, the veterans cheered. Waters arrived a while later and saw that the police had cordoned off the entire Capitol building, leaving little space for any demonstration. Previously, Waters intended to stage a parade, but he had acquiesced to Glassford's suggestion to cancel it after the chief reminded him that his officers were tired from having worked day and night for a week. Waters still wanted a demonstration and came up with something very different. Facing the Capitol, he positioned himself about ten feet in front of his 17,000 men. Then, without uttering a word, he turned and raised his arm and started trotting toward the Capitol with four lieutenants, forming something of a spearhead. He heard a roar behind him as his men followed at quickened pace, soon trotting. Waters passed through the police lines and jumped on top of a platform at mid-Plaza. Then he raised his arms again and signaled for his men to stop, aided by his military police at the front. It was not the demonstration that Waters had originally wanted, but its message was clear: a reminder to Glassford and his officers, the DC commissioners, the representatives and senators, and the president that, at his command, Waters could unleash a force of thousands of angry veterans.[25]

Glassford stood stunned. Confounded by the onrush of veterans, he pointed at Waters and shouted to his officers to go after him. In something of a comedy of errors, Glassford arrested, released, re-arrested, and re-released Waters as he sought to find out what Waters was doing. The potential for a riot was at hand. A quick-witted nurse, Lauretta D'Arsanis, dressed in her blue and white uniform and well known for her assistance to BEF families, snatched a megaphone from someone and shouted for the veterans to sing "America." The veterans did as she commanded, singing not only that song but also several others. Thus, once again, another friend of the Bonus Army used the same song and averted a riot. Meanwhile, Glassford and Waters negotiated an agreement: Waters and his veterans could occupy the middle stairway of the Capitol but had to leave the side stairways open. During the confusion, Glassford, the BEF's "friendly enemy," had come close to losing their support. Then, sometime before 10:00 p.m., about fifty Communist veterans attempted to rush the White House. Glassford had 400 police officers in place and quickly forced them back and dispersed them. Three were arrested without incident, but one vigorously resisted, requiring Glassford and five officers to wrestle him to the ground. Veteran Nathan "Shorty" Kalb had only one arm, but it took twelve police arms to take him down and hold him.[26]

For months, Waters had been the leader of his Portland contingent as well as the thousands of veterans who had arrived thereafter; Robertson was the come-lately but visible leader with his band of recently arrived Californians. Each led his group but declined to associate with the other.[27]

It was customary for the president to visit the Capitol for the annual adjournment of Congress. Hoover waited in the Lincoln Study, his car and a dozen motorcycle officers standing by, for the request to come to the Capitol, but no call came. Finally, at about 10:30 p.m. that evening, the president sent a message that he would not be observing the customary closing of Congress. At 11:26 p.m. Congress adjourned, and most of its members quickly slipped out the back doors or passed through the underground tunnels, hoping to avoid the veterans. The Bonus Army had altered the routine of the president and Congress, but nothing more.[28]

CHAPTER 13

Pretext for Expulsion

TWO days before Congress adjourned, a confidential meeting took place in General MacArthur's office, resulting in a change in the stance of the Hoover administration regarding the BEF. Glassford had purposely not been notified of the meeting, and he would be excluded from such meetings in the future. Thus, he was unaware that the Hoover administration, the War Department, and the DC commissioners had conspired to adopt a hostile approach in dealing with the veterans. With the summer recess and the departures of the representatives and senators who supported the veterans, the Hoover administration decided that it was time to cleanse the city of the troublesome veterans and their grimy camps. Since the first veterans had arrived, the White House had remained silent, never publicly uttering a word, good or bad, about the thousands of down and out veterans. Now the administration was ready to act.[1]

On July 17 Waters issued a bulletin to his veterans, stating that with Congress adjourned, there was nothing more that could be done. He added that transportation was still available, and no veteran would be criticized for leaving. Many did, but thousands remained. Waters later wrote that had the Hoover administration simply permitted the ongoing dissolution for a few more weeks, the BEF would have peacefully disintegrated.[2]

Many veterans decided that it was time to leave. On July 16 the count had been 22,374, but by July 26 it was down to 14,925, with an average of 75 departures daily. Glassford continued to urge the veterans to return to their homes. Some did, but others stayed, no longer having homes to go to. They reasoned that a Hooverville in Washington was closer than a Hooverville someplace else. The veterans disliked the Hoover administration as much as they disliked the Communists, but they maintained their allegiance to their country and never stopped loving America. Waters relaxed somewhat, no longer anticipating expulsion since his army was shrinking. He did not know that the president, the DC commissioners, and the army had neither the patience nor the inclination to tolerate a gradual and peaceful dissolution of the veterans. Riot training continued at Fort Myer.[3]

MacArthur read some secret intelligence reports that indicated that Communists were intent on bringing violence to the Washington streets. The War Department could be depended on to believe any negative information relative to Communists, especially Deputy Chief of Staff George Van Horn Moseley. MacArthur and Moseley likely were not aware of the wisdom of author Arthur Conan Doyle, who said, "It is a capital mistake to theorize before one has data. Insensibly one begins to twist facts to suit theories, instead of theories to suit facts."[4]

Until recently the DC commissioners had disfavored but nonetheless tolerated Glassford's handling of the BEF. Now they searched for a pretext to expel the veterans, one with which Glassford could not argue. On July 20, Ferry K. Heath, assistant secretary of the Treasury, sent letters to Crosby, Glassford, and a demolition company stating that it was now imperative that the old Ford building and the area of Pennsylvania Avenue from Third to Fourth Streets be free of veterans by July 25 so that demolition could begin. The demolition had been expected for some time, but now it seemed suspiciously rushed. The next day the DC commissioners advanced the eviction date earlier to July 22, and now asserted that all buildings housing veterans had to be clear by July 24. Camp Meigs, Camp Simms, and Camp Marks at Anacostia, however, had until August 4 before needing to be cleared. At this point, the day-to-day control of the Bonus Army passed from Glassford's hands to those of the federal government. Glassford argued but was unable to change anyone's mind. But, although he was not an attorney, his reading of the eviction order caused him to suspect that it was not legal. He carried the order to the DC Corporation Council, who agreed that the order was legally unenforceable. The next day Glassford informed Waters that a revised eviction order would be coming soon. Waters replied that the veterans would not evacuate unless the government found other shelter for them. As historian Donald Lisio observes, "Most embarrassing was the ease with which the local police chief had exposed the lack of careful planning and coordination of an important and possibly dangerous undertaking."[5]

About 800 veterans and more than 1,000 women and children associated with the veterans lived in some of the crumbling buildings slated for immediate evacuation. The reason given for the eviction was that workers on contract were standing by to demolish these buildings to make way for a new building. How all the other encampments came under that umbrella was puzzling. Some veterans had managed to get a closer look at the building plans, which indicated that the demolition of the Ford building was to make way for a park, not a new building. Judge Bartlett later wrote that the veterans would not have resisted moving to other nearby buildings, or even to his property. He and others feared that this was aimed at forcing an evacuation.[6]

What had once been a highpoint assemblage of about 26,000 veterans was now down to less than 10,000, with many leaving daily. In the planning stage was an opportunity to move all the remaining veterans to Camp Bartlett within two weeks. Glassford estimated that about 1,000 veterans now departed daily, and he urged Waters to encourage those veterans who could depart to do so immediately. Meanwhile, the chief and Bonus leader rushed negotiations with Judge Bartlett. Now might have been the time for President Hoover to recall that the American people had once thought of him as "the Great Humanitarian."[7]

The DC commissioners quickly recruited Corporation Counsel Vernon L. West to untie and retie the legal knots, necessitating that the commissioners delay the evacuation until July 28. To soften the sudden eviction, the president signed a bill allowing some veterans to borrow up to 50 percent of their bonus at 3.5 percent interest. As a result of the recent transportation bill, the Veterans Bureau reported that 2,800 veterans had now departed by rail and 600 had left in other ways. Robertson, perhaps predicting the outcome better than the others, suggested to his Californians that they return home. When they declined to follow, he simply climbed into a waiting car and drove away. Glassford's latest detailed police count was 11,698 remaining in twenty-four camps. If 1,000 left each day, all the veterans would be gone within twelve days. Glassford later wrote, "There was no reason whatsoever for demanding the evacuation of the Pennsylvania Avenue camps on the 28th. It is utterly untrue that the lots were needed to enable the Government to proceed with new construction." Additionally, Herbert S. Ward, pro bono attorney for the BEF, determined that while the federal government intended to create a park at the location, Congress had not yet set aside any funding to do so; furthermore, two businesses in the building, an auto garage and an undertaking parlor, had secured injunctions preventing destruction of the buildings. Needing to feed the veterans and their families, Glassford once again pulled out his wallet and spent another $238 ($4,787) for food. Cora, likely in Washington for a visit, was pressed into service as well. Her irritation showing, she later wrote, "I personally purchased and delivered to their commissary nearly a thousand dollars' worth of foods paid for by the [Chief] and there was a great deal more purchased by him but childishly never admitted even at home."[8]

Waters met with Glassford and asked him how the police would go about evicting anyone who refused to leave. Glassford said that his officers would arrest them one by one and take them to the DC jail. Waters, feigning relief, said in that case, his worries about feeding and housing the men were over.[9]

On July 25 Pace and his Communist veterans again attempted to rush the White House, but a phalanx of police pushed them back with batons. Glassford and a squad of motorcycle officers roared up and joined in, sending the Communists scampering. Hoover, shocked at Pace's attempt to rush the White House, began to agree with his army chief of staff. While the number of Communist veterans was still about 200, MacArthur, fueled by Army Intelligence reports, somehow concluded that the "Reds" had now permeated the BEF and were likely making the key decisions. That, of course, was exactly what Pace and the New York Communists hoped that the Hoover administration would believe. MacArthur sent for two combat vehicles, a truck-mounted 75 mm gun with 100 shrapnel rounds, and an armored car equipped with .30 and .50 caliber machine guns and ammunition. The day-to-day decision making relative to the BEF now shifted from the DC commissioners to the army; in particular, Chief of Staff MacArthur and his deputy, General George Van Horn Mosley.[10]

Douglas MacArthur had been born in 1880 in Little Rock, Arkansas, the son of an army general. Young MacArthur graduated from West Point in 1903 as the top cadet in his class, then served in the Engineer Branch for ten years until being appointed to the General Staff, where he served four years. During the World War he was a member of the 42nd "Rainbow" Division, quickly becoming the division commander. His courage under fire was legendary, earning him high decorations. Not satisfied that his actions alone made him stand out, he adopted something of a personal uniform, especially notable for his billed cap with its grommet stiffener removed, which, ironically, gave him the appearance of a German officer. Historian John S. D. Eisenhower writes, "MacArthur saw himself as a man of destiny; he never hesitated to take risks, serious risks, but insured that he was noticed in the process." In the 1920s he became the youngest-ever superintendent of West Point, where he pushed through substantial and needed reforms, and soon he became the youngest-ever chief of staff, commanding the entire army. He continued to have the adoration of West Point cadets and the Officer Corps.[11]

George Van Horn Moseley was born in Evanston, Illinois, in September 1874. He always wore a stern look on his face, and if he ever smiled, no photographer managed to capture it. He graduated from West Point in 1899, thirty-seventh in a class of seventy-two. As a second lieutenant, he joined the 9th Cavalry Regiment (Colored), one of the original Buffalo Soldier units, and later transferred to the Field Artillery. During the World War he became chief of staff of the 7th "Hourglass" Division, and after the war he commanded the 1st Cavalry Division. From 1931 to 1933 he served under MacArthur as his deputy chief of staff. Moseley hated Jews, African Americans, and immigrants, growing increasingly vocal about it, telling his superior that the integration of white and black veterans in the BEF was proof that Negro and Jewish Communists were preparing for a revolt. Regarded as one of MacArthur's close friends and a favorite of Secretary of War Patrick Hurley, Moseley once wrote to a friend complaining that "Americans carefully bred their horses, cattle, dogs, and hogs, but allowed humans to absorb objectional blood."[12]

Waters, fearful of an army callout, knew that hundreds of women and children were sheltered in the building scheduled for eviction. He contacted the Red Cross for assistance. Judge John Barton Payne, Red Cross director, could not help him, but he arranged for Waters to meet with Secretary of War Hurley and General MacArthur, which must have come as a complete surprise to Waters. At the meeting with the two generals, former Sergeant Waters explained that the veterans were now leaving the camps on their own every day and that he and Chief Glassford were negotiating with John Bartlett to use "Camp Bartlett." To make it work, Waters was hoping that the War Department might supply tents to temporarily house the veterans and family members. When Waters asked the secretary of war if any tents were available, Hurley looked to MacArthur and asked him. MacArthur, pacing back and forth as was his habit, bluntly said, "No." Hurley then made it clear that their intention was to get the BEF out of Washington, and at the first sign of disorder or bloodshed they would summon the army. Surprisingly, the meeting continued for some time, MacArthur pacing throughout. Waters next tried to distance his veterans from the Communist veterans, saying that his men had nothing to do with them.

Hurley curtly answered that he knew that because they had infiltrators in the various groups, but that the BEF had been too orderly. Too orderly? Waters must have wondered at that comment, but then he turned his attention to whether the BEF would be allowed to gather their possessions and march out of the city. MacArthur assured him that that would be the case. Waters said he was anxious to disintegrate the BEF gradually and orderly. Hurley agreed to work with him to that end. Waters departed, thanking them for their assistance. Still, he had misgivings. Hidden between the lines of Hurley's comments, Waters suspected, was the administration's necessity for an "incident" that would allow for the use of federal troops.[13]

On July 27 Waters met with his 182 supervisors and commanders. As blunt as he could be, he told them what he feared was about to happen and urged them to pass it on to their veterans. He said he hoped to evacuate Pennsylvania Avenue slowly and peacefully but that all veterans in the other camps should be kept away from Pennsylvania Avenue. That afternoon, Waters sent Doak Carter to meet with John Bartlett, saying that an unidentified donor—likely Evalyn Walsh McLean—had agreed to supply money for lumber to build barracks at Camp Bartlett. Bartlett said he agreed but only if Glassford concurred, adding that he also had to be sure that the president would not forbid it. The veteran count was now down to about 7,000, easily small enough to fit into Camp Bartlett.[14]

The White House, now in charge, confided to the DC commissioners that mandatory evacuations would begin the following morning, July 28. Since Glassford's officers would provide security for the evictions, the DC commissioners had no choice but to tell the chief about the plan but waited until the last moment to do so, and then ordered him not to reveal it to Waters. No doubt angered, Glassford could have resigned immediately or simply disobeyed the order. More likely was that he knew that if he remained in the process, he could slow the pace of the commissioners. But he also had some concerns that Waters, given enough time and cause, might feel justified in unleashing his thousands of veterans. Hoping to avoid military intervention, Glassford focused on the Bartlett property. Betting on an inside straight, it appears he endeavored to get Waters and the commissioners in the same room to discuss moving the veterans to the Bartlett property. In essence, the chief needed Waters, in person, to sell the Camp Bartlett opportunity to the DC commissioners. The commissioners, aware of the evictions planned for the following day, had very little interest in meeting with Waters. Apparently, to get Waters to the district building, Glassford sent for him, saying that the commissioners wanted to discuss plans for the eviction, which was not true. Waters, having met with Hurley and MacArthur, was puzzled but came to the commissioners' office anyway. It did not take long for Waters to conclude that the Hoover administration and the DC commissioners were not in sync. He was ready to meet with the commissioners, but Glassford then said that they refused to meet with him in person, necessitating that Glassford carry messages back and forth. Waters later mused, "It isn't every ex-sergeant that can have an ex-general for messenger boy." Following this shuttle diplomacy, Waters departed thinking that he and the DC commissioners had agreed that Waters would have until August 1 to evacuate all the veterans and that he would start the following morning by evacuating 200 by early evening and 40 or more per day thereafter, until they were all out. In fact, the commissioners, and now Glassford, knew of the surprise eviction scheduled for the following morning.[15]

    Glassford's gamble had failed. He apparently had hoped that Waters would have been able to persuade the commissioners to be patient. Had that happened, Glassford likely thought the DC commissioners might be able to persuade the White House to delay the evictions. It was uncharacteristically naive of the police chief to think so. He later wrote, "Waters was more than willing to be reasonable. The DC commissioners were not. It was evident to me that they were being driven by pressure from higher up. The whole thing had an ugly aspect. The administration was forcing the issue, making a surprise attack." Waters would later blame Glassford for not sharing the plan with him and, as a result, failing the veterans. Glassford trusted Waters, but not completely; the chief had already seen what Waters could do by simply waving an arm. Even so, Waters would prove more trustworthy than either the DC commissioners or the Hoover administration.[16]

July 28, 1932, eviction day, began warm and calm. At 9:00 a.m. Bartlett telephoned Glassford, wanting to verify that he approved of the Camp Bartlett arrangement. At the time Glassford was giving instructions to 100 police officers who would provide security for the federal agents, who—technically—would conduct the eviction. The chief returned Bartlett's telephone call, saying that he was very pleased with the Camp Bartlett plan. At about 9:15 a.m., not yet finished with his briefing, Glassford dispatched his personal secretary, Aldace Walker, to the evacuation site to locate Waters. Waters arrived at about 9:30 a.m., wearing his usual uniform of riding boots and jodhpurs, fully prepared to evacuate 200 occupants that day, just as he had pledged to do during the previous day's negotiation. Although it promised to be a hot and sticky day, he urged the building occupants, now somewhere between 1,100 and 1,600, to pack and leave, saying that it was the best thing to do, especially since he now had a donor who would pay for building materials at Camp Bartlett. He knew that accomplishing the evacuation in four days—by August 1—would be difficult if not impossible, but he asked the building occupants to cooperate anyway. They then voted not to evacuate; they were staying. At about 9:50 a.m. Aldace Walker pushed his way through the crowd and located Waters and gave him a copy of the Treasury order, which, much to Water's shock, mandated total evacuation of the building by 10:00 a.m. that day. Looking at his watch, the BEF commander saw that he had just ten minutes to clear everyone—veterans and family members—out. Momentarily puzzled, he quickly turned livid. Loud, angry, and bitter, he announced, "There you are! You're double-crossed. I'm double-crossed."[17]

Needing to finish his briefing, Glassford had had to send Aldace Walker to the scene to give the bad news to Waters before he heard it from the Treasury agents. Glassford and his officers arrived at the scene a few minutes before 10:00 a.m., just ahead of Assistant District Attorney John Fihelly and his six Treasury agents. At 10:05 Waters was still urging the building occupants to leave, and by 11:10, police officers were ushering the men and families out of the building, which formerly had been the old National Guard armory. By 11:50 a.m. the last veteran was out. At about that time Attorney General William D. Mitchell issued a formal order requiring all veterans to clear all government property buildings that they had been inhabiting. At the eviction scene, the veterans grumbled and cursed but offered only minor resistance. After nearly two hours, the first phase of the eviction was complete. Thus far, the process had gone relatively well. Glassford called a short break, intending to resume after lunch and complete the eviction by day's end. At about noon, despite Waters's orders to all veterans to remain at their assigned camps, thousands of veterans streamed to the site, likely having heard about the surprise eviction. The new arrivals joined with the veterans just evicted. Spectators came as well, anxious to see what might happen. By then police officers had the entire eviction area roped off. Everyone milled around but no problems occurred.[18]

Then, quite suddenly, the situation changed. At about 12:10 p.m. a small group of veterans carrying an American flag—Communists, according to

Waters—arrived on the scene, followed by twenty to forty others, with still another hundred gathered in the background. The group then moved toward the evacuated building, intending to reoccupy it. An officer grabbed the flag, leading to a scuffle. A second officer struck the veteran with his baton but then another veteran wrested the baton away. As other officers rushed to the disturbance, Communist veterans in the rear hurled brickbats at the officers, who responded by swinging their batons. Glassford rushed into the middle of the melee, ignoring the two brickbats that struck him on the shoulder and his leather puttee. One of the Communists, Bernard McCoy, a Navy veteran from Chicago, tore Glassford's badge from his uniform, but two non-Communist veterans quickly knocked McCoy down and retrieved the badge. Police maintained the upper hand throughout the disturbance and arrested several of the attackers, while the others took flight. Glassford later wrote, "I stepped between the lines, held up my hands, and called for a cessation of the fight. This game is getting dangerous, and it's getting time for lunch." Paul Y. Anderson, a writer for *The Nation* magazine, was at the scene. He was about forty feet away and concluded that the situation looked like a dreadful mess, but the officers had kept their wits and refrained from shooting. According to Anderson, Glassford had rushed into the middle of the disturbance and managed to stop the fighting within seconds. Anderson later wrote that within two minutes the veterans were cheering Glassford. But brickbats thrown by the attackers had injured five officers, one of whom suffered a skull fracture. No other serious injuries occurred during the incident, which lasted all of five minutes, or six minutes by Waters's count. By 12:15 p.m. it was over. The Hoover administration and the DC commissioners quickly labeled the incident a "riot." Waters said that about twenty police officers went after forty veterans, most of whom were Reds. Glassford later wrote, "Relatively few veterans had participated. Not more than fifty." He added, "No stores had been broken into. There had been no depravations, and none were imminent." Thousands of Washingtonians were quietly watching the events, many circulating among the veterans. No one, except those in high authority, sensed any danger to the city or to the institutions of the country."[19]

Glassford and Waters conferred in a nearby garage, shadowed by a few news reporters. Glassford thought it was serious and asked Waters what he thought about it. Waters was unsure and asked the chief what he thought. Glassford answered, "If I'm not asked to increase the area of evacuation, I'm satisfied that there will be no more trouble." Waters said he agreed but added that if there were another surprise like the Treasury order this morning, he would not be able to control the veterans. One of the news reporters overheard Waters's comment and immediately phoned in a story saying that the Bonus Army commander had admitted losing control of his men.[20]

Commissioner Crosby had secretly inserted his "personal aide" as a confidential informant—spy—into the evacuation team. Lieutenant Ira E. Keck, who had been "assigned by the commissioners as their special agent at the site," slipped away just after the melee and reported to Crosby and Reichelderfer that a "riot" had occurred and that "several thousand" veterans from the other camps had attacked the police with "bricks, clubs, iron bars, concrete, and similar items." He added that he and Inspectors Brown and Edwards thought the situation was beyond police control and that federal troops were needed. Crosby sent Keck back to the site to tell Glassford that the DC commissioners wanted to see him. The commissioners now had the *casus belli* they needed.[21]

Keck's report to the commissioners was alarming, to say the least, and would be greatly at odds with the recollections of Glassford, Waters, and journalist Anderson, a neutral observer. While Keck had said thousands of veterans had attacked the police, Anderson said he saw the veterans cheering Glassford. Waters, who was at the scene, later described the six-minute battle between twenty officers and forty Communist veterans, adding, "That was the only disturbance that occurred that day." Unfortunately, the commissioners had heard Keck's report first. It is highly likely that some sort of personal relationship—driver and police aide to the commissioner—existed between Crosby and Keck, which may have influenced Keck to provide the description that he suspected Crosby wanted. The other possibility is that Keck had had very limited contact with the veterans and had panicked unnecessarily.[22]

At 1:00 p.m., Glassford, Aldace Walker, and Keck arrived at the DC commissioners' offices. Glassford most probably brought Walker, his secretary, along as a witness. Judging from the statements issued following the meeting, one might conclude that the participants had attended different meetings. After giving his report to the commissioners, Glassford told gathered news reporters that he had told the DC commissioners that, in his judgement, his police could hold the present line, and he strongly advised against any further evacuation that day. Further, he opposed calling federal troops, but if the DC commissioners chose to disregard his advice and order him to extend the evacuation area, then troops would be necessary, adding that the DC commissioners had not ordered him to extend the evacuation area at the meeting. He acknowledged that he had said that he did not want to go against the "seething mob" again today. In their version of the meeting, the DC commissioners said that Glassford had repeated Waters's statement of losing control over his men and that Glassford said he wanted federal troops to standby in readiness. While it is conceivable that the DC commissioners might not have heard the conditional "if" in Glassford's message, it defies belief that they failed to hear him assert his officers could handle the situation and he did not want federal troops at this time. Most probably, the commissioners had already made up their minds, having first heard Keck's alarmist description.[23]

At about 1:15 p.m., and without notifying Glassford of such, the DC commissioners sent the following message to the White House:

> It is the opinion of the major and superintendent of police [Glassford], in which the District of Columbia commissioners concur, that it will be impossible for the Police Department to maintain law and order except by the free use of firearms, which will make the situation a dangerous one; it is believed, however, that the presence of federal troops in some number will obviate the seriousness of the situation and result in far less violence and bloodshed.[24]

How the DC commissioners' use of the language "except by the free use of firearms" made its way into the message is inexplicable, but it achieved an immediate response from the White House.

Glassford returned to the evacuation scene, where some 4,000 veterans and hundreds of spectators were now standing around talking. Inspector Edwards had already called for all available officers—as a precaution—and now had more than 400 officers at the scene. There was no disturbance occurring, and no "riot" in progress; there were thousands of people present, but no trouble. Commissioners Reichelderfer and Crosby showed up at the scene unexpectedly, their first-ever visit to any Bonus camp. Since the commissioners had already called for federal assistance, primarily based on Keck's obsequious report, there would seem to be little necessity for their presence there. Perhaps their virginal visit to a Bonus camp was to dispel any doubts that their request had been premature. After a few minutes the commissioners left, not telling Glassford that they had already called for federal assistance. Glassford later wrote, "It seems incredible that Crosby should not have informed me of the situation if he knew of it himself."[25]

Until a few days before, Glassford had held a firm grasp on the situation. He had visited the camps daily for two months and knew many of the veterans by name; he was fully aware of the limited Communist threat and understood how best to contain it; he was confident that his officers could handle the situation. He returned to the evacuation site under the assumption that the DC commissioners understood his message. That was true, but it appears that the commissioners chose to disregard it. Another message from the DC commissioners to the president stated: "This morning officials of the Treasury Department seeking to clear certain areas in which there were numerous members of the Bonus Marchers, met with resistance. They called upon the Metropolitan Police for assistance and a serious riot occurred. Several members of the Police were injured." President Hoover had Secretary Hurley order the War Department to mobilize the army.[26]

Crosby telephoned MacArthur, telling him that Glassford had said "he had cleared a small area and was entirely unable to evict the mob from the federal property which they were holding," and that the police chief "requested that troops should be held in immediate readiness for action." To MacArthur, it must have sounded like a distress call from General Custer. At 1:50 p.m. MacArthur called General Miles and told him to dispatch troops to the Ellipse, south of the White House.[27]

CHAPTER 14

No Good Deed Goes Unpunished

GLASSFORD remained at the eviction scene, which was calm, unaware of the actions taken by the DC commissioners and the Hoover administration. At about 1:45 p.m. Glassford heard a loud disturbance of some sort at the front of the Ford building, about fifty yards away. The chief, followed by Officers George W. Shinault, Miles Znamenacek, and a few others, raced up the exposed exterior concrete stairway of a nearby crumbling building to get a better view of the distant disturbance. What happened next is unclear.[1]

It may be that a scuffle on the stairway broke out between officers and veterans, causing an officer behind Glassford to lose his footing, whereupon he likely panicked and fired into a group of veterans behind him.[2]

Another description is that as Glassford and the two officers ascended the steps, someone yelled, "Let's get him," and then a veteran shoved the two officers aside. A thrown brick struck Znamenacek, and someone grabbed Shinault's baton and struck him with it. Then a veteran on a higher floor of the building threw down a garbage can, which landed near Znamenacek, followed by Shinault drawing his revolver and firing twice.[3]

Waters's version is that he was about twenty feet from the shooting and some veterans, curious about the nearby disturbance, and followed Glassford and his officers up the stairs, resulting in some pushing and crowding. Waters said Shinault, perhaps alarmed by the closeness of the following veterans, and the last officer in the police line, turned around with his gun in his hand and fired at the veterans behind him.[4]

Glassford looked down just as Shinault fired his gun and bellowed, "Stop the shooting!" ordering the officer to put away his gun. Other officers were by then running up the stairway with their guns drawn. Shinault, dazed, raised his gun, the barrel of which was momentarily pointed toward Glassford, who darted behind a pillar. A follow-up investigation determined that both Shinault and Znamenacek had fired shots.[5]

In an instant, the situation had changed. No one moved. No one spoke. John Bartlett had been at the scene since noon when he heard the gunfire: "A breathless silence of horror, as in the presence of death, seemed to depress the thousands of bystanders, for it was whispered through the crowd that two veterans had been killed." Bartlett spoke with some of the veterans, who were mostly sad and discouraged, though some were angry. Waters noted that the huge crowd had become almost pin-drop quiet. No one shouted or hurled brickbats or rioted. Just dead silence.[6]

Veteran William Hushka, thirty-five, from Chicago, died within seconds. Veteran Eric Carlson, age thirty-eight, from Oakland, died on August 2. An inquest later determined that Shinault had shot Hushka and Znamenacek had shot Carlson. Ambulances took three other seriously injured officers to the hospital. The identities of the veterans involved in the original disturbance, and the identities of the other veterans who climbed the stairway, is not recorded, nor is the reason for their involvement. It is possible that some of the veterans were Communists trying to create chaos, but that seems unlikely as the Communists had fled the scene earlier. More likely is that the surprise eviction had frustrated and angered some of the displaced veterans, who lashed out at the police. Waters called the police shooting of the veterans murder, but a later coroner's inquest, after a five-minute deliberation, ruled the shootings self-defense by both officers.[7]

Glassford took stock of the situation. News reporters at the scene wanted a statement. He told them that the trouble began when he was commanded to enforce an order he knew was unnecessary. He added that given a few hours the occupants would have been evacuated peacefully. At about 2:00 p.m. Glassford was still considering the impact of the shooting when a news reporter, Raymond P. Brandt of the Washington bureau of the *St. Louis Post-Dispatch*, appeared and informed Glassford that President Hoover had called out federal troops, some of whom were at or on their way to the Ellipse, about a quarter mile south of the White House. Glassford was incredulous and livid: he had heard this from a news reporter! Not the DC commissioners, not the Hoover administration, but from a news reporter. Some minutes later Assistant Attorney General Nugent Dodds arrived and told Glassford that troops were standing by at the Ellipse. Glassford peppered Dodds with questions, but Dodds just walked away, saying he had delivered the message. Only minutes before, the chief had called Crosby about a rumor that Marines were being summoned. Crosby said he knew nothing about the rumor and said nothing about troops being called. Understandably perplexed, Glassford was certain of one thing: the callout had nothing to do with the shooting that had just happened, as the callout had been made well before that. Those veterans already evicted, and those not yet evicted, were unsure what to expect. An irritated Glassford kickstarted his motorcycle and roared off to the Ellipse. There he saw General MacArthur in full uniform seated in his staff car. Glassford did not bother looking around to see who was in charge; if MacArthur were present, he would be in command. MacArthur invited Glassford to sit in the staff car with him. The police chief asked his former West Point classmate what he was going to do. MacArthur replied, "We are going to break the back of the BEF. Within a short time, we will move down Pennsylvania Avenue, sweep through the billets there, and then clean out the other two big camps. The operation will be continuous. It will all be done tonight."[8]

It was no secret that army units at Fort Myer had been closely watching the happenings in the District of Columbia for some months. They knew that should military intervention be necessary, they were the closest and most available to respond.[9]

Major George Patton had reported to Fort Myer just three weeks previous as the new executive officer of the 3rd Cavalry Regiment. Like MacArthur and the others, he had served in the World War, and his personal feelings about Communists were akin to those of MacArthur and Moseley. Sometime later, after the Bonus Army situation had passed, Patton would author a training presentation for army officers titled "Federal Troops in Domestic Disturbances." In that document he advised, "If you must fire do a good job—a few casualties become martyrs, a large number an object lesson. . . . When a mob starts to move keep it on the run. . . . If they are running a few good wounds in the buttocks will encourage them. If they resist, they must be killed."[10]

On July 28 at 2:00 p.m., Patton, Truscott, and the other members of the cavalry squadron at Fort Myer had saddled and assembled at the stable line and shortly thereafter left Fort Myer for the Ellipse. Lucian Truscott Jr. writes, "The squadron then pounded down through Arlington National Cemetery, over the recently completed Memorial Bridge, and halted on the Ellipse south of the White House at about half past two o'clock." As it turned out, the full gallop was unnecessary. Boats and trucks transporting 400 infantry soldiers and various weapons and vehicles from other army forts would not arrive for nearly two hours.[11]

At 2:55 p.m. Secretary of War Hurley sent the following orders to General MacArthur:

> The president has just informed me that the civil government of the District of Columbia has reported to him that it is unable to maintain law and order in the District of Columbia. You will have United States troops proceed immediately to the scene of disorder. Cooperate fully with the District of Columbia police force which is now in charge. Surround the affected area and clear it without delay. Turn over all prisoners to civil authorities. In your orders insist that any women and children who may be in the affected area be accorded every consideration and kindness. Use all humanity consistent with due execution of this order.[12]

It was unconscionable that no one in the DC government or the Hoover administration had informed Glassford that army troops had been summoned or that he and his department were "now in charge." MacArthur, who must have had a copy of the order, failed to share it with the police chief when the two spoke in the staff car. Of note is that the president had ordered federal troops before the shooting, although Hurley may have known about it before giving MacArthur his orders. While Hurley's order stated quite clearly that the DC police were in charge, its next sentence muddled the message by saying that MacArthur was to clear the area without delay. If the Metropolitan Police Department were "in charge," then it would be Glassford's decision as to whether to clear the affected area. It seems evident that the president and secretary of war wanted it both ways: they instructed MacArthur to clear the area while professing that Glassford was in charge. This neatly avoided the president having to declare martial law, which would have brought immediate and overwhelming national and international attention to the District of Columbia. As orders go, it was one of the worst.[13]

The critical events had happened quickly: the eviction had begun at about 10:00 a.m. and by 2:30 p.m. the cavalry squadron was standing by at the Ellipse. Four companies of infantry, a mounted machine gun squadron, and six British-built Mark A Whippet medium tanks arrived within two hours. With associated units, the total number of soldiers was 793, but the troops who would confront the veterans would be those of the 2nd Squadron of the 3rd Cavalry Regiment, under Major Alexander D. Surles, and the 3rd Battalion of the 12th Infantry Regiment, under Lieutenant Colonel Louis A. Kunzig.[14]

MacArthur had placed Major General Perry L. Miles in command but then told him that he, MacArthur, would accompany the troops. MacArthur justified his personal involvement to Hurley by saying he was "anticipating the possibility of such a situation arising that necessary decisions might be beyond the purview of responsibility of any subordinate commander." Probably no one who knew MacArthur doubted that he was in charge and would determine the outcome. Major Dwight D. Eisenhower, MacArthur's chief military aide at the time, strongly suggested to MacArthur that he should not assume command, that it was "highly inappropriate" for the chief of staff of the entire US Army to "be involved with anything like a local street-corner embroilment." None of Eisenhower's arguments worked. MacArthur asserted that there was "incipient revolution in the air." Perhaps because Hoover was a Quaker, military officers in DC during that era seldom wore their uniforms, and on that day, MacArthur had worn a white suit. In view of the situation, he dispatched another aide to his quarters to bring back his uniform, and he instructed Eisenhower to do the same. Considering Glassford's high personal regard for MacArthur, it is difficult to imagine what Glassford would have done had the chief of staff given him a copy of the presidential order. The police chief normally would not have deferred to another person, but MacArthur likely would have been an exception.[15]

The titular head of the expulsion force, West Point graduate General Perry Lester Miles, had assumed command a few months earlier. Commissioned an infantry officer in 1895, he had earned a Distinguished Service Cross as a first lieutenant in 1899 for "extraordinary heroism" during the Philippine Insurrection. As a colonel in the World War, he had commanded the 371st Regiment of the 93rd "Blue Helmet" Division (Colored), then under French senior commanders.[16]

Had General Miles actually been in command, Glassford could have approached him and asked what the general intended to do. Miles might have said that the army was there to assist the police department in any way it could, or perhaps Miles might have said that the army would escort the veterans out of the camps, using force only if necessary. Instead, Glassford had approached MacArthur. During their conversation, MacArthur laid out the full plan, not for comment but simply as edification. The 11th Street Bridge would be lifted, and the expulsion would start with a demonstration of force along Pennsylvania Avenue to impress and intimidate the veterans; a platoon of tanks and a troop of machine guns would be in the lead but would eventually pull to the sides to make way for the infantry soldiers with fixed-bayoneted rifles and the cavalry troopers with drawn sabers. All the soldiers would carry gas masks. The mounted troopers would work the flanks, keeping the veterans centered and moving forward along the route toward the bridge and the Anacostia camp. Soldiers would evict veterans from their shacks and tents with enough force to ensure compliance but would be considerate of women and children. MacArthur then requested that Glassford's officers shut off traffic and keep pedestrians at a distance so as not to mingle with the veterans. In essence, the soldiers would do the real work while the police officers directed traffic. Nonetheless, Glassford thought MacArthur's plan was "excellent." He later wrote, "In the pre-eviction conference I held with MacArthur, no mention was made of political implications, law, justice, or common everyday American decency; it was all military business." The police chief asked for a ten-minute head start to warn the veterans to leave the camps, which MacArthur granted. Glassford then sped back to the camp to have the veterans he encountered spread the word among all the camps for veterans and families to evacuate immediately.[17]

What possessed the West Point-trained and battle-tested MacArthur to treat middle-aged destitute veterans as a hostile enemy force can only be surmised. Perhaps he believed Moseley's intelligence reports that the veterans really were Communists bent on insurrection, or maybe he thought they had shamed the army—his army. Perhaps he believed that it was their own negligence or irresponsibility that had caused them to become homeless, or maybe he simply wanted to be in the spotlight once again. Whatever the reason, by day's end he would have earned the disdain of a nation.

Glassford proceeded to Pennsylvania Avenue, which remained calm. Glassford told his officers that they were to handle traffic and spectators only. Anticipating that the troops would come at any moment, he had the streets cleared of everyone except uniformed officers; not even plainclothes officers or news reporters were permitted in the possibly deadly space between the veterans and spectators. And then—nothing happened. No soldiers came. Glassford remembered that it was two hours before any troops were sighted. During the interim, everything remained calm and orderly. The veterans were understandably curious and anxious about what might happen. Of course, there was no reason to immediately march against the veterans: no emergency, no rioting, no disturbances, no shouting. But now, nothing, not even a formation of all the veterans smartly double-timing out of town, would have stopped what was about to happen.[18]

At 4:30 p.m. MacArthur and Miles led the soldiers along Pennsylvania Avenue, focused on the three thousand veterans assembled between Third and Fourth Streets. An immense crowd of curious spectators had gathered along the curb line. The onlookers were not sure what was coming, but it was certain to be a spectacle.[19]

Glassford remembered that it was obvious that the veterans had no thoughts of resisting; in fact, they cheered the troops in good faith, the solidarity of soldiers to soldiers. But MacArthur's timing could not have been worse. It was a Thursday in the late afternoon; workers left shops and offices, knowing that the weekend was almost here. Truscott writes, "Simultaneously, so it seemed, every office building and business establishment in downtown Washington discharged its occupants onto the streets. This parade was indeed witnessed by thousands."[20]

MacArthur's "excellent" army plan now risked serious injury to thousands of bystanders and guaranteed a surfeit of news photographs and witness-spectators who would eagerly tell everyone just how bad it was. In a matter of moments, the US Army must have realized that it had a much bigger problem than it had expected. MacArthur's tactical plan essentially entailed nothing more than a crude frontal assault of soldiers employing 2,000 tear-gas bombs, 200 sabers, and 400 bayonets, backed by the threat of machine guns and tanks.[21]

General Miles had briefed his soldiers at about 4:00 p.m., telling them that they would use necessary force and tear gas, but that they were to treat the women and children they encountered with kindness. He labeled the veterans as "the mob" and the spectators as "the crowd," signaling to his soldiers which group deserved the poke of a bayonet or the slap of a saber and which did not. Not surprising, "the crowd" quickly overflowed the sidewalks and spilled into the streets. Rather than "surrounding the affected area," as Hurley's written orders had directed, the army would simply shove the veterans down to and across the bridge. Within a half hour, the troops were on the move. Truscott remembered, "The squadron moved out in a column of platoons followed by the infantry battalion." At first, the soldiers pushed the veterans and the veterans pushed back, seeing it as something of a game. Then, as Glassford recalled, an officer barked an order and the infantry soldiers stopped to put on gas masks and returned to the attack, but now hurling tear-gas bombs. Veterans scrambled about for a few important possessions and then took flight.[22]

Waters was on the street when he saw the approach of the heavily armed soldiers with their cannons, machine guns, sabers, and bayonets. The Bonus leader recalled that flight was the intention of each veteran, not resisting; that the veterans could hardly believe this was happening. The mob and the crowd, almost in unison, stood staring at the seemingly unreal approach of the troops. Suspecting that Waters would be a trophy capture for the soldiers, his bodyguards shoved him into a taxi and spirited him away to a room in the Ebbitt Hotel.[23]

The mounted cavalry troopers, wearing their campaign hats, towered above everyone else, their carbines slung but their sabers drawn and raised; the foot soldiers wore their steel helmets and held their bayoneted rifles at port arms. The black gas masks of the soldiers gave them something of a monstrous appearance; their blue tear-gas bombs dangled from their belts, ready to be quickly drawn. The troopers led the way, easily clearing the path, the huge horses bumping into anybody who dared to remain in the way, their shoed hooves coming down on tender and unsuspecting feet. John Bartlett saw and heard the mounted troopers coming, which he described as "a force of Cavalry with sabers glistening, making the ominous click of iron feet on the pavement, which sounded so much like war."[24]

By 5:45 p.m. the infantry had moved into and through the shacks and abandoned buildings. Those veterans in the buildings who refused to leave changed their minds when the soldiers dropped tear-gas grenades from the tops of the stairwells onto the floors below. Cavalry troopers herded the disgorged veterans, as well as those already on the street, along Third and Fourth Streets to Missouri Avenue in the direction of the bridge, allowing no one to evade. The veterans cussed and insulted the troopers, and some threw rocks and brickbats, but the troopers ignored the insults. Major Patton later recalled, "Bricks flew, sabers rose and fell with a comforting smack, and the mob ran. We moved on after them, occasionally meeting serious resistance.... Two of us charged at a gallop, and had some nice work at close range with the occupants of the truck, most of whom could not sit down for some days." With respect to Patton's comments, it is difficult to imagine a gaunt veteran, attired in tattered clothing, perhaps armed with a handful of broken bricks, offering any "serious resistance" to a cavalry trooper armed with a saber with a thirty-six-inch blade, towering over him while mounted on a 1,000-pound horse and charging at a gallop.[25]

Onlookers later described a scene of gas-masked soldiers lobbing tear gas without warning, cavalrymen riding into men and women and pushing them aside, and thousands of spectators finding themselves caught in the middle. The air thickened with white tear gas, restricting both sight and breath, affecting the police officers as well as the spectators. Most veterans ran. Bartlett described the cavalry attack: "Into the crowds they ruthlessly drove, scattering us like sheep, knocking down many pedestrians. I backed double-quick or a horse would have hit me." Some soldiers next moved to 14th and C Streets SW, the Communist camp, but most of the comrades had fled some time ago. Shortly thereafter, some of the veteran shacks caught fire, which spread quickly in the warm late afternoon breeze. Soldiers continued to herd and push the veterans. Bartlett remembered, "Along came the infantry, glistening bayonets fixed to their rifles. From the crowded spectators a chorus of boos [was] heard. The infantrymen threw gas grenades recklessly into the crowd of citizens."[26]

At 6:30 p.m. the troops paused before crossing the 11th Street Bridge. By now most of the veterans had fled across the river into Camp Marks, rushing about to save what possessions they could carry away. By dusk the first phase of the operation was complete. Glassford located MacArthur and asked him if the troops would cross the bridge. The general said they would and asked Glassford to warn the veterans. MacArthur intended to wait a few hours during which his soldiers would eat their dinner rations. Glassford motorcycled across the bridge and once again urged the veterans and families to grab their possessions and flee. President Hoover, now alerted to what had become a gigantic melee, told Hurley to dispatch Moseley to meet in person with MacArthur and tell him that the president did not want troops to cross the 11th Street Bridge. MacArthur, however, did not need his commander in chief to tell him how to do his job, and he simply ignored the presidential order. At 9:10 p.m. MacArthur and the troops crossed the bridge into Camp Marks. Just after 10:00 that night, veteran Eddie Atwell, displaying a white flag of truce, approached MacArthur, who was then seated in his staff car. Atwell pleaded for another hour to continue the evacuation of the camp of several thousand, including 600 women and children; MacArthur granted the request. With that white flag of surrender, the US Army had soundly defeated the ragged remnants of the Bonus Army.[27]

Two hours later flames engulfed the giant Hooverville. The hovels were mostly plywood and scraps of lumber. They ignited easily in the July heat, moving rapidly from shack to shack. The smoke thickened and the flames leaped upward, the fire so intense that it lit the night sky. Truscott later wrote that the cavalry had halted to allow the veterans to vacate their camp, but that the infantry battalion had moved in to clear it. Flames soon consumed the camp. "By morning," Truscott recalled, "the veterans were gone, and the huge primitive camp was a smoldering mass." One news reporter recalled that he had been very close to General MacArthur and saw him give an order to a sergeant, after which the sergeant and his soldiers wadded newspapers near deserted huts and set them ablaze. Another reporter said he saw soldiers torching shacks. The following day a newspaper photograph showed soldiers using a torch to burn a shanty, and another photograph showed two police officers tearing down a shack. Hurley, when questioned by reporters, finally admitted that a few soldiers had ignited some of the hovels for "sanitation" purposes. Miles asserted that burning the Hooverville had not been part of the plan. Soldiers had tossed more than 2,000 tear-gas bombs.[28]

Waters had assumed that the troops would not go into the Anacostia camp. Once he got word that they had done so, he left his hotel room and rushed to the camp. The troops entered the Anacostia Flats late that night. Men and women raced about, holding bundles and packs, and pulling children by the hand.[29]

The veterans and their families simply ran into the night, not knowing where they were headed except away from the conflagration. Those walking to Virginia found the bridges blocked by soldiers; those walking to Maryland found the roads blocked by state troopers. Many veterans and families simply walked, not noticing the night rain, not caring where they would end up. By midnight the army troops had bivouacked on the flats for the night, and Coast Artillery searchlights swept across the flats until daylight. Maryland authorities eventually trucked some veterans and families to Johnstown, Pennsylvania—away from Maryland.[30]

By morning, when news stories and photographs revealed the events, many Americans grew angry. Hoover must have been irritated as well; he had expressly forbidden MacArthur from sending troops across the 11th Street Bridge. General

Moseley had reported to the president that he had personally carried the message to MacArthur and discussed it with him, but that MacArthur was quite annoyed, saying he did not like anyone interfering with the implementation of his plans. General Miles and Major Eisenhower verified that Moseley had delivered the message to MacArthur. Eisenhower added that MacArthur had said that he was "too busy and did not want either himself or his staff bothered by people coming down and pretending to bring orders."[31]

One of the veterans later saw Glassford standing alone, having now released his officers. The veteran later told Waters that Glassford, looking tired and troubled, was speaking to a woman who had come up to him. The police chief was saying that he was sure that the soldiers had not meant to burn down her home—a shack—conveying it as nicely as he could. The veteran told Waters that it was reassuring to see such a man on such a night. About 150 veterans had taken refuge in the private property of Camp Bartlett but soon found that the soldiers paid no attention to that and pushed them out. Glassford recalled, "Who set the fires? I do not know. I only know that the camps were burned. I was deeply touched as the simple homes these men had built for themselves, the only homes they possessed, went up in flames. The number of shacks, huts and tents was estimated to be 2,100."[32]

After midnight, the pungent smell of tear gas and smoke persisting, and much against Eisenhower's sound advice, MacArthur addressed the waiting press. Eisenhower had urged him to allow Hurley or another civilian official to handle the press, but MacArthur ignored Eisenhower's suggestion. As one might expect, MacArthur now magnified the threat previously posed by the veterans to justify his horrific response, telling the assembled reporters,

> That mob ... had been animated by the essence of revolution. The gentleness, the consideration, with which they had been treated had been mistaken for weakness, and they had come to the conclusion ... that they were about to take over ... the government. It is my opinion that had the President not acted today, had he permitted this thing to go on for 24 hours, he would have had a grave situation which would have caused a real battle. Had he let it go another week, I believe that the institutions of our government would have been very severely threatened ... had he

not acted with the force and vigor that he did, it would be a sad day for the country tomorrow.

The chief of staff went on to say that among the "insurrectionists" he would be surprised if one in ten was a veteran. It was a speech of an egotist and a sycophant, praising himself and the president whom he had just disobeyed, a remarkable display of the general's political acumen.[33]

MacArthur told the reporters that, as far as he knew, there had been no serious injuries. There were no deaths, but perhaps 1,000 citizens, police officers, news reporters, and ambulance crew members had been tear gassed. Some serious injuries were reported later but not verified. For his own reasons, the president chose to support MacArthur, who had just ignored a presidential order. Donald Lisio writes that Hoover's "acceptance of MacArthur's explanation contributed to a more profound tragedy than his own." It would become the challenge of a future American president to dismiss MacArthur and remind him that a commander-in-chief outranks the highest general, even if President Harry S. Truman had been only an artillery captain in World War I.[34]

MacArthur next related an implausible account of people coming up to him and expressing gratitude, "especially in the Negro section, that a regular system of tribute was being levied on them by this insurrectionist group; a reign of terror was being started which may have led to a system of Caponeism, and I believe later to insurgency and insurrection." One would suppose that a threat of "Caponeism" would have surfaced well before average citizens had the courage and confidence to approach a uniformed army general during or just after an armed military expulsion. Correspondent Paul Y. Anderson said he had visited the camps many times and remembered that he had never had a veteran ask for anything more than a cigarette. Anderson later speculated that the Hoover administration might use the expulsion to demonstrate Hoover's handling of the radicals.[35]

On July 29, the day after the expulsion, oversized headlines and lengthy news articles shouted out the harsh details of MacArthur's armed expulsion of the veterans; a plethora of photographs filled entire pages with a graphic record of soldiers using tear gas, sabers, bayonets, and torches. Black-and-white newsreels later showed soldiers walking and then running after the fleeing veterans. Many DC residents knew that the veterans were not Communists but were instead surprisingly disciplined, restrained, and agreeable men who would never have trekked to Washington if they had had jobs.[36]

Glassford listened to MacArthur's speech with disbelieving ears. "I was one of his many hundreds of cadetmates who had idolized him for his brilliance, soldierly qualities, and geniality." The police chief was conflicted by MacArthur's comments about the veterans, and later wrote:

> I do not know to this this day whether or not MacArthur realized that the armed eviction of defenseless men who had served their country in the time of peril would mark a black page in American history. I do not know to what extent he abhorred the mission he had been ordered to do.... It may have been ignorance of the actual situation, or it may have been loyalty to the president, his commander in chief, that was responsible for MacArthur's statements to newspaper journalists after the eviction when he said 'Not one man in 10 among those who were active about the so-called veterans' camps was a real veteran.... MacArthur had never visited any veteran camp or billets. From my observation I do not believe that he was an eye-witness at close range to any of the troop actions on that memorable July 28th. It is quite possible that he was duped by the false reports of government agents that in the Bonus Army there was a large percentage of ruffians with criminal records, and men who had never served in our armed forces during the war. The charge of intolerance, ingratitude and brutality must be leveled, not against the Army nor against MacArthur, but against the Hoover administration's blind attempt to make political capital out of hunger, misery, and despair.

The police chief who so admired MacArthur clearly struggled to comprehend his former classmate's state of mind. But in the end, likely aided by cognitive dissonance, idolatry trumped reason. The MacArthur whom Glassford thought he knew prevailed, as the police chief chose to shift blame from MacArthur to Hoover.[37]

Throughout the nation Americans read newspapers and watched newsreels in theaters and came to a different conclusion. As noted by historians Paul Dickson and Thomas B. Allen, "In movie theaters all across America the unthinkable happened: The United States Army was booed and MacArthur jeered." Bartlett summed up his feelings: "No, there is no use seeking to conceal the fact that eviction from the District of Columbia was the object from the first, and not the quelling of riots, which did not exist." MacArthur biographer William Manchester writes, "Since the president was MacArthur's commander in chief, the General had been flagrantly insubordinate. But before Hoover could act, MacArthur had outmaneuvered him. Law-and-order Republicans, he knew, would approve his show of strength. Therefore, he called a midnight press conference, disclaimed responsibility, and praised Hoover for shouldering it." Following the expulsion, Franklin Roosevelt, then a presidential candidate, remarked to his assistant that it would no longer be necessary launch a campaign against Hoover.[38]

MacArthur, in his 1964 autobiography, after describing his actions during the Bonus march, recalled a conversation he had once had with then New York governor Franklin Roosevelt and quoted Roosevelt as saying, "Douglas, I think you are our best general, but I believe you would be our worst politician." Later, as a presidential candidate, Roosevelt mentioned to his assistant, Rexford G. Tugwell, that Louisiana political figure Huey Long was one of the two most dangerous men in the country. Tugwell asked Roosevelt if the other was Father Charles E. Coughlin. Roosevelt replied, "Oh no, the other is Douglas MacArthur." Roosevelt went on to explain that Americans had suffered from a lack of strong leadership skills and to gain security they would be willing to give away liberty.[39]

Despite the police chief's pronouncement that MacArthur's expulsion plan had been "excellent," it is inconceivable that Glassford would have handled it that way, had he been in charge. To begin with, he would have obeyed a presidential order. His preference, of course, would have been to allow two weeks for the continued self-evacuation of the Bonus Army until it dissipated, and then relocate any remaining veterans and families to Camp Bartlett. It is highly unlikely that the president and the DC commissioners would have allowed that.

How might Glassford have handled the expulsion had he been ordered to do so? Glassford, of course, had been a battle commander. To begin with, he would have tailored the plan to the situation. It seems probable that he would have focused more on herding the veterans rather than stampeding them, and he would have initiated his plan unexpectedly on an early Sunday morning. Those officers, sergeants, and commanders who had worked in the camps and assisted with the parades and demonstrations would have taken the lead, doing their best to cajole, persuade, and then order the veterans into moving to Camp Bartlett. The chief would have employed virtually his entire department, backed at some distance by a prearranged force of National Guard soldiers, supplied with weapons and tear gas. Police arrest-and-removal teams, supplied with prisoner wagons, would have immediately taken into custody any veterans who refused to leave, and engineer soldiers would have worked with sanitation workers to quickly flatten and remove the shacks, shelters, lean-tos, and tents. The 11th Street Bridge would have permitted outgoing traffic only, and once all the camps were clear, police officers and National Guard soldiers would board up all buildings and occupy all camps for three days.

A great deal of debate followed regarding who had set the fires. Newspapers printed photographs showing soldiers setting fires, but General Miles said that the fires had started quickly and were a surprise and not part of his plan. Captain Truscott said that no one knew who started the fires. Eisenhower said that the soldiers had been too far from the fires to have started them, and that the veterans had started the fires. MacArthur claimed that it was the veterans who had fired their own billets. Waters asserted that the Communists had fired their own billets, and that some in the BEF had set some of the fires. Hurley said retreating radicals had set the fires. No one listed above, however, reported any veteran having set a fire; furthermore, no photograph ever showed a veteran setting a fire. Since the veterans and their families were in flight and had few possessions to begin with, it seems improbable that they would have taken the time and effort to set fires.[40]

The army wanted to know how the fires started, and in August conducted tests at Fort Washington. General Miles later concluded that the first fires along Pennsylvania resulted from "defective inflammatory grenades and candles, and that the later fires were set by soldiers mistakenly thinking that an order had been issued to burn the huts." During the Fort Washington tests, defective grenades injured six soldiers.[41]

A fair question is, who was most responsible for this ugly turn of events? While many were to blame, Commissioner Crosby and General MacArthur deserve the greatest censure: Crosby for leading the president to believe that Glassford agreed with the army callout; MacArthur for using a sledgehammer to kill an ant.

Eddie McCloskey, mayor of Johnstown, Pennsylvania, and a veteran, had on several occasions addressed groups of Bonus veterans in their camps. He said that if they needed to, they could stay for a while in his city. Johnstown had had its own tragedy in 1889, when a reservoir failed and flooded the town, killing more than 2,200. McCloskey expected that a few hundred veterans might come. Following the expulsion, about 7,000 veterans and family members wandered in all directions, with most strung out for days on various highways between Washington and Maryland. Some recalled McCloskey's invitation and, along with thousands of others, headed to Johnstown, Pennsylvania, 175 miles northwest of Washington. Waters, expelled just like the others, remembered that the Maryland police had been helpful in keeping the journey as painless as possible as the veterans and families continued the journey through Maryland. Johnstown was never meant to be an ultimate destination but served well as an assembly point. Pennsylvania Governor Gifford Pinchot sent social workers to Johnstown to interview Bonus Army veterans who had sought refuge there. One social worker reported speaking with 75 veterans, each of whom produced papers of honorable discharge. At Waters's request, Eddie Atwell assembled the veterans in Johnstown and read the formal order disbanding the BEF. Eventually, the B&O Railroad offered free rides west to Chicago and St. Louis, and various states supplied trucks to return their veterans and families.[42]

One short, slender veteran did not leave Washington the night of the eviction. The next day, in the hazy, still-smoky morning light, the smell of burnt wood and cardboard heavy in the air, a wisp of a man approached a tall sergeant of the 12th Infantry Regiment and asked to speak to Major George Patton. At the time, Patton, Captain Truscott, and other cavalry officers were standing in the ash remnants of what had been the veterans' encampment, sipping morning coffee from a field kitchen. The sergeant brought the veteran forward and told Major Patton that the man claimed to know him. Patton looked at the small man and barked, "Sergeant, I do not know this man. Take him away." After the sergeant and veteran had left, Patton told Truscott and the others that the man had been his orderly during the World War and had dragged him to safety while under fire, saving Patton's life. Patton hoped to avoid a negative headline should a news reporter capture the story. Joe Angelo, recipient of a Distinguished Service Cross, second only to the Medal of Honor, disappeared into the Great Depression.[43]

Hoover, Hurley, Moseley, MacArthur, and the DC commissioners, certain that they had derailed the Communist-led BEF, likely missed an Associated Press article, dateline Berlin, reprinted in the *Washington Post* on July 29, the day after the

Bonus Army expulsion. The article described the happenings in Germany, the headline reading, "Nationalists Urge Return to Monarchy to Restore Germany's Power." The article reported, "The fiery Hitler, who swept into Berlin by airplane last night, brought forth thunderous cheers of 100,000 persons gathered in the great Berlin stadium by declaring: 'July 31 must remove the rule of democracy and Marxism and its vassals from Germany, and restore a regime of discipline, national confidence, honor, and power.'"[44]

Hoover and DC administrations now had to redefine what had happened: the government had not tear gassed and stampeded thousands of harmless veterans out of Washington; it had rescued the nation on the brink of insurrection and Communist domination. The president needed to persuade Americans that subversives had gained control over those veterans in Washington. He tasked Attorney General William D. Mitchell with drafting a report that vividly painted the Bonus marchers as "criminal, communist, and non-veteran elements." Assistant Secretary of War F. Trubee Davison cleverly labeled the veterans as a "a polyglot mob of tramps and hoodlums [with a] generous sprinkling of Communist agitators." Hurley explained, "The duty of restoring law and order was performed with directness, with effectiveness, and with unparalleled humanity and kindness."[45]

Not everyone agreed. The Veterans Bureau, after a detailed examination, announced that 94 percent of the men in the Bonus Army were bona fide veterans, 67 percent had served overseas, and 20 percent had some disability. Later, a federal grand jury looking into the matter returned just three indictments, and of the 363 arrests of Bonus members in the past few months, 350—96 percent—had been for minor crimes. Hundreds of letters sent to the *Washington News* showed that 90 percent of its readers disfavored Hoover's handling of the Bonus Army. The thousands of downtown workers caught in the streets during the discharge of 2,000 tear-gas canisters no doubt found the experience to be less than "unparalleled humanity and kindness." Most Washingtonians concluded that the veterans were not Communists but simply victims of the Great Depression, like so many others. The reality was that most of the veterans now had a much better chance of becoming Okies and Arkies than ever attending a radical meeting. Many veterans and their families would later nurse their jalopies along US Route 66, the Mother Road, to California, hoping to find work; instead, they would find highway patrol officers, sheriff's deputies, and city police officers at the state line ordering them to turn around and drive the other way.[46]

Glassford later told journalist Owen White, "The majority of the marchers, ninety percent of them, would have been willing to move out to the proposed camp, and thereafter it was expected that they would cooperate with the police of Washington in evacuating by any means necessary any undesirable or radical element that insisted on remaining in the Capital." Glassford added that the agreed-to plan, originated by the BEF leaders, was to have the veterans drift away on their own, and pointed out that Camp Bartlett was two miles on the other side of the 11th Street Bridge. Without funds or transportation, and having little to do, the veterans would have become inclined to move along. When Owen White asked the police chief to comment on the allegation that his friendliness had encouraged more veterans to come, he answered that he supposed that there might have been some truth in it, but that he preferred having 20,000 law-respecting veterans than 7,000 rioters with empty stomachs.[47]

The Communist Party, predictably, took 100 percent responsibility for what had happened, asserting that it had planned and managed the whole thing. Benjamin Gitlow and John Pace later admitted that their orders had come from the American Communist Party, acting on orders from Moscow. While that was true, Moscow was not happy with the results and denounced the failure of the American Communists who had not even dented the Bonus Army, much less launched a revolution. In truth, the only people who believed, or claimed to believe, that the Communists had engineered the happenings were those in whose best interests it was to espouse such—MacArthur and his key staff, the Hoover administration, and the DC commissioners, the same individuals who seemed oblivious to rising fascism.[48]

The DC commissioners now had a vendetta with Glassford, who had essentially accused them of lying and then produced a witness to verify that he had not said what they attributed to him. Waters told reporters that every drop of bloodshed was the doing of the White House. A blistering editorial in the *Washington Post* assigned the fault to the fanatics in the Bonus Army and those in Congress who supported them. Hoover wrote to the DC commissioners, fulminating that civil authorities had failed to enforce city ordinances and laws.[49]

Chief Glassford was irritated about something else. Some days after the BEF expulsion, Hoover administration Assistant US Attorney Leo Rover bypassed the police chief and asked one of his police inspectors, Ogden T. Davis, to accompany immigration officials and Secret Service agents on a dragnet raid at an abandoned church, where they subsequently arrested more than 100 suspected Communists. Glassford fumed that he had been available all Friday night. He knew why immigration officials had not consulted him about the sweeping roundup, of course, but he challenged the legality of picking up people presumed to be radicals and then handing them off to the police department. The roundup netted 26 arrested and 150 detained and then escorted out of the District. The Federal Courts had some concerns about the roundup and released almost all the radicals for lack of evidence. Glassford was understandably displeased that Inspector Davis had not alerted him about the raid. The two met for an hour during which Davis explained that the US Attorney had asked him and his officers to participate in the raid and that former chief of police Henry Pratt had previously issued a standing order to cooperate with federal agents. Likely not satisfied, Glassford nonetheless issued a statement praising Inspector Davis as both efficient and conscientious. A standing order from a former police chief, however, would not have been a sufficient reason for the inspector's failure to contact Glassford before participating in the raid. Much more likely is that US Attorney Rover pressured Davis not to contact his police chief, and Davis acquiesced to the request. The DC commissioners finally passed an ordinance prohibiting organizations such as the Bonus Army from coming into the District of Columbia to lobby Congress. The commissioners had not invited Glassford to the meeting where they discussed and then passed the ordinance, but they did send him a copy on August 2. Whether the new ordinance would pass constitutional muster was one question; the other more important question was why the commissioners had refused to put anything in writing when Glassford needed their guidance.[50]

To cap off probably the worst week of his life, Glassford received final divorce papers on August 2. He and Cora had separated on New Year's Day 1927. She had returned to Alamo Heights, Texas, to live near her retired parents, but returned to Washington on occasion. She had filed for divorce on March 31, 1932, and Judge S. G. Taylor granted the divorce on August 2. The petition noted that the children were of age and the property settlement was acceptable. Neither person shared the reason for the divorce, and Cora embarked on a career as a writer of fiction, history, and biography. She became active in the Daughters of the Republic of Texas, which eventually appointed her as the director of its extensive research library, a position she held until retiring in 1955.[51]

CHAPTER 15

Whitewashing the Expulsion

ATTORNEY General William D. Mitchell's September 9, 1932, report to the president, completed in just eleven days, was full of allegations and lacking in evidence. Halfway through the first sentence Mitchell referenced the "so-called" Bonus Army, a clue as to its foregone conclusion. The entire Bonus Army, it seemed, was to be held accountable for the actions of the small number of Communists, lending the impression that most all the veterans were Communists or criminals or both. The police chief and retired field artillery commander knew misdirected fire when he saw it. Staying up until 4:00 a.m., Glassford zeroed in on the inaccuracies of the report, lowered his barrel, and fired for effect. Pounding his typewriter keys, paragraph by paragraph, he identified, documented, and rebutted its numerous errors. He began by saying that many reporters had asked him to comment upon Attorney General Mitchell's report, which had appeared in the morning papers on September 12. One by one, he disproved the report's allegations:

> *Mitchell Report*: It is probable the Bonus Army brought into the City of Washington the largest aggregation of criminals that had ever assembled in the city at any one time.
> *Glassford*: According to police records and statistics, there was less crime in the District of Columbia during either June or July than during the month of August, after the veterans had been evicted. The report does not show that of the 362 arrests made during the two months of the so-called bonus invasion, only 12 arrests of bonus marchers were made

for offenses of a criminal nature.... The report stresses communism, crime, and subversive influences. There are of record many demonstrations of patriotism and discipline by the great mass of the unemployed veterans. An editorial in the June 18 *Washington Evening Star* newspaper concluded that following the Senate's tabling of the Bonus Bill, the "patriotism demonstrated by the veterans made their countrymen proud."

Mitchell Report: One of the bonus camps—that within 12th and 14th and B and C Streets, S.W., was occupied principally by communists headed by [John T.] Pace.
Glassford: Police records show that there were nine separate [veteran] units billeted in those four-square blocks numbering by police count 824 individuals on July 26. Of those units, only one, comprising approximately 150 men, was associated with the Soldier's Ex-service Men's League, a radical organization.

Mitchell Report: There is irrefutable proof that a very large body of communists and radicals, some ex-service men and some not, were in the city as part of the Bonus Army, circulating among them and working diligently to incite them to disorder.
Glassford: Following two days of circularized propaganda, John T. Pace mustered on July 21 a group not exceeding 210 [communists] by police count for the purpose of attempting to picket the White House. This was the largest group of radicals gathered at any one time. The attempts of the communists and radicals to circulate and incite disorder in the loyal camps were completely frustrated by the veterans' Military Police, an organization sponsored by the police department mainly for that purpose.

Mitchell Report: In response to questions by the DC commissioners, he [Chief Glassford] stated that the situation was out of his control and that the police could no longer hold the bonus marchers in check. He was asked the direct question whether he thought it was necessary to secure the assistance of Federal troops, to which he replied in the affirmative.

Glassford: At a conference held at the DC commissioners' office within half an hour after the brick battle, I stated that the police could hold the area which had been repossessed during the morning. I stated that if further efforts toward evicting by the police was insisted upon that afternoon, there doubtless would be more rioting and possible bloodshed. I recommended that should further evicting be required that day, the Federal troops should be called to do it. Nothing was said by the Commissioners at this conference to indicate they had reached a decision to call for Federal aid. My statement above is substantiated by a certificate of my personal secretary, Mr. Aldace Walker, quoted as follows:

Aldace Walker: "He [Glassford] expressed strong opposition to calling for Federal aid. Both Commissioners asked Major Glassford if the police had lost control of the situation. The Major replied that the situation was not out of control of the police. He explained fully just what had happened, and then maintained that the area which was roped off could be held if he were not required to extend this area. The Commissioners then told the Major to hold what he had. The conference ended and Major Glassford and I returned to the area on Pennsylvania. Although the subject of requesting Federal aid was discussed at this conference there was no manifestation on the part of the Commissioners of calling upon the president for the use of troops."

Glassford: Within half an hour after the conference at the District Building, Commissioners Reichelderfer and Crosby appeared at the disaffected area. I left a group of veterans which included Commander W. W. Waters and other veteran leaders to tell the Commissioners that all was quiet and that plans were being formulated to get all the veterans in this area to return to their camps. Nothing was said by the Commissioners at this conference to indicate they had reached a decision to call for Federal aid. It was not until more than an hour later that I had any intimation that the troops had been called out. The information came to me first from a newspaper reporter, and was confirmed officially a few minutes later by a message from Attorney General Mitchell transmitted verbally by Mr. Nugent Dodds. I was in command of a difficult situation which was vitally affected by the call for Federal troops. I have never been informed why the Commissioners did not notify me instantly when the troops were called.

Mitchell Report: Finally, the mob of bonus marchers again attacked the police with bricks, lumps of concrete and iron bars. Two of the bonus marchers were shot by police who had been set upon and were in danger of their lives. The entire mob became hostile and riotous. It was apparent that a pitched battle on a large scale might start at any moment. Practically the entire police force of the city was called from their posts and assembled at this point but they were outnumbered 10 or 15 to 1.
Glassford: The facts are as follows: This second attack occurred about 1:45 P.M., more than an hour and a half after the brick battle. It was a short spontaneous affair involving seven police officers who were isolated from the main body of police holding the repossessed area, which was in the same block but on the other side of three large buildings. It is true that there was a certain amount of hostility but a very large proportion of the unemployed veterans remained loyal to law and order. Without this mass of loyal men, it would not have been possible for me to have stopped the brick battle before it had been in progress five minutes, nor to have stopped the second outbreak in which two veterans were shot almost as soon as it had commenced. There was no trouble of any kind between 2:00 P.M., and the time the troops arrived, which was after five. The Metropolitan Police Force has 1,300 officers. There were at no time more than 454 in the disaffected area.

Mitchell Report: The results of this effort to bring justice to the principals who incited this riot have been unsatisfactory. The reason is that on the day of the riot [July 28] no detective officers were at Camp Marks, [Anacostia Flats] where originated the large movement of [veterans] to march over and attack the police. The function of having detectives and crime prevention agents in a position to observe and obtain evidence against those who at the last moment incited the riotous march and attack, belonged to the District of Columbia police. The inspector in charge of that branch of police service reports that he had no orders to place men for that purpose, and, on the contrary, on the day of the disturbances was directed to keep his men out of the area.
Glassford: Camp Marks was within the Eleventh Precinct. Officers from this precinct circulated in the camp continuously. In addition to the police officers from the Eleventh Precinct, two plain clothes men from the Crime Prevention Division . . . were detailed to this camp the morning of July 28th. They remained at Camp Marks from early morning until the veterans suddenly started their movement [in response to the eviction] to the Pennsylvania Avenue area about 11:00 a.m. No orders were issued to the Inspector in charge of the Crime Prevention Division, nor to any other inspector, which prohibited plain clothes officers from pursuing their normal functions of obtaining and reporting information. In order to avoid unnecessary provocation or confusion, orders were issued requiring that the eviction of veterans and the quelling of any disturbances which might result, should be accomplished by uniformed officers.[1]

In fairness, President Hoover, Attorney General Mitchell, Secretary of War Hurley, and General MacArthur were at some disadvantage. They believed, understandably, the request for federal assistance from the DC commissioners, who, in turn, it appears, had based their decision on Keck's obsequious report, although it found an eager audience. It is difficult to believe that the DC commissioners somehow misunderstood Glassford. Even had they somehow missed the conditional "if" in his answer, it would have been essentially impossible to miss Glassford's assertion that his police officers could handle the situation and that he did not need or want the army. It seems most probable that the DC commissioners heard just enough of what they wanted to hear, and on that based their request for federal assistance. The DC commissioners said they asked Glassford directly and that "he answered in the affirmative." Answering "in the affirmative" is not as specific as saying that Glassford said "yes," or "absolutely," or "you are correct," or "I would like federal assistance." "In the affirmative" is, at best, deliberatively evasive, a catchall and conclusionary term open to interpretation. The DC commissioners never said what exact words Glassford had used that allowed them to conclude that he had answered in the affirmative. The Hoover administration accepted the request for federal troops from the DC commissioners without questioning it, suggesting a readiness to commit the army. Commissioner Crosby demonstrated an appalling absence of leadership twice: first, when he misled the Hoover administration as to Glassford's statements, and second, when he chose not to tell Glassford that troops had been summoned. A fair conclusion is that the DC commissioners wanted the president to call out the army. Furthermore, it is not a stretch to conclude that the commissioners had in mind to punish both the veterans and Glassford. Glassford's response to the Mitchell report ignored some of the allegations that were canards based on rumor or assumption and lacked even a scintilla of evidence. These included the insinuations that a large number of the Bonus marchers had not been in the military; that Communists continually circulated among veterans in the camp; that after Congress adjourned, the quality of men in the Bonus Army deteriorated and the proportion of disorderly and criminal elements steadily increased; that tribute had been demanded from businesses; that housewives had been intimidated; that the contractor of the building to be demolished demanded possession; and that there might have been a difference of opinion among Lieutenant Keck, the two police inspectors, and Glassford as to whether or not the situation was out of police control.[2]

When Glassford challenged the attorney general, and indirectly the president and the DC commissioners, he drove the first nail in his coffin. He had no intention of resigning, however. Thus, the DC commissioners would have to wait until they saw their opportunity. They were hesitant to dismiss him at this point and settled on pressuring his resignation. When Glassford undertook a routine reorganization that would result in the demotion of the chief of detectives, the DC commissioners backed the detective chief. A few months previous the commissioners would have backed the police chief; now they refused to do so. Apparently, Commissioner Crosby forgot that when he hired Glassford he had told news reporters that the new chief would have "quite a free rein in reorganizing the department after he assumes command." Glassford brokered a compromise in the reorganization situation, which proved acceptable to the commissioners. That night, Glassford reassessed his situation. The next day, October 20, 1932, without explanation, he resigned. He had been chief of police for eleven months. Following the resignation, Corporation Counsel Bride said he was "amazed" at Glassford's resignation. Crosby said that he was "astounded" to hear about it, adding, "As I sponsored General Glassford from the beginning, I have done everything I could to cooperate with him, sometimes even when I believed he was wrong." What was astounding was that Crosby pressured Glassford's resignation and then feigned surprise when it happened. Perhaps most alarming was that Crosby and the other commissioners failed to remember why they had hired Glassford in the first place—to clean up a police department with ongoing corruption problems. When news reporters asked Crosby if the new police chief would come from within the department, he answered, "I hope so." Apparently, disposing of Glassford had now become more important than achieving an honest police department.[3]

Historian Donald Lisio said of the attorney general's report: "The document was so obviously inaccurate, so poorly reasoned, so tactless and politically inept that few republican leaders could either believe or defend it." Journalist Rodney Dutcher of the Newspaper Enterprise Association took a different view. He wrote that for a year the city had had a capable and honest police chief, who avoided politics but was willing to stand up to politicians. Dutcher lamented that the police department would now go back to the politicians. In their future autobiographies, Herbert Hoover and Douglas MacArthur would each rely almost exclusively on the Mitchell report to justify their actions. Of note, excepting Donald Lisio, Hoover's biographers have all mischaracterized the Bonus Army as being of little significance and riddled with criminals and Communists.[4]

On November 8, 1932, in a nation of 125 million, New York Governor Franklin D. Roosevelt received 7 million more votes than did President Hoover. It is doubtful that Hoover would have been reelected even had the Bonus Army expulsion never occurred. He had not caused the Great Depression, but Americans blamed him for not doing more to help the people who suffered its results. The best Hoover had offered them was an early version of "trickle-down economics," a term coined by Will Rogers. Rogers joked that you could give money to a rich man at the top and it might "trickle down" to a needy man at the bottom; or you could give money to a needy man at the bottom and the rich man at the top would have the money before the day ended, but at least it would have passed through the needy man's hands. Secret Service Agent Edmund Starling was the lead agent in the presidential protection detail for President Hoover during his 1932 campaign tour, which at one point stopped in Detroit. The president switched from train to motorcade and was driven along the streets. As Starling remembered, "For the first time in my long experience on the [Secret Service] Detail I heard the President of the United States booed. All along the line there were bad spots, where we heard jeers and saw signs reading: DOWN WITH HOOVER; HOOVER—BALONEY AND APPLESAUCE. The president looked bewildered and stricken."[5]

In the fall during Glassford's final days as chief of police, *Collier's* magazine reporter Owen P. White sought an interview. Glassford invited White to his home for breakfast, which the chief prepared for them. White's hope was to persuade Glassford to write his own version of the Bonus Army saga, but Glassford refused, saying doing so would capitalize and commercialize something that was essentially an accident. White spent the morning with Glassford, riding with him to police headquarters, watching him execute a few law enforcement duties, and then going with him to the National Press Club lunch. In the room full of news reporters, Glassford was the guest of honor. Various journalists stood to praise Glassford for his patience, candor, valor, and courtesy. One news editor said that Glassford had distinguished himself by speaking the truth when the nation's blood pressure was elevated, and some people were tampering with the facts for political reasons. At the end of his visit with Glassford, White was impressed that Glassford was so delightfully frank and a very human kind of person whom others willingly followed. The journalist concluded that the soon-to-be former chief was anything but a "yes man," who now looked forward to painting, fishing, and motorcycle touring.[6]

CHAPTER 16

Aftermath

SEEMINGLY everyone wanted to hear Glassford's story, but he declined most requests to speak. He did accept an invitation to address a veterans' rally in Philadelphia on November 3. He knew it would be a friendly audience, but he still needed to set the record straight. "I am neither a democrat, a republican, a socialist, nor a communist. I am not looking for a political job, nor do I seek further activities in the field of public life. I came here on invitation to tell a story that has already been told and retold." He went on to say that the Bonus Army veterans should rightfully have been the responsibility of the federal government, but those in power refused to give them even a supply tent. As for the DC commissioners, they refused to announce any kind of policy or assume any responsibility for the veterans. "Nothing," he told the audience, "leads more directly to disorder and disturbance than hunger.... It was either feed them or fight them." He said people had criticized him for "too much leniency, too much hospitality, too much kindness." He noted, ironically, that in this policy, "[he] had taken a leaf from the book of Mr. Herbert Hoover in the humanitarian relief work he had done in Belgium." If the president could do that for foreigners, the speaker wondered aloud, "why could he not do it for American citizens who were veterans of the world war?" They had gone to Washington hungry and discouraged, but still proud. They trekked to the nation's capital to peacefully petition for the only thing of value they had—their bonus. They had organized themselves so well, Glassford noted, that he doubted that any active-duty army unit the size of the BEF "could have camped in Washington and maintained a higher standard of discipline and conduct." He said they had supervised themselves so well that he had assigned only five police officers to oversee the Bonus Army, which totaled more than 20,000. He said that by motorcycling through the camps daily, he got to know many of them personally. He acknowledged that he and Waters were "friendly enemies," but he and Waters had cooperated in most every way except one very important difference: Glassford did everything he could to keep the veterans from coming and to encourage them to go home, while Waters did everything he could to encourage more veterans to come and to retain those already in the camps.

Glassford talked about the Communists, who were few, emphasizing that they might have succeeded in their efforts had the Metropolitan Police not helped organize, feed, and shelter the veterans. The former chief told the audience that in his daily chats with the veterans, he discovered that most of them knew very little about Communism, but from the beginning "Waters and all his lieutenants were fiercely opposed to radicalism." He added that under the policies used by the police there were no difficulties or disturbances for two months; the problems began when the Hoover administration chose to "repudiate everything that had been done and to take matters in their own hands." As for the administration's need to immediately tear down the dilapidated buildings, he noted that the veterans had already investigated and determined that the intended space was to become a park; furthermore, a funeral business and a gas station-garage business were still operating in the buildings, and the managers had applied for and received an injunction preventing demolition of the property. Glassford spoke about Camp Bartlett and Waters's and his efforts to move the remaining BEF of 7,000 to the thirty-eight-acre site on the outskirts of the city. He explained that there was no valid reason for the rushed eviction. He recounted meeting with MacArthur, who had asserted, "We are going to break the back of the B.E.F." Glassford closed by saying, "Herbert Hoover, on July 28th last, drove from the National Capital at the point of the bayonet, the disarmed, disavowed, and destitute army of Woodrow Wilson."[1]

At the end of November, Glassford was ready for a getaway. The *Monarch of Bermuda*, a combination cargo and passenger ship with two steam engines, three funnels, and four screws, was now fully functional and ready to take on both cargo and passengers. To Hap's delight his twenty-two-year-old daughter, Elisabeth "Bettie" Glassford, was available and interested in a short stay at the Belmont Hotel in Bermuda, and thereafter from Bermuda to New York City, where they would disembark on December 3. Like Guy and Pete, Bettie was born at West Point. As a young girl she was bright, active, and a leader, recruiting her friends to take part in various events. She was quite sociable, having learned from Cora the art of sophistication and dressing elegantly. Bettie attended the Sacred Heart Convent in Paris, where she studied design, and later in Los Angeles where she studied fashion art and design with Harry Collings, famous for dressing the Astors and Vanderbilts. When Hap and Cora separated, Bettie had moved to San Antonio with her mother. When the Glassford children were young, Hap had taught them various art techniques, and Bettie turned out to be his best student. She was the only child to inherit Pelham's intense desire and compulsion to create art. She continued art studies under Catharine Carter Critcher at the Critcher School of Painting and Applied Arts in Washington, DC, from which she graduated in 1931. She had begun with fashion drawing, but over the decades she branched out, painting portraits and landscapes, the latter usually bodies of water, sunsets, trees, flowers, and animals.[2]

By January 1933 Glassford had apparently resolved the internal conflict he had had with the way MacArthur and his troops handled the eviction. In a letter to John T. Rogers, historian for the 3rd Services Command in Baltimore, Glassford wrote:

> The use of troops under MacArthur was carried out with his usual good judgement and finesse. He initiated the operation with a parade and show of force on Penn. Ave at 6th Street, loudly applauded by the veterans assembled there. Instead of piecemeal eviction as recommended by the DC commissioners, MacArthur had the good judgement to complete the eviction in about a 12-hour period. No one was seriously injured, and the veterans did not have time nor opportunity to consolidate or plan any resistance.... A few bricks and stones were thrown but no shots were fired on either side; tear gas was the principal means of driving out the veterans. MacArthur did what he was told to do; it was a dirty job, but he did it well.[3]

Why Glassford absolved MacArthur is bewildering. The police chief would never have handled the expulsion that way, yet he not only refused to criticize the army chief of staff but praised his actions, placing full blame at Hoover's doorstep. Another possibility, of course, is that Glassford was simply trying to satisfy Mr. Rogers's inquiry without touching on feelings of discomfort with MacArthur's expulsion, which the former police chief had yet to fully settle.

In 1933 the John Day Company notified Glassford that they were about to publish Walter Waters's book *B. E. F.: The Whole Story of the Bonus Army*. Critchell Rimington, an associate editor, assured Glassford that "the book was fully documented and every statement made therein has been authenticated in one form or another." Rimington regarded it as "a colorful account of one of the most important dramatic events in American history since the [world] war." There seems to be no record of Glassford voicing any objection or disagreement with the recollections of his former "friendly enemy."[4]

Over the years some historians have discounted Waters's book, dismissing it as more of a self-serving recollection than accurate history. While that charge may be true to some degree, Waters's book rings much truer than the two other eyewitness, self-serving accounts of the Bonus March: Douglas MacArthur's *Reminiscences* (1964) and Herbert Hoover's *Memoirs of Herbert Hoover: The Great Depression, 1929–1941* (1952). While Waters's book was a contemporaneous, almost diary-like recounting of events, the other books are distant in time and lacking in any new evidence or research, relying almost exclusively on the attorney general's thoroughly debunked report, favorable press releases, and subsequent self-serving testimony by Communists seeking to inflate their role in the Bonus encampment.

Glassford had been helping veterans since they first trickled into Washington. In a most unusual post-expulsion case, he was called upon to aid a veteran who had been jailed for killing his wife. In 1933, Carl William Taylor, a Mescalero Apache better known as Chief Running Wolf, was sitting in the Berks County Prison near Reading, Pennsylvania. From his cell he scribbled a six-page letter to General Glassford: "My Dear Old Pal and Friend: I am very sorry to my heart to write you a letter like this but it can't be helped. I am in trouble here. I killed my loving wife in self-defense."[5]

Glassford remembered that Running Wolf was one of the few veterans who owned a vehicle, an old yellow pickup truck, which he used to scrounge food for his fellow veterans. At Glassford's suggestion, Running Wolf routinely solicited excess milk from local dairies for the infants, toddlers, and children in the camps. Glassford drove to the prison and met with Running Wolf's two court-appointed attorneys. Prosecutors had charged Running Wolf with first-degree murder and requested the death penalty. At the trial Glassford testified as a defense witness but could say only that the former Bonus member had been very helpful in the camps. After five hours of deliberation, the jury found Running Wolf guilty of voluntary manslaughter, and the judge later sentenced him to six to twelve years in prison. While Glassford could only testify as to Running Wolf's character, his testimony may have aided the defendant in avoiding the death penalty.[6]

Before returning to Arizona, Glassford wanted to see how the country could better assist its unemployed and transient youth, many of whom were riding the rails and surviving—or not—in hobo jungles. The National Children's Bureau reported that 250,000 young people under twenty-one were wandering from town to town and sleeping wherever they could, at substantial risk of death or injury.[7]

By February Glassford had acquired use of substantial acreage on the Potomac River, across from Sterling, Virginia, about thirty miles northwest of Washington. He hoped to use the property to establish a camp where unemployed and transient youth could live and learn occupational trades. Working with the American Industrial Training Association, he believed the program could be ready by April 1.[8]

Desperately in need of such camps were an estimated 2 million errant young men and a surprising number of boys, girls, and women, most of them continually moving about. The boxcars in which they rode and the jungle camps where they ate and slept were dangerous places. One teenager who "hopped freights" for a time was future journalist Eric Sevareid. "I entered a new social dimension," he later wrote, "the great underground world, peopled by tens of thousands of American men, women, and children, white, black, brown, and yellow, who inhabit the 'jungle,' eat from blackened tin cans, find warmth at night in the box cars, take the sun by day on the flatcars, steal one day, beg with cap in hand the next, fight with fists and often razors." Like most young people riding the rails, Sevareid found it essential to move about with friends; if they were together, they were safer. He remembered traveling for a time with two other young men; among them they shared one five-dollar bill, "which was tied in a handkerchief and secured out of sight inside my belt. Murder for much less than that was commonplace in the jungle."[9]

On February 8 Glassford spoke to members of the Civitan Club at their regular meeting, held in the Hamilton Hotel. He described how the camp property could support 500 homeless and unemployed young people, who would learn vocational skills and eventually become self-sufficient. On February 19 he delivered a similar message to the Soroptimists Club, adding that this camp might possibly be the first of other such camps across the country, where young people would learn poultry farming and stock raising.[10]

In 1933 Pelham drafted his son Guy to assist him on a road tour of Virginia, West Virginia, the Carolinas, Georgia, and Florida. With Guy's help, the former police chief hoped to observe and report on the conditions in which thousands of boys and young men—homeless and unemployed—got by. Presumably, they would be representative of how up to 2 million others in similar conditions throughout the nation survived. Glassford's tactic was to drop Guy at one of the "jungle camps," usually visible at the outskirts of a town. Guy would then get to know a few of the boys in the camp, who typically mistrusted older males. While Guy mixed with the camp denizens, Glassford visited with local officials, welfare workers, and railroad police. They shared with him the reality of crowded missions, overfilled flophouses, train station floors, and jails. Afterward, Glassford would return to the jungle camp and pick up Guy, who by then had assured his new acquaintances that Glassford was trustworthy. Usually the campers talked with Glassford, sharing with him such things as how long they had been on the move, the threats and assaults they endured, and how often authorities arrested them. In the towns and counties the Glassfords visited, the story was similar. Local charities would give a recent arrival a plate of beans, let him sleep indoors for a night, and send him out the next morning. In one county in West Virginia, sheriff's deputies arrested and jailed boys but did not feed them until the next morning, at which time the deputies provided only coffee and beans. The local sheriff was charging his county administrator sixty-five cents per day per prisoner. Since the sheriff's food cost per day per prisoner was just five cents, he enjoyed a pretty profit on his "hobo hotel."[11]

Another who rode the rails during the Great Depression was Morey Skaret, who many years later served as a Seattle police sergeant (later lieutenant) and related his story to me one night. As a young rookie police officer, I was assigned as Morey's driver one night shift in 1969, when potentially volatile civil rights and anti–Vietnam War protests necessitated that no marked police cars have just one officer on board. In the very early and quiet hours of the morning, as part of an ongoing conversation, Morey recalled that during the Great Depression he and scores of other young "hobos" habitually rode the rails. He remembered one night when he and some others were in boxcars passing through Wyoming. The train stopped suddenly, and sheriff's deputies ushered the freeloaders off the train. They were then packed into trucks, taken to a farm, and required to work thirty days without pay. After that, sheriff's deputies retrieved them, put them on another train, and sent them on their way. Morey remembered that there was no formal arrest or charging, but the farmer had fed them and given them a barn to sleep in. Presumably, the next train brought a new load of transients, the farmer received essentially free labor for a month, and the sheriff pocketed his finder's fee.[12]

Following his personal survey of unemployed youth in various states, Glassford submitted his report and was successful in having a bill introduced in Congress to establish camps for destitute and unemployed youth. His work and that of others comingled and led to the establishment of the Civilian Conservation Corps.[13]

On March 4, 1933, Franklin Roosevelt became the thirty-second president of the United States. That same year 3,000 World War veterans—some from the Bonus Army—returned to Washington, still seeking their bonus. A new president and a new Congress were in office, but neither favored giving the veterans an early bonus, aware that the down-and-out veterans were but a small percentage of the total population living in poverty. But by then Roosevelt had a program ready. It had happened quickly. On March 9, having been in office just five days, he sent for advisors to expand on some thoughts he had about putting 500,000 young men to work doing national conservation projects. By 9:00 that night he had a draft of the required legislation, and by March 31 the Civilian Conservation Corps—the CCC—was born.[14]

To greet the 3,000 recently returned World War veterans, Roosevelt told his assistant, Louis Howe, to provide them with food, shelter, and medical care and to take Eleanor Roosevelt to visit their camp. Howe drove the First Lady to the camp. "When we arrived," Mrs. Roosevelt remembered, "Howe announced that he was going to sit in the car but that I was to walk around the veterans to see just how things were. Hesitatingly I got out and walked over to where I saw a line-up of men waiting for food. They looked at me curiously and one of them asked my name and what I wanted. When I said I just wanted to see how they were getting on, they asked me to join them." She ignored the rain and mud and shared coffee with the men for almost an hour. As she recalled, "There had been no excitement, and my only protection had been a weary gentleman, Louis Howe, who had slept in the car during my visit." Thereafter, often repeated, were the words of an unremembered veteran, who said, "Hoover sent the army and Roosevelt sent Eleanor."[15]

The Roosevelt administration later recruited 2,600 of this group of 3,000, along with an additional 25,000 other World War veterans, as CCC members. The program was restricted to young men from eighteen to twenty-five, but Roosevelt granted an age exemption for the World War veterans, who joined 2.75 million young men and labored for years planting trees, building bridges, and carving roads in the nation's many natural areas and parks. For their work they earned $30 ($612) per month, $22 ($449) of which they had to send home if they had a dependent family. In the end the CCC provided a legacy that millions of Americans still view and enjoy every year. American military veterans who subsequently benefited from the Servicemen's Readjustment Act of 1944, better known as the GI Bill, can trace those benefits back to the BEF. In July 1943, midway through World War II, President Roosevelt, in one of his famous fireside chats, warned, "Veterans of [World War II] must not be demobilized into an environment of inflation and unemployment, to a place on a bread line or on a corner selling apples.... We must this time have plans ready." From the 2 million veterans of World War II and the Korean War who used their GI Bill education benefit, America gained 67,000 doctors, 22,000 dentists, 91,000 scientists, 450,000 engineers, and 238,000 teachers. Nearly 8 million veterans benefitted in some way from the GI Bill. A subsequent bill during the Vietnam War was equally successful for many, and a similar program continues today.[16]

In late 1933 Bettie Glassford went to Los Angeles to visit her sister Dorothy, who had settled there after marrying Lee Osher Combs Jr. For a short time in 1934, Bettie became a Hollywood dress designer. She traveled to San Diego to attend a cocktail party given in her honor, aboard the USS *Constitution*. There she met Navy Lieutenant Lee Wood Parke, who was stationed nearby.[17]

On March 17, 1934, with Cora Glassford at his side, Hap sent off their daughter, Bettie, to Lee Parke, at the time assigned to the destroyer USS *Yarnell* (DD-143). The wedding took place at the Church of the Flowers in Glendale, California, the proud father wearing his full-dress army uniform. Following their honeymoon the newlyweds intended to reside in Washington, DC, Lieutenant Parke's new assignment. Mrs. Lee Combs—the former Dorothy Seymour Glassford—sister of the bride—was matron of honor, and Lee Combs, a *Yarnell* shipmate of Parke's, was best man. Mr. Guy Carleton Glassford, brother of the bride, served as one of the ushers. Pelham Glassford Jr., in his final year at West Point, was unable to attend.[18]

Pelham Glassford returned to Arizona and a life of farming, ranching, motorcycle riding, traveling, and painting. On July 19, 1933, he and his mother traveled from Arizona to the family's summer home in Port Townsend, Washington, on the Olympic Peninsula. An intervening stop, however, was a brief stay in Seattle to visit with Navy Captain William Glassford II, assigned to the battleship USS *California* (BB-44), one of several navy ships in port for Fleet Week, Seattle's annual festival—always held when the chance of rain is less but always a potential. Brother Bill's battleship was a post–World War I Tennessee-class battleship, destined to spend her entire career in the Pacific, mostly as the flagship of the Pacific fleet. Japanese bombs would send her below at Pearl Harbor, but the Navy would reconstruct her so that she could serve again throughout World War II. Following their visit with Bill, Pelham and Allie continued to Port Townsend. For Allie, seeing the Victorian house on Reed Street brought back memories of being there with William Sr., who had first discovered the beauty of Port Townsend while overseeing the laying of an underwater telegraph cable from Seattle to Alaska. Just as he had become a booster for Arizona, he did the same for Port Townsend. He began by buying individual lots on the southern edge of Morgan Hill in the Crow's Nest area above the harbor town of Port Townsend. William and Allie hoped to build a home there with the high bluff location providing a commanding view of Port Townsend Bay, and in the background, Puget Sound, with the snow-covered Mount Baker reflecting brilliantly. As it turned out, William and Allie never built that house because on a subsequent trip they discovered a house for sale that offered the same view. They bought the elegant two-story home, replete with bay windows that provided something of a view from almost every room. The retired colonel also enjoyed visiting with army friends at nearby Fort Worden, one of the coast artillery forts overlooking greater Puget Sound, none of which ever fired a shot in anger.[19]

On a drive north Hap had sketched a map of the route from Phoenix to San Diego and up the Pacific Coast through California, Oregon, and Washington to Port Townsend. The sketch later became a family postcard. Port Townsend developed its reputation as being "much dryer" than most Western Washington towns because of its location in the "rain shadow," caused by clouds dropping their moisture over the

Olympic Mountains, west of the town. But when October and November arrive, even dryer Port Townsend gets wet. Thus, in late September 1933, rain possible any day, Hap and Allie departed Port Townsend. Soon they were once again managing the farms in Phoenix.[20]

On March 11 of the following year, motorcycle-lover Hap took time off from his farm and ranch duties to lead the annual "gypsy tour" of about 200 riders of the Phoenix Motorcycle Club from Phoenix to a desert resort in Arizona.[21]

CHAPTER 17

Factories in the Field and Communists on the Horizon

IN 1934 Glassford found himself a target of death threats as he attempted to mediate between powerful crop growers and itinerant fieldworkers in the Imperial Valley of California. The situation had its roots in a land history unique to California.

Early California farms were unlike traditional American farms. A better description of these growing operations was "factories in the field," a term originated in 1935 by author-journalist Carey McWilliams. Since the arrival of the pilgrims, traditional American farming in the East had been more a way of life than an occupation. Farms were usually family undertakings, with the birth of each child welcomed as a future helper in an ongoing quest for prosperity. But even with large families, many farmers still found it necessary to hire a full-time laborer or two to help with cultivating crops, raising livestock, and maintaining the house, barn, sheds, tools, and equipment. Family members tended to regard these hired hands as minor partners in the enterprise, who sometimes shared meals with the family and bunked in a building on the farm.[1]

Such was not the case in California. Originally, the land had belonged to Spain until Mexico seized it upon achieving independence. Over the decades, the Spanish owners divided the land into huge tracts, subsequently dispersed to a relatively small number of families of favored colonial aristocracy. When the Mexican War forcefully passed California to American ownership, the land retained its character of immense ranches and farms owned by a surprisingly small number of individuals; thus, in 1870, just over 500 men owned close to 9 million acres. The first large-scale agricultural use of these lands was as "bonanza wheat farms," which followed the decline of the California gold rush. By 1889 California had 2.75 million acres of wheat under cultivation. Like the California gold rush forty-niners, the bonanza farmers were out to strike it rich, but mined for wheat instead of gold. These farmers, however, seldom saw their fields. That was because they were office-bound absentee corporate businessmen overseeing plantations from a comfortable distance. McWilliams branded them "land buccaneers."[2]

The landowners relied on low-paid fieldworkers to harvest the wheat. The first seasonal workers were American Indians. Needing more workers, wheat growers searched for an additional population, which needed to be willing to work long hours for low pay under miserable conditions. "Chinamen," as the whites called them, became the preferred workers. Beginning in 1865, Chinese immigrants in the West and mostly Irish immigrants in the East picked, pounded, shoveled, and dynamited their way toward each other through almost 2,000 miles of prairie, mountains, and desert to build a transcontinental railroad. The Chinese workers had not been recruited from China for this purpose but had previously immigrated to the United States. The Irish were primarily former Union and Confederate soldiers, usually unmarried. By the time the two populations met in Utah in 1869, they had built a railroad. The Chinese, now unemployed, often worked in the wheat fields, proving to be the population the big growers had hoped for—not quite slaves but close enough. Doing sweat work, the Chinese proved to be hardworking, reliable, and agreeable. Because they had no cultural, linguistic, or social ties to the local population, they quickly became economic captives of the growers. By the 1870s growers agreed that the Chinese were indispensable, having proved themselves in the fields just as they had on the rails.[3]

Other unemployed Chinese gravitated to the cities, finding urban work by accepting substandard pay. Rather quickly, white workers agitated for laws restricting Chinese employment. Congress subsequently enacted the Chinese Exclusion Act of 1882, which prohibited future Chinese immigration. Somewhat concurrent with this challenge for the California growers was the awareness that cultivating fruits and vegetables was now more profitable than wheat. The completion of huge irrigation projects, coupled with the arrival of refrigerated rail cars and improved canning and drying processes, created new financial opportunities. Desert lands morphed into lush valleys, ideal for feeding the huge appetites of thousands of fruit and vegetable markets in the East. Growers found themselves transitioning from wheat to fruits and vegetables while at the same time contending with the loss of their preferred workforce. Of necessity, it was seasonable work; a 4,000-acre vineyard, for instance, provided year-round employment for only 70 workers but at harvest needed 700.[4]

Growers soon identified another population, Japanese immigrants, who were then arriving on the West Coast and appeared to be as agreeable and dependable as had been the Chinese. Additionally, the Japanese would work for even lower wages than the other populations, soon becoming the picker majority. By 1900 most California growers had concluded that Japanese workers were their preferred workers. What the growers failed to anticipate was that the Japanese culture afforded the workers almost total solidarity and common purpose, something of a built-in labor union. This gave the workers significant power, especially just before a harvest, when Japanese workers might suddenly leave the fields until they received a substantial raise, threatening the loss of the crop. Growers responded by successfully obtaining federal legislation restricting future Japanese immigration, as well as state legislation forbidding Japanese from acquiring their own farmland. By 1907 many Japanese workers had migrated to other job opportunities, leaving the fields and taking up urban occupations or working the fields in other states.[5]

Once again, California growers searched for another workforce and settled on a promising group—Mexicans. By all appearances, it was a sound choice, and through the 1920s growers were as pleased with Mexicans as they had been with the Chinese. In the view of the growers, both populations possessed two attractive qualities—they were available, and they were powerless. Despite ongoing immigration restrictions along the Mexican border, Mexicans who were in the country illegally were readily at hand, and if they became troublesome, friendly authorities could deport them. Additionally, Mexicans remained largely outside the social, economic, and political mainstream—another benefit for the growers.[6]

For the growers a major threat arrived when it appeared that national labor unions contemplated organizing California farmworkers. To the relief of the growers, the national labor unions rather quickly concluded that trying to organize farmworkers, mostly Mexican, was too difficult—they were highly transient and spoke only Spanish. The agribusinessmen, now on their third worker population, concluded that in the future their labor practices needed to afford them "absolute control over wages, hours, and most other conditions of employment." The way the growers would accomplish this would be to greet any request for better wages or improved working conditions with intransigence.[7]

Willing to step in where the national labor unions left an opening was the Communist Party, USA, founded in New York in 1919. American Communists saw opportunity in grooming populations that mainstream unions dismissed, suspecting that agricultural fieldworkers, mostly Mexican, would welcome organizing. This proved to be difficult not only because the workers spoke only Spanish but also because they were staunchly Catholic. Regardless, the New York Party leaders demanded that the local Communists in California and other states recruit farmworkers. Ready to undertake this improbable mission in California was a small number of low-level Communists, young, idealistic, and committed. The place they selected for their organizing was the Imperial Valley, its highly industrialized agriculture having benefitted from massive irrigation programs. On high alert for even a whiff of labor organizing in California, however, was a committed force of growers, business associations, local newspapers, and sympathetic law enforcement agencies.[8]

The first significant confrontation came in January 1930, in the Imperial Valley town of Brawley, California, about thirty miles north of Mexico. Fieldworkers, Mexican and Filipino, spontaneously walked off the lettuce fields, fed up with miserable pay and unbearable conditions. What began with a few hundred workers inflated to 5,000 over a few days, despite little coordination. Under pressure from the local sheriff, the strike was close to collapse when three young California Communists of the Trade Union Unity League, Frank Waldron, Harry Harvey, and Tsuji Horiuchi, inserted themselves into the labor camps. Imperial County Sheriff Charles L. Gillett, a strong supporter of the region's antilabor stance, smelled trouble and mobilized local authorities. The no-nonsense sheriff had arrived in the county in 1922 and quickly built a reputation of being fearless. He alerted the growers, who called on friendly newspapers and public officials to launch an educational campaign asserting that the labor strike was not about wages or conditions but was an attempted Communist takeover. Fearful of arrest, Waldron, Harvey, and Horiuchi slept in the camps by day and engaged workers at night. The sheriff's deputies soon detected the three and arrested them for vagrancy, putting them in separate jails and roughing them up in the process. For several days investigators interrogated the men, demanding that they confess to a plot to blow up lettuce sheds, which the men adamantly denied. Two representatives from the American Civil Liberties Union (ACLU) appeared unexpectedly at Sheriff Gillett's office to protest the arrests and treatment of the three organizers. Shown to his office, the two attorneys saw a man they presumed to be the sheriff, seated at a desk, his thick, black, center-parted hair crowning a round face that appeared to rest on shoulders with no discernable neck.

Interrupting the ACLU lawyers midsentence, the enraged sheriff bounded from his desk and began pushing, punching, shoving, and kicking the two men until they were out of his office and in the street. With that the strike died, but the clash between the growers and workers did not.[9]

Samuel Adams Darcy was the newly arrived Communist Organizer of Branch 1, DC 13, based in San Francisco. Now twenty-three, tall and brawny, he seldom fussed with his untamable hair and wild mustache. An astute organizer, he concluded that the only way to organize Mexican farmworkers was to focus exclusively on improving wages and conditions and forget about preaching Communist doctrine, which could come later.[10]

Confrontation between growers and workers flared on April 14, 1934, at El Centro, fourteen miles south of Brawley. Darcy's embryonic and naive Communist labor union, the Agricultural Workers Industrial League (AWIL), unwisely announced publicly that an informational meeting would take place on April 20, as a prelude to planning a cantaloupe strike. On April 14, as various preliminary labor meetings got underway, city, county, and state law enforcement officers launched a series of raids, swooping in and rounding up more than 100 militant workers and AWIL organizers. The leaders were quickly jailed, with the standard bail of $500 to $3,000 ($10,208 to $61,246) increased to $40,000 ($816,618) for each. Growers had no intention of letting any strike happen, and cooperative local police chiefs and sheriffs recruited and appointed special deputies who used clubs and tear gas to break up strike meetings and force suspected troublemakers from the labor camps. There was no doubt that local law enforcement officers were working with their community, but they limited their community to the growers and their supporters and purposely excluded the fieldworkers, at least those seeking higher pay and better working conditions.[11]

That year, with the inclusion of cannery workers, Darcy's AWIL became the CAWIU. Something of a behind-the-scenes strategist, he engineered more than twenty strikes, aided by two young and foolishly fearless workers, Pat Chambers and Caroline Decker. Chambers, thirty-three and of Irish descent, had been a sailor and oil field rigger and had later gone to jail for working with the Wobblies (Industrial Workers of the World). Decker, the daughter of immigrant Jews, was twenty-one, attractive, and a spitfire with a Georgia accent, so much so that news reporters labeled her "the blonde flame of the red revolt." A veteran of the Harlan County, Kentucky, coal strikes, she had not gone to college, but she easily and confidently stood toe-to-toe with prosecuting attorneys as she defended arrested workers. Working furtively in the camps, Chambers and Decker followed Darcy's instructions and omitted all political doctrine, focused only on improving wages and conditions as a way of turning discontented workers into militant strikers.[12]

Growers feared losing ground and struck back. Local law enforcement officers were in support of the growers, with one Kern County undersheriff stating, matter-of-factly, "[The growers] put us here and they can put us out again, so we serve them." With the support of local newspapers, growers announced boycotts against any merchant who sold anything to the workers, and at the first indication of a strike, urged welfare agencies to scrub the names of any strikers from their client lists. Nevertheless, the strikes continued, and by October 9, 12,000 strikers in Kings, Kern, and Tulare Counties were demanding increased wages. While workers were grateful for CAWIU assistance, they remained impervious to Communist indoctrination. H. L. Walker, manager of the Bakersfield branch of the state employment office, summed it up when he said, "Radicals don't make a strike and needless to say the run of the [mill] strikers don't know the difference between communism and somnambulism."[13]

President Franklin Roosevelt hoped to address strike violence then occurring throughout the country, including California. His predicament was that assistance to organized labor might distance the formidable southern Democrats in Congress, whose support was vital for passage of federal legislation deemed essential for recovering from the Great Depression. The South, of course, had its own force of low-paid workers—overwhelmingly African American sharecroppers, tenant farmers, and domestic workers—usually living in ramshackle dwellings. Southern voters and campaign contributors, almost exclusively white, resisted any legislation or government action that might disturb the status quo. It seemed incongruous to focus on California labor violence while at the same time ignoring widespread lynching occurring in the South, but that was the choice presented to the president. From 1889 to 1933 more than 3,700 lynchings had taken place, primarily of African Americans in the southern states, with torture often a precursor to the hanging and posthumous body mutilation underscoring its savagery and signaling a warning to others. Still, some action in California might lessen labor violence there.[14]

Since local law enforcement agencies seldom chose to protect California fieldworkers at that time, supporters of the pickers requested federal assistance. President Roosevelt would eventually send two conciliators to California to help address labor violence. The first would be George Creel, and the second would be Pelham Glassford. The limited success of Creel would directly determine how successful, or unsuccessful, Glassford would be.

In 1933 California was the site of thirty-seven spontaneous strikes involving 50,000 fieldworkers. The largest strike had come on October 4 in the cotton country of the San Joaquin Valley. Money was the issue: growers offered 60 cents ($12.25) for 100 pounds of picked cotton; workers, three quarters of whom were Mexican or Mexican American, demanded $1 ($20.42). The 40 cents difference led to what became known as the Pixley Massacre.[15]

On October 10, 1933, Pat Chambers stood in the bed of a pickup truck, addressing 350 fieldworkers in the small town of Pixley, about fifty miles north of Bakersfield on Highway 99. Still nursing a broken jaw from a recent vigilante assault, Chambers cautioned the workers to be nonviolent but assured them that they had the right to protect themselves. Suddenly, a caravan of forty growers and their supporters drove up behind the crowd, jumped out of their trucks and cars and began firing rifles, shotguns, and handguns. As the workers fled, the growers emptied their weapons at the fleeing bodies, killing two and wounding eight. California newspapers reported the story widely, their readers outraged at the level of violence. Clearly, someone needed to do something, but local and state officials, including the governor, had little interest in doing so. When the *New York Times* reported the story, President Roosevelt knew he had to send a troubleshooter to California.[16]

The president wanted to put the country back to work. The recently passed 1933 National Industrial Recovery Act (NIRA), which created the National Recovery Administration (NRA), was intended to do just that. It was labor legislation intended to help employees and their unions bargain with employers. But Roosevelt did not want agricultural labor—farmworkers—considered as "employees," since he still needed the votes of southern lawmakers. The language of Section 7(a) of the Act neither included nor excluded farmworkers; even so, farmworkers understandably concluded that the president wanted them to bargain collectively. Regardless of the ambiguous NIRA language, Roosevelt needed the two sides in California to reach a compromise. For this he called on George Creel, who had so ably assisted President Wilson in preparing Americans to support the World War.[17]

Then living in San Francisco, Creel was anxious to assume his new duties as the West Coast Chief of the new NRA. "I accepted the appointment," he recalled, "but days passed without a word from Washington as to the powers and duties of the new bodies, or even an inkling as to who would head them."[18]

Creel tended to be petulant, arrogant, and inflexible, but he got results. He concluded that the only way to learn the extent of his new duties was to travel to the nation's capital. "Flying to Washington to get some exact information," he later wrote, "I had my first experience with the headlong, haphazard methods that were to make a mess of the New Deal. On every hand there was the confusion of activity with action." Of major concern to him was that "there was only a vague surmise as to the workings of 7(a), the all-important section having to do with labor's right to organize and bargain collectively." Unfortunately, his trip to Washington failed to lift the fog, and even a meeting with the president cleared up very little. It was apparent that even Roosevelt did not have the answers.[19]

Creel returned to San Francisco a few days later, having decided that bluffing was his best move. He established dominance early: "On my return I walked into the customhouse, picked myself an office, and calmly announced that I was the head of NRA for the [West] Coast, and the sole source of authority. Fortunately, nobody had the wit to challenge my right, and before any embarrassing questions could be asked, I had an organization going full speed ahead."[20]

Creel was not only the West Coast head of the National Recovery Administration; Roosevelt had also appointed him as the western regional chief of the National Labor Board. On October 18, 1933, upon hearing of the Pixley violence, Creel went to the San Joaquin Valley. He first met with the large growers in Tulare County, and then met with Pat Chambers, which required that Creel go to the Visalia jail where Chambers awaited trial on criminal syndicalism charges. Outraging the large growers, Creel arranged for Chambers to be temporarily released to attend a fact-finding hearing of the governor's commission. Creel next met with Caroline Decker at the Corcoran strike camp, which at the time was jammed with 5,000 hungry Mexicans and Dust Bowl migrants, their home since growers had evicted them from company shacks at gunpoint. Now they slept in their dilapidated jalopies and flivvers and tattered tents, amid chickens and children. Caroline Decker had been there a week and had earned the trust of the inhabitants. When she asked them to listen to Creel, they did.[21]

Creel then warned the growers that if their vigilantes and thugs continued to beat and shoot workers, he would cancel their federal loans and have trucks deliver food to feed the striking workers. Thereafter, he pressured Governor James "Sunny Jim" Rolph, former mayor of San Francisco, to appoint a three-person fact-finding commission, and then he pressured the growers to accept its findings. The commission hearings took place on October 19–20. Harvard graduate and ACLU attorney Abraham Lincoln Wirin represented the workers, assisted by Caroline Decker, both of whom skillfully questioned the witnesses and presented the facts. The commissioners took only two days to conclude that there was no question that the strikers' civil rights had been infringed upon and recommended that growers pay workers 75 cents per 100 pounds.[22]

Creel again warned the growers to accept the compromise or lose their loans, and then he warned the workers to do the same or he would no longer provide food. Decker, representing the CAWIU, advised the workers to accept. The agreement reached on October 25 ended the strike and its violence. The growers complained that the wage increase would cost them $450,000 ($9,186,951), but they also knew that the agreement affected only the current cotton crop and only for the remainder of the current season. By the end of the year, the cotton harvest had brought in an increase of 145 percent over the previous year. With this limited victory, Creel moved on to other New Deal issues.[23]

The vague language of NIRA Section 7(a) was taken out of contention when growers successfully lobbied New Deal administrators to simply use executive fiat to remove agricultural workers from the NIRA. In addition, the administrators, on their own, extended the exclusion to include the Social Security Act and the NRA.[24]

While the New Deal administration was pleased with Creel's limited success, it was uneasy that his take-it-or-leave-it tactics had been unwise. The growers, foolishly believing that Conciliator Creel had the power to fulfill his threats, now had no intention of ever allowing that to happen again. Their studied plan was to undertake a major educational and information campaign to persuade Californians that the problems between growers and workers had nothing to do with wages or conditions; on the contrary, it was a Communist union fomenting a Bolshevik revolution. The ongoing campaign of the growers would vex the next federal conciliator, Pelham Glassford, who would soon arrive to deal with labor violence in a different valley.[25]

On January 23, 1934, ACLU attorney Abraham Wirin drove from Los Angeles to the Imperial Valley town of Brawley to be the principal speaker at an

ACLU event the next day at the Azteca Hall. He would speak about Imperial County and the right to strike as guaranteed by the NRA and the Constitution. He had already asked the Imperial Valley sheriff and the Brawley police chief for protection, but both refused. Wirin was having dinner in the restaurant of the Planters Hotel an hour before his presentation when several men, one wearing the uniform of a Highway Patrol officer, grabbed and dragged him from his table out to the street, where they punched him and forced him into a car. They drove him to a deserted area, beat him a second time, tied his hands behind his back, and pinned him to the ground, covering his head with his coat. When he said he could not breathe, they beat him again. He next heard one of the kidnappers say that they should brand him before they drowned him, and another suggested lynching him. The men then stole his shoes and wallet and left him for dead in the nighttime desert, eleven miles from the tiny town of Calipatria. After Wirin heard them drive off, he managed to free his hands, stand, and walk barefoot along the desert road until he encountered some teenagers having a party. They drove him to a telephone, where he was able to call a friend to pick him up. Three other friends drove fourteen miles from Brawley to meet him at the Barbara Worth Hotel in El Centro, anxiously waiting for him outside the elegant Spanish Renaissance Inn. After Wirin's arrival, armed vigilantes, some drunk, came close, shined lights in their eyes, jabbed them with the barrels of their revolvers, and threatened to lynch them. The sheriff appeared, gathered Wirin and his friends, and said he would protect them, but only if they left the Imperial Valley immediately. They agreed and accepted an escort toward San Diego.[26]

Perhaps surprisingly, local newspapers praised the men as homeland defenders rather than vigilantes. One newspaper editorialized that the removal of the troublemaker was simply local citizens maintaining the community peace when the law failed to do so; thus, treating kidnapping, assault, robbery, and attempted murder as a noble action. The message was clear: in the Imperial Valley, those deemed to be "agitators" were at high risk.[27]

Had Wirin been a foreigner or a Communist, the matter would have fizzled, but he was a respected ACLU attorney, and his legal associates demanded that the federal government do something about this serious crime. Wirin's kidnapping, coupled with earlier vigilante attacks, prompted Senator Robert F. Wagner, chair of the National Labor Board, to appoint a three-person board of Californians to investigate. The board consisted of Will French, previously director of the California Department of Industrial Relations; Simon Lubin, owner of a chain of department stores as well as the director of the California Bureau of Commerce; and J. L. Leonard, professor of economics at the University of Southern California. In February 1934, after a ten-day investigation, the Board presented its thirty-page document, which lambasted growers and government officials, asserted that law enforcement officers routinely interfered with the workers' rights of free speech and assembly, and described the living conditions of the workers, using such terms as "primitive," "filthy," "savage," and "squalor." In a later speech before a civic club, Lubin accused the growers of inventing "Red Scare" tactics to shift attention from starvation wages and terrible conditions. Hackles rose in both California and Washington, DC. The *Los Angeles Times* and the *Brawley News* labeled the report as nonsense, insisting that the growers were just defending their lives and property from "communists" bent on treason. The New Deal administration downplayed the report, maintaining that California could address the situation without federal involvement. Thus, while the White House clearly had no interest in interceding, it would entertain something a notch below that.[28]

On March 23, 1934, the Imperial Valley Growers and Shippers Protective League had held a mass rally of some 6,000 people at the Imperial County Fairgrounds. The goal of the gathering was to drive the Communists out of the county. That same year the recently formed Associated Farmers organization undertook a massive educational campaign to revise the thinking of Californians.[29]

The day before, March 22, Glassford had received a telegram from the office of Secretary of Labor Frances Perkins, under President Franklin Roosevelt. It read:

> GENERAL PELHAM GLASSFORD PHOENIX ARIZ
> HAVE BEEN REQUESTED IN CONFIDENCE BY MISS
> PERKINS OFFICE TO ASK IF YOU WOULD BE WILLING
> TO REPRESENT AS LABOR MEDIATOR FROM HER
> DEPARTMENT AND AGRICULTURE DEPARTMENT
> IN IMPERIAL VALLEY CONTROVERSY WHERE
> THERE IS APPARENTLY A GOOD DEAL OF TROUBLE
> IN HARVESTING OF MELONS ETC STOP REPORT
> THRU NATIONAL LABOR BOARD HAS NOT BEEN
> SATISFACTORY STOP IT WOULD MEAN ABOUT SIX
> WEEKS.

Glassford read the telegram again, no doubt attentive to its key words: "in confidence"; "a good deal of trouble in harvesting"; "about six weeks." It seemed a reasonable request, and the Imperial Valley was only about a day's drive from his ranch. He telegraphed his willingness to assist.[30]

Secretary Perkins had become the first woman in US history to hold a federal cabinet position. She had previously been commissioner of the New York State Department of Labor under then-governor Franklin Roosevelt. Now she was a member of his federal cabinet, a position she would hold throughout his tenure. She needed a conciliator, but not George Creel. She had earlier read about Glassford and had been impressed by his handling of the Bonus Army and how he had preferred charm over confrontation, coupled with compassion and professionalism.[31]

In 1954 Secretary Perkins gave an extensive oral interview in which she reflected on her life, including her interactions with Pelham Glassford in 1934, twenty years previous. She likely spoke without having written notes to consult, and some of her recollections were likely faulty. Her view of Latinos is racist by today's standards but were commonly held opinions in the 1930s and 1950s. Speaking of fieldworkers in 1934, she told the interviewers that those people tended to move about and thought nothing of washing their children, clothes, and vegetables in the same irrigation ditches, which she attributed to their "Latin blood."[32]

She recalled that she thought that a military man might be the ideal person to help the "good deal of trouble" in the Imperial Valley. She knew he was intelligent and had a sense of justice and would be committed to the mission. She telephoned him and invited him to come to Washington to discuss serving as a conciliator with the Department of Labor, adding that she hoped he might be able to bring some calm to the disturbances taking place there. Glassford agreed and surprised her when he showed up at her office the next day. She recalled that he had little experience with the niceties of preliminary interviews and such, and he was ready to do what needed to be done. She liked what she saw and was pleased that he spoke Spanish.[33]

It had been six months since the Roosevelt administration had dispatched its first conciliator to California. Now it had appointed a second one, and for the same reason—labor violence. Glassford likely did not know that he was already at a disadvantage: what had worked well for Creel, his take-it-or-leave-it bluff, would not be available for Glassford. Worse, over the previous six months, the growers had educated themselves and knew that Section 7(a) did not apply to agricultural labor.

For Glassford, bluffing was out of the question. Equally important, Glassford would do his work in the Imperial Valley, not the San Joaquin Valley, where Creel had conciliated. Whatever happened in the San Joaquin Valley received considerable statewide media coverage; whatever happened in the Imperial Valley attracted little notice except from its residents, who for news likely relied on small local newspapers sympathetic to the growers.[34]

Endowed naturally with compassion and empathy, Glassford would seem to be the ideal conciliator. The Imperial Valley growers, however, did not want anyone coming into their county and hotly announced their hostility even before he arrived. The new conciliator likely knew little about Imperial Valley history. In 1901 private developers had dug a canal to allow water from the Colorado River to flow into the Valley. The distant mountains remained brown and bare, populated exclusively by xeric desert plants that survived on three inches of annual rain. That would not work for fruits and vegetables, but now with river water, the Valley found new life, perfect for growing melon and citrus crops under the intense sun. In the 1920s the Federal Bureau of Reclamation had assisted with the maintenance and expansion of water projects, rendering the farm fields fertile. The local growers loved the subsidized water but cringed at the thought that the federal government had its big hand on the spigot.[35]

Geographically, the surroundings of the Imperial Valley included San Diego, 115 miles to the west, the Chocolate Mountains and sand dunes to the east, the accidentally formed Salton Sea to the north, and Mexico to the south. The major east-west route, Highway 60 (now I-10), ran to the north of the Imperial Valley, connecting Phoenix and Los Angeles; a secondary east-west route, Highway 80 (now I-8), ran across southern Imperial Valley, connecting Tucson and San Diego. The latter route carried much less traffic, especially in 1934. A little over 200 miles from Los Angeles, the Imperial Valley was well outside the circulation and distribution area of the larger Southern California newspapers. Except for the folks who lived and worked in the main towns of Brawley (population 10,500) and El Centro (8,500), few people paid much attention to what happened in the Valley. Some of the landowners had small farms while others had extensive operations, and some of the landowners might not have been suspected of being landowners at all, such as the Southern Pacific Railroad, the Security First Bank of Los Angeles, the Equitable California Holding Company, and the Times-Mirror Corporation, parent of the *Los Angeles Times*. Unsurprisingly, these corporate owners seldom visited their fields, relying instead on superintendents who managed the field bosses of the bent-over pickers baking in the sun. Farming in the Imperial Valley did have its risks, of course: fruits and vegetables damaged easily, border violence was common, the climate was harsh, and the economy was anyone's guess.[36]

On March 27 the *Washington Daily News* reported that General Pelham Glassford had been appointed as conciliator for "strike problems" and was expected to arrive in the Imperial Valley by April. The National Labor Relations Board had suggested to Secretary Perkins that she send someone to "take the lead in setting up some permanent machinery to prevent bloodshed and further rioting in the war-torn region." With Glassford's experience with the Bonus Army, Perkins thought he would be the right person to serve as federal conciliator between growers and fieldworkers there. She likely knew that he was now a grower and rancher himself, but she expected that he would be able to empathize with the fieldworkers as he had done with the Bonus Army veterans. What apparently never surfaced in the early communication between Perkins and Glassford was that he would have essentially no power as a conciliator, and while she wanted him to lessen the violence, she needed him to do so without offending the growers. She feared that hostile information from California growers might trickle its way east to the southern Democrats, whose support Roosevelt still required. The catalyst for inserting a second conciliator into California had been the damning report issued by Senator Wagner's investigative committee. In addition to stating its startling conclusions, the investigative committee recommended federal intervention, perhaps dispatching someone to take the lead in establishing policies and procedures to prevent additional bloodshed and rioting. Secretary Perkins saw that as an overreach; she would settle for Glassford simply seeing that the melon crop was peacefully harvested before it became damaged and that he suggest some lasting reforms. That, of course, was much less than what the National Labor Relations Board had in mind. What complicated matters in the Imperial Valley was that the local highway patrol commander, El Centro police chief, Brawley police chief, sheriff, undersheriff, and local judges were themselves growers.[37]

It did not take the new conciliator long to realize that the "good deal of trouble in harvesting" was an understatement. As soon as the Imperial Valley growers heard that a federal conciliator was coming, they balked, certain that there was absolutely no need for Glassford or anyone else to come into their valley. One after another the hostile messages found the desk of Secretary Perkins. Timothy A. Reardon, California state director of industrial relations, asserted that negotiators had settled all wage and working condition issues to the satisfaction of both growers and workers. William C. McCarthy, executive secretary to California Governor James Rolph, said there was no labor dispute and state authorities could handle all matters. C. B. Moore, secretary-manager of the Western Growers' Produce Association, Brawley, California, said that the state could handle labor problems and needed no help from the federal government, and if they did, they would ask it. Mr. N. M. Graham, chairman of the Imperial County Board of Supervisors, wrote that they could handle all labor matters so that both growers and workers were satisfied, and there was no need for Glassford to come. Mr. Alvin N. Jack, president of the Growers and Shippers Protective Association, asserted that there were no ongoing strikes and thus nothing for Glassford to conciliate, adding that it was true that they had had some labor problems, but it was only because the Communists were inciting the workers and now the Communists had been put down. A *Los Angeles Times* editorial announced that there was nothing to conciliate, and if there were, Glassford was without the experience to do it. The editorial charged that it looked like the federal government could not tell the difference between patriotic American taxpayers and Communist aliens trying to overthrow the government, adding that Imperial County needed no external interference, unless, perhaps, Glassford came with a "sharp stick" to use on the Communists.[38]

Even before the last telegram fluttered down on Perkins's desk, an incident occurred that belied the collective message of the telegrams. On March 28, the same day that Glassford sent his acceptance telegram to Washington, a brazen assault occurred in El Centro. ACLU attorney Grover C. Johnson, working pro bono, was escorting two of his clients, Pat Chambers and S. C. Alexander, out of the Imperial County courthouse. The two men had previously been taken into custody and now had been released following Johnson's submission of a writ of habeas corpus. The charge against the two men was disturbing the peace, the usual charge for labor agitation. As Johnson threaded his way through a group of about forty men, one of them slugged him, knocking him down the courthouse steps, causing his glasses to fly off. As he looked around and felt for them, he heard someone warn that if he ever came back to Imperial Valley, he wouldn't need any glasses. This had been a daylight assault on the white marble steps of the Imperial County Courthouse, the symbol of justice.[39]

In 1934 Harry Chandler was the well-known publisher of the *Los Angeles*

Times. Of concern to some observers was that the corporate parent of that newspaper owned vast tracts of land—hundreds of thousands of acres—in both the Imperial Valley and south of the border. No longer expecting a welcome banner, Glassford packed his suitcases and drove west.[40]

As an Arizona rancher and grower, Glassford employed Latino workers, apparently with few problems. Having now agreed to conciliate in the Imperial Valley, he first considered the labor issues there from a grower's point of view, under the reasonable assumption that he and the California growers had much in common. But unlike Glassford the California growers were dealing with a recently formed Communist union intent on organizing fieldworkers. Glassford had experience working with Communists during his tenure as Washington's police chief, and likely regarded them as a manageable problem. Before sending Glassford into the fray, Perkins's staff had informed him that, in their opinion, Senator Wagner's National Labor Relations Board report had been too harsh and too pro-worker. Graphic descriptions of working conditions and tales of ongoing rights violations were bad enough, but what Perkins's staff especially disfavored was the report's recommendation that the federal government form worker unions and dispatch US marshals to protect the workers. What Perkins really had in mind, her staff elucidated for Glassford, was to help the economy by getting the huge melon crop harvested on time. Since the workers had now returned to the fields—some said under threats—the task should not be too difficult. Perkins hoped that Pelham Glassford could be the peacemaker. Glassford may or may not have detected the hidden message that nothing in the Imperial Velley should ruffle the feathers of the southern Democrats.[41]

Like many if not most Anglo-Americans, especially in the 1930s, Secretary Perkins and Pelham Glassford held paternalistic and often demeaning views of Mexicans and Mexican Americans. Perkins reminded Glassford that the fieldworkers were like children, who might ignore a parent but would not ignore a strict grandparent or other family person in charge. Such a person, whom Perkins labeled an "old Aunt Susan," would not put up with childish tantrums; the children would sense it and calm down. In essence, Perkins wanted Glassford to be the strict Aunt Susan who could calm down the fieldworkers of "Latin Blood." Glassford's view of Mexican and Mexican American fieldworkers was not dissimilar. He told the secretary of labor that such people were nomadic and had too many children, too many chickens, too many dogs, and would continue to live that way.[42]

Notwithstanding their views of migrant fieldworkers, neither Glassford nor Perkins condoned the abusive methods that the growers and their vigilantes were using in the Imperial Valley. The secretary was sure that the local governments were out of control, and she needed Glassford to restrain them.[43]

Glassford, it seems, would be the powerless "old Aunt Susan" that Secretary Perkins had in mind. He could see two possible paths. The first was to befriend his fellow growers and persuade them that a small pay increase and some minor improvements in working conditions would weaken the Communists' arguments and send them agitating elsewhere. The second path was to treat both sides neutrally, collect information and solicit testimony, decide who was more believable, and write a report accordingly. He concluded that as a grower he felt more comfortable with the first path, and if that path did not work, he could take the second. As a first step, he thought it wise to begin by giving the growers some favorable press to lessen their hostility.[44]

While Glassford had felt kinship with the Bonus Army veterans, even those who were Communists, he felt no such connection with the migrant workers. They were not white nor were they veterans; they were primarily brown, short of stature, Spanish-speaking people, many, if not most, of whom were not US citizens. That said, Glassford respected their civil rights. One might conclude that California growers, compelled to work with a federal conciliator, would relish a fellow grower. The growers, however, had no intention of cultivating Glassford, although they might try to educate him. Their entrenched position was that there were no labor problems in the Valley. Two California agencies, the California Chamber of Commerce and the Farm Bureau, agreed to form a commission to investigate the situation. Its three members included Claude B. Hutchinson, dean of agriculture at the University of California; W. C. Jacobsen, a member of the state department of agriculture; and John Phillips, a member of the board of the Associated Farmers, the latter known to be ultraconservative. In what became known as "The Phillips Report," the commission concluded that federal intervention was unneeded and that the federal government should allow Imperial Valley growers to deal with the outside agitators without interference.[45]

Glassford surveyed the scene. It seemed clear that the Communist union was promoting the threat of strike to get a wage increase, and it was willing to allow destruction of the melon crop to do so. At the same time he could see that various grower-associated officials and citizens had organized and were interfering with the constitutional rights of free speech and assembly. But the latter, the conciliator concluded, was outside his authority for now. Having arrived in the Valley and now lodged in the Hotel Dunlack in Brawley, Glassford began his work. On April 7 he met with State Assemblyman John Phillips (of the Phillips Report) and Police Chief J. L. "Lon" Cromer of Brawley. They took him to the Azteca Hall in Brawley, where the "radicals" were known to meet. Chief Cromer said that on January 12, three months earlier, he and his officers had gone to the hall to arrest three persons on warrants and were then stormed by hostile Communists. Cromer said he had suffered an injury when someone tossed a stench bomb from inside the hall. The chief then showed Glassford 300 wooden clubs, some nail-studded, that he said his officers had discovered concealed in the building. Glassford saw no reason to disbelieve Cromer's explanation of what had happened. For eight days Glassford conducted hearings and invited various committees representing fieldworkers to speak regarding pay and conditions. By April 13 he had completed his investigation, having found no problems between employers and those workers who had jobs. He noted that there was a serious situation resulting from outside agitators promoting Communism among the workers. The growers were cautiously pleased with his finding.[46]

But there was another version of the incident at the Azteca Hall, which held that three days previous, January 9, scores of police officers, sheriff's deputies, highway patrol officers, and American Legionnaires armed with clubs and tear gas had stopped and attacked a caravan of cars and trucks carrying about 150 workers headed to the town of El Centro for a strike meeting. The Brawley police chief had described the caravan stop as "routine law enforcement," since the group did not have a valid parade permit issued from his office. Then, on January 12, while several hundred fieldworkers, some with families, met in Azteca Hall, a large force of law enforcement officers and associates arrived to serve arrest warrants on several Communist organizers believed to be inside. When those inside held the doors closed, the officers barred the doors from the outside and fired tear gas into the building. Those inside broke windows to breathe and flee from the building, soon chased by officers. When the hall was empty, the officers entered the building and destroyed typewriters, duplicating machines, and even kitchen appliances.[47]

CHAPTER 18

Sob Sisters and Busybodies

THE new conciliator returned to Arizona for a few days to study the information he had collected, and perhaps to get some distance perspective on the Imperial Valley situation. He later told the *Arizona Daily Star*, "These men who pioneered the Imperial Valley and have spent a great deal of time and money there, feel that the 'reds,' as they call the radicals who are attempting to organize the Mexican pickers into a cannery and farm union, are interfering with private property." On April 20 he returned to the Imperial Valley, and for three days interviewed cantaloupe workers about wages and conditions. He also heard from religious ministers as well as the Mexican consul, who had worked to organize workers in a Mexican-led, non-Communist, company union, hoping to minimize the influence of the Communists. By now Glassford must have begun to consider that he may have misread the situation. Previously, Glassford had shared his strategy with Department of Labor officials: "It is absolutely essential at the present time that [the growers] believe me to be entirely under their control." His idea was to use friendly grower-to-grower persuasion and cajolery to convince them to offer slightly better pay and conditions, which he thought would eliminate the strikes and bloodshed. He had sought to befriend prominent growers and key politicians, assuring them that he understood their complaints. He had also harshly and publicly criticized the CAWIU leaders, labeling them "vile agitators"; additionally, he had issued a bulletin to all fieldworkers warning them that the Communist union was there only to cause problems. Still, the growers refused to budge, not even a little. Now fully aware of the grower intransigence, coupled with his recent interviews of melon workers, ministers, and Mexican diplomats, he concluded that his initial approach had been wrongheaded. The former police chief now found himself faced with the inescapable conclusion that serious abuses of fieldworkers were ongoing and that the growers sanctioned it. He had assumed that his fellow growers were honest and reasonable men; regretfully, he saw that was not the case. He must have cringed when he realized that he would have to publicly reverse his stance. He could see that his efforts would take longer than expected and that he would need secretarial assistance. He was fortunate to find and hire Lucille Painter, the niece of an ACLU attorney, Ernest Besig. Lucy, as she preferred to be called, would prove to be a confidant and advisor in the weeks ahead.[1]

Secretary Perkins was favorably impressed with Glassford. She reflected on Glassford's actions in the Imperial Valley: "He went to see the [newspaper] editor and he let everyone know through the press that General Glassford was in town. He called the ministers on the telephone and asked them to tell their congregations that General Glassford was in town." He told them that he represented the Department of Labor and was going to correct things. Then, according to Perkins, he issued a proclamation, stating, "I, Pelham D. Glassford, General of the United States Army, Representative of the Department of Labor, do hereby establish the following minimum wages to be paid in this valley." Perkins soon heard about the "Glassford wage" and reflected, "I was nearly bowled over when I heard this. There had been no consultation with me or anyone else. He had no authority whatsoever, in any act of the law of any judgement of a court." She later remembered, "I'll never forget the utter consternation with which I consulted my legal counsel, saying, 'What in the world shall we do? Someone is sure to bring suit against the Secretary of Labor. What are we to do?'" Her legal counsel, Charlie Wyzanski, said, "Well, if anybody brings suit against you . . . all you can do is state the exact truth—that your unworthy and unfaithful subordinate did this on his own. Of course, you will have to dismiss him. That will be the public sacrifice that is made. But really, I think it was smart." According to Perkins, "They paid the wage." When a grower complained about the wage, Glassford said, "This is the minimum. That's the least you can pay. You have no right to make an interpretation of that. Yes, you've got to give them clean drinking water. No, they don't have to drink water out of the ditch." When a grower protested that the workers had always drunk out of the ditch, the conciliator replied, "That doesn't matter. You've got water on your farm. You've got to haul water to where the camp is and they've got to have clean water to drink." Whether or not the "Glassford wage" existed is questionable; the local newspapers made no mention of it, but perhaps it had been something discussed at various meetings.[2]

At this point savvy growers might have collaborated with Glassford and given workers the slightest improvement in pay and conditions, which might have been just enough to allow him to write a positive report and drive away. Unfortunately, having previously committed to meet any demand for improved pay or conditions with intransigence, the growers had narrowed their options to one. They refused to work with Glassford and simply contended to countenance the abuses in their fields. In the past the growers had cooperated with the non-Communist company union, which the Mexican consul had helped put into place. But once the police had arrested the Communist leaders and the courts had sentenced them, the growers simply gauged the strike potential to be minimal and ignored the company union, disregarding previously agreed-to contracts.[3]

On April 27 the ACLU announced its intention to lead a motor caravan of a dozen or more cars from San Diego and Los Angeles to the Imperial Valley, carrying twenty attorneys, ministers, and activists. They billed it as part of a "goodwill tour," which would culminate with a meeting in Azteca Hall. The ACLU invited Glassford to the meeting, but he assured them that he much preferred that they cancel the tour and the meeting, knowing that the caravan was intended as easy bait for the growers' vigilantes. The ACLU representative did not deny that, saying that the event would dramatically show just how out of control and dangerous the conditions were in the Imperial Valley. Glassford did his best to recruit local law enforcement officers to provide security for the caravan, but they all refused. As predicted, when the caravan later arrived, a mob of vigilantes stopped and surrounded the caravan and threatened its drivers and passengers, resulting in the caravan speeding away, but having accomplished its mission of revealing the Valley's hazardous conditions.[4]

On April 30 the San Diego headquarters of the CAWIU initiated an information attack on Glassford, distributing Spanish-language circulars throughout the melon camps saying that Glassford had lied to them and intended to sell them out. Glassford responded by preparing 7,000 of his own circulars, also in Spanish, refuting the CAWIU charges, and had them distributed in the camps.[5]

The ACLU next planned a second Imperial Valley tour, this time near Brawley, to be held on May 5, Cinco de Mayo, a major Mexican holiday. Glassford asked the ACLU lawyers to postpone the tour for a week, but they declined. They said they hoped to hear from the growers and workers, adding that many ACLU members worked during the week and could participate only on weekends. Glassford responded by saying that the tour was inadvisable and could result in serious trouble. Imperial County Supervisor N. M. Graham took the motor tour to announce that the Imperial Valley was fed up with sob sisters and busybodies. That same day, in Sacramento, the Associated Farmers of California protested the dangerous invasion of state's rights by the federal government, which could set a precedent.[6]

Brawley Police Chief Cromer reported that he would have his officers working on May 5, and then he divined that if any problems resulted, they would be the fault of the ACLU, adding that Azteca Hall would not be available for any meetings. Chester Williams of the ACLU had asked for a police escort, but both the sheriff and highway patrol denied his request. Fortunately, no violence occurred, resulting in a *Los Angeles Times* report that during their two-hour tour of the area, the ACLU representatives received little notice, and they seemed quite annoyed that Glassford was not available to receive them.[7]

Throughout Glassford's time in the Valley, various residents surreptitiously approached him to share their disapproval of the growers' tactics, but said they feared speaking out. A minister who had witnessed a vigilante viciously beat an attorney, and who had sworn out a complaint to police, withdrew it when a group of his parishioners pressured him to do so. Another resident, who admitted to being a vigilante, told Glassford that he disliked his involvement, but he feared that the other vigilantes would close his business if he failed to show. Yet another citizen told Glassford that while he had no fondness for the Communists, he believed the motive of the growers was profit, not patriotism. Glassford now had no choice but to conclude that his hope of working with the growers to find an amicable solution had been a serious error, and now he regretted his earlier public praise of them. He fumed in letters and calls to his Washington contacts, characterizing the growers as both arrogant and obstinate and resistant to any reform or concession.[8]

The Associated Farmers went on the attack, asserting that the Roosevelt administration had previously said that the federal administrative code did not cover agricultural work. Glassford subsequently asked the federal Department of Labor to clarify his authority. The chief attorney replied that while federal authority allowed for insertion of a conciliator into the situation, the conciliator—Glassford—could adjust grievances but had no real police power. Previously having held the authority of an army general and thereafter of a police chief, Glassford now found himself essentially powerless. Furthermore, the Department of Labor denied his proposals to set a minimum wage and to have workers vote on joining a union. Now understanding the politics of the situation, he must have questioned the wisdom of coming to the Imperial Valley.[9]

The next attack on Glassford came from the other direction. On May 18 the ACLU claimed that Glassford was under the control of the growers, that he was openly hostile to the fieldworkers, and that he had publicly attacked union leaders. Secretary Perkins reviewed their claim and said that she was not convinced and denied their request, saying there was no cause for removal. On May 23 the ACLU renewed its demand for Glassford's termination, citing that he was hostile to the workers and had attacked their labor unions, and further suggested that the federal government should protect the unions. At this point Glassford accepted that almost any action on his part would have no lasting effect and altering public opinion would have to come only through long-term education.[10]

On May 15 Glassford had explained—apparently off the record—his plan to a magazine journalist: "The Growers and Shippers control the banks, the press, the police, the American Legion—everything. I can't aggravate them too much. I can't afford to, that's all, and if I am to accomplish anything, I've got to lean over a little on their side." Those would be words to eat. He no longer believed his previous contention that the growers would respond better to persuasion than confrontation. He now realized that any change in their attitude was impossible. Therefore, he would no longer attempt appeasement; he would confront and ruffle feathers, whether Washington officials liked it or not. He could see now that it was the fieldworkers who were the underdogs. He also learned that an organization called the "secret thirty" had tapped his telephone calls, read his telegrams, and most probably shadowed him wherever he went and spied on whatever he did. During his time as police chief, he had never felt his life in danger; now he thought it might be. He had not felt that possibility since the Western Front. Faced with death threats, the wishes of Perkins and her assistants to avoid offending Imperial Valley growers and local officials seemed unimportant. Perkins could recall him if she chose, but he would expose the growers. He found himself hoping that the growers' actions would prompt a strike or other event so that the Labor Department would have to intervene.[11]

It was a short wait. A vigilante struck on June 7, having targeted former New Yorker and Cornell graduate Ernest Besig. The ACLU attorney had come to the Valley to observe the trial of seven Mexican activists arrested for vagrancy. Glassford had met Besig at the train station and driven him to the county courthouse. The attorney monitored the court proceedings, and the next day Glassford drove him to the train station, remaining with him until he boarded the Southern Pacific train and it pulled away from the station. Still new to the Imperial Valley, Glassford failed to realize that to reach Los Angeles, Besig would have to change trains in the small town of Niland, about thirty miles north of Brawley. As Besig sat waiting on a bench in the small train station, a man approached him and without saying a word slugged him on the side of the head and continued raining blows on him, yelling, "That will teach you to keep out of the Valley." Besig covered his face and yelled for help, blood gushing from his head. As onlookers rushed to assist, the attacker fled, shouting, "That's Besig from Los Angeles. He's a Red!" Besig was able to call Glassford, who sped to the train station and picked him up. Glassford took Besig to receive medical attention in Niland and then the two returned to Glassford's hotel in Brawley. Later, Glassford secretly moved the attorney to the basement and in the evening transferred him to a waiting car in the alley, after which that car, with Glassford doing countersurveillance in a trailing car, raced through the dark desert toward Los Angeles. Glassford ensured that Besig was entirely safe before returning to Brawley.[12]

On June 8 an angry Glassford telegraphed California's new governor, Frank F. Merriam:

> IN VIEW SEVERAL RECENT AND UNWARRANTED ASSAULTS BY VIGILANTES CULMINATING TODAY IN BRUTAL COWARDLY ATTACK ON ATTORNEY ERNEST BESIG WHILE LEAVING IMPERIAL VALLEY FOLLOWING A LEGITIMATE INVESTIGATION UNDER MY PROTECTION AM RECOMMENDING FEDERAL GOVERNMENT URGE YOU INITIATE INVESTIGATION IMPERIAL VALLEY LAWLESSNESS AND UNQUESTIONABLE ABUSE OF COURT JUSTICE IN TRIALS OF LABOR ORGANIZERS.

Glassford had put Governor Merriam on notice that as federal conciliator, Glassford intended to ask Secretary Perkins to demand that the governor initiate a state grand jury to investigate the assault and other violence. By now Glassford knew better than to ask Perkins to launch a federal investigation, but perhaps she might urge the Sacramento-based governor to do so.[13]

Previously, Glassford had told Secretary Perkins that he would soon return to Phoenix, but now he changed his mind. After monitoring the filing of two sworn complaints against two Brawley suspects in connection with Besig's assault, Glassford told reporters that he had no definite plans to leave the Valley. Thereafter, speaking to reporters at various meetings, he leveled his charges. On June 13: The Valley is "governed and controlled by a small group which, in advertising a war on Communism, is sponsoring terrorism, intimidation, and injustice." On June 14: "Charges against strikers are 'trumped up'; growers never intend to improve conditions, and are opposed to 'law, order, sanity, and reform' and now 'had put themselves in the position of becoming the most dangerous 'reds' ever to come to the Imperial Valley.'"[14]

On June 15, at an evening meeting of the Imperial County Board of Supervisors, held in Brawley, Glassford publicly charged that Judge Vaughan Thompson and Prosecutor Elmer Heald, both of whom were seated in the room, were crooks who sustained corrupt local officials. White with rage, the judge shot up from his seat and rushed toward Glassford, shaking his fist, demanding to know if Glassford had just called him a crook. Unruffled, Glassford clarified that he had said that in his opinion the judge was a crook. Still shouting, the judge asserted that he had been on the bench for twenty-one years and no one had ever called him a crook and demanded an apology. Glassford paused momentarily, reflecting on his word choice, during which Prosecutor Heald shouted that he had been prosecuting for eight years and his worst political enemy had never called him that and demanded an apology. Glassford, unbowed, apologized to the judge and prosecutor and then refocused his accusation, explaining that while he did not think they took bribes, they had allowed themselves to be associated with and controlled by corrupt growers, making themselves incapable of protecting the civil rights of those not associated with the growers. His words were not apologies, but simply more focused allegations. He later issued a public statement, explaining that while he did not think the judge and prosecutor were the kind of crooks who were financially dishonest, he did believe they were controlled by a certain group of citizens in the valley. He later added that the term "tools" was more precise, a clarification as damning as the original accusation. Without directly saying so, he was accusing both men of failing to protect and defend the Constitution, which they had sworn to uphold.[15]

Aside from being public servants, both Thompson and Heald were also growers, and at the request of the Associated Farmers they had previously addressed such groups as the Rotary Club, Brawley Women's League, and the American Legion, assuring audiences those Communists were pushing propaganda to harm the governmental and social fabric.[16]

Glassford had also announced that a county official had recently threatened him, saying that Glassford could be "removed" for as little as $50 ($1,021) by a "tough element." When an Imperial County Supervisor asked who had said that, Glassford answered that it had been County Agricultural Commissioner B. A. Harrigan. According to Glassford's notes, Harrigan had said, "I could go out of here right now with $50 and come back without the $50, and you wouldn't be here." Glassford added, "During the meeting with Harrigan, when Ernest Besig's name came up, Harrigan said that he was sorry that he had not been the one to punch Besig." Glassford's notes further revealed that Harrigan had warned, "They will never get any place, and if Besig comes back here he won't be allowed in court. You'll never get a jury to convict the assailant." Harrigan wasted no time in responding to Glassford's allegation. On June 27 Harrigan angrily declared, "I can only say that my record is an open book of which I am proud. . . . General Glassford's self-humiliation has evidently warped his judgement and he has made statements smarting under the lash he had applied to himself." In his attack on Glassford, Harrigan neglected to deny the allegation. He later resigned his position.[17]

On June 18 Glassford received the following Western Union telegram from ACLU attorney Abraham Wirin:

> CONGRATULATIONS AND MANY THANKS YOUR
> COURAGEOUS TYPICALLY GLASSFORDIAN
> DECLARATION REPORTED UNITED PRESS JUNE
> FOURTEENTH WE SHOULD HAVE KNOWN THAT
> YOU WOULD ULTIMATELY REBEL AT COWARDICE
> AND LAWLESSNESS OF VIGILANTES STOP
> WARD BALDWIN RICE HOLMES JOIN IN THESE
> CONGRATULATIONS BUT SUGGEST YOU ASK
> CUMMINGS SEND MARSHALS TO VALLEY AND
> ARRANGE WORKER POLL.[18]

During Glassford's time as conciliator, his clerical assistant Lucy Painter came to serve as a sounding board, advisor, and confidante. She was also the niece of Ernest Besig. She wrote to "Uncle Ernie" saying that Glassford had planned to be critical of the growers long before he had sufficient justification to do so. She wrote, "I knew all along that he WANTED to open up and let loose, and yet for a time it looked very much as though no opportunity to do so would present itself."[19]

On June 23 Glassford submitted his formal report in which he listed his recommendations for improving labor conditions in the Imperial Valley, including instituting a standard pay scale; building small homes to replace congested camps; using standardized contracts and forms; implementing a system for regulating the supply of workers; and developing stronger labor laws to protect workers. He then moved on to the more serious issues, beginning with his assertion that those who ruled Imperial Valley did so as tyrants. He went on to say that he was convinced that the growers invented and sustained a Communist hysteria that welcomed agitation, which could then be labeled as "Red," allowing them to keep wages down and profits up, and in this were assisted by certain government officials who served as their tools.[20]

He went on to recommend that the California state attorney general appoint a special counsel to investigate terrorism and intimidation in Imperial County, certain that the local prosecutor would be prejudiced and biased. He next listed some of the incidents for a grand jury to investigate: the kidnapping and assault of Abraham Wirin, the assault of attorney Grover Johnson on the steps of the Imperial County courthouse; and the arrest and charging of ACLU attorney Emma Cutler. He charged that it was common knowledge that a deputy sheriff and a county official had been involved in the kidnapping and assault of Wirin, and further it was common knowledge that three county officials had been involved in the assault on Johnson. He then recommended Harrigan's removal from office, asserting that he had heard several complaints about him being both unfair and a tyrant.[21]

He had no doubt that the Imperial County government would ignore his suggestions, but he did not want to allow the Board of Supervisors to say that the federal government had failed to lay out a plan of action.[22]

The growers, shippers, and county supervisors raged at Glassford's scathing excoriations. The editorial board of the *Los Angeles Times* contended that Glassford's report showed that he and Franklin Roosevelt were bigger "communist-coddlers" than Joseph Stalin. Imperial County officials emphasized the conciliator's volte-face, quoting his earlier statements as indicative of widespread communism. Alvin N. Jack, president of the Imperial Valley Growers and Shippers Association, said that following Glassford's first outburst nothing of value would follow. Sheriff George Campbell vigorously denied that he or any of his deputies had taken part in any lawless acts, and he refuted Glassford's statement that a member of the sheriff's department was present when Grover Johnson was assaulted, explaining that he and his deputies were in the jail at that time. The sheriff explained that when they heard a ruckus, he told his deputies to stay where they were as it was just a ruse distract them.[23]

A June 28 *Los Angeles Times* editorial attacked Glassford, pointing out that it made no sense that he had initially said Communists were behind the trouble and now said that it was the growers and officials. It suspected that "political pressure" might be behind Glassford's accusations that growers and politicians had encouraged Communist strikes to keep labor wages low, labeling it as absurd. It accused Glassford of being unstable and a man with a history of being incapable of pleasing anyone. None of this was a surprise to Glassford. He knew too well that he had violated the adage of never picking fights with folks who buy ink by the barrel. Later, when a news reporter asked the Imperial County Board of Supervisors if it intended to follow up on Glassford's report, a supervisor of the sparsely populated county said that they were way too busy with the budget now, but they might look at it little later.[24]

Regarding the arrest of attorney Emma Cutler for vagrancy within a few hours of her arrival in the county, Judge W. H. Lorenze said that the jury had convicted her "based on past association with five communists who had been sentenced from Imperial County in 1930," four years earlier. The judge added that the court had examined 140 potential jurors before her trial and conviction, not explaining why the court had permitted the questioning of such an exceedingly large pool of people for a vagrancy charge. Superior Court Judge Roy D. McPherinn later upheld Cutler's conviction.[25]

The ACLU was delighted with Glassford's damning comments but wished that he had made them sooner. Abraham Wirin, recalling his desert kidnapping and beating, telegraphed the Labor Department and urged, "Please, please back up Glassford now that he shows signs of moving in the right direction." If ever the Department of Labor needed to dispatch US marshals to protect the life of a federal conciliator, this was the time; instead, the department simply urged him to return to Arizona.[26]

The New Deal administration had permitted Creel to pull loans from growers and to truck food to the workers, but those options had not been available for Glassford. The New Deal administration chose not to dispatch US marshals or the National Guard. Nor did it use its ultimate weapon: water restriction. Clifton Taft, national secretary of the ACLU, had suggested simply shutting off the water, as well as stopping the in-progress construction of canals, until Imperial Valley officials obeyed the Constitution. The federal government did the opposite. The Public Works Administration (PWA) continued its plan of building an eighty-mile canal to supply water to the Imperial Valley, and in response to the Colorado basin drought, trucked water to help the growers who were at the time denouncing Glassford. The Department of Agriculture, for its part, continued to provide the Valley with drought relief and subsidies. Apparently, ACLU Secretary Taft's suggestion of restricting water had nicked a nerve. The *Imperial Valley Press* condemned him by assuring its readers that Washington knew he was "a depraved fanatic with sawdust for brains."[27]

By June 28, Glassford left the Imperial Valley. He had accomplished his mission as well as he could under the restrictions placed on it by the Department of Labor. The Roosevelt administration had sent him into a violent valley armed only with a grin. Though it was a wasted effort, he had told the federal government and the state of California what they needed to do to address labor violence in the Imperial Valley. The former conciliator wrote to Besig, saying that he had been more than ready to leave and hoped that he would not have to return. Besig wrote back saying that for himself leaving the Valley was like being released from prison. Glassford said he hoped that someday right-minded people in the Valley would correct its problems.[28]

The truth is that Secretary Perkins had dispatched Glassford to the Imperial Valley with the very limited mission of bringing in one melon crop and developing some suggestions for long-term changes to reduce strikes and violence. Glassford had attempted, ultimately unwisely, to do much more. When his work was finished, he purposely remained in the Valley long enough to avert any news reports or editorials that he had fled in fear. Having suffered one serious death threat, he saw no reason to invite another and simply drove away, likely glancing in his rearview mirror from time to time. He left having to conclude that his efforts to improve the lives of the Imperial Valley fieldworkers had been no more successful than his efforts to improve the lives of the Bonus veterans. But not for want of trying.

Historian Kathryn Olmsted's careful study of Glassford's Imperial Valley mission argues that it failed for two reasons. First, unlike the San Joaquin Valley, the Imperial Valley was remote and isolated, allowing for the use of brutal violence without the prying eyes of the national investigative media, which allowed growers to orchestrate unrestrained tactics to maintain dominance. Second, growers and shippers, in response to Creel's tactics, had educated themselves. They had come to understand that Creel had had little power and that Glassford had none. Nevertheless, Professor Olmsted concludes that while Glassford had taken "a more critical and emphatic stance against the growers than Creel had during the cotton strike, that he accomplished even less." But that was not how Secretary Perkins recalled it, saying, "To this day I think he did a perfect job. I don't think it could have been done any other way. Yet it startled me. It was so completely off the pattern of what is usually done in government circles, or what government is supposed to be able to do." Secretary Perkins's recollections were most probably faulty, but there is no denying that she had been pleased with Glassford's efforts. For better or worse, the New Deal administration had sacrificed justice in the fields of the Imperial Valley for continued economic progress throughout the nation.[29]

CHAPTER 19

Ranching, Policing, and Politics

GLASSFORD returned to Arizona and his post-army life of ranching and farming. Working the soil had been his grandfather and father's passion, but it was not necessarily his. His father's death had required that someone assume management of the farms. They were now his mother's farms, but in a few years, she would turn eighty. Brother Bill was still in the navy and seemed to have even less interest in the farms than did Hap. Circumstances had required that Pelham end his military career perhaps sooner than he would have preferred. On the other hand, promotion in the army was exceedingly slow, making a life of ranching and painting somewhat more inviting. To some extent it was, but Hap had come to realize that he had an abundance of interests in other things. The conflict was that the farms took up a lot of time. In addition to oversight of his mother's property east of Phoenix, consisting of two farms of 160 acres each, he now had his own farm, which was not small, 60 irrigated acres situated six miles west of Phoenix. Horse breeding, dairy cattle, pigs, cotton, and tending other crops filled his days. He did his best to find time for cruising on his motorcycle, riding his thoroughbred horses, and motoring into town in his black roadster convertible coupe. And, of course, he was always painting, usually having two or three canvases in progress.

 Glassford had stayed in contact with Lucy, his able assistant when he served as conciliator in the Imperial Valley. How she had come to be recommended to him is unclear. Lucille Kathryn Painter was born in St. Louis on November 16, 1906, and now lived in Winslow, Arizona. She was the daughter of Charles Louis Painter, a former two-star army general in the Judge Advocate Corps, who was now an advertising executive in St. Louis. Lucy previously had worked as a secretary for the

Arizona Industrial Commission, as well as the Arizona attorney general's office in Phoenix. The connector between Hap and Lucy was likely Besig. She heard about the position, applied, and was subsequently hired. Despite an age difference, it became clear that Pelham and Lucy were mutually attracted. Two months after leaving Imperial Valley, he proposed to her rather directly by saying, "Let's get married." She replied, just as directly, "All right." On September 5, 1934, in Holbrook, Arizona, the two wed. Glassford was fifty-one; she was twenty-seven. Judge P. A. Sawyer of Maricopa County performed the marriage. Despite the age difference, the union had all the markings of a match made to last.[1]

Between late 1934 and early 1936, Glassford involved himself in various endeavors. He lectured at a forum for the US Office of Education in Colorado Springs, coauthored several textbooks subsequently used at West Point and the Command and General School, contributed articles on law enforcement and sociological subjects to various newspapers and magazines, and participated in several social and art clubs in Phoenix, occasionally exhibiting some of his paintings.[2]

In March 1936 the Phoenix city commission demoted its police chief, Charles M. Johnson, to patrolman and appointed Glassford as interim chief of the Phoenix Police Department. The ninety-day appointment included a mandate to reorganize the department and make it efficient. Former police chief Johnson complained to news reporters that he was the victim of politics and that Glassford's appointment was political as well.[3]

The Tucson-based *Arizona Daily Star* newspaper offered some observations about its neighbor city, Phoenix, 115 miles to the north, speculating on how the new interim chief would do. It noted that Glassford was a man of known ability and one who would not tolerate tomfoolery, adding that the police department had internal disruptive cliques and had been a political toy for some time. The *Star*, in an editorial, put forth several predictions: that while doing his duty, Glassford would come up against political factions; that these competing factions would block his efforts and find a way to neutralize him; that city officials would search for a way to openly criticize his actions; and that other Arizona cities would watch to see how long Glassford would remain in office.[4]

Even before he could initiate any kind of problem-solving program, Glassford lost his temporary position, much sooner than he expected. It was like the joke told among police chiefs, in which the outgoing police chief gives three sealed envelopes to the incoming police chief, with instructions to open each one sequentially when a major problem occurred. The new chief encountered such a problem and opened the first envelope, which said, "blame it on the budget." The chief did, and the problem soon faded. When the next problem came about, the chief opened the second letter, which said, "blame it on the newspapers." The chief did, and after a while everyone forgot about the problem. When the third problem surfaced, the chief opened the third letter, which said, "prepare three sealed envelopes for the new chief."

On May 1 a new city administration in Phoenix took office and devised a different organization plan for the police department. The new mayor, John H. Udall, of the Udall family, a prominent political force over several states for 100 years, announced that he would not be retaining Glassford. The new mayor also replaced the city attorney, city engineer, assessor, and auditor as well.[5]

While serving as interim chief in Phoenix, Glassford received another job offer. Blanton Winship, retired army lawyer and World War veteran, had been appointed by President Roosevelt as governor of Puerto Rico. Blanton now offered Glassford the position of Director of Insular Military Police Force, the island's military police. The island was amid political unrest, however, with the Puerto Rican Nationalist Party resisting US rule. Glassford offered to accept the position on an interim basis for six months. A disappointed Blanton thanked Glassford but said he would continue looking. Then, in June 1936, Homer LeRoy Shantz, president of the University of Arizona in Tucson, resigned his presidency to accept the directorship of the US Forest Service. Glassford applied for Shantz's former position. The only other contender was Homer L. Nearpass of Whittier, California, previously superintendent of Santa Barbara schools. When neither Glassford nor Nearpass proved acceptable, the University operated with an interim president for a year until finally appointing Alfred Atkinson, who served from 1937 to 1947.[6]

Glassford now considered making a run for Congress in Arizona's 1st Congressional District. On June 12, 1936, the *Casa Grande Dispatch* reported that Glassford had started circulating petitions for the Democratic nomination for Congress. Glassford told news reporters that he was just sizing up the situation, but he was hoping to succeed Isabella Greenway, who had decided not to seek reelection. Glassford told reporters that he supported the "humanitarian objectives initiated by President Roosevelt" and would work to support them. Aside from Glassford, eight other people eyed the same position—not a good sign. On August 20 Glassford delivered his keynote speech at a meeting of the Young Democrats of Phoenix. He told them that while he supported the president's "humanitarian principles," he would not be a New Deal "yes man." He told the young Arizonans that he would protect Arizona's right to Colorado River water and would support Arizona farmers in resisting the increasing importation of foreign agricultural products. Finally, he promised to stimulate population growth and industrial development in the state. His election posters began appearing. Texas Representative Wright Patman, author of the Bonus Bill, wrote an endorsement in the September 1936 issue of *Better Men in Government*. Patman wrote that Glassford "stood firmly against foreign entanglement and against maintaining possessions outside the Western Hemisphere." He lauded Glassford's "unbounded energy," adding that he was "a born leader of men." Glassford was the only candidate who stumped about the state on a motorcycle. While the 1936 race was a landslide for Democrats, that was not the case for Glassford. Too many candidates had split the vote, giving John R. Murdock the congressional seat.[7]

Disappointed, Glassford returned to his farm. On January 9, 1937, Pelham and brother Bill lost their mother. Pelham had kept Bill informed as Allie slipped away. "I held her hand and talked to her as she took her last few breaths . . . passing out of life without a tremor, and without gaining consciousness. She died at 9:49 AM today (Jan 9)."[8]

Allie Davis Glassford had come from Ohio to the New Mexico Territory in 1881. There she had met young Lieutenant William Glassford and subsequently shared her life with him. William had now been gone for six years, and Allie would join him at the cemetery on the Presidio at San Francisco. She had been pleased in 1932 when the United States Geographic Board had changed the name of Bald Mountain in Arizona to Glassford Hill, in William's honor. Several years earlier, the Maricopa County Board of Supervisors had named a road east of Mesa in William's honor, describing him as one of the Valley's most prominent and enthusiastic promoters.[9]

Allie's estate, shared between Hap and Bill, included 320 prime farmland acres, two lots, her house and contents at 834 North 1st Avenue in Phoenix, dairy cattle and turkeys, various stocks and bonds, a 1928 Franklin motorcar, and about $10,000 ($189,977) in cash. The total value was $58,000 ($1,101,867).[10]

In July 1937, Ernie Pyle, already well known as a roving reporter, stopped by Glassford's farm for a visit. Approaching the farm, Pyle noticed a couple of signs alongside the highway, one announcing three bales of hay for a dollar and another offering fresh eggs from Himalayan chickens. In the distance he saw the tall farmer. Pyle later wrote that he had just met the youngest man of fifty-three he had ever seen. Over the course of his visit to the farm, Pyle tagged along with Glassford, who, attired in old clothes, fed chickens, sawed wood, and followed a team of work horses pulling a plow as it carved the soil. The roving reporter met Glassford's foreman, who essentially ran the farm during Pelham's frequent absences, and at harvest time oversaw temporary pickers. Pyle found Lucy to be delightful and one who without doubt enlivened the farm. He noted that she called Glassford "Hap" when they were alone but otherwise referred to him as "the General." It was clear that the couple had fun together, sometimes doing crazy things. If one of them could not sleep, for instance, the other awoke and the two would go for a walk, flashlight in hand, treading the mile to the highway and back, he in his pajamas, she in her bathrobe. The self-appointed protectors of the strollers were the two farm dogs, who followed them along, one on guard while the other investigated interesting scents. The two dogs had shown up at the farm one day and never found occasion to leave. Hap and Lucy discussed an issue. The farms, despite their commitment to them, were like millstones around their necks. Already restless, Hap was anxious to travel. Pyle remembered him as the only person whose reputation had improved following the Bonus Army expulsion. Pyle reflected that Glassford wanted to do so many things, but he also wanted to have the peacefulness of Arizona.[11]

Hap and Lucy traveled to the Glassford family house in Port Townsend, Washington, for the summer in 1937, staying for six weeks. He liked the fruits, berries, and corn there, saying they were the best he had ever tasted. He found the fishing to be good and the golf on the Chevy Chase Golf Club on Discovery Bay delightful. In addition to the house, Hap and Bill also owned eight view lots on the bluff overlooking Port Townsend and the Strait of Juan de Fuca.[12]

Perhaps inspired by the roving reporting of Ernie Pyle, Glassford next sought and received an interview with Leon Trotsky, a key figure in the October 1917 Russian Revolution and thereafter, who now lived in Mexico City. At the time, Trotsky was petitioning for a temporary visa in the United States for medical treatment and historical research. Glassford traveled by train to Mexico City and later remembered, "As an army officer for many years, twice chief of police, and now engaged in capitalistic enterprise, I was extremely fortunate to gain an interview with the world-renowned exile in Mexico, who had been deprived of Soviet citizenship in 1932."[13]

On October 9, 1938, Guy Glassford married a second time, this time to Marjorie Robinson of Richmond, Utah. The ceremony, conducted in the Hotel Utah in Salt Lake City, brought together nearly 100 family members and friends. Hap and Lucy had returned from their summer trip in time to attend. Cora Carleton Glassford was there as well, but Pelham Jr. was not able to attend, being stationed at Hickam Field in Honolulu. The young couple planned to honeymoon for four days on Coronado Island near San Diego. Because Hap and Frank Lloyd Wright were friends, the architect invited Guy and Marjorie to spend one of their honeymoon nights at Wright's then-unfinished Taliesin West home in Scottsdale. This was Guy's second marriage. Four years previous, then twenty-three, he had married Gail Elisabeth Goodness, just eighteen. She was an actress then under MGM contract as one of the Goldwyn Girls, and Guy was working as a credit manager. As with many Hollywood weddings, this did not last.[14]

In November 1939 Ernie Pyle dropped by the Glassford farm for another visit, which Hap and Lucy now called "Rancho Valle Del Sol." Motoring up the driveway, Pyle saw a sign with the word "Ducks" on it. He learned that Pelham and Lucy had given up on chickens, which seemed to acquire too many diseases. Hap said he got tired of running a chicken hospital. Pyle had received a Christmas card sketched by Hap, and he was amused that the card featured both an army sword and police baton covered with cobwebs and stored in the upper reaches of a barn. The card pictured Hap rolling up his sleeves ready to go to work while Lucy sat on an upsidedown Haig & Haig Scotch Whisky box, milking a cow. The card read, "Greetings and the Best of Everything from Lucy and Hap Glassford." Pyle saw that Pelham had traded his old roadster for a new Packard coupe and noted that Hap was a tad heavier but still looked not a day older. Hap told Pyle that he was raising racehorses and entering them in the winter races. Before long, the subject of a possible war came up, with Ernie coming to understand that Hap was following the news intently and was opposed to the United States getting involved in another war. With his son Pelham Jr. now an Army Air Corps pilot and Guy subject to the draft, the thought of another war was too close to home for a father to view it any other way. Pyle still found Hap to be a very engaging man and one who had numerous interests, concluding that "General Glassford has immense capabilities for helping make this world a better place."[15]

On his ranch Hap had heightened his interest in breeding and training horses, an activity not unlike the horse training he had done many years before as a new army lieutenant at Fort Riley. He now had nine thoroughbred horses and another four available for sale. For each horse he had pages of information showing its lineage. The horse in which he took the most pride was Warmaker, born from Filemaker and Comet. He described Warmaker as "a beautiful jumper and a well-trained horse. Has jumped to 4'8" and can go much higher. Can walk a mile in eleven minutes." One might assume that an Arizona rancher would be inclined to raise quarter horses and enter them in rodeo and Western horseshow competitions. Such horses required muscular sprinting, quick cutting, and rider-roping ability, which was much different from the competitions in which Hap entered. Glassford's horses competed in events more akin to British dressage, and the horses he bred, raised, and competed with were hunters and jumpers. The essential difference was that in hunter competitions only the horse was judged, whereas in jumper competitions both the horse and the rider were judged. For training and competitions, Glassford relied on professional riders such as Marcel Delporte, who had won a race on Warmaker, and fourteen-year-old Helen Quamame, who was photographed jumping Warmaker over a four-foot, five-inch stack of logs and a barrel. Glassford's three farms continued needing attention as well, yielding cantaloupes, cotton, hay, and lettuce. Lucy took care of the office management, much of it conducted by mail on letterhead reading: "COLONEL WILLIAM A. GLASSFORD FARMS in the Salt River Valley of Arizona," signed by (Mrs. P. D.) Lucille P. Glassford, Route 3, Box 361.[16]

CHAPTER 20

The Later Years

THE Pearl Harbor attack, shocking but not quite a surprise, altered Glassford's life. In February 1942 the army recalled him, as it did many former and retired officers. Now fifty-eight, he returned to his rank of lieutenant colonel, and at the direction of Secretary of War Henry L. Stimson, served in the provost marshal general's office in Washington, DC, the army's law enforcement, criminal investigation, corrections, detention, and resources-protection command. He reported to Provost Marshal General Allen Gullion, who happened to be an old friend. Gullion graduated from West Point in 1905, a year behind Pelham. Thereafter, Gullion served in the Philippine War, earned a law degree, took part in the Punitive Expedition in Mexico, and served in France during World War I in the Judge Advocate Corps as a brevet lieutenant colonel, earning a Distinguished Service Medal.[1]

Instead of wearing the artillery branch crossed-cannons insignia on his uniform, Glassford now wore the crossed-flintlock pistols insignia of the military police. In wartime Washington, already beginning to teem with uniformed military officers of all the branches, as well as some allied nations, he managed to find quarters at the Military Police School in the Arlington Cantonment. By June he was a full colonel.[2]

Others in the Glassford family were serving as well. Bill was now a vice admiral (three stars) and chief of the Asiatic fleet in the southwest Pacific. Pelham Jr.—Pete—recently promoted to major, would command an air squadron and soon leave for Europe. The following month, on April 5, 1942, Guy, age thirty-three, enlisted in the army as a private. Having attended West Point for a year and a half, he was soon commissioned as a second lieutenant. News reports said that Guy hoped to join the field artillery, but he was ultimately assigned to the

Corps of Engineers, where he would rise to the rank of captain, having become adept at directing the building of wartime airstrips on Pacific islands, including Guam and the Philippines. Also promoted, in a sense, was Lucy Glassford, who now found herself the full-time manager of three large farms, totaling 385 acres.[3]

In March, *Washington Daily News* columnist Evelyn Peyton Gordon caught up with the former police chief and requested an interview. She had heard that he was now a farmer and wanted to know what kind of farm he had. He said he raised dairy stock and grew lettuce, cotton, alfalfa, and other grains. When she wondered if he was still the police chief in Phoenix, he replied that he had been too tough on the gamblers and lost his job as a result. Having previously seen some of Glassford's murals and screens, she wondered if he still painted. He said he did, but now mostly did watercolors, adding that he had recently been working with a fine artist, Arthur Beaumont, already known for his nautical and harbor watercolor scenes. Glassford told Gordon that watercolor painting brought him a great deal of relaxation, and recently he had come close to winning first prize in a Phoenix exhibit. As for his new assignment, he said his "job would be a traveling one," adding he did not expect to have much time for painting. He explained he was now responsible for the security and protection of war resources and industries against sabotage, espionage, fire, and all other hazards throughout the United States, as well as inspecting the many new military police units and related organizations. He mentioned he was pleased that he would be able to see his daughter, Bettie, who lived in Washington with her husband, Lieutenant Commander Lee Parke. Evelyn Gordon reminded her readers that during the Bonus March everyone had agreed that Glassford had done an outstanding and humane job.[4]

Glassford was busy but still found time to make a social visit to his old police headquarters. Some of the officers and employees who had been there for at least a decade may have recognized the tall attractive man wearing an army officer's uniform. He carried ten more pounds, had gray hair at the temples, and presented the tanned look of a rancher who frequently baked under the Arizona sun, but his personality was as magnetic as ever. At the DC police headquarters, he strolled into the office of the major and superintendent of police and greeted his old friend, Edward J. Kelly, who now held Glassford's old job. Kelly leapt to his feet and advanced with outstretched hand. Each pumped the other's hand thoroughly, Kelly saying that seeing the General was such a pleasure and Glassford saying that seeing Eddie was a treat for his eyes. They had not seen each other in ten years. Glassford had wanted to promote Kelly to chief of detectives back then, but the DC commissioners had prevented him from doing so. Glassford told his good friend that he had known that Kelly would become chief of police someday.[5]

Putting on yet another lavish dinner party was Evalyn Walsh McLean. Among the various ambassadors, national ministers, senators, House representatives, and people too wealthy to work, were two invitees—Hap and Lucy, perhaps Lucy's first visit to the nation's capital. Also invited was J. Edgar Hoover. Now that former chief Glassford was in the Military Police Corps of the Provost Marshal General's Office, it is difficult to imagine that Evalyn did not introduce them.[6]

By now, Hap and Lucy maintained a small apartment in Washington, something of a home base away from home. He still traveled frequently around the country, and she still had to oversee the farms, but this gave them some time together. Mary Harris, whose column "Ringside Table" kept social tabs on the city, discovered the Glassfords enjoying themselves at the Copacabana supper club one evening. Glassford, Harris quipped, had been a "fine bucko" of a police chief during the Hoover years and since then had acquired his "darkly lovely young wife."[7]

During Glassford's travels, he and Lucy relied on letters. Sometimes he typed them and sometimes not, and often they were composed on the hotel letterhead of wherever he was staying, with an occasional photograph included. Over the course of exchanged letters, the two debated whether it was time to sell the farms and horses and rethink their future. Now having been in his army position since February 1942, Glassford was at full stride, and he was quite surprised when the army notified him that, having reached his sixtieth birthday, regulations required that he retire. His supervisors pleaded for dispensation, but the army denied the request, just as it had done with Glassford's father when he received a similar letter. In October 1943 the army awarded Glassford a second Legion of Merit medal for his exceptional meritorious conduct in developing and administering principles of internal security for the protection of the resources of war throughout the United States.[8]

Glassford likely did not know about the dark side of his superior, Provost Marshall Allen W. Gullion. Glassford's continual travel probably resulted in only limited contact between the two. Following the Pearl Harbor attack, California Governor Culbert Olson, California representative Earl Warren, and the Hearst newspapers had led an effort to intern all Japanese Americans. FBI Director J. Edgar

Hoover wrote a memorandum to US Attorney General Francis Biddle saying that "the necessity for mass evacuation is based primarily upon public and political pressure rather than on factual data." Biddle later issued a press release saying that the FBI had found no evidence of sabotage, and the Departments of Justice and War agreed that "the present military situation does not at this time require the removal of American citizens of the Japanese race." General Gullion attended a meeting at which Biddle presented his position. As Roosevelt biographer Ted Morgan notes, "That was too much for the jingoistic Provost Marshal, Allen W. Gullion, who said: 'Well, listen, Mr. Biddle, do you mean to tell me that if the army, the men on the ground, determine that it is a military necessity to move citizens, Jap citizens, that you won't help me?'" Gullion added that General John L. DeWitt, head of the Western Defense Command, favored "mass evacuations." Later, DeWitt called Biddle, saying that Governor Olson and he agreed "that all Japanese, even American-born, should be removed from the areas of California designated as combat zones," adding that people would take matters into their own hands because, "out here, Mr. Secretary, a Jap is a Jap to these people now." By April 1943 the FBI was investigating Provost Marshall Gullion for having initiated "a clandestine organization within the Army known as the 'SGs,' for Slim (his nickname) Gullion, which aimed, according to an FBI informant, 'to save America from FDR, radical labor, the communists, the Jews, and the colored race.'"[9]

Glassford's retirement date was December 25, 1943, but by then he was already on his way home. He may have been disappointed at having to leave the army before the war concluded, or perhaps he was pleased with his early release so that he could get on with another phase of his life. He and Lucy had agreed to sell the farms and animals and move to the art colony of Laguna Beach, California. Of course, there was always the worry that something might happen to brother Bill or sons Pete and Guy, who were in the war for the duration.

In the near years to come, Hap would be saddened by the death of his West Point classmate and fellow artillery commander Leslie McNair, killed on July 25, 1944, as the result of friendly fire while in France following D-Day. He would also mourn the death of his good friend Ernie Pyle, killed by enemy fire during the Battle of Okinawa in April 1945. Bill, Pete, and Guy would return from the war unharmed. Pete received a Distinguished Service Cross, awarded to him in Italy by Brigadier

General Charles W. Lawrence. Now a full colonel, Pete was the deputy commanding officer of a B-17 Flying Fortress group, having flown thirty-two missions and previously having received the Legion of Merit and the Air Medal. His award honored his "exceptional leadership as lead pilot on a mission to the Brux Oil Refineries [Czechoslovakia] on September 23, 1944." Hap was immensely proud, as was Pete's wife, Alice C. Glassford, waiting for Pete at their home in Tampa, Florida.[10]

Eventually, with brother Bill's concurrence, Hap and Lucy put up for sale most of the Arizona property and animals. It had not been an easy decision. By 1946 Hap and Lucy had liquidated most of their Arizona holdings, and by 1947 they had moved to Laguna Beach, California, where previously they had been occasional visitors. For them the move to Laguna Beach proved positive, especially when they discovered and bought a house just above the beach with a splendid view of the Pacific Ocean.[11]

Bill retired from the navy in 1946 and moved to Santa Barbara, California, bringing the two brothers close once again. Bill could look back on an impressive career since he had graduated from Annapolis in 1906. Like Hap, he had served in both World Wars.[12]

To say that Laguna Beach was an art colony would be an understatement: it was an American art mecca with a national reputation, aided in large measure by the Laguna Beach Art Association. The association had been founded in 1918 with the intent of not only staging exhibitions but also as a cultural, educational, and social center. While it had 150 charter members, its temporary gallery consisted of one community room in the Laguna Beach Hotel. Its goal was to advance knowledge and interest in art with close cooperation between artists and the public. Eleven years later it had its own building, but its fundraising plan had garnered too little, meaning that the art association had a building but was rather stark inside. By then the association had 700 members, and the town's population had grown to 2,000.[13]

Back in August 1932, while Glassford had contended with the fallout from the Bonus Army expulsion, the Laguna Beach Art Association, in cooperation with the Chamber of Commerce, held its first Festival of the Arts, with art studio tours, exhibitions, parades, dances, plays, a costume ball, and a spectacle of lights. The following year the association held its first Pageant of the Masters. The latter was *tableaux vivants*, or living pictures, with modern people re-creating famous works of art. The 1936 pageant, for instance, had live people sitting at a long table to re-create in accurate detail Leonardo da Vinci's *The Last Supper*. When Hap and Lucy arrived, they found exactly what they were looking for, and what would prove to be a superb choice for the couple. In its beautiful setting overlooking the ocean, about fifty miles southwest of Los Angeles, the newcomers found a circle of friends who loved creating art and encouraging the work of their fellow artists. Their beachfront house was just south of the city on Gaviota Drive, with a bank of seventy steps leading down to the sandy beach. It was perfect for entertaining family and friends, allowing Glassford to exercise his culinary skills, often preparing dinners for groups of eight to twelve.[14]

As one might expect, Pelham involved himself the social life of the Laguna Beach community, and in 1952 became the president of the Laguna Beach Chamber of Commerce. He was also very active in the art association's management, volunteering as chair of exhibits for the 1953 Laguna Beach Festival, held from July 30 through August 14. At least 150 paintings were on display, representing the work of art organizations from Santa Barbara, Los Angeles, and San Diego. Glassford was seemingly everywhere, his pipe clenched between his teeth, his left hand usually on his hip, in conversation with someone, likely about art. That same year, between July 29 and August 30, the Laguna Beach Association celebrated its 35th Anniversary Exhibition. Now having the time to devote to art, Glassford became an active painter, and between 1944 and 1959 he would paint more than seventy-five watercolors. His favorite subjects were boats, ships, docks, marinas, beaches, deserts, ranch houses, and scenes of Laguna Beach. He was a lifelong student, always keen to learn more. He had attended classes at the art institutes of San Francisco and Kansas City and taken classes from D. Howard Hitchcock in Hawaii. Now he was studying the work of several artists who would have an impact on Hap's paintings.[15]

Hap and artist Arthur Beaumont met during World War II. The latter was best known for his portraits of senior naval officers and paintings of war ships, naval battles, harbors, and landscapes. He suggested to Hap that he specialize in "transparent" watercolor paintings, which he believed was a medium well adapted for an artist with a military background. Glassford took his advice and used that technique from then on. Hap also considered three other artists as mentors: Emil Bisttram, Eliot O'Hara, and Russel Iredell. To what extent he learned from them by studying their paintings, attending their classes, reading publications about them, or exchanging letters is unclear, but each influenced Hap's art.[16]

Bisttram had founded the Taos School of Art and was well known for his paintings of New Mexico's landscape and people. O'Hara was a highly regarded plein air artist, known for his ability to capture the changing light and color of an outdoor scene, much as Glassford had attempted to do in the late afternoon light of Washington, DC. Iredell's specialty was portraits of Hollywood notables. He later became a member of the Laguna Beach Arts Association, where he and Glassford met and became friends. These artists, along with Glassford's good friend and combat comrade, John Twachtman, influenced Glassford's art.[17]

Douglas MacArthur had been a candidate for president in the elections of 1944, 1948, and 1952. It was never his idea; rather, others had drafted him. Apparently, under the assumption that voters would choose to elect him, he never bothered to campaign, and thus he never made much of a showing in any of the elections. In 1948 Glassford had organized a local MacArthur for President Club, but since MacArthur was out of the running early on, there was little for Glassford to do. Hap's willingness to involve himself in this effort, however, underscored his continued high regard for MacArthur. One who was very familiar with Douglas MacArthur was Clare Booth Luce, author, member of Congress, ambassador, and the wife of Henry Luce, founder of *Time*, *Life*, and *Fortune* magazines. Luce, who had had a romantic affair during World War II with one of MacArthur's lesser generals, later gave her view of the five-star general: "MacArthur's temperament was flawed by an egotism that demanded obedience not only to his orders, but to his ideas and his person as well. He plainly relished idolatry." Glassford was one those who inexplicably obliged.[18]

Living in Laguna Beach had its downside, however. Many friends of Hap and Lucy, perhaps too many, found their way there for a visit. In a March 30, 1954, letter to Pete, Hap groused that "visitors on vacation assume that because we live in a resort we are on perpetual vacation and have nothing better to do than pour drinks and otherwise entertain them." That likely sounded pretty good to Pete, who looked forward to his next visit.[19]

A somewhat disturbing incident happened one day when Glassford was thumbing through the September 29, 1953, issue of *Life* magazine, which showed a photograph of an employee of the Mammal Division of the Smithsonian Institution, who was examining the unstuffed carcass of what had once been a horse. Glassford startled when he realized that the carcass was that of Kidron, his grand thoroughbred horse in France. Glassford wrote to the magazine to say that he had known that horse very well, adding that Kidron had been "literally stolen from me by General John J. Pershing, in my opinion one of the greatest soldiers—and horse thieves—of all times."[20]

Of Hap and Cora's children, Guy probably caused his parents the most stress. They had not forgotten when he mysteriously ran away, and they were likely very disappointed when he left West Point before graduating. While they were proud of his World War II service, in other ways he confounded them. On one occasion when Guy needed a job, Hap found one for him, selling cars at a Ford agency in Port Orchard, Washington. Guy was agreeable and went there. He had no experience selling cars, however, and after three or four months of selling fewer cars than his coworkers, he lost his enthusiasm and quit. With Guy, things would go well for a few months, and then he would find a reason to leave. Guy's wife, Marjorie, wrote to Pelham and Lucy in March 1955 saying that Guy's employer had fired him and that Guy had taken off and left her and the two children. Pelham invited her and the children to come to Laguna Beach for a visit and sent her the money for the trip.[21]

By February 19, 1956, Hap had had it with Guy and wrote an angry letter, calling him a disgrace to the Glassford clan. In another angry letter, Hap wrote, "Guy, if you want a separation or a divorce be decent about it; you can't let Marjorie and your two wonderful children be in a lurch." Eventually, Marjorie, Lynne, and Carl moved to Laguna Beach, living near Hap and Lucy. Despite seeing their father only occasionally, the two children were happy at Laguna Beach. Marjorie worked full time to pay the bills and her mother looked after the children. Guy came and went in the lives of his children, but Marjorie never spoke critically of him to either child.[22]

Young Carl, a budding artist, lived in Laguna Beach from the sixth grade through his high school graduation, and he inherited from Hap a love and talent for art. When not surfing, which he did almost daily, Carl spent time in Hap's studio, watching his grandfather and learning his techniques. Carl remembered Hap as always having his pipe in his mouth as he brushed the watercolor strokes onto the paper, periodically puffing, sending forth the fragrance of burgundy cherry tobacco. In addition to his grandfather, Carl was surrounded by other well-known artists in Laguna Beach, and he began creating his own pictures and developing a portfolio. Although Hap sold some of his watercolors, he regarded his art primarily as an avocation. Carl had something else in mind—a career in art. When it was time to go to college, the young artist presented his portfolio to members of the Laguna Beach Art Association, hoping for a scholarship. While it helped to be Hap's grandson, Carl's artwork was clearly impressive. He received a four-year scholarship and elected to attend Brigham Young University in Provo, Utah. After graduating from BYU, Carl again followed in Hap's footsteps. He joined the army, graduated from Officer Candidate School, completed Airborne and Ranger training, and served in the 82nd "All American" Airborne Division. After completing his military obligation, he pursued a career in art, earning advanced degrees in communication, design, and education. He credited his grandfather when he later wrote, "[Hap's] approach to life as an artist set the hook in [his] grandson that later produced a career in Art."[23]

Hap's life changed drastically when Lucy's health deteriorated. The diagnosis was advanced breast cancer. For a time she sought treatment at the Capistrano-by-the-Sea Sanitarium at Dana Point, eight miles south of Laguna Beach, but it became clear that little could be done. She died on a Sunday evening, May 26, 1957, at 10:15 p.m., at age fifty, so young that her parents, Charles and Kathryn Painter, were there to anguish at her funeral. Doctor C. C. Henrie, MD, the attending physician, listed the direct cause of death as a collapsed lung over the course of two days, with breast carcinoma of two years duration the antecedent cause. Father John McNulty of Saint Catherine's Catholic Church led the rosary and service, held at the Laguna Beach Funeral Home. Lucy was buried on Wednesday afternoon at Fort Rosecrans National Cemetery, Point Loma, near San Diego. On May 28, 1957, Glassford wrote, "End of a Happy Era—God Bless!"[24]

Hap returned to his art but with less ardor, suffering the loss of Lucy as well as his own serious medical issue, the arrival of Parkinson's disease. His children were a source of comfort, as was brother Bill. The next year, 1958, would be a difficult year as well, for Hap would lose two important people in his life. Cora died on June 26 at her home in San Antonio of coronary occlusion, arteriosclerosis, and hypertension at age seventy-one. Still reeling from the deaths of Lucy and Cora, Hap was disheartened when his brother Bill died on July 30 at age seventy-two, having suffered a heart attack while at the Naval Hospital in San Diego.[25]

Pete was then teaching at West Point, New York, and Bettie was living in Florida with her family. Hap's youngest child, Dorothy, was living in Los Angeles. Dorothy had suffered a tragic loss in her own life. After her marriage to Lee Osher

Combs ended, she married William Walter Graham III, a naval officer, who was killed in action in the Pacific during World War II. Guy eventually found a career as a chef and manager in various restaurants and hotels in Salt Lake City, and he became a member of the Church of Jesus Christ of Latter-day Saints. He divorced Marjorie Robinson in 1955 and later married Lea Beatrice Harlow. He resettled in Denver, where he became an accomplished carpenter and took up fly fishing with a passion.[26]

Bettie had been the only Glassford child who inherited her father's compulsion for art, subsequently having a career in dress designing. She and her husband, Lee Parke, raised four children. She had gone with him to his various naval assignments, including Long Beach, California; Washington, DC; and Norfolk, Virginia. She drove across the country in her trusty 1937 Studebaker, which lasted for seventeen years. During World War II, Lee had managed the cryptanalysis decoding office in the navy, which broke the Japanese "purple code," the method the Japanese used to encrypt diplomatic messages. Bettie and Lee retired in Cape Coral, Florida, where Lee designed and built their house, and where they loved to cruise about in their boat, the *CoraLee*. In retirement Bettie spent much of her time creating art, as Hap had done.[27]

The following year brought news regarding Hap's "friendly enemy," Walter Waters, who had settled in Wenatchee, Washington, with Wilma and their children. Following three months of hospital treatment, the disabled veteran of two world wars died on April 22, 1959, at age sixty-one, with his wife at his side. Following the Bonus Army expulsion, he had written, "I sold out to no one. I was broke when I began the Bonus Army. I was broke and in debt when I finished." History seems to have given short shrift to his contribution to the Bonus March.[28]

Pelham Glassford died on August 9, 1959, at 2:30 a.m., the day after his seventy-sixth birthday. He passed away in the South Coast Community Hospital, South Laguna, California, having been ill for several weeks. He had enjoyed his retired years at his home above the beach, situated between the South Coast Highway and the Pacific Ocean. His death certificate fittingly listed his last occupation as "artist." The doctors noted that the cause of death was acute, decompensated left heart failure, accompanied by Parkinson's disease.[29]

Numerous newspapers published obituaries regarding Glassford's death, most providing a detailed chronicle of his life, paying the most attention to his defense of the Bonus Army. One person with good standing to comment on Pelham Glassford was Pelham Jr., who later wrote:

Dad never wavered from his life of fearless honesty, and keeping to his principle, he never lost a friend. Even after his complete honesty in dealing with the Bonus Marchers in Washington became an important factor in the defeat of President Hoover, there was not a single enemy, neither the ex-president nor any of his followers. This phase of Dad's life, and many others like it, demonstrated the thing that is immortal. His steadfast honesty was an inspiration to thousands of men.[30]

The Laguna Beach Art Association said of him, "Hap, as he was affectionately called by his host of friends, was a graduate of West Point, and was an instructor of Topography and Graphics. In addition to studying at many Art Schools, he was a pupil of Arthur Beaumont and Eliot O'Hara. Ships and docks were his favorite subjects." The association then listed more than seventy-five of his paintings by name, which he had created between 1944 and 1959. In his last year, despite advanced Parkinson's disease, Hap completed ten paintings.[31]

Perhaps the most heartfelt memory of Hap came from his granddaughter, Lizabeth "Lynne" Glassford Christy, which she wrote in 1979, twenty years after his death. She was the daughter of Guy and Marjorie Robinson and sister of Carl Glassford. Lynne called her grandfather Hap, not Grandpa. She thought he was the "living image of what a distinguished military leader should be" and recalled that what first registered with anyone who met him was his height and the way he carried himself, never stooping, not even a little. She thought he had a "kind, wise face" and skin that seemed wrinkle resistant. Hap had deep-set eyes, she recalled, and she always suspected that they "saw more than did the eyes of most people." Long after his death, whenever she noticed the aroma of sweet-smelling pipe tobacco, she thought of Hap. In 1952, when she was twelve, Hap and Lucy had come to visit the family in Port Orchard, Washington. She recalled Hap setting up his easels and painting the view from their living room window, "the bay, the Bremerton Navy Yard, the gray Northwest sky, and the fringes that were the many trees edging the hills behind the bay," a painting she always cherished. She recalled a special day when her grandfather took her to Seattle for the day, riding the Washington State Ferry from Bremerton, looking at Bainbridge Island as they passed by, and seeing the approaching Seattle skyline. He took her to "an elegant lunch" in the Frederick and Nelson tearoom of the department store, a "must" thing to do in those days. After lunch, he took her to the preteen section of the store and allowed her to select an outfit. She recalled the return ferry ride: "What a wonderful trip it was on the ferry home to Port Orchard. I wore a dressy silk dress with a short black over-jacket." Lucy, keeping things fair, took Carl on the Bremerton ferry to Seattle, where they had lunch and then shopped for boy's clothing. Like Lynne, Carl called his grandfather Hap.[32]

Hap had promised that he would pay for Lynne's college expenses, but that turned out not to be necessary. With scholarships she received bachelor's and master's degrees in English and went on to become a professor at Brigham Young University. Back when she was in high school, she had needed a new coat. By then Hap's Parkinson's disease prevented him from going with her, but he gave her money to buy it. She recalled, "The last few years of Hap's life were heartbreaking for us. He had developed Parkinson's disease which became worse. My mother and new step-father had an ambulance come to take him away from his home on the cliff above the ocean to the South Coast Hospital." In August 1959, at age nineteen, she said goodbye to Hap for the last time "as he breathed heavily under the oxygen tent, his long legs stretched out under the sheet."[33]

All of Hap's children survived him. Guy Carleton Glassford died in 1974 at the age of sixty-five, of a heart attack, while living in Denver. Dot, the youngest, died in 1977 at age sixty-four. Bettie, artist and dress designer, died in her sleep of heart congestion in 1986 at age seventy-six. Pete was the last of the Glassford children to go, dying on August 20, 1992, at age eighty-one.[34]

Pelham Davis Glassford lies buried at Fort Rosecrans National Cemetery, San Diego, with Lucy's grave beside his. Anyone visiting Hap's grave is guaranteed to have a superb view of Coronado Island and the Pacific Ocean, a continuing gift from him to anyone who drops by to say hello, underdog or not.

Afterword

PELHAM Davis Glassford was an exceptionally talented man, smart, fearless, and empathic. His primary career was that of army officer, in which he served in combat as a skilled field artillery commander, and later as one of the army's premier instructors. He is most remembered, however, for his single year of service as the Washington, DC, police chief, a position for which he had no experience. Nonetheless, essentially alone, he defied the Hoover administration and District of Columbia government to feed and shelter thousands of destitute World War I veterans, who had come to the nation's capital to lawfully petition for early payment of a promised bonus.

In 1934 the Roosevelt administration dispatched him to California's Imperial Valley to mediate labor violence. Again, essentially alone, but now without coercive power, he confronted powerful crop growers, corrupt officials, and violent vigilantes who threatened his life.

He felt compelled to defend the underdog. Whether it was West Point cadets unfairly threatened with dismissal, or destitute veterans considered to be itinerant tramps, or Mexican field pickers regarded as lesser humans, he was their champion.

He was amazingly generous with his money. When corrected for inflation, his personal expenses to feed the starving Bonus veterans amounted to about $47,000 in 2021 dollars. In contrast, the Washington powerful used starvation as a cruel tool to force hungry men, women, and children back onto the rails and roads of the Great Depression in search of their next meal.

He was charitable with his time. He seems to have been incapable of saying no when someone asked for assistance, accepting more positions on committees, commissions, boards, agencies, and clubs than anyone around, and their members continued to solicit him because they knew he could do whatever he put his mind to.

He made a couple missteps. On occasion, his moral compass settled on an incorrect heading. Thus, he seems to have suffered something of a blind spot for his fellow West Point cadet Douglas MacArthur, whose troops used sabers, bayonets, and tear gas to drive out the down-and-out veterans from the nation's capital. Similarly, when asked to conciliate labor violence in the Imperial Valley, he initially and unwisely sided with the growers. Realizing his error, he corrected his position, knowing that newspapers would ridicule his volte-face.

He was always the artist. Throughout his life he loved creating art—screens, murals, watercolors—even more than he did his other passions, riding motorcycles and training thoroughbred horses.

The former army commander and police chief seemed destined for something greater, perhaps a World War II generalship or a seat in Congress. Neither happened, but he may have taken satisfaction in knowing that while history has recorded many World War II generals and even more members of Congress, it has recorded only one police chief who defied a president and his administration to feed and shelter thousands of hungry veterans. The poet William Ernest Henley might have characterized Pelham Glassford as the master of his fate, the captain of his soul.

NOTES

Preface

1. Davis Jr., *Generals in Khaki*, 144–46, 183–84; Calhoun, *General Lesley J. McNair*, 29, 52. Both Pelham Glassford and Leslie McNair have been identified as the youngest brevet generals in the AEF. But in fact, John Neal Hodges was the youngest, serving with the AEF in the Engineer Branch in the British Sector on the Western Front, France. Glassford was the second youngest. Hodges: born February 13, 1884; USMA 1905, promoted to brevet general on June 26, 1918. Glassford: born August 8, 1883; USMA 1904, promoted to brevet general on October 1, 1918. McNair: born May 25, 1883; USMA 1904, promoted to brevet general on October 1, 1918.

Introduction

1. Glassford speech to veterans' rally, Philadelphia, November 3, 1932; Pelham D. Glassford Papers, Charles E. Young Research Library, UCLA, Box 1, unnumbered folder. Hereafter, PDG Papers.
2. PDG Papers, Box 1, blank folder, PDG letter to James T. White & Company (for eventual inclusion in the *National Cyclopedia of American Biography* and/or *Dictionary of American Biography*); Davis Jr., *Generals in Khaki*, 144–45.

Chapter 1

1. US Civil War Soldiers Index, 1861–1865, S. B. Davis pension folder, National Archives and Records Administration, Washington, DC; *Santa Fe Weekly Post*, April 10, 1869, 2; *Santa Fe Daily New Mexican*, January 19, 1874, 1; *Las Vegas Optic*, February 10, 1913.
2. *History of Jasper County, Missouri*, 766; Professor William Parke (grandson of Pelham Glassford), personal archive.
3. William Weir, "An Outline of Achievements of Col. William A. Glassford

by his nephew," PDG Papers, Box 3, "clippings" folder; David Rankin Barbee, "The Artist Who Became a Cop," *Washington Post*, November 15, 1931, 3–4; William Parke, personal archive; PDG Papers, Box 3, "family folder."

4. Perrigo, *Gateway to Glorieta*, 1, 8, 11–12; Santa Fe Trail Official Map and Guide, National Park Service.

5. Fort Union National Monument, New Mexico Official Map and Guide, National Park Service; Santa Fe Trail Association Official Map and Guide, National Park Service.

6. Perrigo, *Gateway to Glorieta*, 17, 19, 36; Historic Las Vegas, New Mexico pamphlet; William Parke, personal archive.

7. Historic Las Vegas, New Mexico pamphlet; Perrigo, *Gateway to Glorieta*, 27, photo 177; Plaza Hotel brochure, www.Plazahotellvnm.com. Today the hotel continues to do a brisk business.

8. Perrigo, *Gateway to Glorieta*, 22, 71, 73–76.

9. *Las Vegas Daily Gazette*, April 11, 1874; *Las Vegas Daily Optic*, November 19, 1881, June 16, 1882; Perrigo, *Gateway to Glorieta*, 70; *Rio Grande Republican*, Las Cruces, NM, March 11, 1882.

10. *Las Vegas Daily Optic*, June 16, 1882. All 2021 monetary calculations based on US Bureau of Labor Statistics CPI Inflation Calculator. Some early calculated amounts have been approximated as the website begins at 1913.

11. Perrigo, *Gateway to Glorieta*, 170; *Las Vegas Daily Gazette*, October 17, 24, 1882.

12. *Las Vegas Optic*, March 16 and April 7, 1883, August 9, 1900; *Las Vegas Daily Gazette*, August 21, 1883.

13. *Las Vegas Daily Gazette*, October 11 and December 18, 1885. Since William was the second son, he was William II rather than William Jr.

14. Worcester, *The Apaches*, 4.

15. Ibid., 300–2; Raines, *Getting the Message Through*, 67.

16. *Arizona Weekly Journal-Miner*, March 9 and May 18, 1887; *Arizona Silver Belt*, March 10 and June 30, 1888, 3; *Arizona Champion*, March 24, 1888; *Las Vegas Optic*, April 26, 1888.

17. William Parke, personal archive; *Arizona Silver Belt*, February 26, 1888.

18. *Arizona Weekly Enterprise* (Florence), June 29, 1889; *Santa Fe New Mexican*, October 10, 1888; *Arizona Silver Belt*, October 19, 1889; *Arizona Republican*, December 31, 1890 (the *Arizona Republican* became the *Arizona Republic* in 1930).

19. *Santa Fe New Mexican*, December 7, 1889; Barbee, "The Artist," 2–3; *Arizona Weekly Enterprise* (Florence), June 14, 1890; *Arizona Republican*, December 31, 1890; *Arizona Weekly Journal-Miner* (Prescott), July 29, 1891, 1.

20. PDG Papers, Box 3, "clippings" folder, Pearson-Allen column, *Philadelphia Record*, June 3, 1942.
21. *Las Vegas Free Press*, June 13, 1892; *Santa Fe Daily New Mexican*, June 18 and July 2, 1892; C. Glassford, *One Life Is Not Enough*, 115, hereafter CCG Papers; William Parke, personal archive.
22. *Arizona Silver Belt*, July 29, 1893; *Santa Fe Daily New Mexican*, May 27, July 15, November 9, and December 30, 1893, September 19, 1894; New York Passenger Lists, 1820–1957, Ancestry.com; William Parke, personal archive; *Arizona Silver Belt* (Globe), April 21, 1894.
23. *Santa Fe New Mexican*, April 16, June 9, and July 18, 1898; *Las Vegas Daily Optic*, June 29, 1898.
24. Smithsonian National Museum of American History, *Price of Freedom, Americans at War*, Spanish American War Exhibit.
25. *Santa Fe Daily New Mexican*, July 9 and September 10, 1898; Encyclopedia de Puerto Rico, *Puerto Rico in the Twentieth Century*, https://enciclopediapr.org/en.
26. *Arizona Republican*, May 26, 1899.
27. *Las Vegas Daily Optic*, August 9, 1899; *Arizona Republican*, August 10, 1899.
28. *Santa Fe Daily New Mexican*, March 17, 1900, March 3, 1906; *Las Vegas Daily Optic*, June 30, 1900; US Census, 1900, Pelham Glassford, Port of San Juan, Puerto Rico.
29. *Las Vegas Daily Optic*, June 30, 1900; *National Tribune* (Washington, DC), June 26, 1900, 5; *Santa Fe Daily New Mexican*, September 1, 1900; D'Este, *Patton*, 71; Robert M. Danford, Forward to "One Life Is Not Enough," by Cora Glassford, CCG Papers.
30. William Parke, personal archive; *Santa Fe Daily New Mexican*, March 3, 1906; *Carthage Press*, July 14, 1936.
31. Biographical Directory of the US Congress, 1774–2020; Catton, *The Civil War*, 112, 121, 134, 141; William Parke, personal archive.

Chapter 2

1. McCullough, *1776*, 20, 294; D'Este, *Eisenhower*, 60; Ambrose, *Duty, Honor, Country*, xiv, 9–10, 15, 22, 25, 63, www.britannica.com/topic/United-States-Military-Academy.
2. D'Este, *Eisenhower*, 60–61, 63; D'Este, *Patton*, 70; Ambrose, *Duty*, xiv, 39, 70–75; James, *The Years of MacArthur*, 72, 80.
3. USMA *Howitzer* yearbook, 1904, 6–13; Tuchman, *Stilwell and the American Experience in China 1911–45*, 13; D'Este, *Eisenhower*, 61; Ambrose, *Duty*, 231–33. Because no women were admitted to the USMA during this era, I have used "upperclassmen" rather than "senior cadets," the modern term.

4. Tuchman, *Stillwell*, 13; Ambrose, *Duty*, 222–24; James, *Years of MacArthur*, 80; D. Eisenhower, *At Ease: Stories I Tell to Friends*, 17; D'Este, *Patton*, 71.

5. Biographical Register of the Officers and Graduates of the US Military Academy at West Point, 1900–1910, hereafter, Biographical Register of USMA; PDG Papers, Box 2, Extract Orders, 1919 Résumé; D'Este, *Eisenhower*, 59; D. Eisenhower, *At Ease*, 4; James, *Years of MacArthur*, 67; Tuchman, *Stilwell*, 13; CCG Papers, Danford foreword.

6. CCG Papers, 2; PDG Papers, Box 2, Extract Orders, 1919 Résumé.

7. CCG Papers, 2–5.

8. Ibid. 4–5.

9. Eisenhower, *At Ease*, 4–5.

10. Tuchman, *Stilwell*, 13, 15, 125; Davis, *Generals in Khaki*, 263; James, *Years of MacArthur*, 71.

11. D'Este, *Eisenhower*, 60, 65; D. Eisenhower, *At Ease*, 5; Tuchman, *Stilwell*, 13; Manchester, *American Caesar*, 51.

12. D'Este, *Patton*, 72; Bradley and Blair, *A General's Life*, 31; MacArthur, *Reminiscences*, 25; Ambrose, *Duty*, 222–23.

13. Bradley, *General's Life*, 31–32; D'Este, *Patton*, 72.

14. Ambrose, *Duty*, 193, 202, 211, 213; Tuchman, *Stilwell*, 14; Coffman, *Regulars*, 147; *Dictionary of American Biography*.

15. Bradley, *General's Life* 32; D. Eisenhower, *At Ease*, 9; D'Este, *Eisenhower*, 64.

16. Bradley, *General's Life*, 35; Calhoun, *General Lesley J. McNair*, 32; Tuchman, *Stilwell*, 15; D. Eisenhower, *At Ease*, 25.

17. D'Este, *Eisenhower*, 60, 63.

18. Ambrose, *Duty*, 225–30; CCG Papers, 7.

19. Manchester, *American Caesar*, 51–52.

20. Ambrose, *Duty*, 229–31; MacArthur, *Reminisces*, 25–26; Manchester, *American Caesar*, 52.

21. CCG Papers, 5–8.

22. USMA *Howitzer* yearbook, 1904, 79, 82; Regulations for the USMA, 1902, Article XII, Discipline, 143, Section III, Washington Government Printing Office.

23. PDG Papers, Box 2, Extract Orders, 1919 Résumé; World War 1 DSM citation for Admiral William Glassford.

24. USMA *Howitzer* yearbook, 1904, 28, 51, 82, 120, 173, 174; PDG Papers, Box 2, Extract Orders, 1919 Résumé; Calhoun, *McNair*, 30–31; Tuchman, *Stilwell*, 15; *Dictionary of American Biography*.

25. USMA *Howitzer* yearbook, 1904, 51.
26. Parke, Personal Archive.
27. CCG Papers, Danford foreword.

Chapter 3

1. Coffman, *Regulars*, 191–95; CCG Papers, 39–40.
2. Coffman, *Regulars*, 142–43; Tuchman, *Stilwell*, 16–17.
3. Coffman, *Regulars*, 3, 14–17.
4. Ibid., 27.
5. Ibid., 150. All original and inflated dollar amounts based on the US Bureau of Labor Consumer Price Index; Davis Jr., *Generals in Khaki*, 144.
6. Truscott Jr., *The Twilight of the U.S. Cavalry*, 76; CCG Papers, 10. Note: A "shave tail" is a newly broken, unseasoned pack mule, the tail of which has been shaved so the muleteers can easily identify and watch it within the mule train, hence its pejorative use for newly commissioned second lieutenants.
7. Ambrose, *Duty*, 218; *Santa Fe Daily New Mexican*, March 3, 1906.
8. CCG Papers, 17.
9. Biographical Register of USMA; PDG Papers, Box 2, Extract orders, 1919 Résumé; Truscott, *Twilight*, 75–76; Calhoun, *General Lesley J. McNair*, 36; Coffman, *Regulars*, 156. Note: This school began in 1887 as the Cavalry and Light Artillery School. From 1907 until its suspension in 1917, it was called the Mounted Services School. Following World War I, it reopened as the Cavalry School until its termination in 1947.
10. Blumenthal, *Patton*, 123, 136; CCG Papers, 18; PDG Papers, Box 4, "horses we raised and sold" folder.
11. PDG Papers, Box 2, Extract Orders, 1919 Résumé; CCG Papers, 29.
12. Tuchman, *Stilwell*, 21; *Washington Evening Star*, August 3, 1907.
13. PDG to American Biography; Davis, *Generals in Khaki*, 68; CCG Papers, 18–19; Daughters of the Republic of Texas, guide to Cora Glassford Papers; Death certificate.
14. CCG Papers, 29–35.
15. Grandcamp, Lancaster, and Ferguson, *Rhody Redlegs*, 1; Kernan and Samson, *History of the 103rd Field Artillery*, 3–4.
16. CCG Papers, 39–40; McKenna, *Battery A 103rd Field Artillery*, 14–15; *Washington Evening Star*, March 10, 1910; *Washington Times Herald*, April 30, 1910.

17. CCG Papers, 36–37.
18. *Washington Evening Star*, August 10, 1912, March 10, 1913; Pelham Glassford and Cora Carleton, Our Family Tree, Parke, personal archive.
19. Coffman, *Regulars*, 34, 38–39.
20. Ibid., 56–57, 60, 62, 67, 78–82.
21. PDG Papers, Box 2, Extract Orders, 1919 Résumé; Coffman, *Regulars*, 84; CCG Papers, 41–42. Nipa houses usually rested on stilts and had grass roofs.
22. CCG Papers, 41; Coffman, *Regulars*, 86.
23. CCG Papers, 42–45.
24. CCG Papers, 45–46.
25. CCG Papers, 47–48; Philippines, Manila, Civil Registration, 1899–1984; www/navsource.org/archives/30/13/13058.htm.
26. CCG Papers, 47–48; *Honolulu Star Bulletin*, August 20, 1913, 8.
27. CCG Papers, 47–48, 52–54.
28. *Honolulu Star Bulletin*, December 29, 1914, February 15, 1915; *Las Vegas Daily Optic*, December 22, 1914, 8; PDG Papers, Box 2, Extract Orders, 1919 Résumé.
29. *Honolulu Star Bulletin*, June 14, 1915; Historic Hotels of America, https://www.historichotels.org/us/hotels-resorts/moana-surfrider-a-westin-resort-and-spa/?from=rezconsole.
30. *Honolulu Star Bulletin*, February 12, February 15, August 7; April 11, May 26, June 13, 1916.
31. CCG Papers, 61–62.
32. Ibid., 62.
33. Ibid., 63.
34. https://isaacsartcenter.hpa.edu/artist-works.php?artistId=158146&artist=D.+Howard+Hitchcock+%281861-1943%29.
35. CCG Papers, 69–72.
36. Ibid., 63–66.
37. Ibid., 67–69.
38. CCG Papers, 63.
39. Diary of Sarah Truscott, courtesy of Debbie Truscott.

Chapter 4

1. *Honolulu Star Bulletin*, July 26 and August 3, 1916; *Washington Evening Star*, May 4, 1914; *Arizona Republican*, April 3, 1916, 3; *Bisbee Daily Review*, April 15, 1916, 3.
2. CCG Papers, 89; *Washington Evening Star*, August 9, 1916; *National Cyclopedia of American Biography*, Vol. 12.

3. CCG Papers, 89; Coffman, *The Regulars*, 178; Bernstein, *The Lean Years*, 442; Fleta Campbell Springer, "Glassford and the Siege of Washington," *Harper's Magazine*, November 1932, 642; *Honolulu Star Bulletin*, November 8, 1916; *Washington Post*, Capital Echoes, November 1, 1931.
4. J. Eisenhower, *Intervention!*, xii–xv, 191–92, 214–27, 235–36, 334–35; Coffman, *Regulars*, 197–99; J. Eisenhower with J. Eisenhower, *Yanks*, 28; Levy, *World War I*, 20.
5. CCG Papers, 93–96; PDG, Box 2, Extract Orders, 1919 résumé; *El Paso Herald*, March 13, 1917.
6. CCG Papers, 93–95, 100.
7. Thomas, *The Mexican Punitive Expedition Under General John J. Pershing*, v–11.
8. CCG Papers, 102–4.
9. Calhoun, *General Lesley J. McNair*, 50–51; Collins Jr., foreword, vi–vii; Marshall, *Memoirs of My Services in the World War 1917–1918*, 8.
10. Persico, *11th Month, 11th Day, 11th Hour: Armistice Day, 1918*, 15–17; Levy, *World War I*, 8, 10.
11. Levy, *World War I*, 9, 13; Persico, *11th Month*, 19–23, 399.
12. J. Eisenhower with J. Eisenhower, *Yanks*, 4–5, 8–10; Levy, *World War I*, 22, 25.
13. J. Eisenhower with J. Eisenhower, *Yanks*, 19–21.
14. Ibid., 19–21, 288–89, 296.
15. Marshall, *Memoirs*, vi–vii; J. Eisenhower with J. Eisenhower, *Yanks*, 12–13, 17, 35; Levy, *World War 1*, 37.
16. J. Eisenhower with J. Eisenhower, *Yanks*, 11–13, 15–17, 23, 33–34.
17. Pershing, *Final Report of General John J. Pershing*, 5; Collins Jr., foreword, vii; J. Eisenhower with J. Eisenhower, *Yanks*, 3; 1st Division Museum, www.fdmuseum.org. Note: The World War I "square" divisions of four regiments proved to be unwieldly and were replaced in World War II by "triangular" divisions of three regiments, totaling about 10,000 soldiers.
18. Levy, *World War 1*, 41; J. Eisenhower with J. Eisenhower, *Yanks*, 35, 37–39, 41–42; Marshall, *Memoirs*, 1.
19. Marshall, *Memoirs*, 1, 6–7.
20. Ibid., 6–8.
21. Ibid., 11, 17; J. Eisenhower with J. Eisenhower, *Yanks*, 56–57.
22. US Army, WWI Transport Service, *Tenadores*, July 30, 1917, Hoboken, NJ, to St. Nazaire, August 13, 1917, www.fold3-com.ezproxy.kcls.org/image/603991689; Passenger List; CCG Papers, 104, 107.
23. J. Eisenhower with J. Eisenhower, *Yanks*, 53, 54; Marshall, *Memoirs*, 19, 39.

24. G. Marshall, *Memoirs*, 19; J. Eisenhower with J. Eisenhower, *Yanks*, 53–54.
25. Marshall, *Memoirs*, 41, 53; E. Taylor, *New England in France*, 2–3, 60; J. Eisenhower with J. Eisenhower, *Yanks*, 62, 84, 121; McKenna, *Battery A*, 8. Note: While the French Army of World War II would become the target of jokes, the French Army of World War I was generally considered to be the best Allied army.
26. Taylor, *New England in France*, 71–72.
27. PDG Papers, Box 2, extract order, 1919 résumé; Barbee, "Artist Who Became a Cop," 2–3.
28. CCG Papers, 109–10; Barbee, "Artist Who Became a Cop"; *National Cyclopedia of American Biography*, Vol. 12.
29. CCG Papers, 108–10.
30. Calhoun, *McNair*, 52.; CCG Papers, 108–10.
31. McCullough, *Truman*, 113–15; CCG Papers.
32. CCG Papers, 110; McKenna, *Battery A*, 147.
33. CCG Papers, 110.
34. Barbee, "Artist Who Became a Cop"; CCG Papers, 111–12.
35. CCG Papers, 110–12.
36. Ibid., 112–13; PDG Papers, Box 2, Extract Orders, 1919 résumé.
37. D'Este, *Patton*, 140–42; Blumenthal, *Patton*, 75.
38. Barbee, "Artist Who Became a Cop"; Ambrose, *Duty*, 204–5; USMA *Howitzer* yearbook, 1904; USMA Post Cemetery, Find A Grave; CCG Papers, 114.
39. Biographical Register of Officers and Graduates, USMA, supplement, vol vi–A, 1910–1920; PDG Papers, Box 13, "Saumur" folder; CCG Papers, 113.
40. CCG Papers, 113.
41. Jenkins, *The Last Ridge*, 126–27. During WWII, Hayes commanded the Tenth Mountain Division; CCG Papers, 115–17; Parke, "The Story of Kidron," personal archive.
42. Parke, "The Story of Kidron"; PDG Papers, Box 5, "Kidron" folder; CCG Papers, 115–17.
43. CCG Papers, 115–17; J. Eisenhower with J. Eisenhower, *Yanks*, 144–47, photo insert.

Chapter 5

1. US Army Center of Military History, *World War I Birth of the Modern Army Division*; J. Eisenhower with J. Eisenhower, *Yanks*, 94, 99; Taylor, *New England in France*, 1917–1919, 211.
2. Clarke, *Over There with O'Ryan's Roughnecks*, 33.
3. Ibid., 32.

4. Gutierrez, *Doughboys on the Great War*, 13, 57–58, 118, 167.
5. J. Eisenhower with J. Eisenhower, *Yanks*, 94, 99, 173–74; Coffman, *The Regulars*, 218; Gibran, *The 92nd Division and the Italian Campaign*, 1–2; Lloyd, *The Western Front*, 386.
6. J. Eisenhower with J. Eisenhower, *Yanks*, 68, 99, 107, 303 n6; Lloyd, *The Western Front*, 332.
7. J. Eisenhower with J. Eisenhower, *Yanks*, 102 map; Levy, *World War I*, 43–44.
8. J. Eisenhower with J. Eisenhower, *Yanks*, 104–5.
9. Ibid., 89–90; S. Marshall, *World War I*, 371–72.
10. J. Eisenhower with J. Eisenhower, *Yanks*, 121, 125, 127, 131–32, 135–36.
11. Ibid., 135–36, 153, 156–58, 161; Levy, *World War I*, 47; Pershing, *Final*, 35.
12. CCG Papers, 116–17, 120–23.
13. Ibid., 120–21; Taylor, *New England in France*, 67–68.
14. Taylor, *New England in France*, 151–53; Kernan and Samson, *History of the 103rd Field Artillery*, 51; CCG Papers, 121.
15. CCG Papers, 122–23; Kernan and Samson, *History of the 103rd Field Artillery*, 16.
16. Taylor, *New England in France*, 154.
17. Taylor, *New England in France*, 15; McKenna, *Battery A*, 45, 133; Haas, "Bringing in the Thunder"; Kernan and Samson, *History of the 103rd Field Artillery*, 19.
18. *U.S. Army Handbook of Artillery*, 80–82, 207–9.
19. McKenna, *Battery A*, 105; CCG Papers, 120–24; Rosskam, "The Glassford They Remember"; Taylor, *New England in France*, 67–68.
20. J. Eisenhower with J. Eisenhower, *Yanks*, 109–11, 163.
21. Ibid., 166–70, map.
22. Taylor, *New England in France*, 159–61, 170–74.
23. Ibid., 161–64, 170–71.
24. Kernan and Samson, *History of the 103rd Field Artillery*, 64–65.
25. Ibid., 66–67.
26. Ibid., 66–67, 69, 75 (Foch quoted in); CCG Papers, 126–27.
27. CCG Papers, 124.
28. CCG Papers, 124–25.
29. Ibid., 125–27; Rosskam, "The Glassford They Remember."
30. CCG Papers, 126–28.
31. Ibid., 129–30.
32. Taylor, *New England in France*, 208.
33. Clarke, *Over There*, 43–44, 73.

Chapter 6

1. CCG Papers, 131–32.
2. Ibid., 129–32; McKenna, *Battery A*, 50–51.
3. CCG Papers, 132–33.
4. Kernan and Samson, *History of the 103rd Field Artillery*, 74–75.
5. McKenna, *Battery A*, 52–55; J. Eisenhower with J. Eisenhower, *Yanks*, 191–93.
6. J. Eisenhower with J. Eisenhower, *Yanks*, 182–83; G. Marshall, *Memoirs*, 120–21.
7. J. Eisenhower with J. Eisenhower, *Yanks*, 186–88, 198; G. Marshall, *Memoirs*, 149–51.
8. J. Eisenhower with J. Eisenhower, *Yanks*, 191–94, map; Kernan and Samson, *History of the 103rd Field Artillery*, 90–93.
9. J. Eisenhower with J. Eisenhower, *Yanks*, 194; Taylor, *New England in France*, 224–30; McKenna, *Battery A*, 52–59.
10. Rosskam, "The Glassford they Remember"; CCG Papers, 137.
11. J. Eisenhower with J. Eisenhower, *Yanks*, 198–99, map.
12. J. Eisenhower with J. Eisenhower, *Yanks*, 202–4, 211, map.
13. G. Marshall, *Memoirs*, 149–51.
14. J. Eisenhower with J. Eisenhower, *Yanks*, 200–1, map.
15. Pershing, *Final Report*, 46–52; S. Marshall, *World War I*, 432–37; J. Eisenhower with J. Eisenhower, *Yanks*, 203–4.
16. J. Eisenhower with J. Eisenhower, *Yanks*, 226–27; G. Marshall, *Memoirs*, 161.
17. CCG Papers, 137; Kernan and Samson, *History of the 103rd Field Artillery*, 118–19. Note: Glassford was appointed a brigadier on October 1 and was accepted as a brigadier on October 17. It is almost certain that he wore the stars and took over the brigade on October 1, but that formal Washington, DC, approval and pay began on October 17. Either way, the rank was temporary.
18. Taylor, *New England in France*, 271; S. Marshall, *World War I*, 437.
19. S. Marshall, *World War 1*, 437.
20. Taylor, *New England in France*, 249.
21. Ibid., 249, 268–69; https://www.cdc.gov/flu/pandemic-resources/1918-pandemic-h1n1.html; Taylor, *New England in France*, 268–69.
22. CCG Papers, 138.
23. Ibid., 138–39.
24. Ibid., 139.
25. Ibid., 140; Taylor, *New England in France*, 300.

26. J. Eisenhower with J. Eisenhower, *Yanks*, 288; Professor Cosgrove, presentation.
27. Pershing, *Final Report*, 49, 51; G. Marshall, *Memoirs*, 138.
28. Professor Cosgrove, presentation.
29. PDG Papers, Box 2, Extract Orders, 1919 Résumé; J. Eisenhower with J. Eisenhower, *Yanks*, 228–37.

Chapter 7

1. PDG Papers, Box 2, Folder 1, https://www.veteranmedals.army.mil.
2. Lofthus, *From Wentworth to the Western Front*, 3, 13, 29, 36, 59–61.
3. Clarke, *Over There with O'Ryan's Roughnecks*, 129–30.
4. CCG Papers, 144; *Washington Evening Star*, September 6, 1925.
5. CCG Papers, 159.
6. PDG Papers, Box 2, Extract Orders, 1919 Résumé; Coffman, *Regulars*, 205, 224.
7. Hedglen, "The Boys from Las Vegas," 12–15.
8. *Washington Evening Star*, December 23, 1912, March 10 and May 4, 1913; *Arizona Republican*, February 14, 1915, April 3 and April 15, 1916.
9. *Washington Evening Star*, April 11, 1917, June 2, 1920; *Arizona Republican*, April 25 and October 22, 1917; *Washington Evening Star*, June 2, 1920.
10. *Bisbee Daily Review*, April 29, 1922.
11. PDG Papers, Box 2, Extract Orders, 1919 Résumé; CCG Papers, 160–62; extracted from 1920 US Census; Truscott Jr., *The Twilight of the U.S. Cavalry*, 136. Note: Glassford called this school the General Service Schools and later the General Staff College and School of the Line. The name seems to have been in transition in 1919. General William Tecumseh Sherman began the school in 1881 as the School for the Application of Infantry and Cavalry, soon shortened to the Infantry and Cavalry School. In 1901 the school became the General Service and Staff College, and in 1907 was renamed the School of the Line, eventually becoming the Command and General Staff School, as it is now called.
12. CCG Papers, 160–64; *National Cyclopedia of American Biography*, Vol. 12.
13. CCG Papers, 165–72, 190; *Washington Evening Star*, April 2, 1923, June 1, 1924; Springer, "Glassford and the Siege of Washington," 642.
14. Olmsted, *Right Out of California*, 20–21; Dickson and Allen, *The Bonus Army*, 53.
15. Coffman, *Regulars*, 239–42.
16. *Washington Evening Star*, April 2, 1923; CCG Papers, 206, 224; *National Cyclopedia of American Biography*. Note: Today the building and campus that had been the Army War

College is the National War University, attended by members of all the branches of the US military, Department of State and other federal agencies, and international fellow students.

17. CCG Papers, 206–7.
18. *Washington Evening Star*, March 1, 1925; *Washington Evening Sunday Star*, March 24, 1925.
19. CCG Papers, 207, 213–14.
20. Ibid., 208–12.
21. Ibid., 219–26.
22. *Washington Evening Star*, September 19, 1925; Greenwich Historical Society, www.greenwichfacesthegreatwar.org/j-alden-twatchman.php.
23. CCG Papers, 214–15.
24. *Washington Post*, March 3, 1926, 24; *Washing Evening Star*, February 23, 1927, 3.
25. *Washington Post*, May 16, May 23, September 16, September 26, December 26, 1926.
26. PDG Papers, Box 6, "Children" folder; Carl Glassford interview, August 10, 2019.
27. PDG Papers, Box 2, Extract Orders, 1942 Résumé; CCG Papers, 216.
28. *Corsicana Daily Sun*, August 3, 1932; *New York Times*, August 4, 1932; *National Cyclopedia of American Biography*; Carl Glassford interview, August 10, 2019.
29. *Washington Evening Star*, July 31, 1927; November 27, 1927.
30. *National Cyclopedia of American Biography*; *Washington Post*, August 26, 1928; PDG Papers, box 2, Extract Orders, 1942 Résumé.
31. *Washington Post*, December 22, 1929, 59; Springer, "Glassford and the Siege of Washington," 642; collected notes provided by Wm. Parke.
32. Carl Glassford interview, August 10, 2019; 1930 US Census; *Washington Post*, January 8, 1936; *List of Cadets, West Point*, 3, 62; Parke, personal archive.
33. PDG Papers, Box 2, Extract Orders, 1942 Résumé; Springer, "Siege of Washington," 642; PDG Papers, Box 14, Folder 2, Draft Document, "My Opportunity."
34. *Bakersfield Californian*, August 7, 1931, 2; *Arizona Daily Star*, August 7, 1931, 8.
35. Superior Court of Arizona, Distribution of Estate, August 4, 1932; *Dictionary of American Biography*.

Chapter 8

1. Springer, "Glassford and the Siege of Washington," 642; PDG Papers, Box 14, Folder 2, Draft Document, "My Opportunity," 1; PDG Papers, Box 14, Folder 2, Draft Document, "The day I took over command," 2.

2. Barbee, "The Artist Who Became a Cop."
3. www.arlingtoncemetery.net/hbcrosby.htm.
4. Dickson and Allen, *The Bonus Army*, 19–20, 32–34.
5. Dickson and Allen, *Bonus Army*, 43–44. Barbee, "Artist Who Became a Cop."
6. PDG Papers, Box 14, Folder 2, Draft Document, "The day I took over command," 3.
7. Barbee, "Artist Who Became a Cop"; *Washington Post*, October 25, 1931; Springer, "Siege of Washington," 643.
8. *Washington Post*, November 10, 1931.
9. *New York Times*, November 11, 1931, 28; *Washington Post*, November 12, 1931, 2.
10. Shales, *The Forgotten Man*, 113–14; Dickson and Allen, *Bonus Army*, 20–23, 26–28.
11. Dickson and Allen, *Bonus Army*, 1, 28–31.
12. Ibid., 31–34; Olmsted, *Right Out of California*, 21–22; Lisio, *The President and Protest*, 5; Goodwin, *Lyndon Johnson and the American Dream*, 74.
13. Watkins, *The Hungry Years*, 132–33; Dickson and Allen, *Bonus Army*, 34–35.
14. Shales, *The Forgotten Man*, 129; D'Este, *Patton*, 351.
15. Watkins, *The Hungry Years*, 82; Dickson and Allen, *Bonus Army*, 35–37.
16. *Washington Post*, October 21 and 22, 1932.
17. Lisio, *The President and Protest*, 54; PDG Papers, Box 14, Folder 2, Draft Document, "The day I took over command," 1. This draft document is Glassford labeled to Boyd.
18. PDG Papers, Box 14, Folder 2, Draft Document, "The day I took over command," 1–4. This draft document is Glassford labeled to Boyd.
19. *Washington Post*, October 21, 1932.
20. Bernstein, *The Lean Years*, 442; Daniels, *The Bonus March*, 90.
21. *Washington Post*, November 24 and 22, December 1, 1931, 3; Springer, "Siege of Washington," 641, 643.
22. Bernstein, *Lean Years*, 429, 446; Dickson and Allen, *Bonus Army*, 53, 55, 124.
23. PDG Papers, Box 14, Folder 2, Draft Document, "The day I took over command," 4; Bernstein, *Lean Years*, 429–30.
24. Bernstein, *Lean Years*, 429–30; *Washington Post*, December 4, 1931, 1, 3; Daniels, *The Bonus March*, 67.
25. *Washington Post*, December 6, 1931.
26. Ibid., December 5, 1931; Bernstein, *Lean Years*, 430.
27. Dickson and Allen, *Bonus Army*, 45; Bernstein, *Lean Years*, 430.
28. Bernstein, *Lean Years*, 431; *Washington Post*, December 8, 1932.

29. *Washington Post*, December 7, 1931.
30. Ibid., December 9, 1931; Bernstein, *Lean Years*, 431; James, *The Years of MacArthur*, 385–86.
31. Dickson and Allen, *Bonus Army*, 52–53; Bernstein, *Lean Years*, 432–34; Watkins, *Hungry Years*, 126–30.
32. *Washington Post*, December 16 and 17, 1932.
33. Ibid., December 26, December 27, December 30, 1; Springer, "Siege of Washington," 643.
34. Dickson and Allen, *Bonus Army*, 47.
35. *Washington Post*, January 7, 1932; Dickson and Allen, *Bonus Army*, 49–50.
36. Dickson and Allen, *Bonus Army*, 51–52; Lisio, *President and Protest*, 62.
37. *Washington Post*, January 23 and February 26, 1932.
38. *Washington Post*, February 28 and March 1, 1932.
39. *Washington Post*, March 2, 4, 5, 1932.
40. *Washington Post*, March 20, 1932; MacArthur, *Reminiscences*, 64, 67.
41. *Washington Post*, April 1 and 2, 1932.
42. *Washington Post*, April 11, 1932.
43. *Washington Post*, April 12, 13, 16, 21, 27, 1932.
44. *Washington Post*, May 11, 1932.

Chapter 9

1. Dickson and Allen, *The Bonus Army*, 37.
2. Waters as told to White, *B. E. F.*, 4; James, *The Years of MacArthur*, 387.
3. Walters and White, *B. E. F.*, 4; Dickson and Allen, *Bonus Army*, 56–57; Lisio, *The President and Protest*, 64–65.
4. Schlesinger Jr., *The Age of Roosevelt*, 256–57; Waters and White, *B. E. F.*, 4–7, 10–13; Article I, US Constitution; Lisio, *President and Protest*, 66; Daniels, *Bonus March*, 66.
5. Waters and White, *B. E. F.*, 8–9.
6. Ibid., 10, 14–15.
7. Ibid., 14–16; Dickson and Allen, *Bonus Army*, 59; Schlesinger, *Crisis of the Old Order*, 257.
8. Waters and White, *B. E. F.*, 16–21, 28; James, *Years of MacArthur*, 385.
9. Ibid., 21–23.
10. Ibid., 24–25.
11. Ibid., 26–28; Watkins, *The Hungry Years*, 133; Lisio, *President and Protest*, 64–65.
12. Waters and White, *B. E. F.*, 30–31.
13. Ibid., 33–34.

14. Ibid., 34–38.
15. Ibid., 39–40; Lisio, *President and Protest*, 68.
16. Waters and White, *B. E. F.*, 41–46.
17. Ibid., 47–50.
18. Ibid., 51–55. Some news accounts reported that veterans, possibly elsewhere, soaped the tracks, but Waters wrote that the veterans closed the brakes against the wheels.
19. Ibid., 56–59; Watkins, *The Hungry Years*, 133.
20. Waters and White, *B. E. F.*, 60–61; Lisio, *President and Protest*, 68–69.
21. Dickson and Allen, *Bonus Army*, 73–74.
22. Waters and White, *B. E. F.*, 61–62.
23. https://hoover.archives.gov/hoovers/president-herbert-hoover.
24. https://hoover.archives.gov/hoovers/president-herbert-hoover; Shales, *The Forgotten Man*, 130; Daniels, *The Time Between the Wars*, 193.

Chapter 10

1. Dickson and Allen, *The Bonus Army*, 5, 10, 59–60; PDG Papers, Box 14, Folder 2, Draft Document, "Glassford to Boyd," 1.
2. PDG Papers, Box 14, Folder 2, Draft Document, "Glassford to Boyd," 4–6.
3. Owen P. White, "General Glassford's Story," *Collier's*, October 29, 1932, 10; PDG Papers, Box 14, Folder 2, Draft Document, "Glassford to Boyd," 5–7.
4. Daniels, *The Bonus March*, 87.
5. PDG Papers, Box, 14, Folder 2, Draft Document, "Glassford to Boyd," 7; *Washington Post*, May 25, 1932.
6. https://okhistory.org/publications/enc/entry.php?entry=HU008.
7. PDG Papers, Box 14, Folder 2, Draft Document, "Glassford to Boyd," 7–8.
8. Ibid., 9, 12; Springer, "Glassford and the Siege of Washington," 644.
9. PDG Papers, Box 14, Folder 2, Draft Document, "Glassford to Boyd," 10–11.
10. Dickson and Allen, *Bonus Army*, 76–77.
11. Ibid.; Springer, "Siege of Washington," 645; PDG Papers, Box 14, Folder 2, Draft Document, "Glassford to Boyd," 9, 12.
12. White, "Glassford's Story," 10; Dickson and Allen, *Bonus Army*, 77; PDG Papers, Box 14, Folder 2, Draft Document, "Glassford to Boyd," 5–6, 9.
13. PDG Papers, Box 14, Folder 2, Draft Document, "Glassford to Boyd," 9.
14. Truscott Jr., *The Twilight of the U.S. Cavalry*, 121.

15. *Washington Post*, May 27, 1932.
16. Dickson and Allen, *The Bonus Army*, 86, 89.
17. *Washington Post*, May 27, 1932.
18. Ibid.
19. Waters and White, *B. E. F.*, 62.
20. Ibid., 62; Lisio, *The President and Protest*, 70–71.
21. Waters and White, *B. B. F.*, 62–64, 258–59.
22. Dickson and Allen, *Bonus Army*, 83–84.
23. Bernstein, *The Lean Years*, 442.
24. Starling as told to Sugrue, *Starling of the White House*, 296; Terkel, *Hard Times*, 46.
25. Dickson and Allen, *Bonus Army*, 82; *Washington Post*, May 30, 1932, 1.
26. Dickson and Allen, *Bonus Army*, 85–86.
27. Waters and White, *B. E. F.*, 65–69; Daniels, *The Bonus March*, 105.
28. *Washington Post*, May 30, 1932; Watkins, *The Hungry Years*, 134.
29. Dickson and Allen, *Bonus Army*, 83–86.
30. Waters and White, *B. E. F.*, 65–67, 74; Dickson and Allen, *Bonus Army*, 85–86.
31. Waters and White, *B. E. F.*, 71–72; Schlesinger Jr., *The Age of Roosevelt*, 260–61.
32. Dickson and Allen, *Bonus Army*, 97, 107; *Washington Post*, May 31 and June 1, 1932.
33. Dickson and Allen, *Bonus Army*, 90, 96–97.
34. Bernstein, *Lean Years*, 445; Dickson and Allen, *Bonus Army*, 107; *Washington Post*, May 31 and June 1, 1932.
35. PDG Papers, Box 14, Folder 2, Draft Document, "Glassford to Boyd," 9–11; Dickson and Allen, *Bonus Army*, 89–91, 94.
36. *Washington Post*, June 3, 1932, 11; Dickson and Allen, *Bonus Army*, 97.
37. Springer, "Siege of Washington," 648; PDG Papers, Box 14, Folder 2, Draft Document, "Glassford to Boyd," 10.
38. *Washington Post*, June 1, 1932.
39. McLean, *Father Struck It Rich*, 12, 31.
40. Ibid., 227.
41. Ibid., 228; Bartlett, *The Bonus March and the New Deal*, 115. Note: It is unclear if Waters's two daughters came with Wilma, but Bartlett reports that the two were later at Camp Marks.
42. McLean, *Father Struck it Rich*, 226–30, chap 11.

Chapter 11

1. Dickson and Allen, *The Bonus Army*, 94–96; Waters and White, *B. E. F.*, 103–5, 108–9, photograph section.
2. Dickson and Allen, *Bonus Army*, 94, 96.
3. Watkins, *The Hungry Years*, 134–35; *Washington Post*, June 2, 1932.
4. James, *The Years of MacArthur*, 388.
5. Dickson and Allen, *Bonus Army*, 83, 90–91, 134; Waters and White, *B .E. F.*, 90–94; Glassford's response to attorney general's report, 2; Lisio, *President and Protest*, 116–17, PDG Papers, Box 14, Folder 2.
6. *Washington Post*, June 4, 1932, 1.
7. Bernstein, *The Lean Years*, 446; *Washington Post*, June 7, 1932; Dickson and Allen, *Bonus Army*, 103; Waters and White, *B. E. F.*, 83–84, 258–59.
8. Bernstein, *Lean Years*, 446–47.
9. Waters and White, *B. E. F.*, 106–7, 109–10; Carl Glassford interview, August 10, 2019; *Washington Post*, June 11, 1932; Lisio, *The President and Protest*, 169.
10. Waters and White, *B. E. F.*, 107; Dickson and Allen, *Bonus Army*, 106–7.
11. Dickson and Allen, *Bonus Army*, 110–11, 115.
12. Ibid., 99–100, 105–6, 124.
13. Ibid., 99–100; *Washington Post*, June 10, 1932.
14. *Washington Post*, June 10, 1932; Dickson and Allen, *Bonus Army*, 123–25.
15. PDG Papers, Box 14, Folder 2, Draft Document, "communists," 5.
16. Dickson and Allen, *Bonus Army*, 124–25; *Washington Post*, June 10, 1932; Waters and White, *B. E. F.*, 94–96.
17. *Washington Post*, June 11, 1932; Lisio, *President and Protest*, 80, 84.
18. *Washington Post*, June 11, 1932.
19. MacArthur, *Reminiscences*, 90.
20. Waters and White, *B. E. F.*, 90–91, 93.
21. James, *Years of MacArthur*, 391–92.
22. Dickson and Allen, *Bonus Army*, 108–15.
23. Watkins, *Hungry Years*, 135; Dickson and Allen, *Bonus Army*, 111; Waters and White, *B. E. F.*, 122–23.
24. Dickson and Allen, *Bonus Army*, 112; Carr, *Dos Passos*, 301; Wilkins with Mathews, *Standing Fast*, 118–19; Schlesinger Jr., *The Age of Roosevelt*, 260.
25. *Washington Post*, June 12, 1932.

26. Truscott Jr., *The Twilight of the U.S. Cavalry*, 124; *Washington Post*, June 13, 1932; PDG Papers, Box 13, Folder 18, Draft Document, "MacArthur and the Bonus Army," 2.
27. *Washington Post*, June 13, 1932.
28. PDG Papers, Box 14, Folder 7, "Land Scheme."
29. Dickson and Allen, *Bonus Army*, 135–36; Waters and White, *B. E. F.*, 158–59; Lisio, *The President and Protest*, 121–22.
30. Dickson and Allen, *Bonus Army*, 127–28; *Washington Post*, June 17, 1932; Springer, "Glassford and the Siege of Washington," 646.

Chapter 12

1. Dickson and Allen, *The Bonus Army*, 129–30; Waters and White, *B. E. F.*, 149–50.
2. Bernstein, *The Lean Years*, 447; Dickson and Allen, *Bonus Army*, 130; Waters and White, *B. E. F.*, 152; Schlesinger Jr., *The Age of Roosevelt*, 258.
3. Waters and White, *B. E. F.*, 152–53; Dickson and Allen, *Bonus Army*, 130–31.
4. Dickson and Allen, *Bonus Army*, 131–32; PDG Papers, Box 16, "Bonus Marchers" file.
5. *Washington Post*, June 20, 1932.
6. Schmidt, *Maverick Marine*, 1–2, 6–8, 10, 109, 111, 126–27, 212, 218–19.
7. Dickson and Allen, *Bonus Army*, 132; PDG Papers, Box 16, Folder 12, "Shelter for Bonus Marchers."
8. Dickson and Allen, *Bonus Army*, 132.
9. Ibid.; Waters and White, *B. E. F.*, 177–80.
10. Bernstein, *The Lean Years*, 448.
11. *Washington Post*, June 23, 1932.
12. Ibid., June 24, 1932, 1, 3.
13. Dickson and Allen, *Bonus Army*, 133.
14. Dickson and Allen, *Bonus Army*, 135–36; Waters and White, *B. E. F.*, 155–59.
15. Dickson and Allen, *Bonus Army*, 136; Waters and White, *B. E. F.*, 157–58.
16. *Washington Post*, June 27, 1932; Dickson and Allen, *Bonus Army*, 136–37.
17. *Washington Post*, July 5, 1932. Note: During World War II, General George P. Hayes, 10th Mountain Division, issued orders to unload all weapons before climbing to attack Riva Ridge and Mt. Belvedere in Italy.
18. James, *The Years of MacArthur*, 392; Waters and White, *B. E. F.*, 161–62.
19. *Washington Post*, July 8, 1932; Dickson and Allen, *Bonus Army*, 143; The American Presidency Project, UC Santa Barbara, Document, Statement of the Justice Department Investigation of the Bonus Army.

20. Dickson and Allen, *Bonus Army*, 101, 145–46; Lisio, *The President and Protest*, 126–27.
21. Lisio, *The President and Protest*, 128–29; Dickson and Allen, *Bonus Army*, 146–47.
22. Dickson and Allen, *Bonus Army*, 147; Lisio, *The President and Protest*, 130–31.
23. PDG Papers, Box 14, Folder 2, Draft Document, "Glassford to Boyd," 14–15; Dickson and Allen, *Bonus Army*, 147–48.
24. Dickson and Allen, *Bonus Army*, 148.
25. Ibid., 148–49; Waters and White, *B. E. F.*, 167–68.
26. Dickson and Allen, *Bonus Army*, 149–50.
27. Waters and White, *B. E. F.*, 167–70.
28. Dickson and Allen, *Bonus Army*, 150; Waters and White, *B. E. F.*, 170–71.

Chapter 13

1. James, *The Years of MacArthur*, 394; Springer, "Glassford and the Siege of Washington," 651; Waters and White, *B. E. F.*, 133–34.
2. Waters and White, *B. E. F.*, 176–78.
3. Ibid., 180–81; Springer, "Glassford and the Siege of Washington," 652.
4. Dickson and Allen, *The Bonus Army*, 152; Wordsmith, www.goodreads.com/quotes92128-it-is-a-capital-mistake; Waters and White, *B. E. F.*, 180–81.
5. Bernstein, *The Lean Years*, 450–51; Dickson and Allen, *Bonus Army*, 157; Lisio, *The President and Protest*, 144–47; James, *Years of MacArthur*, 394.
6. Anderson, "Tear-Gas, Bayonets, and Votes," *The Nation*, August 7, 1932, 138; Dickson and Allen, *Bonus Army*, 157–58; Bartlett, *The Bonus March*, 13–14; James, *Years of MacArthur*, 394–95.
7. Watkins, *The Hungry Years*, 12; Waters and White, *B. E. F.*, 178–79; James, *Years of MacArthur*, 395; Bernstein, *The Lean Years*, 450; Springer, "Glassford and the Siege of Washington," 653.
8. *Washington Post*, July 20 and 21, 1932; Dickson and Allen, *Bonus Army*, 158–59; Glassford, "Calling of Troops,"; PDG Papers, Box 6, "children" folder.
9. Waters and White, *B. E. F.*, 185–86.
10. Dickson and Allen, *Bonus Army*, 159.
11. Davis Jr., *Generals in Khaki*, 237–38; MacArthur, *Reminiscences*, 89; J. Eisenhower with J. Eisenhower, *Yanks*, 86.
12. Davis, *Generals in Khaki*, 276; Dickson and Allen, *Bonus Army*, 7, 73–74; James, *Years of MacArthur*, 383–84; Bernstein, *The Lean Years*, 441.
13. Waters and White, *B. E. F.*, 190–94, 196, 198; Schlesinger Jr., *The Age of Roosevelt*, 262.

14. Waters and White, *B. E. F.*, 202; Dickson and Allen, *Bonus Army*, 162; Bartlett, *The Bonus March*, 19–22, 87; Lisio, *President and Protest*, 171.

15. Waters and White, *B. E. F.*, 202–6.

16. Ibid., 205–6; James, *Years of MacArthur*, 395; Waters and White, *B. E. F.*, 202–6.

17. Watkins, *The Hungry Years*, 137; Dickson and Allen, *Bonus Army*, 162–64; Waters and White, *B. E. F.*, 209–10.

18. Bartlett, *The Bonus March*, 20–21; Dickson and Allen, *Bonus Army*, 164; James, *The Years of MacArthur*, 395–96; Bernstein, *The Lean Years*, 451; Waters and White, *B. E. F.*, 212–13.

19. Anderson, "Tear-Gas, Bayonets, and Votes," 139; Glassford, "Calling of Troops,"; James, *The Years of MacArthur*, 395–96; Dickson and Allen, *Bonus Army*, 165–67; Waters and White, *B. E. F.*, 213–15, photograph section.

20. Waters and White, *B. E. F.*, 215–16, photograph section.

21. *Washington Post*, July 28, 1932, 2; Dickson and Allen, *The Bonus Army*, 167–68; Lisio, *President and Protest*, 181–83.

22. Dickson and Allen, *The Bonus Army*, 167.

23. Ibid., 168; Bernstein, *The Lean Years*, 451–52.

24. Bernstein, *The Lean Years*, 452.

25. Ibid.; Dickson and Allen, *The Bonus Army*, 168; PDG Papers, Box 13, Folder 18, Draft Document, "MacArthur and the Bonus Army."

26. Bernstein, *The Lean Years*, 452; James, *The Years of MacArthur*, 397; Waters and White, *B. E. F.*, 211.

27. James, *The Years of MacArthur*, 397; Springer, "Glassford and the Siege of Washington," 654–55; Bartlett, *Bonus March*, 29.

Chapter 14

1. Dickson and Allen, *The Bonus Army*, 168–69.

2. James, *The Years of MacArthur*, 397.

3. Dickson and Allen, *The Bonus Army*, 168–69.

4. Waters and White, *B .E. F.*, 217–18.

5. Dickson and Allen, *The Bonus Army*, 168–69.

6. Bartlett, *Bonus March*, 32; Waters and White, *B. E. F.*, 218.

7. Dickson and Allen, *The Bonus Army*, 192–93.

8. Anderson, "Tear-Gas, Bayonets, and Votes," 139; Dickson and Allen, *The Bonus Army*, 169–71; Glassford, "Calling of Troops"; Glassford speech to veterans' rally in Philadelphia,

November 3, 1932.; PDG Papers, Box 13, Folder 18, Draft Document, "MacArthur and the Bonus Army."

9. Truscott Jr., *The Twilight of the U.S. Cavalry*, 124.
10. Blumenson, *The Patton Papers*, 975–76, 980–82.
11. Truscott, *The Twilight of the U.S. Cavalry*, 127; Dickson and Allen, *The Bonus Army*, 171–73.
12. James, *The Years of MacArthur*, 397.
13. Dickson and Allen, *The Bonus Army*, 171; PDG Papers, Box 13, Folder 18, Draft Document, "MacArthur and the Bonus Army."
14. James, *The Years of MacArthur*, 397–98; Dickson and Allen, *The Bonus Army*, 173; Bernstein, *The Lean Years*, 453.
15. James, *The Years of MacArthur*, 398–99; Watkins, *The Hungry Years*, 138; D. Eisenhower, *At Ease*, 216.
16. https://arlingtoncemetery.net/perryles.htm.
17. PDG Papers, Box 13, Folder 18, Draft Document, "MacArthur and the Bonus Army," 8; Dickson and Allen, *The Bonus Army*, 171.
18. Glassford, "Calling of Troops."
19. Dickson and Allen, *The Bonus Army*, 171, 173.
20. Glassford, "Calling of Troops"; Truscott Jr., *The Twilight of the U.S. Cavalry*, 127.
21. Dickson and Allen, *The Bonus Army*, 173.
22. Watkins, *The Hungry Years*, 139; Dickson and Allen, *The Bonus Army*, 173; Truscott, Jr. *The Twilight of the U.S. Cavalry*, 127; Glassford, "Calling of Troops."
23. Waters and White, *B. E. F.*, 221–22; James, *The Years of MacArthur*, 400.
24. Bartlett, *The Bonus March*, 32.
25. Truscott Jr., *The Twilight of the U.S. Cavalry*, 128; Dickson and Allen, *The Bonus Army*, 176; Blumenson, *Patton Papers*, 978.
26. Bartlett, *The Bonus March*, 33, 50.
27. Dickson and Allen, *The Bonus Army*, 177, 179.
28. Truscott Jr., *The Twilight of the U.S. Cavalry*, 129; James, *The Years of MacArthur*, 400; Dickson and Allen, *The Bonus Army*, 180–82, 188.
29. Waters and White, *B. E. F.*, 227–28, 230–33.
30. Dickson and Allen, *The Bonus Army*, 190; James, *The Years of MacArthur*, 403.
31. Dickson and Allen, *The Bonus Army*, 179–81; James, *The Years of MacArthur*, 401–2.
32. Waters and White, *B. E. F.*, 236; Dickson and Allen, *The Bonus Army*, 189.
33. D. Eisenhower, *At Ease*, 217–18; Hoover, *Memoirs*, 228–29.

34. James, *The Years of MacArthur*, 403; Bernstein, *The Lean Years*, 453; MacArthur, *Reminiscences*, 94–96, 139–40; Lisio, *The President and Protest*, 319.
35. Hoover, *Memoirs*, 228–29; Anderson, "Tear-Gas, Bayonets, and Votes," 138.
36. *Washington Post*, July 29, 1932.
37. PDG Papers, Box 13, Folder 18, Draft Document, "MacArthur and the Bonus Army," 1, 9, 10.
38. PDG Papers, Box 13, Folder 18, Letter to John Rogers; Bartlett, *The Bonus March*, 94; Manchester, *American Caesar*, 152; Dickson and Allen, *The Bonus Army*, 184.
39. James, *The Years of MacArthur*, 411; MacArthur, *Reminiscences*, 96.
40. James, *The Years of MacArthur*, 400; Truscott Jr., *The Twilight of the U.S. Cavalry*, 129; D. Eisenhower, *At Ease*, 217; Waters and White, *B. E. F.*, 228; MacArthur, *Reminiscences*, 95; Watkins, *The Hungry Years*, 140; Hurley quoted in Dickson and Allen, *The Bonus Army*, 188.
41. James, *The Years of MacArthur*, 400, 405–6.
42. Dickson and Allen, *The Bonus Army*, 185–86, 190, 196; Waters and White, *B. E. F.*, 240–42.
43. Truscott Jr., *The Twilight of the U.S. Cavalry*, 129.
44. *Washington Post*, July 29, 1932.
45. Dickson and Allen, *The Bonus Army*, 197; James, *The Years of MacArthur*, 406.
46. James, *The Years of MacArthur*, 406–7.
47. White, "General Glassford's Story."
48. James, *The Years of MacArthur*, 407–8.
49. *Washington Post*, July 29 and 31, 1932; Dickson and Allen, *The Bonus Army*, 191–92.
50. Dickson and Allen, *The Bonus Army*, 132, *Washington Post*, August 2, 1932.
51. *New York Times*, August 4, 1932; *Corsicana Daily Sun*, April 3, 1932; www.drtinfo.org.

Chapter 15

1. PDG Papers, Box 16, Folder 1, "reply letter to attorney general."
2. Statement on the Justice Department Investigation of the Bonus Army, US Attorney General William D. Mitchell to President Herbert Hoover, September 9, 1932, published on September 12, 1932; The American Presidency Project, University of California, Santa Barbara; Response by Pelham D. Glassford, Major and Superintendent, Metropolitan Police Department, September 13, 1932; PDG Papers, Box 16, Folder 1, "reply letter to attorney general"; Dickson and Allen, *The Bonus Army*, 197–98.
3. Dickson and Allen, *The Bonus Army*, 200–201; *Washington Post*, October 21, 1932.
4. Lisio, *The President and Protest*, 252; The NEA Service, October 21, 1932; Kenneth Whyte, *Hoover*, 499–501.

5. Dickson and Allen, *The Bonus Army*, 184, 201; Will Rogers Weekly Article #518 (November 27, 1932), willrogerstoday.com/trickle-down-tax-plan-thankful-or-not/; Starling as told to Sugrue, *Starling of the White House*, 299.
6. White, "General Glassford's Story"; CCG Papers, 252.

Chapter 16

1. PDG Papers, Box 1, Folder 1, speech by Glassford at veterans' rally, Philadelphia, November 3, 1932.
2. Parke, personal archive.
3. PDG Papers, Box 13, Folder 18, letter to John Rogers.
4. PDG Papers, Box 4, "writings" folder, Critchell Rimington to Glassford.
5. Running Wolf to Glassford, PDG Papers, box 23, "Bonus March" folder.
6. *Washington Daily News*, March 13, 1933, 3; *Reading Times* newspaper, March 13, 15, 16, 1933.
7. Watkins, *The Hungry Years*, 70–71.
8. *Arizona Daily Star*, February 27, 1933.
9. Dickson and Allen, *The Bonus Army*, 60–61; Sevareid, *Not So Wild a Dream*, 41–42, 45.
10. *Washington Post*, February 8, 19, and 26, 1933.
11. *Youngstown Telegram*, November 25, 1933; PDG Papers, Box 23, Bonus Army, v. 6; PDG draft document for *National Cyclopedia of American Biography*.
12. Author's interview, 1969. Morest "Morey" Skaret later became a member of the Civilian Conservation Corps, after which he worked as a log boom towboat pilot. He became a Seattle police officer in 1941 but was drafted during World War II to serve in the US Coast Guard, eventually becoming a commissioned officer and ship captain in the South Pacific. After the war he returned to the Seattle Police Department but was reactivated for the Korean War, again serving as a ship captain. He returned to the Seattle Police Department but was then appointed by the governor as director of the State of Washington Fish and Wildlife Department, a position he held for four years. He once again returned to the Seattle Police Department and was eventually promoted to lieutenant. He retired in 1980 after nearly forty years of police service. He retired as well from the Coast Guard as a full captain. He died at the age of one hundred. Interview and obituary by Dan Oliver, Seattle Police Department, 2014.
13. PDG Papers, Box 1, Folder 1, Draft Letter to Owen P. White for the National Cyclopedia for American Biography, 2–3.
14. PDG Papers, Box 13, "Camp America" folder; Dickson and Allen, *The Bonus Army*, 269, 276.
15. Roosevelt, *The Autobiography of Eleanor Roosevelt*, 175–76.

16. Dickson and Allen, *The Bonus Army*, 269, 276.
17. Parke, personal archive; *Washington Post*, March 14, 1933.
18. *Washington Post*, March 14 and 18, 1934; Glassford-Parke marriage certificate.
19. *Port Townsend Leader*; Parke, personal archive; Jefferson County Historical Society, 2006.
20. Parke, personal archive.
21. *Arizona Daily Star*, September 30, 1933; March 11, 1934.

Chapter 17

1. McWilliams, *Factories in the Field*, xiv.; Daniel, *Bitter Harvest*, 15–18.
2. Daniel, *Bitter Harvest*, 18–22; McWilliams, *Factories in the Field*, 20, 24–25, 49–50.
3. Daniel, *Bitter Harvest*, 26–30; McWilliams, *Factories in the Field*, 67–70; Ambrose, *Nothing Like It*, 20–21, 27, 150, 155–56.
4. Daniel, *Bitter Harvest*, 26–29, 32–35, 45, 108.
5. Ibid., 47–50, 52, 64, 73–75; McWilliams, *Factories in the Field*, 116, 130–31.
6. Daniel, *Bitter Harvest*, 67–68.
7. Ibid., 67–69, 76–77.
8. Ibid., 106, 109–12, 115.
9. Ibid., 111–16.
10. Ibid., 132–34; Olmsted, *Right Out of California*, 24.
11. Olmsted, *Right Out of California*, 121–26, 138, 144.
12. Daniel, *Bitter Harvest*, 177, 186; Olmsted, *Right Out of California*, 11–12, 43–44, 47–48, 45–48, 131.
13. Daniel, *Bitter Harvest*, 144–45, 182, 186–87, 194.
14. Watkins, *The Hungry Years*, 496, 499; Olmsted, *Right Out of California*, 31.
15. Olmsted, "Bleeding Edge," *Journal of Policy Development*, 52–54.
16. Olmsted, *Right Out of California*, 62–64.
17. Olmsted, "Bleeding Edge," 51–53; Olmsted, *Right Out of California*, 8–9.
18. Creel, *Rebel At Large*, 274; Olmsted, *Right Out of California*, 65.
19. Creel, *Rebel At Large*, 274–75; Olmsted, *Right Out of California*, 66–67.
20. Creel, *Rebel At Large*, 275; Olmsted, *Right Out of California*, 66.
21. Olmsted, *Right Out of California*, 66–67, 70–72.
22. Ibid., 75–77, 119.
23. Ibid., 78–80.
24. Olmsted, "Bleeding Edge," 51–52.

25. Olmsted, *Right Out of California*, 148–49.
26. Ibid., 121–22; Daniel, *Bitter Harvest*, 230–31.
27. Olmsted, *Right Out of California*, 121–22.
28. Ibid., 122–25.
29. Ibid., 107–8, 126–28.
30. Postal Telegram, PDG Papers, Box 26, Folder 2; *Washington Post*, March 28, 1934.
31. Olmsted, *Right Out of California*, 136–37.
32. Frances Perkins Oral History, 1976, Columbia University Oral History Collection, New York, New York. Note: Her actual interview occurred in 1954, likely without notes, twenty years after Glassford's conciliator duties. Hereafter Perkins Oral History.
33. Ibid.
34. Olmsted, *Right Out of California*, 148.
35. Ibid., 108–11. Note: The little-known Salton Sea resulted from the Colorado River's breaching a dam in 1905 and spilling water for two years.
36. Olmsted, *Right Out of California*, 108–10; Olmsted, "Bleeding Edge," 57.
37. Olmsted, *Right Out of California*, 114, 137–39.
38. *Los Angeles Times*, March 28, 29, 30, 1934.
39. Ibid.; Olmsted, *Right Out of California*, 131–32.
40. Olmsted, *Right Out of California*, 114–15.
41. Ibid., 138–39; Olmsted, "Bleeding Edge," 60.
42. Perkins Oral History.
43. Ibid., 137, 139; Perkins Oral History.
44. Olmsted, *Right Out of California*, 133, 139–40.
45. Ibid., 138.
46. *Washington Post*, April 13, 1934; *Arizona Daily Star*, April 8 and 13, 1934.
47. Daniel, *Bitter Harvest*, 228–29; Olmsted, *Right Out of California*, 116–17.

Chapter 18

1. *Arizona Daily Star*, April 14, 1934; *Los Angeles Times*, April 21, 1934; Olmsted, *Right Out of California*, 139–40.
2. Perkins Oral History.
3. Olmsted, *Right Out of California*, 139–40.
4. Daniel, *Bitter Harvest*, 246; Olmsted, *Right Out of California*, 140; *Los Angeles Times*, April 28, 1934.

5. *Arizona Daily Star*, May 1, 1934.
6. *Los Angeles Times*, May 6, 1934.
7. *Los Angeles Times*, May 5 and 6, 1934.
8. Olmsted, *Right Out of California*, 141.
9. Ibid., 141–42.
10. *Los Angeles Times*, May 18 and 24, 1934; *Washington Post*, May 18, 1934; Olmsted, *Right Out of California*, 142–43.
11. P. Taylor, *On the Ground in the Thirties*, 165; Olmsted, *Right Out of California*, 142–43.
12. Olmsted, *Right Out of California*, 119, 143–44.
13. PDG Papers, Box 24, Folder 9, telegram. Note: Previously lieutenant governor, Merriam had become governor following the heart attack and death on June 2 of James "Sunny Jim" Rolph, just a week before Glassford sent his telegram.
14. PDG Papers, Box 24; Olmsted, *Right Out of California*, 144.
15. Ibid., 144–45; *Los Angeles Times*, June 16, 1934.
16. Olmsted, *Right Out of California*, 127.
17. *Los Angeles Times*, June 16 and 27, 1934; *Calexico Chronicle*, June 13, 1934, 1, 4; *San Bernardino County Sun*, June 16, 1934, 1; PDG Papers, Box 24, Folder 1, "conversation with Red Harrigan" folder.
18. PDG Papers, Box 24, Folder 9.
19. Olmsted, *Right Out of California*, 143.
20. *Calexico Chronicle*, June 23, 1934.
21. Olmsted, *Right Out of California*, 129, 145–46; *Calexico Chronicle*, June 23, 1934.
22. *Washington Post*, June 25, 1934.
23. Olmsted, *Right Out of California*, 145; *Los Angeles Times*, June 27, p. 4, and June 28, 1934.
24. *Los Angeles Times*, June 27 and 28, 1934.
25. Ibid., June 28, 1934.
26. Olmsted, *Right Out of California*, 146.
27. Ibid.; Kennedy, *Freedom from Fear*, 293; Olmsted, *Right Out of California*, 146 (includes *Imperial Valley Press* quotation).
28. Olmsted, *Right Out of California*, 147.
29. Ibid., 148–49; Perkins Oral History.

Chapter 19

1. PDG Papers, Box 6, "Arizona Ours" folder, photo of Lucy's father in army uniform; Olmsted, *Right Out of California*, 143, 278, n40; *Arizona Daily Star*, September 5, 1934.

2. PDG draft of information for the *National Cyclopedia of American Biography* and the *Dictionary of American Biography*, PDG Papers, Box 2.
3. *Arizona Daily Star*, March 17, 1936.
4. Ibid., March 18, 1936, editorial.
5. Ibid., April 25 and June 6, 1936.
6. Ibid., January 22, 1936; president.arizona.edu/person-categories/pastpresidents.
7. *Casa Grande Dispatch*, June 2, 1936; *Arizona Daily Star*, July 10 and August 21, 1936; "Better Men in Government," Glassford for Congress Committee, text of speech, August 20, 1936; *Arizona Independent Republican*, September 6, 1936.
8. PDG Papers, Box 3, "family" folder, January 7, 1937.
9. Letter from Cameron to Pelham Glassford, copy provided to author by William Parke; *Port Townsend Leader*, April 22, 1937; *Arizona Daily Star*, December 26, 1937; *Arizona Republican*, August 26, 1927; *Washington Daily Star*, January 9, 1937.
10. *Arizona Daily Star*, January 10 and 28, 1937.
11. "Gen. Glassford Now Runs Arizona Ranch, Paints and Writes," *Washington Daily News*, January 9, 1937; "Career Isn't Aim of All Men," *Pampa Daily News*, Pampa, Texas, January 18, 1937; Gerald C. Gross, "This Capital of Ours," *Washington Post*, March 8, 1942.
12. Parke, personal archive; Jefferson County Historical Society.
13. PDG Papers, Box 11, "Trotsky" folder.
14. *Arizona Independent Republican*, October 10, 1938, 5.
15. Pyle, "Gen. Glassford Still bubbles Over with Zeal and Curiosity"; Parke, personal archive.
16. Gross, "This Capital of Ours"; PDG Papers, Box 4, "horses we raised and sold" folder, August 19, 1940, April 20, 1941.

Chapter 20

1. University of Kentucky Alumni Association, Hall of Distinguished alumni, honoredmps.org.
2. Military insignia order (N. S. Meyer, 419 Fourth Avenue, New York), December 12, 1939, PDG Papers, Box 2; Evelyn Peyton Gordon column, *Washington Daily News*, March 5, 1942.
3. *Richmond Gazette*, March 5, 1942, PDG Papers, Box 2, Folder 1; *Washington Post*, March 6, 1942; *Arizona Daily Star*, March 5, 1943; Carl Glassford interview, August 10, 2019.
4. *Washington Daily News*, March 5, 1942.
5. *National Cyclopedia of American Biography*; *Washington Times Herald*, March 5, 1942.

6. *Washington Post*, July 16, 1942.
7. Harris, "Ringside Table."
8. *Arizona Daily Star*, November 17, 1943; PDG Papers, Box 3, "family" folder; *Washington Post*, November 2 and December 19, 1943.
9. Morgan, *FDR: A Biography*, 625–27.
10. *Arizona Daily Star*, November 17, 1943; *Tampa Daily Times*, January 7, 1945; PDG Papers, Box 3, "letters and clippings" folder.
11. PDG Papers, Box 1, untitled folder; Carl Glassford interview, August 10, 2019.
12. US Navy Official Biography.
13. Warner, *Laguna Art Museum*, preface, 49, 54, 56, 68.
14. Ibid., 68–69; PDG Papers, Box 1, Folder 1; Box 3, "letters and clippings" folder; www.foapom.com/timeline_slider_post/history-timeline.
15. PDG Papers, Box 3, "past art exhibits" folder.
16. PDG Papers, Box 3, "past art exhibits" folder; The Jonathan Art Foundation, excerpt from Nancy Moure, "The Arthur Beaumont collection," jonathanart.org; Warner, *Laguna Art Museum*, 100.
17. Warner, *Laguna Art Museum*, 100.
18. Manchester, *American Caesar*, 5–6, 361–63, 521–25, 684–88.
19. PDG Papers, Box 3, "letters and clippings" folder.
20. PDG Papers, Box 5, "Kidron" folder; Carl Glassford interview, August 10, 2019.
21. PDG Papers, Box 3, "family" folder.
22. PDG Papers, Box 5, "Guy" folder.
23. Carl Glassford interview, August 10, 2019; Glassford, *Drawing with Pen and Ink*, front cover flap.
24. PDG Papers, Box 1, Folder 1, "death certificate."
25. Carl Glassford interview, August 10, 2019; State of Texas death certificate; *Washington Post*, July 1, 1958; US Navy Official Biography.
26. Obituary, *Salt Lake City Tribune*, February 16, 1974; interview with Carl Glassford, August 10, 2019.
27. Parke, personal archive.
28. *Walla Walla Union Bulletin*, April 23, 1959; Waters and White, *B. E. F.*, 3; Schlesinger Jr., *The Age of Roosevelt*, 257.
29. Warner, *Laguna Art Museum*, 110.
30. Author's collection.

31. Moure, Index to California Art LGAA, 1918–1972.
32. Carl Glassford interview, August 10, 2019; Tribute by Lynne Glassford, used with permission.
33. Tribute by Lynne Glassford, used with permission.
34. Our Family Tree, surname: Glassford.

REFERENCES

Collected Papers

Pelham D. Glassford Papers, Charles E. Young Research Library, UCLA.
Cora Carleton Glassford Papers, Daughters of the Republic of Texas Library, San Antonio.

Unpublished Sources

Glassford, Cora Carleton. *One Life is Not Enough*. CCG Papers.
Hedglen, Thomas L. *The Boys From Las Vegas: The Glassford Brothers in World War 1*, presentation at the Arizona–New Mexico Joint Convention, April 26–29, 2007.
Frances Perkins Oral History. Columbia University Oral History Collection, New York, New York, 1976.

Magazines

American Heritage
American Mercury
Citizen-Soldier
Collier's
Harper's
Journal of Policy Development
Nation

Newspapers

Arizona Champion
Arizona Daily Star
Arizona Independent Republican
Arizona Republican/Arizona Republic

Arizona Silver Belt
Arizona Weekly Enterprise
Arizona Weekly Journal-Miner
Bakersfield Californian
Bisbee Daily Review
Calexico Chronicle
Carthage Evening Press
Carthage Press
Casa Grande Dispatch
Corsicana Daily Sun
El Paso Herald
Honolulu Star Bulletin
Las Vegas Daily Gazette
Las Vegas (New Mexico) Daily Optic
Las Vegas Free Press
Long Beach Press Telegram
Los Angeles Examiner
Los Angeles Times
National Tribune, Washington, DC
New York American
New York Times
Pampa Daily News, Pampa, Texas
Philadelphia Record
Port Townsend Leader
Providence Journal
Reading Times
Richmond Gazette
Rio Grande Republican, Las Cruces, NM
Salt Lake City Tribune
San Antonio Express
San Bernardino Sun
Santa Fe Daily New Mexican
Santa Fe Weekly Post
Tampa Daily Times

Walla Walla Union Bulletin
Washington Daily News
Washington Daily Star
Washington Evening Star
Washington Post
Washington Sunday Star
Washington Times Herald
Youngstown Telegram

Books and Articles

Alcina Franch, José. "Penetración española en Esmeraldas tipología del descubrimiento." *Revista de Indias*. 143–44 (1976), 65–121.

Ambrose, Stephen E. *Duty, Honor, Country: A History of West Point*. Baltimore: Johns Hopkins University Press, 1999.

———. *Nothing Like It in the World: The Men Who Built the Transcontinental Railroad, 1863–1869*. New York: Simon & Schuster, 2000.

Anderson, Paul Y. "Tear-Gas, Bayonets, and Votes." *The Nation*, August 7, 1932, 138.

Barbee, David Rankin. "The Artist Who Became a Cop." *Washington Post*, November 15, 1931, 3–4.

Bartlett, John Henry. *The Bonus March and the New Deal*. Chicago: M. A. Donohue, 1937.

Bernstein, Irving. *The Lean Years: A History of the American Worker 1920–1933*. New York: Penguin Books, 1966.

Blumenthal, Martin. *Patton: The Man Behind the Legend, 1885–1945*. New York: Berkley Books, 1987.

Blumenthal, Martin. *The Patton Papers: 1885–1940*. Boston: Houghton Mifflin, 1972.

Bradley, Omar, and Clay Blair. *A General's Life: An Autobiography by General of the Army Omar N. Bradley*. New York: Simon & Schuster, 1983.

Calhoun, Mart T. *General Lesley J. McNair: Unsung Architect of the Army*. Lawrence: University Press of Kansas, 2015.

Carr, Virginia Spencer. *Dos Passos: A Life*. New York: Doubleday, 1984.

Catton, Bruce. *The Civil War*. Boston: Houghton Mifflin, 2004.

Clarke, William F. *Over There with O'Ryan's Roughnecks*. Seattle: Superior, 1968.

Coffman, Edward D. *Regulars: The American Army 1898–1941*. Cambridge, MA: Belknap Press of Harvard University Press, 2004.

Collins, General James L., Jr. Foreword to *Memoirs of My Services in the World War 1917–1918*, by George C. Marshall. Boston: Houghton Mifflin, 1976, v–x.

Creel, George. *Rebel at Large: Recollections of Fifty Crowded Years.* New York: G. P. Putnam's Sons, 1947.

Daniel, Cletus E. *Bitter Harvest: A History of California Farm Workers, 1870–1941.* Berkeley: University of California Press, 1981.

Daniels, Jonathan. *The Time Between the Wars: From the Jazz Age and the Depression to Pearl Harbor.* New York: Doubleday, 1966.

Daniels, Roger. *The Bonus March: An Episode in the Great Depression.* Westport, CT: Greenwood, 1971.

Davis, Henry B., Jr. *Generals in Khaki.* Raleigh, NC: Pentland, 1998.

D'Este, Carlo. *Eisenhower: A Soldier's Life.* New York: Henry Holt, 2002.

———. *Patton: A Genius for War.* New York: Harper Perennial, 1995.

Dickson, Paul, and Thomas B. Allen. *The Bonus Army: An American Epic.* New York: Walker, 2004.

Eisenhower, Dwight D. *At Ease: Stories I Tell to Friends.* Philadelphia: Eastern National, 1967.

Eisenhower, John S. D. *Intervention! The United States and the Mexican Revolution, 1913–1917.* New York: Norton, 1995.

Eisenhower, John S. D., with Joanne T. Eisenhower. *Yanks: The Epic Story of the American in World War I.* New York: Simon & Schuster, 2002.

Gibran, Daniel K. *The 92nd Division and the Italian Campaign in World War II.* Jefferson, NC: McFarland, 2001.

Glassford, Carl. *Drawing with Pen and Ink.* Laguna Hills, CA: Walter Foster, 1985.

Glassford, Pelham. "Calling of Troops to Evict Bonus Army Without Justification." *New American*, November 4, 1932, 1–5.

Goodwin, Doris Kearns. *Lyndon Johnson and the American Dream.* New York: St. Martin Griffin, 1976.

Grandcamp, Robert, Jane Lancaster, and Cynthia Ferguson. *Rhody Redlegs: A History of the Providence Marine Corps of Artillery and the 103rd Field Artillery, Rhode Island National Guard, 1801–2010.* Jefferson, NC: MacFarland, 2012.

Gross, Gerald C. "This Capital of Ours." *Washington Post*, March 8, 1942.

Gutierrez, Edward A. *Doughboys on the Great War: How American Soldiers Viewed Their Military Experience.* Lawrence: University Press of Kansas, 2014.

Haas, Major Darrin. "Bringing in the Thunder." *Citizen-Soldier*, May 8, 2018, 1–3.

Harris, Mary. "Ringside Table." *Washington Post*, June 28, 1943.

Hart, Peter. *The Great War: A Combat History of the First World War.* Oxford: Oxford University Press, 2013.

Hoover, Herbert. *The Memoirs of Herbert Hoover: The Great Depression 1929–1941.* New York: Macmillan, 1952.

James, D. Clayton. *The Years of MacArthur, Volume 1: 1880–1941.* Boston: Houghton Mifflin, 1970.

Jenkins, McKay. *The Last Ridge: The Epic Story of America's Mountain Soldiers and the Assault on Hitler's Europe.* New York: Random House, 2003.

Kennedy, David M. *Freedom from Fear: The American People in Depression and War, 1929–1945.* New York: Oxford University Press, 1999.

Kernan, W. F., and Henry T. Samson. *History of the 103rd Field Artillery, Twenty-Sixth Division, A. E. F. World War 1917–1919.* Providence, RI: Remington, 1919.

Levy, Daniel S. *World War I: The Great War and the American Century.* New York: Time Books, 2017.

Lisio, Donald J. *The President and Protest: Hoover, Conspiracy, and the Bonus Riot.* Columbia: University of Missouri Press, 1974.

Lloyd, Nick. *Hundred Days: The Campaign That Ended World War I.* New York: Basic Books, 2014.

———. *The Western Front: A History of the Great War, 1914–1918.* New York: W. W. Norton, 2021.

Loftus, Rich. *From Wentworth to the Western Front: The World War Odyssey of Private John Warns.* Research Triangle Park, NC: Lulu Publishing, 2018.

MacArthur, Douglas. *Reminiscences.* New York: McGraw Hill, 1964.

Manchester, William. *American Caesar: Douglas MacArthur 1880–1964.* Boston: Little, Brown, 1978.

Marshall, George C. *Memoirs of My Services in the World War 1917–1918.* Boston: Houghton Mifflin, 1976.

Marshall, S. L. A. *World War I.* Boston: Houghton Mifflin, 2001.

McCullough, David. *1776.* New York: Simon & Schuster, 2006.

———. *Truman.* New York: Simon & Schuster, 1992.

McKenna, Frederick Ambrose. *Battery A, 103rd Field Artillery, in France.* London: FB&C, 2015.

McLean, Evalyn Walsh. *Father Struck It Rich.* Lake City, CO: Western Reflections, 1936.

McWilliams, Carey. *Factories in the Field: The Story of Migratory Farm Labor in California*. Berkeley: University of California Press, 1935.

Morgan, Ted. *FDR: A Biography*. New York: Simon & Schuster, 1985.

Olmsted, Katheryn S. "Bleeding Edge." *Journal of Policy Development* 26, no. 1 (2014), 48–72.

———. *Right Out of California: The 1930s and the Big Business Roots of Modern Conservatism*. New York: New Press, 2015.

Perrigo, Lynn Irwin. *Gateway to Glorieta: A History of Las Vegas, New Mexico*. Santa Fe: Sunstone, 2010.

Pershing, John J. *Final Report*. Washington, DC: Government Printing Office, 1920.

Persico, Joseph E. *11th Month, 11th Day, 11th Hour: Armistice Day, 1918, World War I and Its Violent Climax*. New York: Random House, 2004.

Pyle, Ernie. "Gen. Glassford Still bubbles Over with Zeal and Curiosity." Syndicated Article, November 12, 1939.

Raines, Rebecca Robbins. *Getting the Message Through: A Branch History of the U.S. Army*. Washington, DC: 1996.

Roosevelt, Eleanor. *The Autobiography of Eleanor Roosevelt*. New York: Harper Perennial, 1937.

Rosskam, Charles A. "The Glassford They Remember." *Providence Journal*, August 7, 1932, 1–6.

Schlesinger, Arthur M., Jr. *The Age of Roosevelt: The Crisis of the Old Order, 1919–1933*. Boston: Houghton Mifflin, 1957.

Schmidt, Hans. *Maverick Marine: General Smedley D. Butler and the Contradictions of American Military History*. Lexington: University Press of Kentucky, 1987.

Sevareid, Eric. *Not So Wild a Dream*. New York: Knopf, 1946.

Shales, Amity. *The Forgotten Man: A New History of the Great Depression*. New York: Harper Perennial, 2007.

Springer, Fleta Campbell. "Glassford and the Siege of Washington." *Harper's* (November 1932): 642.

Starling, Edmund, as told to Thomas Sugrue. *Starling of the White House*. Chicago: Peoples Book Club, 1933.

Taylor, Emerson Gifford. *New England in France, 1917–1919: A History of the Twenty-Sixth Division*. Boston: Houghton Mifflin, 1920.

Taylor, Paul. *On the Ground in the Thirties*. Layton, UT: Gibbs M. Smith, 1983.

Terkel, Studs. *Hard Times: An Oral History of the Great Depression*. New York: Washington Square, 1970.

Thomas, Robert S. *The Mexican Punitive Expedition Under General John J. Pershing, United States Army, 1916–1917*. Ann Arbor: University of Michigan Library, n.d.

Truscott, Lucian K., Jr. *The Twilight of the U.S. Cavalry: Life in the Old Army, 1917–1942*. Lawrence: University Press of Kansas, 1989.

Tuccille, Jerome. *The War Against the Vets: The World War I Bonus Army During the Great Depression*. Lincoln: Potomac Books, University of Nebraska Press, 2018.

Tuchman, Barbara W. *Stilwell and the American Experience in China, 1911–45*. New York: Macmillan, 1970.

Warner, Malcolm. *Laguna Art Museum: A Centennial History, 1918–2018*. Laguna Beach, CA: Laguna Beach Art Association, 2018.

Waters, W. W., as told to William C. White. *B. E. F.: The Whole Story of the Bonus Army*. New York: John Day, 1933.

Watkins, T. H. *The Hungry Years: A Narrative History of the Great Depression in America*. New York: Henry Holt, 1999.

White, Owen P. "General Glassford's Story." *Collier's*, October 29, 1932, 10.

Whyte, Kenneth. *Hoover: An Extraordinary Life in Extraordinary Times*. New York: Vintage Books, 2017.

Wilkins, Roy, with Tom Mathews. *Standing Fast: The Autobiography of Roy Wilkins*. New York: Da Capo, 1994.

Worcester, Donald E. *The Apaches: Eagles of the Southwest*. Norman: University of Oklahoma Press, 1979.

General Sources

Biographical Directory of the US Congress, 1774–2020.

Biographical Register of the Officers and Graduates of the US Military Academy at West Point, 1900–1910.

Cosgrove, Professor Richard. Presentation, World War 1, University of Arizona, October 11–November 1, 2018.

Dictionary of American Biography

Fort Union National Monument, New Mexico Official Map and Guide. National Park Service.

Historic Las Vegas, New Mexico (pamphlet). Las Vegas Citizens Commission for Historic Preservation, lvhistoric@gmail.com.

History of Jasper County, Missouri. Des Moines, IA: Mills, 1883.

List of Cadets, West Point, New York, From its Origins till June 30, 1937. USMA Printing Office, 1937.

National Cyclopedia of American Biography.

Regulations for the USMA, 1902, Article XII, Discipline, 143, Section III. Washington Government Printing Office.

Santa Fe Trail Association Official Map and Guide, Santa Fe National Historic Trail: Colorado, Kansas, Missouri, New Mexico, Oklahoma, National Park Service.

Superior Court of Arizona, Distribution of Estate. August 4, 1932.

US Army Center of Military History, World War I Birth of the Modern Army Division.

US Census, 1900, Pelham Glassford, Port of San Juan, Puerto Rico.

US Civil War Soldiers Index, 1861–1865, S. B. Davis pension folder, National Archives and Records Administration, Washington, DC.

US Navy Official Biography (1953), Navy Department Library, Navy Historical Center, Washington Navy Yard.

U.S. Army Handbook of Artillery. Washington, DC: Government Printing Office, 1920.

USMA *Howitzer* yearbook, 1904.

INDEX

ACLU. *See* American Civil Liberties Union
AEF. *See* American Expeditionary Force
African Americans, in AEF, 55
Agamemnon, USS (Navy transport), 76
Agricultural Workers Industrial League (AWIU), 208, 224
Air Force, US, 78
Aisne-Marne salient, 61, 64–65
Alamo Heights, Texas, 185
Alexander, S. C., 218
Allen, Thomas B., 179–80
Alman, George, 107, 127, 135, 137
Ambrose, Stephen, 14, 51
American Civil Liberties Union (ACLU), 104, 207–8, 224–25, 226
American Communist Party, 80, 96, 100–101, 134–36, 184, 206–7
American Expeditionary Force (AEF), 43, 47, 50–52, 58, 72, 255n1; African Americans in, 55
American Industrial Training Association, 198
American Legion, 93, 110, 111
American Revolution, 13
Anacostia Flats, 133–34, 136, 176, *fig. 15*. *See also* Camp Marks
Anderson, Paul Y., 163, 178
Angelo, Joe T., 94, 182
Aquitania (troop transport), 77
Arizona, 3–4, 7, 8, 78, 86–87, 235–37

Arizona Daily Star (newspaper), 222, 235
Arizona Silver Belt (newspaper), 8
Arlington Cantonment, Military Police School in, 241
Armistice Day, 71, 88, 91–92
Army, US, 4, 10, 23–24, 32, 37, 194; BEF eviction by, 169–76; Observational Balloon Unit, 9; Punitive Expedition of, 39, 40, 48, 105; racial segregation in, 55, 135; Signal Service of, 6, 7–8, 78
Army War College, Washington, DC, 2, 24, 79, 81, 85, 265n16
Arthur, Cora Belle, 27
artillery school, 47, 50–52, 58
Associated Farmers of California, 225
Atchison, Topeka, and Santa Fe Railroad (AT&SF), 5
Atwell, Eddie, 175–76, 182
Aultman, Dwight E., 58
Austria-Hungary Empire, 41, 42
AWIL. *See* Agricultural Workers Industrial League

Baker, Newton D., 44
Baltimore and Ohio Railroad (B&O), 111–12, 148, 182
Barry, David S., 152–53
Bartlett, John Henry, 147, 157, 159, 168; at BEF eviction, 174, 175, 180; Camp Bartlett of, 142, 160–61, 177, 195

Beast Barracks, at USMA, 11, 17–18
Beaumont, Arthur, 242, 246
BEF. *See* Bonus Expeditionary Force
B. E. F. (Waters), 197
The B.E.F. News (newspaper), 149
Bennett, Harry Herbert, 100
Bennett, John E., 125, 128
Bernstein, Irving, 95, 100, 125
Besig, Ernest, 226–27, 229, 230, 232
Better Men in Government (publication), 237
Biddle, Francis, 243–44
Bingham, Hiram, III, 153
Bisttram, Emil, 246–47
B&O. *See* Baltimore and Ohio Railroad
Bonus Bill, 92, 105, 107, 120; US Congress relation to, 119, 121, 122–23, 126, 130, 143, 144–46
Bonus Expeditionary Force (BEF). *See specific topics*
Booz, Oscar L., 19–20
Bordeaux, France, 72–73
Bosnia, Sarajevo, 41
Boston, YD Club in, 83–84
Bradley, Omar, 18
Brandt, Raymond P., 168
Brawley, California. *See* Imperial Valley, California
Brawley News (newspaper), 214
Bride, William W., 90, 192
Brigham Young University, 249, 252
Britain, 42
Brooke, John R., 10
Browder, Earl, 134
Brown, George Rothwell, 84
Butler, Henry V., Jr., 152
Butler, Smedley Darlington, 146–47
Butler, William A., 135

California, 31, 210, 211, 233; Laguna Beach, 244, 245–46, 248–49; San Diego, 228, 249, 252; San Francisco, 6, 35, 37, 86–87, 237. *See also* growers, in California; Imperial Valley, California
California Chamber of Commerce, 220
Camp Bartlett, 142, 160–61, 177, 195
Campbell, George, 231
Camp Marks, 138, 139, 141, 175, 190, 270n41
Camp Meigs, 123, 139
Camp Simms, 139, 142
Camp Zachary Taylor, 76
Capitol Police, 151, 152
Carleton, Cora Arthur (wife), 16, 64, 85, 158, *fig. 2, fig. 4*; death of, 249; divorce from, 185; on Fort Bliss, 39–40; in Hawaii, 33, 36; marriage to, 26–27; in Philippines, 30; in Utah, 239
Carleton, Guy Edward, 27, 76
Carlson, Eric, 168
Carranza, Venustiano, 38
Carrol Fish Company, 128
Carter, Doak E., 139, 150, 160
Carthage, Missouri, 3
Casa Grande Dispatch (newspaper), 236
Cassidy, George L., 89–90
Cavalry School, 259n9
CAWIU. *See* Agricultural Workers Industrial League
CCC. *See* Civilian Conservation Corps
Central Union Mission, 97
Chaffee, Everitte, 67
Chambers, Pat, 208–9, 210, 211, 218
Champagne-Marne, 62
Chandler, Harry, 218–19
Château-Thierry, 59, 66, 71
Chaumont, France, 58
Cheyenne, Wyoming, 110

Index 293

Chinese Exclusion Act (1882), 205

Chinese immigrants, 205

Choctaw Nation, in Oklahoma, 118

Chotek, Sophie, 41–42

Christy, Lizabeth Glassford "Lynne" (granddaughter), 251–52

Citizen Training Camps, 48

Civilian Conservation Corps (CCC), 200–201, 277n12

Clark Air Force Base. *See* Fort Stotsenburg, Philippines

Clarke, William F,. "Bill," 54–55, 65, 76

Cleveland, Frances Folsom, 8–9

Cleveland, Grover, 8–9

Coast Artillery branch, 25–26

Cockrell, Francis M., 11–12

Coffman, Edward M., 29

Collier's (magazine), 193

Collings, Harry, 196

colonization, in Philippines, 29

Colorado, Fort Logan, 9

Columbus, New Mexico, 2, 37, 38–39

Combs, Lee Osher, Jr., 201

Comintern. *See* Communist International

Command and General Staff school, 85

Committee on Public Information, US, 43

Communist Ford Hunger March, 100

Communist International (Comintern), 80, 134

Communist labor union, 2

Communists, 138, 139–40, 162–63, 181, 183, 186; California growers relation to, 212, 214, 230, 231; in Imperial Valley, 218, 219, 221; MacArthur relation to, 156, 158; in Mitchell report, 187

Congress, US, 24, 129, 150, 154; Bonus Bill relation to, 119, 121, 122–23, 126, 130, 143, 144–46; World War Adjusted Compensation Act in, 92–93

Coolidge, Calvin, 92–93

Corps of Cadets, at USMA, 17–18, 20

Corps of Engineers, 13, 241–42

Coughlin, Charles E., 102, 180

Cowan, C. B., 134

Creel, George E., 43, 210–11, 212, 233

Crime Prevention Division, of Washington, DC, Police Department, 104, 190

Crisis (magazine), 141

Critcher School of Painting and Applied Arts, Washington, DC, 196

Cromer, J. L. "Lon," 221, 225

Crosby, Herbert B., 89, 90–91, 94–95, 101, 118–19, 188; BEF relation to, 114, 165–66, 181; P. Glassford, Sr. relation to, 120–21, 148, 152, 169, 191–92; Keck relation to, 164

Cubbison, Donald C., 47, 48

Curtis, Charles, 96, 98, 99, 132, 151–52, 153

Daily Worker (newspaper), 135

Danford, Robert N. "John," 15, 16, 22, 66

Daniels, Roger, 95, 117

Danville, Kentucky, 76

Darcy, Samuel Adams, 208, 209

Daughters of the Republic of Texas, 185

da Vinci, Leonardo, 246

Davis, Allie Seymour (mother), 8, 29, 87, *fig. 1*, *fig. 3*, *fig. 4*; death of, 237; in Kansas, 6; in Washington, 202–3

Davis, Elizabeth (maternal grandmother), 3, 5–6, *fig. 4*

Davis, Ogden T., 184–85

Davis, Samuel Burwell (maternal grandfather), 3, 5, 12

DC Board of Surgeons, 94

DC commissioners, 89–90, 114, 134, 157, 160–61, 187–88; BEF relation to, 2, 117, 118–19, 120–21,

128, 137–38, 148–49; P. Glassford, Sr. relation to, 156, 164–65, 166, 184, 185, 190–92; Washington, DC, Police Department relation to, 94, 95
DC Corporation Council, 156
Decker, Caroline, 208–9, 211, 212
Department of Drawing, USMA, 26
Department of Labor, US, 225–26, 231
Department of Modern Languages, USMA, 26
DeWitt, John L., 244
Díaz, Porfirio, 38
Dickson, Paul, 179–80
Distinguished Service Medal, 75, 78, 94, 135, 182
Dodds, Nugent, 168–69, 189
Dolan, Mickey, 109, 127
Doyle, Arthur Conan, 156
Dutcher, Rodney, 192

École de Cavalerie, in France, 51
Edwards, Clarence R., 84
Edwards, L. I. H., 144
Eighteenth Amendment, 89
Eisenhower, Dwight D., 14, 16, 17, 171, 177, 181
Eisenhower, John S. D., 158–59
El Centro, California. *See* Imperial Valley, California
El Paso, Texas, 37, 38, 39–40
Ely, Hanson E., 79, 83

Farley, J. C., 79–80
Farm Bureau, 220
fascism, 140, 143, 147, 149
Federal Bureau of Reclamation, 216
Ferdinand, Franz, 41–42
5th Field Artillery Regiment, 37, 38, 46
1st Division, 44–45, 46–47, 67–68
1st Field Artillery Regiment, 85

Flipper, Henry O., 14
Foch, Ferdinand, 61, 63, 67
Ford, Henry, 100
Fort Bliss, El Paso, 37, 38, 39–40
Fort Hunt, Virginia, 136
Fort Leavenworth, Kansas, 6, 37, 79, 265n11
Fort Logan, Colorado, 9
Fort Myer, 142, 169
Fort Riley, Kansas, 25–26, 28
Fort Rosecrans National Cemetery, San Diego, 249, 252
Fort Sill, Oklahoma, 58, 76–77, 85
Fort Stotsenburg, Philippines, 29, 30–32
Fort Union, New Mexico, 4–5
Fort Wadsworth, New York, 9–10
Fort Washington, Maryland, 181
41st "Sunset" Division, 106
42nd "Rainbow" Division, 46, 158
Foulkrod, Harold B., 123, 127, 129, 135–36, 143, 150
France, 51, 54–55, 58, 59, 72–73, 262n25; Germany invasion of, 42; Gondrecourt-le-Château, 47–48; Haute-Marne, 75; La Ferté-Sous-Jouarre, 66; Malicorne, 74; Meuse-Argonne, 67–68, 69–71, 74; Paris, 9, 57, 196; Saint Nazaire, 45, 46; Saumur, 47; Seicheprey, 68; Torcy, 63; Verdun, 49
Freer Gallery, Smithsonian, 81

G-5. *See* General Staff Planning
General Service Schools, 265n11
General Staff Planning (G-5), 47
General Staff School, 37
Gerk, Joseph, 111
Germany, 42, 183
Geronimo, 4, 7, 86–87
Gettysburg battlefield, 19

GI Bill. *See* Servicemen's Readjustment Act
Gillett, Charles L., 207–8
Gitlow, Benjamin, 184
Glassford, Alice C., 245
Glassford, Augusta (paternal grandmother), 8
Glassford, Carl (grandson), 248–49, 252
Glassford, Cora Elizabeth "Bettie" (daughter), 29, 86, 195–96, 201, 250, *fig. 5*; death of, 252
Glassford, Dorothy Seymour "Dot" (daughter), 32, 86, 201–2, 249–50, *fig. 5*; death of, 252
Glassford, Guy Carleton (son), 29, 79, 82–83, 199, 202, *fig. 5*; at Anacostia Flats, 136; in Corps of Engineers, 241–42; death of, 252; disappearance of, 84–85; in Port Orchard, 248; at USMA, 86; in Utah, 239, 250
Glassford, John Knox (paternal grandfather), 3–4, 8, 11, 21
Glassford, Pelham Davis, Jr. "Pete" (son), 29, 86, 239, 241, 250–51, *fig. 5*; death of, 252; Distinguished Service Cross of, 244–45
Glassford, Pelham Davis, Sr. "Hap," *fig. 2, fig. 3, fig. 4, fig. 5, fig. 6, fig. 7, fig. 10, fig. 13. See also specific topics*
Glassford, William Alexander, II "Bill" (brother), 6, 12, 77–78, 202, 241, *fig. 4*; death of, 249; retirement of, 245; at USMA, 21
Glassford, William Alexander, Sr. (father), 3, 4, 9, 78–79, *fig. 1, fig. 4*; in Arizona, 7, 86–87, 237; at Fort Union, 5; in Philippines, 29; at the Presidio, 35; in Puerto Rico, 10–11; in Signal Service, 6, 7–8; in Washington, 202
Glassford Hill, Arizona, 237
Godeau, 52
Gondrecourt-le-Château, France, 47–48
Goodness, Gail Elisabeth, 239
Gordon, Evelyn Peyton, 242
Gotwals, John C., 89
Graham, N. M., 218, 225

Graham, William Walter, III, 249–50
Grant, Ulysses S., 3, 8
Grant, Ulysses S., III, 97, 133
Great Depression, 101–2, 105, 114, 115, 183, 193
Greenway, Isabella, 236
growers, in California, 204, 205–6, 207, 209, 212, 222–23; Communists relation to, 212, 214, 230, 231; P. Glassford, Sr. relation to, 225, 226
Gullion, Allen W., 241, 243–44

Haleiwa, Hawaii, 36
Harding, Warren G., 92, 114, 132
Hard Times (Terkel), 125
Harlow, Lea Beatrice, 250
Harper's Magazine, 96
Harrigan, B. A., 229
Harris, Mary, 243
Harvey, Harry, 207
Haute-Marne, France, 75
Hawaii, 32–33, 34, 35, 36
Hayes, George P., 52
hazing, at USMA, 1, 14, 15–18, 19–21, 28
Heald, Elmer, 228–29
Hearst, William Randolph, 10
Hearst newspapers, 243–44
Heath, Ferry K., 156
Helen Quamame (horse jockey), 240
Henley, William Ernest, 254
Henrie, C. C., 249
Henry, Thomas R., 142, 151
Hitchcock, D. Howard, 34, 246
Hitler, 140, 183
Hodges, John Neal, 255n1
Honolulu, Hawaii, 33, 34
Hoover, Herbert, 2, 91, 93, 94, 194, 253; BEF relation to, 129, 150, 166, 195; Bingham relation to, 153; Bonus

Bill relation to, 145–46; DC commissioners relation to, 184; Great Depression relation to, 101–2, 105, 114, 115; MacArthur relation to, 118, 175, 176–77, 178, 179; *Memoirs of Herbert Hoover*, 197; Mitchell relation to, 183, 192; National Hunger March relation to, 99; F. Roosevelt defeat of, 192–93; US Congress relation to, 154

Hoover, J. Edgar, 80, 243–44

Hooverville, in Washington, DC, 137, 140, 155, 176

Horiuchi, Tsuji, 207

Hospital 114, Bordeaux, 73

Hotel San Marcos, Arizona, 78

House of Representatives Office Building, 88

House Ways and Means Committee, 94, 107

Howe, Louis, 200–201

Howitzer (USMA yearbook), 21

Hurley, Patrick J., 117–18, 159–60, 170, 176

Hushka, William, 168

Hutchinson, Claude B., 220

von Hutier, Oskar, 56

Idaho, 105, 109–10

Imperial Valley, California, 2, 204, 213, 224–25, 233, fig. 15; American Communist Party in, 206–7; Communists in, 218, 219, 221; P. Glassford, Sr. in, 216, 253

Imperial Valley Growers and Shippers Protective League, 214

Imperial Valley Press (newspaper), 232

Iredell, Russell, 246–47

Jack, Alvin N., 218, 231

Jacobsen, W. C., 220

James, Clayton, 13–14

Japanese Embassy, 103

Japanese immigrants, 206

Jefferson City, Missouri, 11

Joffre, Jacques C., 44

John Day Company, 197

John Marshall Place Park, 129

Johnson, Charles M., 235

Johnson, Grover C., 218, 231

Johnson, Royal C., 91, 94

Johnstown, Pennsylvania, 181–82

Joseph, Franz, 41

Kalb, Nathan "Shorty," 154

Kansas, 6, 25–26, 28, 37, 79, 265n11

Keck, Ira E., 164–65, 190, 191

Kelly, Edward J., 242–43

Kentucky, Danville, 76

"Khaki Shirts" organization, 143

Kidron (horse), 52–53, 76, 247–48

Kilohana Art League, 34

Knowlton, Don S., 129, 136

Kolekole Pass, Hawaii, 35

labor unions, 206, 209–10. *See also* Agricultural Workers Industrial League

La Ferté-Sous-Jouarre, France, 66

Laguna Beach, California, 244, 245–46, 248–49

Laguna Beach Art Association, 245–46, 249, 251

Larned, Charles W., 26, 27

Las Cruces, New Mexico, 40

The Last Supper (da Vinci), 246

Las Vegas, New Mexico, 5

The Las Vegas Daily Gazette (newspaper), 6

Las Vegas Optic (newspaper), 5–6

Lawrence, Charles W., 244–45

League Against War and Fascism, 147

Legion of Merit medal, 243

Lenin, Vladimir, 56

Leopold II (King), 132

Life (magazine), 247

Lippmann, Walter, 115

Lisio, Donald, 102, 156, 178, 192

Lorenze, W. H., 231

Los Angeles Times (newspaper), 214, 218–19, 225, 230, 231

Lucas, August M. (paternal grandmother), 3

Ludendorff, Erich, 56, 57, 58, 73

Lusitania (passenger vessel), 42

MacArthur, Douglas, 1, 80, 158, 254, *fig.* 14; at BEF eviction, 169, 171–72, 173, 175–76, 177–78, 179, 196; BEF relation to, 129, 155, 166, 181, 195; on Communism, 139–40; Communists relation to, 156, 158; on hazing, 18; Hoover relation to, 118, 176–77, 178, 179; Hurley relation to, 170; Mitchell report effect on, 192; Plan White relation to, 119; presidential runs of, 247; *Reminiscences*, 197; at USMA, 19, 20; at USMA reunion, 103; Waters relation to, 159–60

Madero, Francisco, 38

Mahony, Felix, 81–82

Maine (battleship), 9, 10

Malicorne, France, 74

Malinta Hill, Philippines, 31–32

Manchester, William, 180

Marines, US, 57

Marks, Sidney J., 136, 137–38

Marshall, George Catlett, Jr., 45, 48, 67–68, 71

McCloskey, Eddie, 181–82

McCullough, David, 13, 49

McKinley, William, 12, 20

McLean, Evalyn Walsh, 130, 131–32, 160, 243

McNair, Lesley J. "Whitey," 17, 19, 21, 48, 244, 255n1

McWilliams, Carey, 204, 205

Mein Kampf (Hitler), 140

Memoirs of Herbert Hoover (Hoover), 197

Merriam, Frank F., 227

Meuse-Argonne, France, 67–68, 69–71, 74

Mexican workers, 206, 219–20

Mexico, 4, 42, 238–39; Punitive Expedition in, 39, 40, 48, 105

Mexico City, Mexico, 238–39

MID. *See* Military Intelligence Division, War Department

Miles, Perry L., 140, 152, 166, 171–72, 173, 181

Military Intelligence Division, War Department (MID), 96

military police, of BEF, 136, 187

Military Police School in the Arlington Cantonment, 241

Militia Act (1903), 23

Millspaugh, Frank R., 27

Missouri, 3, 11, 23, 26, 28, 49

Mitchell, William D., 162, 183, 186–90, 192

Moana Hotel, 33

Model School, in San Juan, Puerto Rico, 11

Monarch of Bermuda (ship), 195

Moore, C. B., 218

Morgan, Ted, 244

Morse, Samuel B., 10–11

Moscow, Russia, 134, 184

Moseley, George Van Horn, 152, 156, 158, 159, 176–77

Mounted Service School, 26, 259n9

Munie, Jerome, 113

Murdock, John R., 237

Murray, Maxwell, 47, 48, 50

NAACP, 141

Nation, The (magazine), 163

National Children's Bureau, 198

National Guard, 23, 26, 28, 41, 49, 58; of Idaho, 105; of New York, 74; of Oregon, 106; PMCA in, 27

National Hunger March, in Washington, DC, 96–100

National Industrial Recovery Act (1933) (NIRA), 210, 212

National Labor Board, 211, 219

National Mall, Washington, DC, 82

National Press Club, 193

National Reclamation Association, Organization Committee of, 79

National Recovery Administration (NRA), 210–11, 212

Naval Academy, US, 4

New Deal, 212

New Mexico, 2, 37, 38–39, 40

Newton, Walter B., 119–20

New York, 9–10, 74

New York Republic (newspaper), 141

New York Times (newspaper), 145, 210

New York World (newspaper), 90

92nd "Buffalo" Division, 55

93rd "Blue Helmet" Division, 55

NIRA. *See* National Industrial Recovery Act

North Island, California, 37

NRA. *See* National Recovery Administration

Obregon, Alvaro, *fig. 4*

Observational Balloon Unit, Army, US, 9

Office of the Chief of Field Artillery, at Fort Sill, Oklahoma, 76–77

O'Hara, Eliot, 246–47

Ohio, Zanesville, 113

Oklahoma, 58, 76–77, 85, 118

Olmsted, Kathryn, 233

Olson, Culbert, 243–44

155 mm Howitzer, 60, *fig. 6*

152nd Field Artillery Brigade, 71, 74

102nd Infantry Regiment, 69

103rd Field Artillery Regiment, 58–60, 64

Operation Blücher, 57

Operation Georgette, 56

Operation Gneisenau, 58

Operation Marneschutz-Reims, 61

Operation Michael, 56

Order of the Purple Heart, 75

Oregon, 106–8

Organization Committee, National Reclamation Association, 79

Pace, John T., 134–35, 136, 150, 158, 184, 187; P. Glassford, Sr. relation to, 138–39

Pageant of the Masters, of Laguna Beach Art Association, 245–46

Painter, Charles Louis, 234, 238, 249

Painter, Kathryn, 249

Painter, Lucille Kathryn "Lucy," 223, 230, 234–35, 243, 249, *fig. 16*; as farm manager, 242

Palmer, J. Mitchell, 80

Paris, France, 9, 57, 196

"Paris on Armistice Night, 1918," 88, 91–92

Parke, Lee Wood, 201–2, 250

Parkinson's disease, 249, 250, 252

Passos, John Dos, 99, 141

Patman, Wright, 93, 113, 119, 122, 143, 237; Waters relation to, 124

Patton, George S., 51, 94, 169, 174–75, 182

Payne, John Barton, 131, 159

Pearl Harbor, 202, 241

Pennsylvania, 181–82, 193

Pennsylvania Railroad, 148

Perkins, Frances, 214–15, 217, 219–20; P. Glassford, Sr. relation to, 223, 226, 228, 233

Pershing, John J. "Black Jack," 39, 40, 43, 54, 69–71, *fig. 4*; 1st Division of, 44–45, 46–47, 67–68; Kidron relation to, 52–53, 76, 248; G. Marshall relation to, 67–68; at "Paris on Armistice Night, 1918," 91; on 3rd Division, 58

Philadelphia, Pennsylvania, 193

Philippines, 1, 10, 24, 29, 30–32

Phillips, John, 220, 221

The Phillips Report, 220

Phoenix, Arizona, 235–37

Phoenix Motorcycle Club, 203

Pinchot, Gifford, 182

Pixley Massacre, 210

Plan White, 96, 119

Plaza Hotel, Las Vegas, 5–6

Plenum meeting, of American Communist Party, 96

PMCA. *See* Providence Marine Corps of Artillery

Pocatello, Idaho, 109–10

Police Department, of Washington, DC, 89, 94–95, 101, 138, 189, 195; Crime Prevention Division of, 104, 190; Prohibition effect on, 103

Portland, Oregon, 106–8

Port Orchard, Washington, 248, 251–52

Port Townsend, Washington, 78, 202–3, 238

Potomac River, in Washington, DC, *fig. 9*

Pratt, Henry G., 94, 95, 185

Presidio, of San Francisco, 6, 35, 37, 86–87, 237

Princip, Gavrilo, 41–42

Prohibition, 89–90, 101, 103

Providence Marine Corps of Artillery (PMCA), 23, 27

Providence Marine Society, 27

Provo, Utah, 249

Public Works Administration (PWA), 232

Puerto Rico, 10–11, 236

Pulitzer, Joseph, 10

Punitive Expedition, in Mexico, 39, 40, 48, 105

PWA. *See* Public Works Administration

Pyle, Ernie, 237–38, 239, 244

Quekemeyer, John G., 52–53

Quonset Point, 28

racial integration, in BEF, 141–42

racial segregation, 55, 135

Rainey, Henry Thomas, 119, 129

Reconstruction Finance Corporation (RFC), 102

Red Cross, 131, 159

Red Squad, Washington, DC, Police Department, 138

Reichelderfer, Luther H., 89, 120, 164, 165, 188

Reminiscences (MacArthur), 197

RFC. *See* Reconstruction Finance Corporation

Rhode Island, National Guard of, 23, 26, 28, 58

Rio Grande Republican (newspaper), 6

Robertson, Royal W., 151, 153, 157

Robinson, Marjorie (Marge), 239, 248, 250

Rockwell Field, Signal Aviation School, 78

Rogers, John T., 196

Rogers, Will, 102, 193

Rolph, James "Sunny Jim," 212

Roosevelt, Eleanor, 200–201

Roosevelt, Franklin D., 2, 139, 180, 192–93, 215, 253; CCC relation to, 200–201; labor unions relation to, 209–10

Roosevelt, Theodore, 24, 39

Root, Elihu, 23–24

Rover, Leo, 184–85

Russia, 42, 56, 134, 184

Sacred Heart Convent, Paris, 196
Saint Nazaire, France, 45, 46
Salt Lake City, Utah, 239
Salt River Valley, Arizona, 3–4, 8, 78
San Diego, California, 228, 249, 252
San Francisco, California, 6, 35, 37, 86–87, 237
San Francisco Examiner (newspaper), 38, 91
San Francisco Institute of Art, 35
San Joaquin Valley, California, 210, 211, 233
San Juan, Puerto Rico, 11
Santa Fe New Daily New Mexican (newspaper), 11, 25
Santa Fe Trail, 4–5
Sarajevo, Bosnia, 41
Saumur, France, 47
Schofield Barracks, Hawaii, 32–33, 35
School of the Line, at Fort Leavenworth, 37, 79, 265n11
Scrapper (dog), 76, 79, 82, 83
2nd "Indian Head" Division, 46
Secret Service, 96, 113, 125
Seicheprey, France, 68
Serbia, 42
Servicemen's Readjustment Act (1944), 201
Sevareid, Eric, 198
77th "Liberty" Division, 74
Shafer, W. Bruce, Jr., 92
"shave tail," 25, 259n6
Shaw, USS, 77–78
Sherburne, John H., 73
Sherman (US Army transport), 37
Sherman, William Tecumseh, 265n11
Shinault, George W., 167–68
Signal Aviation School, at Rockwell Field, 78
Signal Service, of Army, US, 6, 7–8, 78
Silver Star Citation, 75
6th Field Artillery Regiment, 26

Skaret, Morest "Morey," 199–200, 277n12
Smith, James W., 14
Smithsonian Institution, 11, 81, 247
Social Security Act, 212
Soldier's Ex-service Men's League. *See* Workers' Ex-Servicemen's League (WESL)
Soroptimists Club, 198–99
Spanish-American War, 10, 24, 29, 39
Spanish Flu, 72
Springer, Fleta Campbell, 96
Stalin, Joseph, 230
Starling, Edmund William, 115, 125, 193
Stilwell, Joseph W., 17, 19, 21, 26
Stimson, Henry L., 241
St. Joseph, Missouri, 26
St. Louis Police Department, 110–11
St. Louis Post-Dispatch (newspaper), 168
St. Mihiel Salient, 67–69, 71
Sullivan, Mark, 136
Surles, Alexander D., 171
Sweeney, Cameron, 82–83

Taft, William, 118
Taos School of Art, 247
Taylor, Carl William "Running Wolf," 197–98
Texas, 37, 38, 39–40, 185
Thayer, Sylvanus, 13
3rd Division, 57–58
Thomas (US Army transport), 32
Thomas, Elmer, 144–45
Thompson, Vaughan, 228–29
369th "Harlem Hellfighters" Regiment, 55
Torcy, France, 63
Trade Union Unity League, 207
Traffic Advisory Council, 96

Treaty of Paris, 29

Truman, Harry S., 49, 55, 178

Truscott, Lucian K. Jr., 122, 142, 169, 173–74, 176, 182; on BEF eviction, 181

Tugwell, Rexford G., 180

Tuolumne (horse), 33, 52

Twachtman, Alden, 71, 83

Twachtman, John Henry, 83, 247

Twain, Mark, 35

20th Battery Field Artillery Regiment, 25–26

26th "Yankee" Division, 46, 58–60, 61–63, 64, 68, 72

Udall, John H., 236

Union Pacific Railroad, 108

United States (US), 4, 43, 57, 78; Department of Labor of, 225–26, 231; Philippines colonization by, 29; War Department of, 96, 156, 159, 166. *See also* Army, US; Congress, US

United States Military Academy (USMA), 13, 20, 22, 33, 103; Beast Barracks at, 11, 17–18; Department of Drawing of, 26; G. Glassford at, 86; P. Glassford Sr. instructing at, 27; hazing at, 1, 14, 15–18, 19–21, 28

USMA. *See* United States Military Academy

Utah, 239, 249, 250

Verdun, France, 49

Veterans Bureau, 157, 183

Veterans of Foreign Wars (VFW), 88, 93, 111

Vicksburg Campaign, 12

Villa, Francisco "Pancho," 1–2, 37, 38–39, 40, *fig. 4*

Volcano School of artists, 34

Volunteers of America Mission, 103

Wabash Railroad, 110

Wagner, Robert F., 213, 217, 219

Waldron, Frank, 207

Walker, Aldace, 161, 162, 164, 188

Walker, H. L., 209

Walsh, Tom, 130–31

Ward, Herbert S., 157

War Department, US, 96, 156, 159, 166

War Is a Racket (S. Butler), 147

Warmaker (horse), 240

Warns, John, 75–76

Warren, Earl, 243–44

Washington, 78, 202–3, 238, 248, 251–52

Washington, DC, 1, 8, 82, 116–19, 124, 196; Army War College in, 2, 24, 79, 81, 85, 265n16; Hooverville in, 137, 140, 155, 176; National Hunger March in, 96–100; "Paris on Armistice Night, 1918" in, 88, 91–92; Police Department of, 89, 94–95, 101, 103, 104, 138, 189–90, 195; Potomac River in, *fig. 9*. *See also* DC commissioners

Washington Arts Club, 81

Washington Auditorium, 88, 90, 98–99, 130

Washington Daily News (newspaper), 217, 242

Washington Evening Star (newspaper), 142, 145, 151, 187

Washington Navy Yard, 152

Washington News (newspaper), 183

Washington Post (newspaper), 86, 90, 94, 95, 102, 182–83; on BEF, 130, 142, 184; on P. Glassford, Sr., 146; on National Hunger March, 100

Washington Society of Arts and Crafts, 84, 85, 86

Washington Sunday Star (newspaper), 81

water restriction, 232

Waters, Walter Warfield, 105–6, 109, 135, 167–68,

250, *fig.* 13; at Anacostia Flats, 133; B. E. F., 197; at BEF eviction, 174; BEF relation to, 110–14, 125–29, 137, 139, 146, 147–48, 153–54, 155, 161–62; at Camp Marks, 270n41; DC commissioners relation to, 160–61; fascism relation to, 149; in P. Glassford, Sr. report, 188; P. Glassford, Sr. relation to, 156, 158, 163–64, 195; on "Khaki Shirts" organization, 143; MacArthur relation to, 159–60; E. McLean relation to, 131, 132; Patman relation to, 124; Robertson relation to, 151; Thomas relation to, 144–45

Watkins, T. H., 94

Webb-Haney Alien Land Law, in California, 31

Weiser, Idaho, 105

WESL. *See* Workers' Ex-Servicemen's League

West Point Military Academy. *See* United States Military Academy (USMA)

White, Owen P., 184, 193

White House, 96–97, 158, 160, 165

Wilhelm II (Kaiser), 73, 137

Wilkins, Roy, 141–42

Wilson, Woodrow, 39, 42–43, 114, 195, 210

Wirin, Abraham Lincoln, 212–13, 229, 231

Workers' Ex-Servicemen's League (WESL), 123, 134–35, 138, 150. *See also* Pace, John T.

World War Adjusted Compensation Act (1922), 92–93

Wright, Frank Lloyd, 239

Wyoming, Cheyenne, 110

Xivray-Marvoisin, 59

Yankee Division Club, Boston (YD), 83–84

Young, P. J., 111–12, 113

Young Democrats of Phoenix, 236–37

Zanesville, Ohio, 113

Zapata, Emiliano, 38

Zelaya, Carlos Alfonso Don, 127

Zimmermann Telegram, 42

Znamenacek, Miles, 167–68

www.ingramcontent.com/pod-product-compliance
Lightning Source LLC
Chambersburg PA
CBHW031428160426
43195CB00010BB/649